D1522583

KEYS TO THE
KINGDOM

VOLUME TWO

Thank you for supporting independent publishing and the Systemology Society.

mardukite.com

MARDUKITE ACADEMY OF SYSTEMOLOGY COLLECTOR'S EDITION

KEYS TO THE
KINGDOM

VOLUME TWO
SPIRITUAL CLEARING
(LEVEL-8)

Systemology Advanced Training Course
presented by Joshua Free

© 2024, JOSHUA FREE

ISBN : 978-1-961509-57-3

A MARDUKITE SYSTEMOLOGY PUBLICATION

Mardukite Research Library Catalogue No. "Liber-8"

Developed for Mardukite Academy & The Systemology Society

cum superiorum privilegio veniaque

FIRST EDITION
April 2024

Published from
Joshua Free Imprint – JFI Publications
Mardukite Borsippa HQ, San Luis Valley, Colorado

The Keys to the Kingdom are Yours for the Taking!

The Mardukite Academy "Advanced Training Course" for Systemology Level-8 is now available in print for the first time.

Those Seekers that have already completed "The Pathway to Ascension" Systemology Professional Course can now access the secret upper-level teachings of our tradition.

This textbook is not for everyone. . .
It contains Advanced Training Manuals 5 to 8 along with an Advanced Training Supplement, including: "Entities & Fragments," "Spiritual Perception," "Mastering Ascension," "Advancing Systemology" and the "Systemology Piloting" supplemental manual.

Learn how to expertly apply our most advanced spiritual technology toward reaching the highest levels of Awareness and Beingness accessible and attainable during the lifetime of a "human" on planet Earth.

Each of the "Keys to the Kingdom" Advanced Training Course Manuals included can further a Seekers reach on the Pathway leading out of this Universe.

Never before has Joshua Free presented this Infinity Grade material outside the confines of the Mardukite NexGen Systemology Society.

Containing the four manuals from the
Complete 2024 Advanced Training Course for
Systemology Keys-to-the-Kingdom Level-8
in addition to a bonus supplemental manual
all in one Collector's Edition Hardcover.

MARDUKITE SYSTEMOLOGY SOCIETY
"THE KEYS TO THE KINGDOM"
ADVANCED TRAINING
VOLUME TWO

– Introducing the Manual . . . 13
– Charting Flights on the Pathway . . . 14
– Taking Flight on the Pathway . . . 15
– Systemology Level-8 . . . 17

. . . . FIVE . . . .
:: ENTITIES & FRAGMENTS ::
– Level-8: The Wizard Grade . . . 23
– Spiritual Fragmentation . . . 25
– Fragments and Bonded-Entities (B.E.) . . . 31
– The Identification Procedure . . . 35
– Bonded-Entities (B.E.) and Fused-Groups . . . 38
– Incident-Running Procedure . . . 44
– Standard Procedure: Entities . . . 54
– Platforms #1-18 (AT#3 Addendum) . . . 59
– Programmed Machine-Entities (PME) . . . 63
– Standard Procedure: PME . . . 69
– Advanced Entity-Handling . . . 77
– End-Points and Realizations . . . 81

. . . . SIX . . . .
:: SPIRITUAL PERCEPTION ::
– Advancing Spiritual Ability . . . 87
– Realizations From The Pathway . . . 92
– "Ejection" From A Body (Vehicle) . . . 97
– Advanced Ability Training (A.A.T. Routine) . . . 104
– Wizard Level-1 Stabilization . . . 110

– Ejection, Perception & Barriers
  (Wizard Level-2 Keynote Lecture) . . . 117
– R.S.V.P.—Remote Spiritual Viewpoints
  and Perception (A.A.T. Wizard Level-2) . . . 120
– Wizard-Level Session (Script Example) . . . 133

. . . . SEVEN . . . .
:: MASTERING ASCENSION ::
– Self-Direction and Intention . . . 139
– Intention: Directing Thought
  Wizard Level-3X Keynote Lecture . . . 141
– Wizard Level-3X Procedure . . . 147
– Advanced Ability Training (3X) . . . 168
– Implanting The Human Condition . . . 182
– Heaven-Implants (Parts #1-6) . . . 190
– Heaven-Implants (Goals Sequence) . . . 201
– Heaven-Implants (Ethics Series) . . . 214
– Spiritual-Disability Implant . . . 221

. . . . EIGHT . . . .
:: ADVANCING SYSTEMOLOGY ::
– New Standard Systemology . . . 253
– The Jewel of Knowledge . . . 259
– The False Jewel of Knowledge . . . 268
– "Black-Box" Control-Implants . . . 288
– Researching Penalty-Universes . . . 293
– The Agreements Universe . . . 303
– Actual Goals and Basic Purposes . . . 309
– The "Big-Splitter" Incident . . . 323
– Opening Gates to the Kingdom . . . 390

. . . .
:: SYSTEMOLOGY PILOTING MANUAL ::
– Systematic Processing . . . 395
– Preventative Fundamentals . . . 396
– Traditional Piloting . . . 398

– Elements of Piloting . . . 401
– Piloting Seekers . . . 404
– Entry-Points to a Session . . . 406
– The Preliminary Interview . . . 407
– The Skills of Piloting . . . 410
– The Formal Session (Script) . . . 416

. . . . APPENDIX . . . .

– Basic Systemology Glossary . . . 420
– Additional Resources . . . 442

This material is continued from:
Keys to the Kingdom (Volume One)

Systemology "New Standard" Course Books
Fundamentals of Systemology (Basic Course)
The Pathway to Ascension (2 Volumes)
Keys to the Kingdom (2 Volumes)

Systemology "Basic Level" Core Books
The Power of Zu
Systemology: The Original Thesis
The Way Into The Future

Systemology "Master Level" Core Books
The Tablets of Destiny Revelation
Crystal Clear: Handbook for Seekers
Metahuman Destinations (2 Volumes)

Systemology "Wizard Level" Core Books
Imaginomicon
The Way of the Wizard
Systemology-180: A Fast-Track to Ascension
Systemology: Backtrack

∞

EDITOR'S NOTE

"The Self does not actualize Awareness
past a point not understood."
—*Tablets of Destiny*

This book contains a collection of materials from four
of the lesson-manuals developed by Joshua Free for
the "Keys to the Kingdom" Advanced Training Course.

A clear understanding of this material is critical for
achieving actual realizations and personal benefit
from applying our philosophy as spiritual technology.

Any time you run across an unfamiliar term,
refer to the "Systemology Glossary" in the appendix.
It is also helpful to keep a quality dictionary nearby.

The *Seeker* should not to simply "read through" this
book without practicing the "exercises" given and
attaining proper comprehension as "knowledge."
Even when the information continues to be
"interesting"—if at any point you find yourself feeling
lost or confused while reading, trace your steps back.
Return to the point of misunderstanding and go
through it again.

Take nothing within this book on faith.
Apply the information directly to your life.

Decide for yourself.

∞

The Pathway to Ascension
Professional Course

#1 – *Increasing Awareness (Level-0)*
#2 – *Thought & Emotion (Level-0)*
#3 – *Clear Communication (Level-0)*
#4 – *Handling Humanity (Level-1)*
#5 – *Free Your Spirit (Level-2)*
#6 – *Escaping Spirit-Traps (Level-2)*
#7 – *Eliminating Barriers (Level-3)*
#8 – *Conquest of Illusion (Level-3)*
#9 – *Confronting the Past (Level-4)*
#10 – *Lifting the Veils (Level-4)*
#11 – *Spiritual Implants (Level-5)*
#12 – *Games and Universes (Level-5)*
#13 – *Spiritual Energy (Level-6)*
#14 – *Spiritual Machinery (Level-6)*
#15 – *The Arcs of Infinity (Level-6)*
#16 – *Alpha Thought (Level-6)*

Keys to the Kingdom
Advanced Training Course

#1 – *The Secret of Universes (Level-7)*
#2 – *Games, Goals & Purposes (Level-7)*
#3 – *The Jewel of Knowledge (Level-7)*
#4 – *Implanted Universes (Level-7)*
#5 – *Entities & Fragments (Level-8)*
#6 – *Spiritual Perception (Level-8)*
#7 – *Mastering Ascension (Level-8)*
#8 – *Advancing Systemology (Level-8)*

Advanced Training Supplementals
#1 – *Systemology Biofeedback*
#2 – *Systemology Procedures*
#3 – *Systemology Piloting*

THE SYSTEMOLOGY
ADVANCED TRAINING COURSE MANUAL SERIES

Mardukite Systemology is a new evolution in Human understanding about the "systems" governing *Life, Reality,* the *Universe* and all *Existences.* It is also a *Spiritual Path* used to transcend the Human experience and reach *"Ascension."*

This is an *Advanced Training* (*AT*) course manual detailing *upper-levels* of our spiritual philosophy. It is intended to assist *advancing* a *Seeker's* personal progress toward the *upper-most levels* of the *Pathway.*

This manual follows after our *Professional Course* series of lessons—available as individual booklets, or collected in two volumes titled *"The Pathway to Ascension"* The *Professional Course* follows after material given in the *Basic Course* booklets, or *"Fundamentals of Systemology"* volume.

The systematic methodology that we use to assist an individual to increase their *"Actualized Awareness"* (and reach gradually higher toward their *"Spiritual Ascension"*) is referred to as *"The Pathway"* —and that individual is called a *"Seeker."*

To receive the greatest benefit from this manual: it is expected that a *Seeker* will already be familiar with the fundamental concepts and terminology (previously relayed in the *Basic Course* and *Professional Course* lessons) of our *applied philosophy.*

As a *Seeker* increases their *Awareness* in this lifetime, their spiritual *"Knowingness"* also increases—which is to say their *certainty* on *Life*, on this and other *Universes*, and on *realizing Self* as an unlimited "spiritual being" *having* an enforced restrictive "human experience." A *Seeker* also *knowingly* increases their command and control of the "human experience." And this is a part of what is meant by *"Actualized Awareness."*

CHARTING FLIGHTS ON THE PATHWAY

Although there is a systematic structure to *fragmentation*, the personal journey experienced along the *Pathway* will be different for each *Seeker*. For example, certain areas will seem more *"turbulent"* or difficult for one *Seeker* than another. We tend to say that these areas have more *"charge"* on them—or that they are more *"heavily charged."* It is best to handle such areas when you are already feeling "good" and not in a situation (or condition) where that specific area is consistently being *"triggered"* or *"restimulated."*

As an applied philosophy, *Systemology* "theory" can be easily utilized in the "laboratory" of the "world-at-large" in everyday life. This is implied within the basic instruction of each lesson. Unlike other "sciences" that conduct experiments by making a change to some "objective variable" *out there* and waiting to see an effect, our focus is the individual (or *Observer*) themselves, and how *they* affect the *"Reality"* perceived.

Our philosophy is applied by using specific exercises and systematic techniques. These *"processes"* provide the most stable personal gain (and *realizations*) for each area; but only when actually applied with a *Seeker's* full *"presence"* and *Awareness.* Hundreds of such *processes* may be found in the *"Pathway to Ascension"* (*Professional Course*) material.

Applying a technique is called *"running a process."* *Processes* are designed with very   simple instructions or *"command-lines."* To *run* a *processing command-line*, a *Seeker* may be assisted by the communication of that *line* from a *"Co-Pilot"* (as in *"Traditional Piloting"*). But even then, a *Seeker* must still personally "input" the *command* as *Self.* For this reason—and quite thankfully—*Solo-Processing* is possible.

TAKING FLIGHT ON THE PATHWAY

Processing Techniques are intended to treat the *Spiritual Being* or *Alpha-Spirit*; the individual themselves. The *"command-lines"* are *directed to* the individual themselves —not some *mental machinery* of theirs, and not even a *Biofeedback* metering device.

Systematic Processing is applied by the *Alpha-Spirit*—who then *Self-directs* command of their "Mind-System" or "body" (*genetic-vehicle*), both of which are "constructs" that the *Alpha-Spirit* (*Self*, or the "I-AM" *Awareness unit*) operates, but neither of which is actually *Self. Fragmentation* causes *Humans* to falsely identify *Self as* the *"Mind"* or even a *"Body."*

Some *processes* can be treated quite lightly at first; others may require a bit of working at in order to get *"running"* well. It is important to set aside a period of time when you can be dedicated to your studies and *processing.* This period of time is referred to as a *"processing session."*

When a *process* does start *running* well, it is important to be able to complete it to a satisfactory *"end-point."*

Processing allows us to be able to *actually* "look" at *things* and even determine the *considerations* we have made—or attitudes we have decided—about *Reality* as a result of those experiences.

It doesn't do us much good to simply "glance"—or to *restimulate* something uncomfortable and then quickly *withdraw* from it once again, leaving more of our *attention* yet again behind and held fixedly on it.

Generally speaking, a *Seeker* continues to *run* a *process* so long as something is "happening"—which is to say, the *process* is still producing a change. Usually this is evident by the type of "answers" that a *command-line* prompts a *Seeker* to originate from the database of their own *Mind-System*.

Processing Command-Lines ("PCL") are not "magic words"; they do not "do" anything on their own. They systematically assist a *Seeker* to direct their own attention toward increasing *Awareness*.

A *Seeker* may also cease to generate new "data" from a *process* without reaching an *"ultimate"* realization as an *"end-point."* It is possible that additional "layers" (or even other "areas") require handling before anything "deeper" is accessible. If this is the case, end the *process.* But, if a *Seeker* is *withdrawing* from something uncomfortable that was incited or stirred up, then a *process* is *run* until they feel "good" about it.

One of the benefits to *Flying-Solo* on the *Pathway* is that the *processing* is entirely *Self-determined.* This naturally provides a certain built-in "safety" for a practitioner. Anything you *restimulate* by *Self-determinism* is *your thing*. It is not triggered or incited by some external "*other-determined*" influences (or other "source-points") that make you an *effect*. It can be more easily handled in *processing* —or you can simply let things "cool down" and come back to it again in another *session*.

While it may seem "mysterious" to beginners, a *Seeker* gets a sense for knowing how long to *run* a *process* only with practice. Once you have spent some time actually applying material from "*The Pathway to Ascension*" *Professional Course*, there are many aspects of it that become "second nature" because they are, in fact, a part of our true original native nature. All we have done in *Systemology* is "*reverse engineer*" the routes of *creation* and *consideration* that are already *our own.*

SYSTEMOLOGY LEVEL-8

We are publishing "*upper-level*" *Systemology* in 2024 for the very first time. Its effective application is dependent on a *Seeker* having already reached a stable point of "*Beta-Defragmentation.*" This requires proper use of materials for *processing-levels 0 to 6*—as given in the "*Pathway to Ascension*" *Professional Course* (available in two volumes, or sixteen individual booklets).

Additionally, this current *Systemology Level-8* work is a direct continuation of *Level-7*, which *must* be completed before continuing. The *Systemology Level-7* manuals —"*The Secret of Universes,*" "*Games, Goals & Purposes,*" "*The Jewel of Knowledge*" and (to a lesser extent) "*Imp-*

lanted Universes"—should be treated as a single "unit" of work *prior* to approaching *Level-8*. These manuals are available individually, or as collected in *Volume One* of the *"Keys to the Kingdom" Advanced Training (A.T.) Course.*

After uncovering *"The Jewel"* and discovering the "secret" of *Universes*, a *"Seeker"* has *found* the "hidden gem" of the *Pathway* at *Level-7,* and is no longer a *"Seeker."* Of course, things are not always what we expect —and *"all that glitters is not gold."* Yet, still, it is *"The Jewel of Knowledge"* (*Parts #1-5*) and the *Entry-Point Heaven Incident, &tc.*, that represents the "ceiling" of *this Universe* and even what is behind it, beneath it, or embedded into its structure. It was what a *"Seeker"* had been *drawn* to in their *search*, but was never meant to find by any other method or avenue, except *systematically.*

Systemology Level-8 is the first official *"Wizard Level"* of the *Systemology Society*. As stated in *A.T. Manual #4*: while "formal" *Advanced Training* may end with manuals representing *Systemology Level-8* (and completing the *"Keys to the Kingdom"* series), this will also open up, what is referred to by the *Mardukite Academy* as, the *"Infinity Grade."* [For instructional purposes, we tend to still refer to a practitioner as a *"Seeker"* in the *upper-level* manuals.]

There is no finite end-point to the *"Infinity Grade"* because its ultimate goal is the *"increase of spiritual perception,"* which is, in essence, *unlimited.* This means that plenty of room remains for future researchers to contribute; but only after first completing their *Advanced Training* regarding the parts of our *"Map"* that are *already* researched, well-plotted, effective in application, and thus published.

A *Seeker* could complete *A.T. Manual #3*, and then move on directly to *Level-8* with *A.T. Manual #5* ("*Entities & Fragments*"). If, however, a *Seeker* doesn't have enough "*reality*" on that *Level-8* material—as in, it doesn't seem "*real*" enough to them—then some time studying *A.T. Manual #4* ("*Implanted Universes*") may be of benefit. The covert purpose of introducing "*Implant Platforms #1-18*" *(AT#3)* and the "*IPU Platforms*" *(AT#4)* at *Level-7*, is really to make "*Entities & Fragments*" *(AT#5)* more accessible.

To apply *upper-level Systemology*, an *advanced Seeker* must follow the prescribed outline of instruction that is now available for the first time to the public as the "*Keys to the Kingdom*" series.

All Advanced Training Manuals should be studied in the sequential order in which they are numbered.

A.T. MANUAL #5
ENTITIES &
FRAGMENTS

Keep this reference material accessible:
PC Lesson-1 to 10; Processing-Levels 0 to 4.
PC Lesson-11, "Spiritual Implants"
PC Lesson-12, "Games & Universes"
PC Lesson-13, "Spiritual Energy"
PC Lesson-14, "Spiritual Machinery"
AT Manual #1, "The Secret of Universes"
AT Manual #2, "Games, Goals & Purposes"
AT Manual #3, "The Jewel of Knowledge"
AT Manual #4, "Implanted Universes"
AT Supplement, "Systemology Procedures"
AT Supplement, "Systemology Biofeedback"
AT Supplement, "Systemology Piloting"

LEVEL-8: "THE WIZARD GRADE"

Welcome to *Systemology Level-8*.

In this manual, we begin handling the *upper-level "Wizard Grade"* work of *defragmenting "spiritual entities and identity-fragments."* We have a very specific and *systematic* way of approaching this subject. A *Seeker* is advised not to mix or blend *other* beliefs and practices (for these topics) during this *training* and *processing*.

After a true successful completion of *"The Jewel; Parts #1-5" (AT#3)*, a *Seeker* no longer applies *processing-levels 0 to 4* to *"defragment"* their *own* case. [If more than a month has passed since completing the *Level-7 Stabilization Exercises (AT#3)*, it may be beneficial for a *Seeker* to repeat these before *Level-8*.]

A *Seeker* does not use *A.T. Levels* to handle *fragmentation* that should have been treated earlier on *The Pathway*. Any specific *"imprinted"* area of concern—or where *attention* is *"fixed"* in this lifetime—that *can* be handled with *processing-levels 0 to 6*, must be treated prior to *Advanced Training*—but most certainly before applying (or even studying) *Systemology Level-8*.

Assuming that all prerequisite *defragmentation* work is completed through *Level-7 (AT#3)*, a *Level-8 "Wizard"* should not be *running "imprint-chains"* on *themselves*. If it hasn't been completed, then the *Seeker* should have at least reached an *end-realization* with *"The Jewel,"* that they, themselves, are the ones keeping these *"chains"* in persistence, and holding them in place with *"attention units"* compulsively *"fixed"* outside their *actual Awareness* (or *Knowingness*).

At this point, simply *"Spotting"* areas of former *Not-Knowingness* is often enough to *defragment* them with *high-power attention-Awareness*. Understand that: *knowingly "Imagining"* (*creating* and *destroying*) *"mental imagery"* of the *past* for inspection, at will, is quite different than persistent *"imprinted imagery"* from those points on the *Backtrack* where parts of our *attention-Awareness* have been compulsively *"fixed"* or *"stuck."*

If a *Level-8 "Wizard"* still tries to *run "imprint-chains"* on themselves—even though a *Level-8* doesn't have any more of these *"fragmented chains"*—the *Wizard* will still *"find" imprinting-chains* to *process*. But this time, the *"imagery"* or *"content"* doesn't necessarily even make sense, because it is generally supplied by *other entities* (in close proximity to us); it is, in essence, *someone else's imprinting* that is being *"pulled-in"* as our own. As a *Seeker* knows—from studying *"source-points," "cause,"* and *"creation"*—we cannot effectively *defragment* something *"As-It-Is,"* when it is *"mis-owned"* or *"misidentified."*

While there are some *"spiritual perception"* exercises from *processing-levels 0 to 4* that may still be applied to *Self,* those that pertain specifically to *"imprinting"*—or *"confronting-the-past"* by *"incident-chains"*—should no longer be applied at *Level-8*. The *exception* here is: unless they are *directed to an entity other than Self* (and even then, they are often only *run* for *Circuit-1*).

By *"defragmenting spiritual entities...,"* we mean very literally: a *Level-8 "Wizard"* (acting as *Co-Pilot*), directing *defragmentation processing* to other *entities (as Seekers)* in order to *release them.* In this wise, our philosophy differs from other approaches. At *Level-8*, the directive is: *freeing entities from ourselves*, rather than *freeing ourselves from them.* This is to say: *releasing them* from their *entrapped fragmented* state, rather than the idea of *ridding* ourselves of them.

The handling of *spiritual entities and fragments* is a critical part of the *"Wizard"* work. While a *Seeker* may have *de-fragmented* their own case to a point of *Self-Honesty*, they are still operating (on *Earth* and in the *Human Condition*) in close proximity to heavily *fragmented low-Awareness entities, identity-fragments* and other *"spiritual machinery."* Hence, this is where we place our emphasis at *Systemology Level-8.*

Study all material in *A.T. Manual #5* (*"Entities & Fragments"*) several times before applying any of its procedures. There are several techniques and methods provided in the text. A *Seeker* should be familiar with *all* of them before proceeding with any application. They are each *systematically* applied for a specific purpose, or in a specific sequence, to handle any layers of *spiritual "Alpha" fragmentation* that remain from previous *processing-levels.*

Having now introduced this new *gradient level* of work, let us take up this subject from the top...

SPIRITUAL FRAGMENTATION

As an *Alpha-Spirit*, you are capable of *being* in many places at once. The *Alpha-Spirit* is able to operate *from* many places at once—because, of course, our *actual Be-*

ingness is not actually "located" anywhere. It can, however, *consider* that "*parts*" or "*units*" of its *attention* (or *Awareness*) *are* located somewhere in sometime. Earlier *processing-levels* included exercises to aid in *unfolding* such *realizations*.

By "*located*," we mean systematically: wherever an individual places their *attention*, wherever they *perceive* from, wherever *intention* is *projected*, whatever *point-of-view* they are *operating* from, is where an individual is *located*. Maintaining multiple located viewpoints simultaneously is something that an *Alpha-Spirit* can do *knowingly—at will*. This natural ability—innate to all *Alpha-Spirits*—has simply been *fragmented* to one's own detriment.

Fragmentation occurs when we allow our *attention* to get *entrapped* in specific "*locations*"—then afterward burying our *knowingness* of it; intentionally "*Not-Knowing*" it, instead of either *knowingly operating from* it, or properly *withdrawing attention-units from* it. By this point on the *Pathway*, a *Seeker* should be increasingly *aware* that there are "hidden" or "compartmented" *fragments* of *Self* that continue to *unknowingly operate* (on *automatic*).

We are actually putting out "bits" of ourselves, our *thoughts* and *attention*—our *Awareness*, so to speak—all the time. We "*project*" this into the *Physical Universe* in order to perceive *impressions*, which allow us to *create* (or *duplicate*) appropriate imagery and sensation for our own experience. This is how we *perceive* "walls" and *interact* "or communicate" with others that share in the *Game* of this *Universe*. We *create* and *dissipate* these "bits" of *Awareness* (or "ZU") at will, simply by focusing *intention* and *attention*.

We *descended* as *spiritual beings*—through many *Universes*—and the decline of our *actualized Awareness* is proportional to the amount of *spiritual fragmentation* that has occurred. As a *spiritual being* "decays," they begin to "abandon" things, rather than "dissolving" them; this leaves many "bits" of themselves behind—"*unconscious*" but persistently running on *automatic*.

Earlier *processing-levels* will have allowed a *Seeker* to regain control over some of these "*split-pieces*." A littl was regained, for example, when we have extended our *Awareness* on the *Backtrack* and "spotted" or "confronted" something that we had formerly left some part of our *attention* on. Another critical area, "*spiritual machinery*," is introduced in *PC Lesson-14*; but we only scraped the surface when treating such "*fragments*."

LOCATIONAL PROCEDURE

This *process* was developed specifically for "*split-fragments*"—but it also applies to other *entities*, which is why we introduce it first. Since it applies to both "*fragments*" and "*entities*," a *Seeker* doesn't have to be too concerned whether they are treating a "*split-off*" piece of themselves or "something else."

A "*split-off*" piece of an individual is not a "*separate being*" (or actual "*entity*"), but it can "act" as though it is. It is really a "*part*" of themselves—usually sent off somewhere, hidden, and otherwise kept *operating unknowingly*. These "*fragments*" can be *aware*, in the sense that they *perceive*, *record*, and *react* to what is happening (based on *computations*)—but they are not *aware* of their own "*thinkingness*."

One of the challenges originally faced with this work concerns the fact that we, as individual *Alpha-Spirits*, have been *split-off* and *divided* many times—been *spiritually fragmented* over and over again. *Systematically* speaking: a *Seeker* cannot usually reclaim a "piece" of themselves directly, *if* both "*it*" and "*you*" have been *fragmented* further (subsequent to the original point of *division*). [The figure here is for illustrative purposes only.]

In this example: if (C3) is the *conscious viewpoint (Seeker)*, and it locates the presence of (D6) and tries to "rejoin" that part directly (using other procedures), the *Seeker* will be unsuccessful (and potentially feel "ill"). This is because such "bypasses" *missing "fragments"* that are essentially "*in between.*" The "*Locational Procedure*" resolves this issue for *our own "spiritual fragments"* (on which other techniques are unworkable). The *in-session procedure* is rather simple:

If you *get a sense of* (or *spot*) something that might be a *split-off* part of yourself, an *isolated (compartmented) fragment* of something (or someone), or an *entity* (or some *identity-fragment*) that is blocked from (or blocking) your *Awareness*—then you *direct to "it"* the *processing command-line* (PCL):

"*Point To The Being That You Divided From.*"

This is an important technique for a *Seeker* to "fall back on"—as a remedy or "*repair action*"—if any difficulties arise when applying other material from this manual. [It is also effective on *fragments* of *others* that are "stuck" on *us*; so you don't have to know the exact nature of *what* you are applying it to.]

The *"pointing"* is really a *direction* of *attention*—or *"spotting"* with *Awareness.* It is a "mental action" and is not limited to *three-dimensions* or a *Physical Universe "direction."* It is not even *"pointing"* toward (or *"spotting"*) where the *"other being"* is *now*; rather it focuses *attention* on the original *"direction"* where the *"split"* occurred. [If some remnant seems to remain thereafter, a *Seeker* may then apply the *"Identity Procedure"* directly to it (as given later).]

The PCL (above) is also beneficial for handling *entities* (*self-aware spiritual beings* or *Alpha-Spirits*), which includes the *Seeker* themselves. One will notice (if the PCL is applied directly to *Self*) that *you* do not "dissolve" or "rejoin" someone else. A separate individual *entity* (*Alpha-Spirit*) gets a better sense of *Self*, or who they are. However, when treating a *fragment*, it dissolves the separation. A *fragment* has no reason to remain separate, unlike the case of an actual individual *Alpha-Spirit*.

"Split-off pieces" and *"spiritual fragments"* (of ourselves or others) are different from individual *entities*. An *Alpha-Spirit* can also *"divide"* into two completely separate *entities*. In other words, both parts will have the complete prior *Backtrack* of the other; neither is senior. There is no loss of *spiritual ability*; both are identical—and both have identical memory of *being* the *original* that *divided*. Such results in two completely separate individual evolving spiritual beings that will never "rejoin" because each is now a full *Alpha-Spirit*.

In *Meta-Systemology*, it is theorized that approximately only *10,000* individual *Alpha-Spirits* separated from the "*Infinity-of-Nothingness*" at one time and went through the original *Jewel* incident into this particular "*womb of existence*" (prior to *Home Universe*). [Ref: *AT#1 & 3*.] These individuals eventually *divided* many times, leading to the *trillions* that now inhabit *this Physical Universe*.

True individual *Alpha-Spirits* do not "rejoin"—because such would reduce the *infinitude of creation* that is balancing the *Infinity-of-Nothingness*. "*Fragments*" on the other hand, whether your own or someone else's, are not separate units of "*Self-Awareness*." These *fragments can* "rejoin"—and usually with great benefit, by restoring *Awareness* to areas that the *Alpha-Spirit* was handling *unknowingly* (and can now treat *knowingly*).

A *Seeker* should *not* make the mistake of thinking that *they* (*themselves*) are a subordinate piece of some kind of bigger "*Uber-Alpha*" or "*over-soul*." There *are* "*upper-level compartments of ourselves*" that *operate unknowingly*, or that we are typically blocked from being *aware* of directly; but that is not a separate *entity*—it is the "*higher parts*" of our *Self*, which we "unfold" an increasing conscious *Awareness* of, as we *Ascend*.

There is also some "*splitting*" (of *Awareness*) that occurs naturally. For example: you put "bits" of yourself on people and places (*terminals*)—using *intention* and *attention*—that you want to keep track of, or influence. Since these are not "*enforced*" by anyone, they can simply be brought under conscious control. There's nothing that inhibits you from dissolving (or controlling) these "pieces" except your own worries over being able to put them back, or losing track of things.

A *Seeker* can actually master consciously dissolving these "*splits*" and putting them back out. All that is necessary is to practice "*projecting*" and "*dissolving*" these "*split-pieces*" at will. Once a *Seeker* has certainty on this ability, they will be able to let go of the ones that aren't wanted. Part of their *compulsive persistence* is the lack of *certainty* on this skill—because there is a natural tendency to form these "connections" to others people (and *terminals*) in order to stay in the *Game* of *this Physical Universe.*

The "*splitting*" of *attention*—or our *projecting* "*pieces*"—is not the actual *fragmentation*. The *fragmentation* occurs when a "*split*" takes place without one's conscious control (or *Awareness*), and also when one loses control and *Awareness* over the *pieces* that have already *split*. This is what takes place under the heavy spiritual impact of *Implanting*.

FRAGMENTS & BONDED-ENTITIES

When we refer to "*entities*" in *Systemology*, we usually mean other individual disembodied *Alpha-Spirits* (without ownership and control of their own "*Human Body*"). We introduce this subject at *Level-8*, after a *Seeker* has a handle on their own case from previous levels. *Entities* (and *fragments, &tc.*) are not a primary source of *fragmentation*; at best, they might "block" *Awareness*, or amplify our own *fragmentation*.

The *entities* we are most concerned with at this point are those which are adhesively attached to *you* or your *Human Body*. These *Bonded-Entities* has been with the *Alpha-Spirit* for a long time. They generally remain *stuck* in a *low-Awareness level* that is tied to *misemotional states* such as: anger, resentment, anxiety, terror/fear, depression, and hopelessness. They seem to be most "active" when an individual is also operating at those levels, which tends to contribute to such states persisting.

But understand that if you're "angry" (for example), it is *your* "anger"—it does not stem from an *entity* or some kind of *demon*. However, just as a living person might "fan the flames" to encourage a greater *dramatization* of your anger, so too with *entities*, or even *fragments* of yourself. While these *fragments* mainly operate on *automatic*, they still respond to what you are "feeling" and other "reactivity." As a *Seeker* increases their *actualized Awareness*, they can operate greater control over these "*mechanisms*" and other areas.

[If at any point, "something" gets restimulated or stirred up by reading the descriptions and instructions in this manual, apply the *Locational Procedure* to "*it.*"]

A *Seeker* will recall a common theme of "*being divided*" in the *Implant Penalty Universes* (IPU) described in *A.T. Manual #4*. Whether this *actually* occurred to the *Alpha-Spirit* during those *incidents*, or were only *represented* in one's virtual/holographic experience of them, is still under research. But, in either case: the concepts present in the IPU all become reoccurring themes for *actual* events in later (more recent) *Universes.*

There are many ways in which a division or "*split*" might occur. When one is "divided against themselves," they make an individual be in two places, and then might *Implant* each location with different *goals* that are "antagonistic" to each other. This will cause each *viewpoint* to essentially *fight against* the other one—continuously applying *counter-efforts* against each other. A *"splitting"* could also take place if an individual were impacted heavily with *force.*

There have been large-scale mass-*Implanting Incidents* that forced an individual to put *"pieces"* of themselves onto *others,* in order to *control* them and *keep* them *"human."* Similarly, there have been "advanced" societies that employed *"Police Implants"*—which caused you to make *"split-pieces"* into *"Control Entities"* that were placed on "criminals." [Some of these societies made all citizens do this regularly as part of their civic duty or taxation.]

There is information on the *Backtrack* about specialized "collectives." In their advanced military campaigns, officers would put *"split-off pieces"* as *"Control Entities"* onto their subordinates—all the way down the chain-of-command—so that an *"invasion force"* could operate as a single "unit" under the command of a single *Alpha-Spirit* (at the top).

In the *"wizarding"* societies of the *Magic Universe,* "entities" were often the high-value *"coin"* or *currency.* They were often used as servants or laborers—or even entrapped in *"objects"* to make "magical devices." One of the reasons the *Human Condition* is susceptible to *"Bonded-Entities"* is because of the accumulated *postulates* and *considerations* regarding the *"acquiring"* of *entities* for some kind of use.

And while we have introduced the subject of *"spiritual machinery"* in earlier *processing-levels* (see *PC-14*), the subject will be treated more thoroughly in this manual. But briefly stated: we have, at times, intentionally put out *pieces* to set up *"machinery"* (in various *non-physical directions*) in order to project the *reality* we *perceive* for ourselves. This too, eventually became fragmented and out of our conscious control as a result of the heavy impacts from certain *Implanting-Incidents.*

In *processing-levels 0 to 6*, the *"Seeker"* themselves is the main focus or target of *processing-sessions.* Of course, on the *Pathway* toward *Ascension*, a *Seeker* is actually treating a "composite case" of:

Self + Human Body + Bonded-Entitites

The fundamental *processing-levels* ensure that an individual—the *Seeker*—ceases in compulsively "mucking up" things for themselves. In this wise, a clear view is available for handling everything that is apart from us; that keeps us entrapped in *this Physical Universe*, *the Human Condition*, and *on Earth.*

Once a strong foundation is in place—a *Seeker* has reached stable *Beta-Defragmentation* with *processing-levels 0 to 6*—and the more significant *turbulent charge* is *defragmented* from the *Implanting* described in *Level-7*, no further *imprinting* must be *processed-out* on the individual's *own case.*

Using those procedures *on Self*, from *Level-8* onward will have a tendency to "pull-in" the *imprinting* and *fragmentation* of other *entities* that hang suspended in "close proximity" to us—such as *Bonded-Entities.* There are ways of applying earlier *processes* directly *to entities* in order to *intentionally* make these *entities* accessible for proper handling; but a *Seeker* must *knowingly* be doing so to be successful. Otherwise, the risks associated with this phenomenon is a *misidentification* of *source/cause*—which results in persistence of the *fragmentation* that is not handled *As-It-Is*.

It is possible, even after *processing-levels 0 to 7*, that a *Seeker* still experiences some *fixation* on specific *"reoccurring items"* or *turbulently charged* "areas" that did not seem to fully *"release"* or *defragment.* Assuming previous *levels* were fully completed, it is likely—at *Level-8*—that such *charge* persists due to the *"protest"* (*restimulation*) of a *Bonded-Entity* or B.E. We want to, however, make certain that we are not treating something *as someone else's,* which is really *our own* (and the other way around).

At this high-level of operation, a *"Wizard's"* primary *processing-action* is now *"Spotting As-It-Is; and Defragmentation by Awareness."* This requires the ability to properly *recognize* a true *identification* of *"Source"* and *"What Is,"* *&tc.,* which a *Seeker* will have strongly developed along the *Pathway.* This is applied directly in *systematic processing* with the *"Identification Procedure"* (given below)—which is effective whether handling a *Bonded-Entity,* a *split-fragment (spiritual machinery),* or even the *genetic-vehicle (Body)* that is also an *entity.*

THE IDENTIFICATION PROCEDURE

This technique is incredibly basic, though its actual application and background requires additional explanation. Its origins are as old as there have been *Wizards* attempting to exercise control over other *entities.*

Once you *locate* (*get a sense of, &tc.*) a *being, entity,* or *fragment,* you *direct to "it"* the following *process*—which includes two *steps* (or PCL):

35

A. *"What Are You?"*

B. *"Who Are You?"*

Use of this technique requires knowing the difference between something being *"in-phase"* versus *"out-of-phase."* There is some mention of *personality-phases* in past *Systemology* literature, but what we really mean is *Identity-phases* or *Identity-phasing*.

By *"phase,"* we mean: *being* something other than *who* and *what* you are (an *Alpha-Spirit*), but *mistakenly* operating from that *viewpoint* or *point-of-view* (POV) as though it is your *actual Identity* (*compulsively* and/or *unknowingly*). This is what people mean by the phrase "lose themselves" —which is to say *"out-of-synch"* with *Truth* or *Self-Honesty.* [Use of the term *"phase"* comes from *electrical-wave engineering*, but its application here is *systematically* accurate.]

Fundamentals of this procedure do not require a lot of technical complexity. The first step is understanding that you are in close proximity to other *entities* (*Alpha-Spirits*) that have not shared the full benefit of the same *processing* that has delivered *you* to this point on the *Pathway.* Therefore, the same type of personal *fragmentation* treated at *processing-levels 0 to 4*, which once held up a *Seeker*, could also be what is keeping an *entity* from *"releasing"* —but in this case, we would direct such *defragmentation processing* to the *entity*.

When we speak of *Identities* and *phases*, we are *systematically* referring to the *"conception and/or perception of one's own Beingness."* *Bonded-Entities* can become *fixated* on any *Identity-phase*, just as any other *Alpha-Spirit* can. The *Identity-phase* that an *entity* may be in, is not restricted to "an individual person"; it is not restricted to a *"body"* or even traditional *terminals.* Of course, one's true and actual nature is *Self*—the *(Alpha)-Spirit.*

An *entity* may be *identifying* (*out-of-phase*) with anything: a role, a name, a significance, a word (or phrase), a group, a body part, or really any material object—from molecules to planets. It may also have been *Implanted* with a *goal,* which is to say a *"doingness"* that it *identifies* with even more than a *"Beingness"*—such as *"a goal to block (you),"* or of *"being a barrier,"* &tc.

In many ways, the *Identification Procedure* is a *"listing-process"* for an *entity.* You may need to get multiple answers for the *"What..?"* PCL until you can determine what they are currently *being.* It is important to *"acknowledge"* any of the answers/responses/impressions that are perceived/received (just as in *Traditional Piloting/Co-Piloting*). A familiarity with *Systemology Piloting* is necessary for *systematically processing entities.*

Initially, this procedure is best practiced by writing out the question on your worksheet, then listing out the answers—preferably using *GSR-Meter "reads"* as an *indicator* of the "most correct" answer.

Just as with *Co-Piloting* any other *Seeker,* it is important not to *"invalidate"* any response; but you can *process* an *entity toward* a *release-point* by getting it *"in phase."* When using the procedure, whether you are freeing an individual *Alpha-Spirit,* or you are returning a *fragment* to its *source,* you are unburdening yourself from carrying the *fragmentation,* and increasing the *Awareness* of other *Alpha-Spirits* in the *Universe.*

Once they *recognize* that they are not the *"phase-item,"*

you direct the *"Who..?"* PCL with the intention that they will answer *"Me"* or *"I'm Me"* (from the perspective of the *entity*). This is meant to restore their *Awareness* that they are nothing else but simply themselves. The *entity* will often *release* after you *acknowledge* the correct answer —as if it finally *realizes*: *"Oh, I really am me!"*

If the answer you get is not *"Me,"* you still *acknowledge* the response, but you will probably have to repeat the PCL. It may also require some basic *two-way communication* with the *entity* in order to steer them toward the *"Me"*-type answer. For example:

"What were you before that?"

This shifts the *entity's attention* to an earlier point on their *Backtrack*. Effectiveness of the *Identification Procedure* is dependent on resolving misconceptions about *Identity* that the *entity* (*fragment, &tc.*) is fixated on.

BONDED-ENTITIES & FUSED-GROUPS

There are two main aspects of instruction for this subject that are alternated throughout this manual: a) the understanding of *Bonded-Entities* and *Fused-Groups* in order to recognize, locate, and contact them; b) the *systematic methods* by which these *entities* can be released by a *"Wizard-level"* practitioner. It may be the case at times that many *entities* are "showing up" for *defragmentation processing*; and a true *"Wizard"* must handle them orderly, civilly, respectfully, lovingly, firmly, ...*systematically.*

Presence of *Bonded-Entities* (or "B.E.") will block or inhibit the clarity and horsepower of our *spiritual perception*

(*ZU-Vision*, *&tc.*)—yet most are not malevolent themselves, they are just sort of *low-Awareness beings* "in the way." It might be helpful to think of "*layers*" (or *sheets*) of interconnected 1-cm. (half-inch) *marbles* or *beads* that surround the *body* (like a tight skin-suit) and even penetrate it. These sheets, although mainly transparent and resembling the structure of modern *bubble-wrap*, "stack up" as *layers,* often extending out approximately three-feet from the *body.*

The *Seeker* should practice being able to *focus, concentrate,* and *concenter* (permeate from all directions), their own "*attention*" to a *spot* that is 1-centimeter (or half-inch)—the approximate area that an *entity* is perceived to relatively occupy as a *viewpoint-for-Awareness* in *Space.* A *Seeker* would have some practice in this area from the "*objective exercises*" found in former *processing-levels.* This is an important skill for *communicating with* (*processing*) a single specific *entity.* A *Level-8* practitioner has a high-level of *Awareness,* but still must limit *attention* to one *entity* at a time until its *release.*

In addition to individual B.E., there is another phenomenon that occurs, which we refer to as a "*Fused-Group.*" These "*groups*" consist of multiple B.E. that are held (or *fused*) together by a shared traumatic, heavily fragmentary, experience—usually a heavy *Implanting-Incident.* By *processing-out* the *fusing incident,* a *Fused-Group* may be *dispersed, released* as a whole, or at least broken up into individual B.E. for *release.*

Fused-Groups "formation" and B.E. "adhesion" often results from heavy *impacts*—such as with at least one significant *Implanting-Incident* we know of that took place in *this Physical Universe.* When an *entity* (*Alpha-Spirit*) forcefully collides (*impacts*) with another *entity*, either (or both) may get so heavily *imprinted* with a *"mental image picture"* of the *impact* that it gets its *consideration-of-Being-ness* "stuck" or "fused" — *out-of-phase* — to the *imprint* and the other *entity* that shares the *imprint*.

While an *Alpha-Spirit (Seeker)* operates with a *Human Body*, it acts as a *filter* and *magnifier* for an individual's *perception* and experience of *reality*. True *spiritual perception* (*ZU-Vision* and other innate *Alpha abilities*) is far more accessible to an individual after clearing all *identifications* with *bodies* that are not *Self*. This includes handling B.E. (and *Fused-Groups*), because once they are fixated on their *identification* with the *Human Body*, they form an *encysted* solidity and *crystallized* "shell" or "aura" that acts to hold an individual (*Seeker*) *in* the *Human Condition*.

Some B.E. are intentionally *implanted* to be part of a *body* (a specific *body-part* or *spot* on a *body*) — which is *out-of-phase* with their *being* an *Alpha-Spirit* or *fragment*, &tc. Operating in this wise, most *entities* believe they are serving a specific purpose, going so far as to think they are being helpful, or even necessary.

A B.E. (or *Fused-Group*) is not really *aware* of their *presence* in *"present-time"* — their *attention/Awareness* being very much *fixed* on a *past incident*. In order to *release* an *entity*, it may be necessary to *process them* to a point of *confronting that incident*. This is accomplished *systematically* with the *Level-8 "Incident-Running Procedure (for Entities)"* given in the next section.

Due to the proximity of B.E. and *fragments*, there is a *"telepathic link"* by which *contact/communication* is possible (for *processing*). This *link* is *knowingly* (*consciously*) accessible to a *Seeker/Wizard* at *Level-8*, given the nature of study and heightened *Awareness* already achieved on the *Pathway*. This manual concerns *defragmenting* one's own *composite-case* (B.E., *fragments*, *&tc.*) and is not an esoteric treatment concerning other types of "*spirits*." The information and skill required to handle other kinds of *spiritualism* is generally acquired by a *Wizard* through the experience of handling what *is* accessible (and affecting their own case).

When a B.E. *defragments/releases* (usually upon "*acknowledgment*" of its proper *Identity*-answer, or some other *process*), the "*telepathic*" *link*, *cord*, or *bond*, also disperses. At the moment this takes place, a moment of "*exterior perception*" is sometimes *fed back* to the *Seeker*, but from the *viewpoint* of the *entity*. To be sure the *entity* "*happily blows off*," this occasional phenomenon should not be *invalidated*; but it should not be mistaken as one's own *ZU-Vision*. [Of course, increase of one's *spiritual perception* is a natural side-effect to *releasing* the *Alpha-fragmentation* that persists in blocking our *clarity*.]

During *processing-levels 0 to 7*, we don't generally handle much concerning *somatic-pings* or *bodily sensations* that "turn on" during *systematic sessions*. They might be *acknowledged*, but generally "turn off" when the *process* is *run* to a full *defragmentation-point*.

At *Level-8*—when treating *entities* and *incidents*—*sensations* and *pressures* felt from the *body* are more critical. If they occur while handling a *process*, record exactly *where* on the *body* they occur. Use this to data as a suggestion for where to focus your 1-cm. (half-inch) beam of *attention* during your next *process*. When applying *Level-8*, it is likely to be a B.E. coming "awake" or "active" and essentially saying: "*Here I am!*" [It is important not to just *pass-by* or *fly-by* such *indicators* at this *level*.]

When this does occur, it is important to *acknowledge* the *somatic-ping* and make a record (to return to later). You can even tell the *entity*: "*I hear you there, but you'll have to wait your turn.*" It is also important not to prematurely *end-off* the handling of a *current entity* until its *release*.

The standard practice is to check for any other *entities* at the same location you were just handling, to be sure it wasn't a *Fused-Group* or if another B.E. moved in to duplicate its position. Then, if the former *somatic-ping* persists (that occurred while working with the other), you can check for an *entity* at *that* location. It is good practice to work with different areas of the body each session, rather than checking over the same parts consecutively. Extend your *Awareness* or *perception* to areas from different sides or angles.

In addition to *somatic-pings* (*pressure, pain, sensations*), B.E. and *Fused-Groups* may communicate by relaying *emotion* (*feelings*), an *audible voice* (*perceived internally*), or some type of "*thought*" or "*imagery.*" *Contacting* (*communicating* with) B.E. for *processing* can also be accomplished directly with even the most faint of *perceived impressions*, if a *Seeker* is proficient with a *GSR-Meter/biofeedback device* (which is the preferred *systematic method* of handling this area/subject). If a "*Wizard*" can focus their *attention-Awareness* specifically on the *energetic-mass* of *one entity*, then that B.E. will *react/register* "*answers*" on a *Meter* (just like any *Seeker*).

Advisement: there could easily be *over 100 Fused-Groups*

and individual *Bonded-Entities* adhesively fixed to a *Seeker*. If you find *zero*, or only a few, it is quite possible that you are not yet at a "level" to *confront Level-8* work. Make certain all your fundamentals (*processing-levels 0 to 6*) "check out" okay. If you are certain that your own handling of *"The Jewel (Parts #1-5)"* is properly *defragmented* (from *AT#3*), run *"Platforms #1-18"* (again) from that manual. Additional details regarding *"Platforms #1-18"* also appears in this manual.

Let's start with a basic exercise to increase your *spiritual perception* for *handling entities*.

1. *Close your eyes.*
2. *"Imagine"* (*create by visualization*) a B.E. as a sort of *"circle of energy"* or *"pressure."*
3. *Acknowledge it* (for being there).
4. *"Imagine/Intend"* for the B.E. to *release*—leaving and disappearing into the distance (as a result of your *recognizing* and *acknowledging* it).

Repeat this exercise many times, *"imagining/creating"* these in various locations: in precise *points* in the *body*, in precise *spots-in-space* around you, in the *walls, floor*, and *ceiling, &tc.* Continue until you feel good about this exercise and your certainty in doing it. Then run the *"Standard Procedure (for Entities)"* and see if there are any more accessible now.

A *Seeker* should be able to notice the slight difference between the "feel" (or "sense of") the *actual* B.E. versus those they have intentionally *imagined/created*. There are times (at *Level-8*) where a *Seeker* will think they've *Spotted* (or *sensed*) a real one, when they're really *imagining/creating* it there. But that's okay.

If you *release* a few *"imagined"* ones from an area, it will be easier to handle the real ones anyways. They even sometimes *"copy the imagery"* of you *releasing* the *imagined* ones and will leave along with it. Once you have *certainty* with the *systematic processing* of *entities*—and have elevated your own *Actualized Awareness*—most types of *entities* and *fragments* can be *dispersed* by simply *"acknowledging"* them and *"defrag-by-Awareness"* (*As-It-Is*).

INCIDENT-RUNNING PROCEDURE
(*for bonded-entities, fused-groups*)

[A *Seeker* should review *"Confronting the Past"* (*PC-9*), *"Spiritual Implants"* (*PC-11*) and *"Games & Universes"* (*PC-12*). Keep these materials accessible—in addition to *"Secret of Universes"* (*AT#1*) and *"The Jewel of Knowledge"* (*AT#3*)—when applying the *"Incident-Running Procedure (for Entities)."*]

Unlike when a *Seeker* has *run incidents* and *incident-chains* for previous levels—such as in *"Confronting the Past"* (*PC-9*)—we only use *Implanting-Incidents* for which we have significant data, when handling *entities*. This means that we do *not* have to find out "what happened" from each *entity* in order to *defragment* them.

When applying *processing* to *entities*: we don't need to go through every detail of an *incident*, or *implant-item* of a *Platform*; simply get the *entity* to *spot* the main highlights. In this wise, we can very pointedly direct a PCL to an *entity* to *"Go To.."* or *"Move To.."* such-and-such part of an *incident sequence*.

To be effective, the *Seeker/Wizard* must maintain control of the *session*, just like a *Pilot*—directing PCL to B.E. in order to "guide" their *attention* through the *sequence* of the *incident*; directing them to *spot* various points from a *"sequence outline"* that is already known to the *Seeker/Wizard*. As you gain experience with handling this procedure, you'll have greater certainty on your ability to *telepathically* "blanket" and "push" an *entity* through the *incident* they are "stuck" in. [This serves to *release* them so they can *leave/blow-off*.]

When starting *Level-8*, there are two primary *Implanting-Incidents* that a *Seeker* first applies this procedure to. A *Seeker* has actually been studying the components of these in previous *processing-levels*.

— *The Heaven Incident* (at the start of our *track* in *this Universe*);

     and

— *The Hellfire Incident* (which occurred *66* or *75 million years ago*).

HEAVEN & HELLFIRE

The *"Hellfire Incident"* used for this *"Incident-Running Procedure"* does not need to be *processed* by a *Seeker* "on *Self*." Its appearance here is specifically for handling *Earth-bound entities* (B.E. and *Fused-Groups*) that are commonly affected by this particular *Implanting-Incident*. It assists in "breaking up" (or *dispersing*) *Fused-Groups* into individual B.E., freeing them up for additional individualized *processing* (through the *"Heaven Incident"*).

Applying the *"Hellfire Incident"* only treats a certain *layer* or segment of *entities* that were actually affected (or *fused*) by this *incident*, or are still "stuck" on it; but we apply this as a basic method because of the amount of gain that is achieved with it. It is not the only mass (widespread) *Implanting-Incident* that this general procedure applies to. [The "*Hellfire Incident*" is a specialized application that does not appear in the basic instructions for "*Standard Procedure: Entities*" (given in the next section).]

The "*Heaven Incident*" is the only *incident* that is *common to all entities* (*Alpha-Spirits*) that have experienced *Entry-Into-This-Universe*; but *only* an *individual* B.E. can be *released* by using it for this procedure. Therefore, the "*Hellfire Incident*" is *processed first*, in order to break up "*groups*" that were *fused* by that *incident* (before *running* individual *entities* through the "*Heaven Incident*").

When the "*Hellfire Incident*" is applied to *handling entities*: you start with "*1. The Explosion*," and *never* push the B.E. (or *Fused-Group*) beyond "*2B. Platforms #1-18*" in the *sequence outline*. To go further requires having full data on the "*36-Day Implant*" (that uses IPU symbols). There is not enough *data* to do so and still be in full control of the *session*. And it is not necessary for this procedure. If the B.E. hasn't *released* by that point, then you may need to *run* the *incident* a second time (starting with *The Explosion*). But, that may be unnecessary, because this much of the *incident sequence* is usually sufficient enough to disperse a *Fused-Group*—in which case, if *entities* remain, you can then take each *individual* B.E. through the "*Heaven Incident*" (and/or apply "*Standard Procedure*").

Usually only the "*1. Heaven Implant*" section of the "*Heaven Incident*" is necessary for this procedure; and even a vague approximation of its events is effective. One of the issues with running "*The Jewel, Parts #1-5*" is that the same *Implant-Pattern* was later (more recently) repeated in the *"Hellfire Incident"* sequence. If a *Seeker/Wizard* finds they *do* need to direct an *entity* to *"Spot"* (or *"Go To.."*) specific parts of *The Jewel Implant* in order to *release* them, it is important to make sure that the *Pattern* is being treated for the right *incident*.

There is additional data for the *Hellfire Incident*, much of which is *speculative* at this juncture of our research. Since the data for the basic *"sequence outline"* is correct (effective), we haven't concerned ourselves with the other details that may be accessible. Whether or not the *incident* took place on *Earth*, or was all an elaborate *"projection,"* does not alter its demonstrable workability and effectiveness in breaking through the *Fused-Groups* of B.E. that are "stuck" on whatever this *Implanting-Incident* happens to really be. In *Systemology*, we are more concerned with *results*, than *dogma*—so we include the *incident* for the gains it provides.

What we do know is that the *atomic blasts*, *meteors* and *volcanism* indicated by the *Hellfire Incident* is a direct reference to what some refer to as *"The Great Dying"*—a cataclysmic period of synchronous events that *did* take place on *Earth*. Although some geologists and physicists date this event at approximately *66 million years ago*, the elevated *radiation* levels of the *incident* have caused the *carbon-dating* to be skewed on this one. When using *GSR-Metering*, the *incident* may be *"located and dated"* (as in it *"registers"*) at *75 million years ago*.

The *Hellfire Incident* was an intentionally planned event. It occurred in order to establish *Earth* as a *"prison planet"* for this *galaxy*—and also program the basic *"Human Condition"* for the *Alpha-Spirits* entrapped here. The *Earth* was actually a beautiful planet inhabited by diverse life-forms; but like everything else in *this Universe*, it became *fragmented*—now *re-purposed* to serve as a dumping ground for *entities* that were otherwise too numerous, or too free, to be adequately controlled (by whatever society did the *implanting*).

More advanced societies in *this Universe* have something akin to *"Implant Dealers."* The *Implants* that appear in the *Hellfire Incident* are not original to that *incident*; but they were collected, chained together, and were effectively impactful. *"The Jewel (Parts #1-5)"* are repeated from the *Heaven Incident*, to install a false sense of the *Hellfire Incident* being the *"start of time."* The *"#1-18 Series"* was primarily kept on file since the *Magic Universe* era (and even prior). Restimulation of the *Implanted Penalty-Universes* extends back several *Universes*. It is only important to *run through* the "items" on the *sequence outline*; you do not have to *run* all *command-lines* of all *Platforms* on each *entity* when applying this *"Incident-Running Procedure."*

HEAVEN INCIDENT

0. ENTRY-INTO-UNIVERSE

1. HEAVEN IMPLANT *(See PC-12 & AT#1)*

   A.) Loud Sharp Snapping Crackles

   B.) Waves Of Light

   C.) Theater & Stage

   D.) Angel On Chariot Enters

   E.) Trumpet Blasts

   F.) Thundering Crackles and Snaps

   G.) Angel On Chariot Exits

   H.) "Goals-Sequencing" Pageant/Skit

   I.) Waves of Darkness

2. THE JEWEL (PARTS #1-5)
       (See AT#3 for additional details)

HELLFIRE INCIDENT

0. CAPTURE/TRANSPORT
    (if Alpha-Spirit is not already on Earth)

1. EXPLOSION

    A.) Atomic, Volcanic, Meteor, *&tc*.
        (specific events and locations)

    B.) Terrible Winds

    C.) Alpha-Spirit Carried Into Sky

    D.) Electronic Field/Screen Rises In Sky

    E.) Alpha-Spirit Stuck To Screen

    F.) Pulled Down For Mass-Implanting

2. HELLFIRE IMPLANT

    A.) The Jewel, Parts #1-5 *(for this incident)*
        Establishes false "Start-of-Time"

    B.) Platforms #1-18 Series *(see AT#3)*
        Programming of "Human Condition"

    C.) Arrival Of "The Pilot"

    D.) 36-Days Of IPU-Restimulation
        Holographic moving pictures (like film)
        (lacking data here; see AT#4)

3. ASSEMBLY CENTERS
    (may belong above as "1G")

    A.) Fusion Of Entities Into Groups
        (at specific locations)

HELLFIRE INC. (ADDITIONAL DATA)

This section is included to increase a *Seeker's reality* on, and ability to effectively handle, the *Hellfire Incident-Running Procedure*. Our research phase demonstrated that it is an area—or point on this *Advanced Training* course—that some *Seeker's* seemed to get "stuck" on, which prevented continuing their studies/progress.

Although there are many *Implanting-Incidents* on the *Backtrack*, this one is included in this manual because it is "*spiritual contamination*" (or *fragmentation*) that is "common to all" *Earthlings*. While this seems like it should make our *Standard Procedures* more effective, many of the B.E. from this *incident* are initially found in an incredibly *low-Awareness state*, and often need a lot of assistance (*Beingness* or *livingness* granted to them by the "*Wizard*") in order to achieve their *release*.

In the past, "Mystics" often used various *tools* and *spiritual-aids* to accomplish their "*divination*" and "*necromancy*." Today, we have the benefit of using *Biofeedback-Devices* that allow us to approach these same areas far more *systematically*.

B.E. are located by "*Meter-read*," checking off from the following list (in the order given): the location of a *current somatic-ping* (*pressure, itching, tingling, &tc.*); the location of a *between-session* discomfort; the location of a *Fused-Group* (from a previous *session* that is not fully handled); and general "scanning" or "looking around" the *body*.

Some B.E. require a greater *reality* on the *incident* they are "stuck" in before they are able to *confront* it "*As-It-Is*."

This means, what we generally refer to as, *"dating and locating."* Remember that the *Hellfire Incident* is the kind of event that an individual might even *want* to *forget*. So, the first part of *"incident-running"* might require more than the *processing-command* to just *"Go to...{start of incident}."*

We can easily determine the date as *"75 Million Years Ago."* [This may be indicated to the B.E./*Fused-Group*.] *"Locating"* the incident on the *Backtrack* as a *"date"* (in *Time*) does not always provide enough *reality* for the B.E. to properly *confront* it. Therefore, a *Seeker* may also need to *"locate"* the *incident "in Space"* —which means determining a literal/physical *geographic location*.

In the past, *"Mystics"* often used *"maps"* combined with such things as *"pendulums"* and *"dowsing-rods"* to accomplish these same *spiritual tasks*. Today's *"Wizard"* benefits strongly from using *"Biofeedback-Technology."*

To be in *contact* with an *entity*, a *"Wizard"* focuses high-level *attention* on the *entity*—realizing *"It-Is"* there, *acknowledging* its *existence*, *&tc*. This grants a higher-level of *Beingness* or *livingness* to the *entity*—and between the two *beings*, there is a heightened *"combined-Awareness"* present for the *session*.

The *attention* and *proximity/affinity* (*telepathic link*) allow the *entity* to *"register"* on a *GSR-Meter*, even though it is the *Seeker/Wizard* (having first *defragmented* the bulk of their own case) that is physically using the *Biofeed-back-Device*. This idea might underlie any assumed effectiveness of such *spiritual-aids* as the *"ouija board"*—but again, we now have far more effective *systematic* means available to us today.

Therefore, with your *attention* on the *entity*, and a *combined-Awareness* on the *incident*: you can use a *GSR-Meter* *"sensor"* (in one hand), and your finger or pointer (with the other hand), and *scan* over a "map" of the *Earth* to find *"Meter-reads"* on actual *locations*. [This applies to more than just *running* the *Hellfire Incident*.]

Note that the continental arrangement of *Earth* was far different *75 million years ago* than it is today. You can "print out" (or otherwise obtain) *geologic estimations* of how the *Earth* appeared at that time, or you can use a modern-day *map*.

Our interest—when specifically handling the *Hellfire Incident*—is the location of the *"explosion site."* For this particular *incident*, it does not have to be exact; the *locations* can be approximated. We also aren't too concerned with whether the nature of that particular *explosion* was *"atomic/nuclear," "meteoric,"* or *"volcanic."* The only time that may be critical data is if a *"Fused-Group"* isn't easily *dispersing*. But, in that case, it is far more *systematically effective* to *locate* (on the *map*) the *"assembly center"* where they were *fused*.

Another key to *releasing* B.E. from a heavily impactful *incident* is to *defragment* any significant specific *protest-charge* that may be *holding* their *attention* on the *incident*. This is *processed-out* just like STEP-B of the *"Standard Procedure: PME–Long Version"* (described later in this manual). In this case, however, the type of *fragmented-charge* will not be on *"going interior,"* but another type of specific *resistive-effort* (or *counter-effort*) applied in the incident. [The basic method is *"Spotting"* the *correct item*, and *defrag-by-Awareness "As-It-Is."*] This may be assessed from the following list:

"In This Incident, Is There An Effort..."

1. *To Stop?*

2. *To Withdraw?*

3. *To (Both) Stop And Withdraw?*

4. *Suppress Something?*

5. *Invalidate Something?*

6. *Protest About Something?*

7. *Hold Onto A Picture (Of The Incident)?*

8. *Hurry Or Rush?*

9. *To Make Something "Not Be"?*

STANDARD PROCEDURE: ENTITIES

We have already introduced the three primary techniques used for this *Standard Procedure for Entities (Fragments, &tc.)*:

1. *Locational*

2. *Identification*

3. *Heaven Incident*

These may be worked forwards and backwards (*1-2-3-2-1-2-3..*) until a B.E. (or *Fragment, Split &tc.*) *releases*.

Combining what you've learned in this manual, let's add some additional introductory guidelines so you can put this into practice. Here are some basic steps to get you started.

A. Close your eyes and *"look"* over the *Body* and the space around the *Body* (the "shell" could extend three feet or more). You are *"looking"* for areas or spots that seem to have "pressure" or some "energetic-mass."

B. *"Get the sense"* of contacting or permeating the *"entity"* that is generating the "pressure" (or "mass").

C. Apply the *"Locational Technique"* (using information given previously in this manual). If you still sense that the presence remains, continue to STEP-D.

D. Apply the *"Identification Technique"* (using information given previously in this manual).

   D1. Ask them *"What Are You?"* and sort of "feel" for an answer coming back from them. You may just get a subtle "idea" or "impression" of what they are "being." You might have to "infuse" them with a bit of life—or "enliven" them directly with your *Awareness of them being there*; *"granting"* them a bit more *"Beingness"*—in order to "draw out" a response. [This is simply done by focused and directed *intention*.]

   D2. Ask them *"Who Are You?"* and, if necessary, steer them toward the *"Me"* answer. *Acknowledge* any responses; but the *release* generally occurs only when the *"Me"* answer is *acknowledged*. Repeat STEP-D2 until you get the *"Me"-release*. If the *entity releases (leaves/blows-off)*, continue to STEP-E; if the *entity* does not *release*, go to STEP-F.

E. Check for *"Copies."* Sometimes another *entity* will immediately *create a "Copy"* of the one that just left, or even assume its *phase* themselves. If you get a sense of this happening, *spot* that others are *copying*; then *project* (or *intend*) an *acknowledgment* to them for doing that. This usually gets them to stop; then you can *defragment/dissolve* the *"Copy"* by *Awareness/Spotting* and/or apply the *"Locational Technique"* to it, *&tc.*

F. Check for *"Holders."* Sometimes another *entity* will attempt to "hold onto" the one that is *releasing.* If you get a sense of this happening, *Spot* that it *Is,* and *acknowledge* the other *entity* for doing that. When the first one *releases,* you can then shift your *attention* to handling the *"Holder."* If the *entity* you are attempting to release is not being "held" by another *entity,* continue to STEP-G.

NOTE: You can shift *attention* to handle a *"Holder"* as your next *entity* to *defragment.* However, this is not usually standard practice for *"Copiers"* — unless it is a *single entity* for certain, and not a *group*; because these *entities* really like to *create "Copies"* (it is the basic skill of an *Alpha-Spirit*) and you can quickly become overwhelmed trying to handle too many *Copiers* and *Copies* at once.

G. If you run into trouble with the previous steps, are not getting any answers/responses, or otherwise are unable to get an *entity* to *release,* then apply the *"Incident-Running Technique"* specifically on the *Heaven Incident* (relying on the *sequence outline* provided in this manual, in addition to your own experience with the *incident*). Gently "push" the *entity* through the *incident.*

H. If at any time, while performing these techniques, you find your attention being drawn to anything that you get the sense of being a *"piece"* of yourself, apply the *"Locational Technique"* to it.

Communication between the *Seeker* and *entity* occurs on a *"telepathic link."* In most cases, the procedural PCL can be "intended" or "projected" to the *entity* silently. The

"Identification Technique" works best as a written exercise. There are some practitioners that have reached the level of freely *processing entities* out loud—but when first starting out, *silent intention* works best for *focusing* on a *single* B.E., so as not to stir up others.

A *Seeker/Wizard* should handle *entities* as various "layers" become *accessible* during *upper-level* work. The in-session handling of *entities* may be accomplished in between treating other areas and developing *spiritual perception* (such as *A.T. Manual #6*). *Entities* become more *accessible* the longer a *Seeker* works with their *Advanced Training*. It is important to not become too obsessive about directly "searching for" or trying to "locate" *entities*; because if you "push" or "intend" too hard in a certain spot, you will frequently find yourself forcing a B.E. to occupy that location.

Self-Honesty is critical for *upper-grade* work. At *Level-8*, the insistence, expectancy, or demand of a *Wizard* that "something" *is* "there" *will put* "something" "there."

As you know, *Alpha-Spirits* are not *actually* "located" in any *space-time* "location" or position. An individual is not *actually* "within" the *Universe* that they are operating their *Awareness* from, but unfortunately, the *Human Condition* tends to be confined or restricted to such *considerations-of-Beingness*. However, this also applies to other *entities* (B.E., *&tc.*) that you encounter. They are only located by their own *consideration*; and since they are highly suggestible and you are now more *Actualized*, they can also be located by *your considerations*.

Let's examine an example of this. For training purposes: there is an *out-of-phase* B.E. that is compulsively occupy-

57

ing a *bookshelf*—"*being a bookshelf,*" "*being in a bookshelf,*" *&tc.* You "touch" or "contact" the *entity* and it gets the *realization* that it's not there (and never *actually* was, except as a *consideration*) and it "*releases*" and ceases to be there.

This phenomenon occurs so quickly that you keep *trying to locate* them—and since you can *actually* "reach" your *Awareness* anywhere in *space-time* (and in *any Universe*), you can still "reach" the *entity*, and the effect is essentially relocating them back. This not only falsely *locates* the *entity* in *space-time* again, but also *invalidates* their previous *realization/release*. If this happens, all a *Seeker/Wizard* needs to do is rehabilitate the *release* by "*Spotting*" the instance that the *location was enforced*, then *release* the *entity* again (if it remains).

In this wise, a *Seeker* should beware "*pulling-in*" or even "*creating*" *entities to be run on processing*. This is a real phenomenon that takes place, which is why "*Entities & Fragments*" is only treated at *Level-8*. After handling of *entities* has begun, the danger comes from "blaming things" on *entities* when/if they are not the direct cause. This is the same as saying or thinking *something is there* when it isn't. This also means potentially *creating* "*things*" *to be there* that are *misidentified* as *something else*; which makes *defragmenting* it "*As-It-Is*" quite difficult later.

An individual's *inabilities* and *fragmentation* are still part of one's own case—one's own *considerations, reality-agreements* and *postulates*. This *fragmentation* can certainly be made worse, *amplified* by the presence of B.E., but they are not the ultimate "reason why" of our problems. There are other parts of *Level-8* that focus more directly on a *Seeker's* own *spiritual perception*; don't make the mistake of thinking that all *Alpha-fragmentation* and *perceived spiritual ability barriers* are being imposed exclusively from the "outside."

"PLATFORMS #1-18" (AT#3 ADDENDUM)

A *Seeker's* own *run* of "#1-18" helps break up solid blocks of *fused-entities* (and may even *release* some directly). The true purpose of *running* it at *Level-8* is to make *entities* "*available*" or "*accessible*" for *processing*. Additionally, it is a primary component of the "*Hellfire Incident*" (appearing in the *sequence* of *Implants* that were applied during that incident). *Implants* "#1-18" originally appeared individually at various times on the *Backtrack*, but were also eventually employed as part of heavy mass (widespread) *Implanting-Incidents*.

[The following is additional data for the "#1-18" series given in *AT#3*.]

PLATFORM #1X

The *Platform* given in *AT#3* provides a long-form using "{*electric-shock*}" as the *implanting-gimmick*. This is actually only one of *twelve* different "{*feelings*}" that this *Platform-pattern* was used for. *Run* the entire *pattern* completely on each of the following in sequence:

1. *Pleasure*; 2. *Pain*; 3. *Heat*; 4. *Cold*; 5. *Electric-Shock*;
6. *Numbness*; 7. *Sensation*; 8. *Dizziness*; 9. *Pressure*;
10. *Suction (vacuum)*; 11. *Flash (explosion)*; 12. *Blackness*.

PLATFORM #3X

The *Platform* given in *AT#3* provides a long-form using

"SURVIVE" as the reoccurring *item*. This is actually only one of *ten* different reoccurring "{*implant-items*}" that this *Platform-pattern* was used for. *Run* the entire *pattern* completely on each of the following in sequence:

1. *Obey*; 2. *Rebel*; 3. *Work*; 4. *Be Lazy*; 5. *Love*; 6. *Hate*; 7. *Survive*; 8. *Die*; 9. *Create*; 10. *Destroy.*

PLATFORM #14X

The *Platform* given in *AT#3* provides a long-form using "PICTURE MACHINE" as the reoccurring *item*. This is actually only one of *seven* different "{*machine terminals*}" that this *Platform-pattern* was used for. *Run* the entire *pattern* completely on each of the following in sequence:

1. *Postulating Machine*; 2. *Picture Machine*; 3. *Thinkingness Machine*; 4. *Somatic (or Sensation) Machine*; 5. *Reality Machine*; 6. *Confusion Machine* ; 7. *Forgettingness Machine.*

PLATFORM #16B

This *Platform* is *not* given in *AT#3*. It is a short-form formula. *Run* the entire *pattern* completely on each of the following *terminals* in sequence:

1. *Treasure*; 2. *Wealth*; 3. *Love*; 4. *Knowledge*; 5. *Pleasure*; 6. *Bodies*; 7. *Glory*; 8. *Honor*; 9. *Identity*; 10. *Immortality.*

16B.0.0 **STAY**. *& Spot the Alpha*

16B.1.1X **SEEK ___**. *& Spot the Alpha*

16B.1.2X **DO NOT SEEK ___**. *& Spot the Alpha*

16B.1.3X **ABANDON ___**. *& Spot the Alpha*

16B.1.4X **DO NOT ABANDON ___**. *& Spot the Alpha*

16B.2.1X **DISCOVER ___**. *& Spot the Alpha*

16B.2.2X **DO NOT DISCOVER ___**. *& Spot the Alpha*

16B.2.3X OVERLOOK ___. *& Spot the Alpha*

16B.2.4X DO NOT OVERLOOK ___. *& Spot the Alpha*

16B.3.1X FIND ___. *& Spot the Alpha*

16B.3.2X DO NOT FIND ___. *& Spot the Alpha*

16B.3.3X MISS ___. *& Spot the Alpha*

16B.3.4X DO NOT MISS ___. *& Spot the Alpha*

16B.4.1X GRAB ___. *& Spot the Alpha*

16B.4.2X DO NOT GRAB ___. *& Spot the Alpha*

16B.4.3X DISCARD ___. *& Spot the Alpha*

16B.4.4X DO NOT DISCARD ___. *& Spot the Alpha*

16B.5.1X CLUTCH ___. *& Spot the Alpha*

16B.5.2X DO NOT CLUTCH ___. *& Spot the Alpha*

16B.5.3X RELEASE ___. *& Spot the Alpha*

16B.5.4X DO NOT RELEASE ___. *& Spot the Alpha*

16B.6.1X OBTAIN ___. *& Spot the Alpha*

16B.6.2X DO NOT OBTAIN ___. *& Spot the Alpha*

16B.6.3X DISDAIN ___. *& Spot the Alpha*

16B.6.4X DO NOT DISDAIN ___. *& Spot the Alpha*

16B.7.1X TAKE ___. *& Spot the Alpha*

16B.7.2X DO NOT TAKE ___. *& Spot the Alpha*

16B.7.3X GIVE ___. *& Spot the Alpha*

16B.7.4X DO NOT GIVE ___. *& Spot the Alpha*

16B.8.1X HAVE ___. *& Spot the Alpha*

16B.8.2X DO NOT HAVE ___. *& Spot the Alpha*

16B.8.3X GIVE UP ___. *& Spot the Alpha*

16B.8.4X DO NOT GIVE UP ___. *& Spot the Alpha*

16B.9.1X SAVE ___. *& Spot the Alpha*

16B.9.2X DO NOT SAVE ___. *& Spot the Alpha*

16B.9.3X WASTE ___. *& Spot the Alpha*

16B.9.4X DO NOT WASTE ___. *& Spot the Alpha*

16B.10.1X PRESERVE ___. *& Spot the Alpha*

16B.10.2X DO NOT PRESERVE ___. *& Spot the Alpha*

16B.10.3X DESTROY ___. *& Spot the Alpha*

16B.10.4X DO NOT DESTROY ___. *& Spot the Alpha*

16B.11.1X GUARD ___. *& Spot the Alpha*
16B.11.2X DO NOT GUARD ___. *& Spot the Alpha*
16B.11.3X NEGLECT ___. *& Spot the Alpha*
16B.11.4X DO NOT NEGLECT ___. *& Spot the Alpha*

16B.12.1X SAFEGUARD ___. *& Spot the Alpha*
16B.12.2X DO NOT SAFEGUARD ___. *& Spot the Alpha*
16B.12.3X RISK ___. *& Spot the Alpha*
16B.12.4X DO NOT RISK ___. *& Spot the Alpha*

16B.13.1X PROTECT ___. *& Spot the Alpha*
16B.13.2X DO NOT PROTECT ___. *& Spot the Alpha*
16B.13.3X ENDANGER ___. *& Spot the Alpha*
16B.13.4X DO NOT ENDANGER ___. *& Spot the Alpha*

16B.14.1X EXHIBIT ___. *& Spot the Alpha*
16B.14.2X DO NOT EXHIBIT ___. *& Spot the Alpha*
16B.14.3X HIDE ___. *& Spot the Alpha*
16B.14.4X DO NOT HIDE ___. *& Spot the Alpha*

16B.15.1X OWN ___. *& Spot the Alpha*
16B.15.2X DO NOT OWN ___. *& Spot the Alpha*
16B.15.3X DISOWN ___. *& Spot the Alpha*
16B.15.4X DO NOT DISOWN ___. *& Spot the Alpha*

16B.16.1X WIN ___. *& Spot the Alpha*
16B.16.2X DO NOT WIN ___. *& Spot the Alpha*
16B.16.3X LOSE ___. *& Spot the Alpha*
16B.16.4X DO NOT LOSE ___. *& Spot the Alpha*

16B.17.1X BUY ___. *& Spot the Alpha*
16B.17.2X DO NOT BUY ___. *& Spot the Alpha*
16B.17.3X SELL ___. *& Spot the Alpha*
16B.17.4X DO NOT SELL ___. *& Spot the Alpha*

16B.18.1X STEAL ___. *& Spot the Alpha*
16B.18.2X DO NOT STEAL ___. *& Spot the Alpha*
16B.18.3X REJECT ___. *& Spot the Alpha*
16B.18.4X DO NOT REJECT ___. *& Spot the Alpha*

16B.19.1X GATHER ___. *& Spot the Alpha*
16B.19.2X DO NOT GATHER ___. *& Spot the Alpha*

16B.19.3x **SEPARATE ___.** *& Spot the Alpha*

16B.19.4x **DO NOT SEPARATE ___.** *& Spot the Alpha*

16B.20.1x **REMEMBER ___.** *& Spot the Alpha*

16B.20.2x **DO NOT REMEMBER ___.** *& Spot the Alpha*

16B.20.3x **FORGET ___.** *& Spot the Alpha*

16B.20.4x **DO NOT FORGET ___.** *& Spot the Alpha*

16B.21.0 **GO AWAY.** *& Spot the Alpha*

PROGRAMMED MACHINE-ENTITIES

"Spiritual Machinery" is introduced in *PC Lesson-14.* Now that we have discussed *entities* at *Level-8*, we can extend our reach further in this area. *"Simple (or Light) Machinery"*—that is directly *created* as as a *machine* or *response-circuit mechanism*—is relatively easy to *defragment.* A *Seeker* simply applies *"creativeness processes"* (*imagining copies, alteration of copies,* and the *creation* and *destruction* of *copies, &tc.*) or even the *"Standard Procedure (for Entities)"* on *Light Machinery.*

There is also more advanced *"machinery"* that consists of a *systematic series* of *programmed postulates*—or *"circuitry"*—that *creates/manifests* something, or causes something to occur. This *programming* can become quite complex—similar to *programs* and *operating systems* for *personal computers,* except that they range all the way up to the level of *creating* and *managing* entire *Universes.*

This *"programmed machine-circuitry"* can actually be quite useful, and is only mildly *fragmentary* in itself. One primary liability to their *creation* is that an *Alpha-Spirit* could set one to run forever, forget about it, and subsequently lose *responsibility* and *control* for its *creation.*

Later (more recently) on the *Backtrack*, these forgotten *machines* also get "infested" by B.E. that *copy* them, and *fragment* their operation, *&tc*. This, again, can all be handled with *Standard Procedures* and even methods given for earlier *processing-levels.*

Early on the *Backtrack*, an *Alpha-Spirit* would *"imprint"* the *programming* onto some kind of *template* or *platform.* [This will be off in some separate (extra-dimensional) *Space* that you've *created* for it.] You would *knowingly* "activate" or "trigger" the *machinery* by *reaching* back and *projecting* a bit of *intention* (or *energy* in more recent *Universes*) on a communication-line (*focused attention*) toward that *template.*

Also, early on the *Backtrack*, *Alpha-Spirits* had the ability to more easily and *knowingly* "erase" each other's *machinery.* Of course, we could just *create* it again—but this led to a tendency toward making multiple *copies* of *templates* and "stacking" them behind various "levels" of *alteration* (*postulates of "It-As-Changed"*) in order to make getting at (or *destroying*) the basic *structural template* of the *machine* more difficult for others.

By the era of the "*Symbols Universe*" (*see AT#1*), the decline of *Spiritual Awareness* resulted in too many *considerations* of *inability* (*Alpha-fragmentation*) to keep all of one's *machinery* "manifested" (in the face of persistent opposition). The solution to this was to *create* a new type of *machinery* that could *persist.* This led to the idea of *making beings* (*spirits*) into *machines, implanting* them to keep the *machinery created.* But, *Alpha-Spirits* were still fairly powerful *beings* during the *Symbols Universe* era, and they wouldn't stay in that *phase of Beingness* forever.

At some point, the *being* would just basically say *"To hell with this,"* and *release* itself.

Programmed Machine-Entities (or "PME") currently in existence primarily stem from the *Magic Universe.* During that era, *"entities"* were essentially the high-value money —such as with *"magic rings"* or *"relics."* But there are also some *entities* that were *crafted/made* into PME during *this Universe.* And by this, we mean *Alpha-Spirits* (and *fragments*) made into *"machine cores"* (resembling tiny *black crystalline cylinders*), which follow a series of *pre-programmed postulates* (or *"circuitry"*) laid out on a *"machine template."* PME are not operating on their own *postulates*; so don't hate on them too much (and handle them civilly).

"Implant Dealers" (from technologically advanced civilizations) are the primary manufacturers of PME in *this Universe.* This means they also serve as *"spirit collectors."* For example: after a mass (widespread) *Implant*—such as the *Hellfire Incident*—there are a lot of *fragmented pieces* of *beings* basically lying around. These are then *collected* and made into PME. The existing PME and B.E. *fragments* could also be *re-purposed.*

More recently on the *Backtrack,* one of the more modern types of PME is the *"Virus."* These are not simple *organic lifeforms,* or like other forms of *biological decay;* they were all intentionally *created.* They are usually used against enemy populations, but they are also unleashed on *"prison planets"* to suppress its inhabitants. Most of the current *viruses* on *Earth* were implanted here in the last *6,000* to *12,000 years* in order to keep the growing population of *"inmates"* under greater control (and reduce the *Human lifespan*).

A "*splitter mechanism*" is often *encoded* in PME programming. This is *systematically* referred to as a "*Split-Viewpoint*" or "*SV-Mechanism.*" We are legally not permitted to even suggest using *Systemology* to attempt to "*cure*" any *viruses*—but for illustrative purposes: if you were to *process* a *virus* as a PME, you would actually find thousands of PME in the *body*. *Processing* a single one might *release* it, but it is immediately replaced by whichever is the original one, splitting again, and then reappearing in that location.

Many older PME types also have this "*replacement-quality*"—and you would have to work through a few *layers* of *templates* to approach the original. Some B.E. will do this, too—which can sometimes make the *entity-handling* portion of *Level-8* seem endless.

Similar to the "*Locational Procedure*" for B.E., the ultimate undercut-PCL for PME is:

"*Spot Being Made Into A Machine.*"

Ever since its introduction during the *Symbols Universe* era, PME *construction* typically occurs within a long *cylinder*. It resembles the shape of the "*machine core*" that the *entity* is made into. The "*surface walls*" of the *cylinder* were covered in *holographic imagery* of IPU-*terminals*. The *entity* would typically have a low-level of "*confront*" on at least some of these *images*—so an increased *resistance* to "*touching the walls*" develops.

Where the *entity* would have otherwise been able to pass through the material-surface of the *cylinder*, a *reactive-withdraw* (or "*attention flinch*") tendency is being *conditioned*. As layers of *holographic imagery* increasingly compounded, the *cylinder* is made to appear as though it were *"shrinking,"* and as a *reactive-effect*, the *entity* would also *"squeeze"* its own *considerations-of-Beingness* tighter and tighter. This is also how *"high-pressure"* Group-Fusing *Incidents* are accomplished, for which the entry-point is: *"(Spot) The Cylinder."* The event just prior to this: you will find them being *entrapped* or *captured* in some manner.

In addition to *"Viruses,"* another PME that has appeared more recently on *Earth* in the last few thousand years is the *"Wraith."* Although these *machines* don't really have *Human-language* names, we use the word *"Wraith"* to describe an *"energy-draining machine-entity."* These are semi-moble; they do not attach permanently to the *Alpha-Spirit*, but once they get into a *body*, they tend to remain with it until it dies (unless they are *systematically released*).

The *"Wraith"* makes one feel *tired* and *weak*. It is possible they were originally released to accelerate *"aging"* on *Earth*. Most individuals accumulate (pick up) at least a few every year, so it makes sense that there is at least some connection. Once in the body, they are *single points* that tend to "pull in" *energy* rather than emanate it, so they are not always easy to "see." They can also move around a bit, a zig-zag within a small area, but once you can focus your *attention* on them (and track them a bit), they tend to settle down. They are easy to *release.*

There are certain types of *"mobile-machines"* that are heavily *imprinted* with *low-Awareness* misemotion, such as: *fatigue, laziness, hopelessness, apathy, &tc*. These types of *machines* tend to drift in, hang around for a while, and then move off to somewhere else. Sometimes they get stuck to your other *machinery* and can linger around an *Alpha-Spirit* for a few lifetimes. They are often perceived as *vague colored-spheres*.

"*Monitors*" or "*Watchers*" (they may give a *Meter-read* on either title) are another commonly encountered PME. They are attached to both *Alpha-Spirits* and *bodies* in order to "keep an eye" on them. A *Seeker* will likely be carrying a few from as far back as the *Magic Universe*.

The "*Monitor/Watchers*" try hard to keep hidden and simply "*watch*" ("*monitor*"). They are usually perceived "over the head" or "behind the back." Many of them are reporting to old empires and forces that don't even exist anymore and so they aren't generally troublesome. But some of them report to the more recent "*invader-forces*" about such things as your *Ascension-work* in *Systemology*, or if you successfully demonstrate the ability to "*break the game*" by *levitating an object*, or something like that.

There is also *machinery* that tries to hide other *machinery* and even inhibit or block your handling or *processing* of *machinery*. Remember that we all have a lot of *Implanting* ("Platforms #1-18") that attempt to prevent us from *dispersing*, *blowing*, or *defragmenting* all types of *machinery*.

There are even instances where we have each contributed a "*split-fragment*" of ourselves to a *machine* that is *installed* on someone else. There are many reasons this may have happened (civic duty, price of a magic spell, *&tc.*). There are "*splitter implants*" embedded in all 64 IPU. Most of this can simply be *Spotted* and *defragmented-by-Awareness*. [Handling "*split-viewpoints*" directly really requires a separate procedure.]

Because you are apply a *GSR-Meter* on behalf of an *entity*, anything that involves assessing IPU *for them* can be difficult if you, yourself, still have a lot of *fragmented charge* on those *terminals*. For this reason, the material from *A.T.*

Manual #4 (*"Implanted Universes"*) should be *defragmented* before handling too much *systematic processing* on *machinery*. The IPU reflect a more *fragmentary* part of your own personal case than all of the *machinery* that has since been accumulated.

STANDARD PROCEDURE: PME

Unlike B.E. (previously), the PME are not always so easy to "wake up" and *defragment*. They have *considered* themselves *to be machinery* for a very long time. There are really two different versions of this procedure: a *long* and a *short*.

- The *long version* treats the entire cycle of their *entrapment* in detail, and *releases* them on a simple gradient. It does, however, require a lot of *session-time* to *run*. A *Seeker* should start with this to get familiarity with all the parts of the procedure.

- Effectively applying the *short version* simply requires having a much higher-level of *Actualized Awareness*— sufficient to grant or imbue the PME with enough *Beingness* (*livingness, &tc.*) to *"Spot"* a couple of key things, without having to treat the other stuff on the *long version*.

Sometimes you can find the PME directly. Most of the time you just handle the *"machinery"*—which consists of the PME, the *programmed-template*, various *imprints* and *circuitry*, and usually other B.E. and *Fused-Groups*. You simply *run* the *Standard Procedure* on the whole *machine*. Most of it will *defragment* within a few steps, which leaves the *"machine core"* that you handle by completing the procedure.

Sometimes *"remnants"* will remain—where the *"core"* releases, but a *Seeker* discovers a few days later the whole thing is apparently *created* again. You can check for a *remnant-machine-core* after the *main-core* blows-off, and continue *processing* it if it gives a *GSR-Meter "read."* [This is an *"advanced systematic GSR-Biofeedback metering procedure."*]

<u>LONG VERSION</u>

A. *Locate the PME.*

Locate the PME, or the *machinery* containing the PME. [The basic method is to *"focus attention"* and get *"Meter-reads"* where something *Is*, and wherever *fragmented charge* is present.] If a *machine*, check for a *Meter-read* on: "PME (?)"—because there may just be *light machinery*, which only requires B.E. procedures. If it's quite obvious to you that there is a "more basic original" *behind* what you've located, then shift your *attention* to that one.

B. *Defragment protest on "going interior."*

This is a *GSR-Meter* assessment on a list of *keywords/buttons* (similar to what is introduced in *PC Lesson-10*). PME (and *complex-machinery*) almost always have some *fragmented charge* related to at least one of these areas. The one that *"reads"* strongest is the *primary charge*. You also note and *acknowledge* when there are smaller *"reads"* on something. [The basic method is *"Spotting"* the *correct item*, and *defrag-by-Awareness "As-It-Is."*]

PME *fragmentation* on *"going interior"* may be related to *incidents* prior to being made into a *machine*; but generally *that is* the greatest *protest* (for these areas) on their

Backtrack. In rare cases, the *"reading"* charge may be *"On"* instead of *"In"*; but this is only the case for a few PME built up in multiple layers, and the following list should suffice for most applications.

1. *Want To Go In*

2. *Can't Get In*

3. *Kicked Out (Of Spaces)*

4. *Can't Go In*

5. *Being Trapped*

6. *Forced In*

7. *Pulled In*

8. *Pushed In*

9. *Made To Go In*

10. *Made Into A Machine*

C. {optional} *Date when they went into the body.*

This is really only useful toward *defragmenting* mobile PME (*e.g.* a *Virus*) that went in relatively recently. For other *machinery* that was built, installed in you (or attached to your *beingness*) long ago, and has remained ever since: this is more of a *research action.* [*"Dates"* are determined by narrowing down a fixed time period using *Meter-reads*.]

D. *"Spot Being Made Into A Machine."*

Have them *Spot* being *made into a machine.* [If necessary, *"Date"* and *"Locate"* it with the *GSR-Meter*.] The basic method for this is to first check *"which Universe"* it occurred in: *"This One (?); Magic Universe (?); Earlier Universe (?)."* You can also apply the *"locational"* method of having them *"point to where..."*

More recent PME were in a mass (widespread) *Implant-*

ing-Incident prior to experiencing the *machine-building*. You can have them *Spot* this (even *"date"* and *"locate"*) and *Spot* the prior instance of "capture"—or whatever was the "beginning" of the *incident*. You may have to take some of the *charge* off of the *incident* that occurred prior to the *machine-building* in order to get the PME to confront the actual *machine-incident*.

[Only work with this step long enough to get the *machine* to start coming apart or loosening up—freeing *attention* from its *fixation* on *solidity*. Eventually a *"Wizard"* will be at a point where enough *Beingness* can be *enlivened* in the PME for it to directly *"Spot"* such things as *"being made into a machine"* with enough high-level *attention* that it will simply *defrag-by-Awareness*.]

  E. *"Spot The First (Earliest) Time You Were Made Into A Machine."*

This means finding the most basic (earliest) *incident* of being made into a *machine*. In every case researched, the *incident* was found in the *Symbols Universe*. It nearly always predates the current *machinery* they are *"being."* This means that PME (and their *remnants/fragments*) have had a long history of *being a machine* of some type.

This data may not be accessible to the PME—and if so, it is likely too entangled with other *entities* and unknown factors to be properly *"dated and located"* with *Meter-reads*. The other possibility is that there are *"harmful-acts"* connected to this area, which is inhibiting their *ability-to-confront*. So, as an alternative to this step (as given), you can run the PCL: *"In The Symbols Universe, Spot Making Others Into Machines."*

  F. *"Spot Being Captured (Before Being Made Into a Machine)."*

In our original version of this procedure, it was suggested to use a list of *IPU-traps* as an assessment action, in an attempt to *systematically identify* an answer. This proved to be a long tedious (and eventually unnecessary) task. Instead, *direct their attention* earlier to the *"Implant Penalty-Universes"* (*see AT#4*) and indicate to them that these IPU are what underlie all the entrapment techniques used in the *Symbols Universe*.

  G. *Assess for the Penalty-Universe underlying their entrapment.*

Use the data provided in *A.T. Manual #4*, *"Implanted Universes."* First use a list of the *16 Dynamic Systems*, and assess for the best/strongest *"reading"* on the list. When you have one, you assess from the list of *4 Goals* for that *Dynamic System*. Take the one that *"reads"* as the IPU-*Goal* for STEP-H. If you are dealing with a *"composite-case,"* you may have to repeat this step to *process-out* a few *Goals* (in the same or different *Dynamic Systems*) to fully *defragment* everything.

  H. *IPU-Defragmentation.*

As you find each IPU-*Goal*, have the PME *run* the following PCL-sequence:

−*"Spot: 'To {Goal} Is Native State'."*

−*"Spot Being Pushed Into This."*

−and/or *"Spot Pushing Another Into This."*

−and/or *"Spot Others Pushing Others Into This."*

−*"Spot: 'To {Goal} Is Native State'."*

It may be that you need to *process-out* another PCL-*Goal* (from STEP-G). If necessary, this can be followed up with *"Who Are You?"* (from the *"Identification Procedure"*) in order to get a *"Me"* answer. The PME may or may not *defragment* at this step, or any of the other steps, from this *Standard Procedure.*

I. *Agreements-Universe Defragmentation.*

If there is still something remaining, have the PME *run* the following PCL-sequence regarding the *"Agreements Universe" (see AT#1, &tc.):*

–*"Spot Rushing To Get Into Agreement."*

–*"Spot Going Through 'The Inverted Golden Triangle'."*

–*"Spot: 'To Agree Is Native State'."*

–*"Look Earlier And Spot When You Decided To Agree."*

Again, this can be followed up with *"Who Are You?"* (from the *"Identification Procedure"*) in order to get a *"Me"* answer. The PME may *release* at this step, or any of the previous steps. If necessary you can also have them *"Spot Encouraging Others To Agree"* and *"Spot Others Encouraging Others To Agree."*

Running the wrong *Goal* for this procedure is not really problematic. All *Alpha-Spirits* have *some fragmented charge* on each of the *64* IPU. Sometimes you will suddenly find the *machinery* blow apart into a cloud of *individuals*—you *acknowledge* them and handle each of the partial-*releases* one by one. We have also found that if you take a break at a time like this, some of them just seem to sort their stuff out and blow off. You can then check back later and see if some require more *defragmentation processing*, or whether there is still a *core-remnant* that still needs to be *processed-out.*

Elements of *"Standard Procedure: Entities"* also applies to PME (it just usually isn't enough for handling PME without some of the steps given above). This means having to check for *"Holders"* and *"Copiers/Copies."* One *machine* may be trying to "hold" or "hide" another. There may even be a *"repair-machine"* that keeps the *machine* you are *processing* in place or copies it when it leaves. Simply check for this stuff and handle it.

<u>SHORT VERSION</u>

This is a shorter script but a more advanced version of the above procedure. It relies on the *high-Awareness level* of a *"Wizard"* to grant enough *Beingness* or *livingness* to the PME, that it raises the *entity's Awareness* high enough to simply *"Spot"* critical *items* with their *attention* and *"defrag-by-Awareness."*

This is the preferred *A.T. version*. With enough *practice/ certainty*, it may even be operated *out-of-session*—once a *"Wizard"* has learned how to apply the entirety of *Systemology without Biofeedback-Devices* (which is an important skill-set for when you find yourself free of your body and material objects).

As you are still developing skill, this is best practiced on a *GSR-Meter*. You should get *"reads"* on each step and get a sense for *machinery* gradually "coming apart" or *releasing*. It follows the same formula as the *"Long Version,"* which a *"Wizard"* should get familiar with first.

A. *Locate the machine.*

It will *read* on: "PME" or *"machine."*

B. *"Spot Being Made Into A Machine."*

It should considerably loosen up with this step (though not always as much as STEP-D of the *Long Version*). If necessary, you can *"date and locate"* (anything from STEP-B to D of the *Long Version*). But really, this step can be accomplished by simple *"Spotting"*—if you can endow the *being* with enough *livingness* to overcome their reactive

75

and conditioned *flinch/withdrawal* from the *"time and location"* of the *incident*.

C. *"Spot The First (Earliest) Time You Were Made Into A Machine."*

This is the same as STEP-E from the *Long Version*. However, in the *Long Version*, you can get away with being a little vague, whereas here, this must be *Spotted* by the PME with high certainty in order to *defrag-by-Awareness*.

D. *"Spot Making Others Into Machines."*

Run the PCL.

E. *"Spot Being Tricked Into Thinking That Machines Are Necessary."*

If the *entity/machinery* remains, continue.

F. *Identification*.

Run the *"Who Are You?"* PCL from the *Identification Procedure*. You may have to get them to affirm *"Me"* (and you *acknowledge* it) several times in order to *release*. Sometimes, the *release* occurs prior to this step. If they don't *release* on this, the assessment steps from the *Long Version* are too lengthy, but you can treat *"Agreements"* in the next step (if necessary).

G. *Agreements-Universe Defragmentation*.

This is the same as STEP-I from the *Long Version*. Have the PME *run* the following PCL-sequence:

–*"Spot Rushing To Get Into Agreement."*

–*"Spot Going Through 'The Inverted Golden Triangle'."*

–*"Spot: 'To Agree Is Native State'."*

–*"Look Earlier And Spot When You Decided To Agree."*

Again, this can be followed up with *"Who Are You?"* (from the *"Identification Procedure"*) in order to get a *"Me"* answer. The PME may *release* at this step, or any of the previous steps. If necessary, you can also have them *"Spot Encouraging Others To Agree"* and *"Spot Others Encouraging Others To Agree."*

ADVANCED ENTITY-HANDLING

Most *fragments* may be *systematically* handled with the same *"Standard Procedure (for Entities)."* Here, we will apply a basic exercise to increase your own *reality* on this —and which also applies to *actual handling*.

1. *Close your eyes.*
2. *"Imagine" (by visualization)* or *"get the sense of"* a *viewpoint* of "looking over someone's shoulder."
3. *Get a sense* of *being* there to "keep them human." [You may or may not get an *actual impression* of environmental scenery, or of someone below you.]
4. Whatever part of yourself you are *projecting* to accomplish this: direct to *it* (the PCL) *"point to the being you divided from."* [At which point it should *defragment/dissolve*.]
5. If any connectivity remains, or seems to linger in the area, alternate applying the *"Who Are You?"* (from the *"Identification Technique"*) and the *"Locational Technique"* until it fully *defragments/disperses*.

Understand that you, as an *Alpha-Spirit*, have the ability to place a *viewpoint* anywhere in *space-time* and perceive *anything*. Therefore, it is possible to continue *perceiving* or "looking at" an area even after *releasing* any *fragments* fixedly located there. One purpose of *Alpha-Defragmentation* is to regain full *conscious control* over such *viewpoints* — nothing should be "fixedly holding" our attention any-where, or enforcing perceptions from anywhere on "automatic."

Repeat the exercise using many different people—altern-ating *real* (one's you know) and *imagined*—until it seems like there are no more "*real*" ones to treat in this manner. Then apply the same exercise; but this time, *get a sense* of being a particular "*body-part*" on someone else, and *being* there to "keep it solid; keep it human."

CONTROL ENTITIES (C.E.)

"*Control Entities*" (or "C.E.") are active, semi-*aware* (intel-ligent) *entities, implanted* (or *installed*) for the explicit purpose of "keeping an *Alpha-Spirit* imprisoned and/or controlled." They are quite challenging to *release* using "*Standard Procedure (for Entities)*" and they don't respond any better with PME-type handling. They are intention-ally *implanted* to be "*Jailers,*" or to block *spiritual perception* (*ability*), or to keep you from *thinking about* or *knowing* certain things, *&tc*.

From the perspective of the C.E., they aren't doing any-thing *wrong*. In fact, quite the opposite, which is why they are more difficult to *release*. They actively *know* what they are doing, but they are under the delusion that they are just being "honest citizens" doing their respective duty. They were *implanted* with this *false-fragmentary data* and forced to "*split-off*" a *fragment/piece* of themselves to further *implant* a "*imprisoned entity*" (to keep them en-trapped and under control).

C.E. are most easily perceived at the *existence-level* or *real-ity-level* of the "*Astral Body*" (from the *Magic Universe*)—

which means a *Seeker* must shift their *attention-Awareness* "up and sideways" to *perceive* (*get a sense of*) a *non-physical dimension*. [This is somewhat always the case, but we are referring to a *perceived layer* of our *Beingness* that extends to a former version of "*bodily-identity*."]

There have been C.E. in use for many layers of *Universes* extending on the *Backtrack*. They are *implanted* (or *installed*) at *one level* (*Universe*) in order to aid in keeping an *Alpha-Spirit* confined to a *lower level* (*Universe*). At any rate, the C.E. (themselves) believe they are "blocking" you for good orderly reasons—which means they are resistant to *defragmentation* unless you first get them to *Spot* the point of being *implanted* with *false data* (*e.g.* a *fragmented purpose*).

Until earlier procedures (in this manual) were standardized, *advanced Seekers* had no formal method for handling C.E. directly. This refined synthesis of *Level-8* (presented in the "*Keys to the Kingdom*" series) now includes an effective procedure for this, relying on a *Seeker's* experience with the other techniques given. Note that in addition to *processing-out* C.E. that are affixed to and blocking you, this procedure can also be extended to include *releasing* "*split-fragments*" of yourself (where you are being a C.E. to someone else).

STANDARD PROCEDURE: C.E.

A. "*Spot Being Made Into A Control Entity (or C.E.).*"

B. *Spotting the Goal.*

As a *listing/assessing* action, use PCL:

 "*Made To Split To Save Society?*"

 if no read,

"Made To Split To Gain Something?"

if no read,

"Made To Split To Serve A Higher Purpose?"

C. *"Spot Being Implanted With False Data."*

if no read (wrong wording),

"Spot Being Implanted With A False Purpose."

if no read (wrong wording),

"Spot Being Implanted With Fragmented Data."

if no read (wrong wording),

"Spot Being Implanted With A Fragmented Purpose."

if still no read, try a different "circuit":

"Spot Implanting Others With False Data" (*&tc.*)

or

"Spot Making Others Into Control Entities."

D. *"Spot The First Time You Were Implanted With False Data."*

Note that if the *"Meter-read"* occurred on different *"wording"* for *"False Data"* from STEP-C, then use that instead. You may also have to "steer" *attention* of the C.E. to a *"False Jewel" incident*—something similar to *"The Jewel"* for *this Universe*, but occurring several layers of *Universe* ago.

E. *Locational Technique.*

"Point To The Being You Divided From."

F. *Identification Technique.*

"Who Are You?" (*"Me"*)

If necessary, you can alternate between STEP-E and STEP-F toward a *release.*

G. *IPU-Defrag. {if necessary}*

If the C.E. showed up (was perceived) while handling *Implanted Penalty-Universes*, and it has not *released* from the former steps, have it "*Spot*" the top of the *Implant-Platform* for that IPU-*Goal*:

"*To {Goal} Is Native State.*"

H. *Agreements. {if necessary}*

Although it is rarely needed, if more handling is required (the C.E. is loosened up and seems ready to *release*, but still seems to be waiting for something)—have the C.E. *run* the following PCL-sequence:

–"*Spot Rushing To Get Into Agreement.*"

–"*Spot Going Through 'The Inverted Golden Triangle'.*"

–"*Spot: 'To Agree Is Native State'.*"

–"*Spot An Earlier Decision To Agree.*"

END-POINTS & REALIZATIONS

As a *Seeker* increases their *certainty* for handling *entities* and *fragments*, they may come to the *realization* that they are reaching a point of being greater "*cause over spiritual life.*" This is one of the primary purposes for introducing this manual at this point of one's *Advanced Training*.

However, it is important that once this *realization* is *actualized* in practice, that a *Seeker* does not focus too hard on treating endless *sessions* on *entities*, exclusive to all other practices. This means that the presence of "more entities" should not hinder a *Seeker* in continuing their *Advanced Training* with *A.T. Manual #6, "Spiritual Perception.*"

In fact, a *Seeker* is likely to achieve greater, more stable, gains in progress by: shifting *attention* between practicing exercises to increase *spiritual perception* –and– *processing-sessions* directed toward *entities*. As one's *spiritual perception* improves, so to will their ability to *locate* and *release* any *entities* and *fragments*.

In addition to the *entities* and *spiritual fragments* of others that "cling" to us and hold us in the *Human Condition*, the majority of an individual's difficulties stem from their own *spiritual fragmentation*. By this, we mean our own *fragments*, *pieces*, and "*split viewpoints*" that are a part of the *machinery*, or act as *entities*, holding *other Alpha-Spirit's* in the *Human Condition*.

The *Locational Procedure* was originally developed to handle these "*split-viewpoints*" (or "S.V."). Since an *Alpha-Spirit* is not truly *located* in *space-time* except by *consideration of viewpoints*, it is quite easy to be operating from multiple *viewpoints* that are *located* separately in *space-time*.

Early on the *Backtrack*, operating from multiple *viewpoints* simultaneously was simply a basic *godlike* skill used to *knowingly animate* one's own *creations* (*Home Universe*)—and it was not very *fragmentary*. At that stage, we were quite capable of consciously extending (or *projecting*) various *remote viewpoints* and then *knowingly dispersing* them or *disconnecting*.

The *fragmentation* occurred when S.V. were enforced (or even used as payment for "magical services") and then we were blocked from consciously operating or controlling them. This greatly contributed to our decline of *spiritual ability*, and the dampening of our total *Actualized Awareness*.

There are numerous *Implanting-Incidents* that forced an individual to divide. This was the case with the *Hellfire Incident*. In the more distant past, we have seen evidence of this in the original *Implanted Penalty-Universes*. This type of *fragmented Awareness* is what we will continue to *defragment* and *reclaim* as our own throughout *Level-8*.

Let's finish this unit/manual of instruction with a basic *objective exercise* to increase your *spiritual perception* and understanding of *handling entities* and *fragments*. This is done in a public place where there are many people.

1. *Spot a person*.
2. Alternate between *getting a sense of* "keeping them human" and "leaving them free."
3. When you have done this to a point of satisfaction with one person, repeat with different one.

Then practice this exercise by applying the other "*circuits*" — *getting the idea* of *others* alternately "keeping *you* human" and "leaving *you* free"; then with *others* alternately "keeping *others* human" and "leaving *others* free." Once you have completed this, in your next *subjective session*, see if any additional *entities* and *fragments* are now accessible.

To truly be a "*Wizard*," a *Seeker* must eventually reach a point where they are no longer influenced, blocked, or held back, by B.E.; and to where they (themselves) are no longer holding others in the *Human Condition*. This is the essence of *Alpha-Defragmentation* — and the first major *upper-level* step toward regaining one's own true and original *spiritual perception* and *ability*.

A.T. MANUAL #6
SPIRITUAL
PERCEPTION

Keep this reference material accessible:
PC Lesson-1 to 16; Processing-Levels 0 to 6.
AT Manual #1, *"The Secret of Universes"*
AT Manual #2, *"Games, Goals & Purposes"*
AT Manual #3, *"The Jewel of Knowledge"*
AT Manual #4, *"Implanted Universes"*
AT Manual #5, *"Entities & Fragments"*

Review this prerequisite material:
PC Lesson-5, *"Free Your Spirit"*
PC Lesson-10, *"Lifting The Veils"*

ADVANCING SPIRITUAL ABILITY

This book is a *systematic training manual*; it is *not* a complete record of *all* experimental research or potential commentary on the subjects included (which would require many volumes). The author spent *30* years dedicated to *"spiritual cartography,"* exploring every potential avenue—from the *most ancient* extant writings available, to the *New Thought* developments of the *20th Century*—before presenting this series of *Systemology* work. Only those "bits" truly useful for *crafting* the *ultimate map* for *The Way Out* were retained.

The ultimate freedom of *Self*—the *Alpha-Spirit*—*knowingly* operating "outside" (or *"exterior to"*) a mortal organic *Body* is our true basic spiritual state. It is the *rehabilitation* of this state—or an *actualized realization* of it—that has driven the populations towards various philosophies, metaphysics, and religion, for thousands of years. Of course, various communication barriers and organizational corruption has kept any of these other "avenues" from fully delivering a *Seeker* to their desired *destination*.

The new standard *Systemology* program—*Basic Course, Professional Course* and *Advanced Training Course*—is the result of feedback from many *systemologists* over the course of many years. It didn't matter how well something *worked* or was *understood* by the author; the real test of its *effectiveness* was reaching a point of *perfection* for its *presentation*—where *Systemology* could be properly communicated to, and used by, others.

Unlike most other *"New Age"* pursuits: we took a *systematic* and *scientific* approach to *Life, Universes* and *Everything*—but while neither adopting, nor excluding, a *physically-mechanistic technological* viewpoint of understanding. The results were a *"spiritual technology"*—something *actually* useful to the *Alpha-Spirit*—that exceeds the boundaries of *this Life, the Human Condition,* and even *this Universe.*

Previous *spiritual* traditions sought to find a way out by *denying* or *altering "What Is."* But while *eastern mysticism* and *western magic* may have been successful in producing many various *effects,* not one of them produced the manifestation of a *True Map* for *The Way Out.*

Advanced Training procedures of this manual are only expected to be effective for those *Seekers* that have *actually processed through* the *"Pathway-to-Ascension" Professional Course (Lesson-1 to 16)* and the *"Keys to the Kingdom" A.T. Manuals (#1 to 5)* prior to studying/applying this manual (*AT #6*). This manual is combined with *"Entities & Fragments" (AT#5)* to function as a single unit of *"Level-8"* training. [*AT#7* and *AT#8* are recent expansions to the A.T. course that encourage additional work and research for this *Infinity Grade.*]

Ideally, a *Seeker* handles what is initially accessible during *AT#5*, then completes a *"run through"* of *spiritual perception* development in *AT#6*. At that time, they may revisit the procedures in *AT#5* to check if there is anything newly accessible. Increased *spiritual perception* makes *releasing entities* (and *fragments, &tc.*) easier; and *releasing entities* makes techniques for increasing *spiritual perception* more effective.

"Free Your Spirit" (*PC-5*) and *"Lifting The Veils"* (*PC-10*) should be reviewed—and considered *"introductions"* to this manual. All other *Systemology* material should also be kept accessible. Many *advanced exercises* already given in previous lessons and manuals will be referenced directly—but their full background and instruction will not be repeated here, so more ground can be covered in a shorter space for this manual.

A.T. Manual #6 is prepared with an expectancy that it will not require any *strenuous effort* (for a *Level-8 Seeker*) to understand or apply—however, *"repetitive practice"* is likely necessary. Most of the *exercises* will be presented with little theory or explanation attached—because a *Seeker* that has *actually* worked through *previous* material will already be familiar with many of the techniques and *processing*-types described here.

The original *Wizard Level-0 "Creative Ability Training"* procedure premiered in the *Systemology Core Research Volume: "Imaginomicon"* (in 2021). These exercises were spread all over the new standard *Professional Course Processing-Levels 0 to 6* as *"objective-environment processing,"* *"creativeness processing,"* and *"advanced techniques."* They were intentionally included to accelerate a *Seeker's* progress on the *Pathway*—and as preparation for *upper-level A.T.* work. Of course, at *those levels*, such exercises were treated quite lightly in between more intensive *defragmentation processing.*

A *Seeker* enters *Level-8* (as a *processing level*) at *Wizard Level-0*. It is at *this* level that *AT#5* (*Entities*) material is treated the *first* time through. Remaining *Wizard-Levels* pertain to theoretical *Infinity Grade "Arcs"*—leading further upward toward total *mastery of Ascension Technology*

—most of which are in experimental stages of development, or still remain to be researched and realized.

The new *Wizard Level-1 "Advanced Ability Training Program"* (proposed in this manual) revisits many earlier *advanced techniques*—but also adds many more. This manual also includes a *Wizard Level-2* training procedure. When a *Seeker* approaches *AT#5* material a *second* time, they will be doing so from a *Wizard Level-1* (or higher) foundation or *viewpoint*. [An experimental *Wizard Level-3* routine appears in *AT#7*.]

"End-point Realizations" for *Wizard-Levels* primarily regard an increased sense of, and certainty in, *Self* as the *Alpha-Spirit*. *"Ability"* and *"certainty"* tend to be correlated. But this alone does not provide much of a *systematic* gradient. Any upward emphasis requires codification using our theoretical *Infinity-Grade "Arcs."*

Wizard Level-1 : *"ejecting" Awareness (fixed viewpoint)* from the *Body*; handling the *Body* (from nearby) while operating from a *viewpoint* that is *remote* from (or *"exterior to"*) any *Body*.

Wizard Level-2 : *"perceiving"* from *exterior viewpoints* that are *projected/extended away/remote* from a *Body*.

Wizard Level-3 : *"intention"*; a proposed experimental gradient. [This level is still subject to future revision and includes material that may later be classified as a *"higher"* gradient of *Wizard-Level*.]

Most early *Systemology* research into procedures for this area was conducted during *experimental workshops* and *Traditional (Co-Piloted) Sessions*. Having a *Co-Pilot* allowed a *Seeker* to focus *attention* more on *"doing"* the *processing command-lines* (PCL) rather than *"thinking"* about book-instructions. A *Seeker* often felt "safer" handling *processing "exterior to"* a *Body* when the *session-environment* was properly controlled (*piloted*)—and without any distractions or chance of sudden disturbances.

However, *Co-Piloting "Advanced Ability Training"* is not without its complications. A *Level-8 Co-Pilot*, requires having some personal *reality* on these *processes* in order to effectively *guide* a *Seeker*. Otherwise, there is a greater risk of a *Co-Pilot "invalidating"* a *Seeker's* experiences, gains, and *abilities. Invalidation* results in having less *certainty*—which slows (or stops) progress with *Spiritual Perception*.

A *Co-Pilot* will *acknowledge* the *ejection*, but *never* makes the *Seeker "prove"* their *Beingness* (or *ability*) by producing any phenomenon, *&tc*. The standard practice was to simply continue the *process* that a *Seeker "ejected"* with, but from their current *viewpoint*.

However, since *ejection* can occur rather suddenly—and a sudden *shift* in *processing* can sometimes cause more *confusion*—this mainly applied to *objective exercises*. In addition to this, sometimes the *Seeker* found themselves suddenly *"looking at"* something else (*imagery, an incident, &tc.*), and so the alternative practice of making *copies* of that *imagery, &tc.*, was developed.

For example: if a *Seeker* is practicing *"Creation-Of-Space"* and suddenly gets a lot of certainty on operating from a *viewpoint* that is *exterior-to* a *Body*, then they would continue their *"Creation-Of-Space"* exercise from that *viewpoint*. But if that became distracting because the *Seeker* was now dealing with some other phenomenon, they would handle that by making/*create "copies"* (*knowingly*, *intentionally*) of whatever it was they *did see*; making many copies of the *imagery*, then alternating "throwing them away" (or *dispersing* them) and "pushing them in" on the *Body*.

REALIZATIONS FROM THE PATHWAY

Shared Universes and *Games* are "contrary" or "antithetical" to the true basic native state (or even "*Home Universe*") of an *Alpha-Spirit*. Our highest level of *spiritual perception* and *ability* does not permit "*game-conditions*" to exist—does not allow for us to experience any kind of *Game*.

The *Alpha-Spirit* is "*Pure Awareness*"—without *energetic-mass* or *location*—but it has an unlimited potential for *postulating, creating,* and even *considering* the condition of "*Having*" something. It can *be anywhere* it cares *to be; looking* at *anything* it wants *to be looking* at. But, in order to *have games*—"*game-fields*" and "*enforced rules*"—*Alpha-Spirits* became expert specialists in *designing* and *creating* various *barriers* and *restrictions*.

We have come to believe that "*something is better than nothing*"—and it is only by achieving high-tolerance levels that a *Seeker* can rehabilitate the "*confronting* of *Nothingness*." In addition to this, we must rehabilitate *creativeness*—the certainty that a *Seeker* can *still* "*Have*" *something* independent of a *Body*—or even the *Game* of *this Physical Universe* altogether. Without rehabilitating these basic states, an individual will not let go, or release *Self*, from their *chronic* and *compulsive participation* with the *Human Condition*.

Restoring *freedom* is synonymous with restoring *spiritual perception* and *ability*. But, *total freedom* does not have a *systematic structure*, because it is a *basic Truth*—reflecting the true native state of the *Alpha-Spirit*. The innate *abilities* of an *Alpha-Spirit* cannot actually be destroyed, because *It Is* the basic *Beingness* of its *Existence*. However, *consciously understanding* and/or *knowingly using* these *abilities* (and *perceptions*) can certainly become *fragmented* and *blocked*.

Freedom is the absence of *barriers* and *restriction*. "*Total Freedom*" would be the *total absence* of *all barriers* and *restriction*. The *Alpha-Spirit* has long since lost its tolerance for *confronting* such a state. At the upper-most level, there is *nothing* to be *free from*. That the "*something*" to be *free from*, is more or less an *illusion*, is also true; but it is the *Alpha-Spirit's* own *illusion*—*agreed* to (at some level) in order to *have* a *game*. [Ref. *AT#1 & AT#2*]

Our *Awareness* is currently "spread" all over *this* and *other* "*Universes*"—"*attention-units*" *fragmented* by *imprinting*, "*splitting*" and other *incidents* where *attention* remains "*fixed.*" *Fixation* is *entrapment*. All *fixation* is really the *suspension* of *Awareness* (*attention*) on a point of a "*communication-cycle*" that has not resolved, closed, or ended. It is *suspended* in a *confusion* or a "*maybe.*" And this obviously reduces *Knowingness*.

Note that the phrase "*communication-cycle*" refers to more than "conversations" with other *people*; it also includes incomplete *cycles-of-action* (or "events" that we've experienced)—or really any "encounters" with the *energy-matter* and/or *space-time* of *this* (or any *other*) *Universe*.

An insistence upon substituting *Knowingness* by obsess-

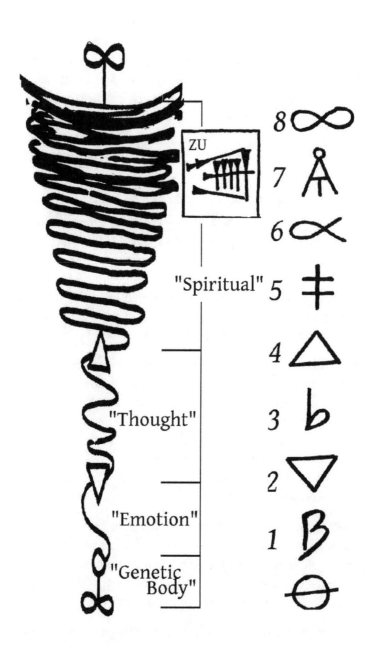

ively holding onto *imprinted imagery* (*mental pictures*) in order to "learn by experience"—and then assigning *automatic control* of *associating* the *data* to *reactive-response machinery*—has inhibited the *total freedom* of the *Alpha-Spirit*.

Spiritual Perception is really only inhibited and limited by one key factor:

What—and how much—an Alpha-Spirit is willing to Know.

The *perception* of *freedom* is connected to:

What an Alpha-Spirit is willing to Create, Do, or Have.

And this is where an individual got themselves involved with the *games* and *puzzles* that an *Alpha-Spirit* is so fond of. Unless a *Seeker* has *certainty* on the *ability* to *Create* another (preferably better) "*game*"—or at the very least *Have* one—"*somewhere*" else, they will not sufficiently *release* their *hold on* "*this*" one.

Systematic Processing on the *Pathway* has established to a *Seeker* that our true basic native *ability* is restored by *Knowingness*—the increase of *Actualized Awareness*. The *unknowing* ("*not-conscious*") *automation* and "*push-button*" *mechanistic control* is a much *lower-level* of "*mental operation*" than *Knowingness*.

The "*Standard Model*" (and "*ZU-Line*") on which our *Systemology* is based, very accurately "maps" or "charts" the conditions of descent in any area. At the top we have:

7. ALPHA-THOUGHT—(*To Be*)—the *postulates* of *Creation*; *Creating* a "*thing*" to *Know* about.

6. KNOWINGNESS—(*What Is*)—the *condition* of *Knowing*; *Total-Knowingness* is all-pervasive perfect *Knowing* about a "*thing*" as maintained by its *Creator*.

5. INTENTION — (*It-As-Altered*) — the *ability* to affect or change the *condition* of an *existing "thing"* to make it *continue*, *persist*, or *perpetuate*, in some way.

For there to be "*intention*" (rather than "*Creation*") the *Alpha-Spirit* already must have decided to "*Not-Know*" about something. The *intention* to *Know something* requires *Not-Knowing* about it in the first place. The *intention* to "*learn*" requires an *interest* — and "*interest*" is something that is difficult for an *Eternal Spirit* to maintain indefinitely (hence, "*games*"). An individual in *Total Knowingness* would simply *disperse* an *undesired "thing"* and *Create* something else, rather than *Alter-What-Is*.

The extent to which one can *Imagine* (or *Create*) does not only concern *Creating* (*Imagining*) "*infinities*" of something (see *PC-15*, *&tc.*), but also the "*distance-factor.*" *Distance* is another *perceived barrier* in *space-time*. So, when *running* any type of "*creativeness processing*," we must also treat the matter of: how "close" does one's *creations* have to be (to their *viewpoint*/POV) to still be *considered* (handled) under their *control?*

Lower down the chained-sequence: when operating with a *Body* in the *Human Condition*, the *Alpha-Spirit* typically directs "*intention*" to the "*Mind-System*" in order to get the *Body* to "*do*" things, in order to affect the *energetic-mass* of *space-time* in the *Game* of *this Physical Universe*. This involves a *consideration* that some kind of "action" or "effort" is required in order to *cause* something — and this part of the chain starts with:

4. THINKINGNESS — (*Computation*) — the *evaluation* of *effort* of some "*doingness*" to *Cause* or *Have* something; and/or the *estimation* of *control* (to "*start,*" "*alter,*" or "*stop*" an existing *system* or "*thing*").

"Thinkingness" (the *Mind-System*) operates far below a level of *Knowingness*. It is unnecessary; it is where most *beings* get themselves into trouble. Of course, to get to this point, a *being* would have to *Not-Know* about a lot of *created things* in order to *"think about things to know about."* But this is exactly what sets up the conditions for a *game*.

"EJECTION" FROM A BODY/VEHICLE
(*Wizard Level-1*)

The phrase *"ZU-Vision"* is used in *Systemology* to indicate the experience of the true *Spiritual Awareness* (and thus the *Spiritual Life*) of the *Alpha-Spirit*. This is beyond the *sensation* or *perception* of a *Body*; it is beyond the *mental machinery* and *fragmented computations* of any *Mind-System*.

ZU-Vision regards *Beingness* that is completely *"exterior to"* *Body* and *Mind*. Other methods and traditions that do not properly *defragment* a *Seeker* first, may occasionally get them *"out-of-body"*—but the individual is still very much *"in-the-mind"* and attached to all their "stuff" and their interconnection to *bodies* of *this Universe*.

Although it may seem to cross-over in subject matter at times: when handling *Spiritual Perception* at *Wizard Level-1*, we are not directly interested in what is often referred to as *"psychic phenomenon"* or making objective demonstrations of *ability* in *this Physical Universe*.

When unrestricting *fixed viewpoints* in *Space*, one is also treating *Time*—and at first, a *Seeker* may not have *clear* "*present-time*" *perception* with *ZU-Vision* on the immediate environment of the *Body*. One's *actual perception* must also be distinguished from the "*mental imagery*" that one is likely to still be *compulsively creating* (to *look at*). A *Seeker* may initially not *perceive* the *Physical Universe* because the *Seeker*, themselves, is not "*putting it up there to see.*" [This strongly hints toward a very specific and significant *A.T. realization.*]

ZU-Vision is not a *process, procedure* or *skill*. It is the natural *ability* of an *Alpha-Spirit* that simply has varying degrees of *clarity in perception*—and thus, like any *ability* or *function*, it can be *inhibited* or *fragmented*. To treat this subject as a *process* directly would be like writing a book instructing on how to "*eat*," "*walk*," or "*breathe*" (although such exist). There are obviously ways of "improving" how one does such things, but the basic development of the function is essentially *in-born* or *innate*.

Alpha-Spirits have developed a *compulsive dependency* on *bodies, automation,* and *games*. We can rehabilitate *Spiritual Perception* by resolving (*defragmenting*) the *compulsions*. This is the real emphasis of the *Pathway*—because any time we tried to directly focus *processing* specifically on "*getting out,*" we encountered many *barriers*. Instead, initial gains were accomplished by *processing-out* the "*entry-points*"—the "*getting in*" part. Secondly, we achieved gains by *processing-out incidents* of unwanted or unexpected (*other-determined*, rather than *Self-Determined*) "*ejections*" from anything, but mostly *bodies*.

To effectively apply the techniques of *Wizard Level-1* as a *systematic procedure*, a *Seeker* must *Know* (have *actual* certainty on):

1. *"What"* is being *ejected/released* (the *Alpha-Spirit*);

2. *"What"* it is being *ejected/released "from"* (the *Body*); and

3. *"mechanisms/machinery"* (called the *Mind*).

Years of experimental research allowed us to collect data regarding key factors that more commonly affected *Seekers* experiencing difficulties with *ejecting/releasing* from their *Body*. Many of these points are treated earlier on the Pathway, but a *Seeker* may need to revisit key areas specific to their own case, or even other areas that may have yet to be personally handled at all, for *Wizard Level-1*. These include:

–FEAR associated with some element of *space-time, energy,* and/or *mass;* or else *terminals* attached to *this Universe.*

–FEAR associated with *lack* or *loss* of *"having" space-time* or *energy-mass;* including reduced *ability-to-confront "Nothingness."*

–NO RESPONSIBILITY (OR CONTROL); therefore the *effect of,* or *controlled by,* other things (*other-determinism*).

–NO CERTAINTY; low-*Awareness;* no *Self-Determinism,* therefore everything is *other-determined,* or from an *unknown (hidden) source.*

–MACHINERY; excessively burdened by personal *mechanisms* of *automation* and *reactivity.*

–BEINGNESS (VIEWPOINT or POV) deeply enmeshed in the *rigid-energy* (*standing-waves*) of a *Body;* either a *fixation* on the *Body,* or total lack of interest/responsibility in handling the *Body* ("disowning" while still remaining connected to it).

–BEINGNESS (VIEWPOINT/POV) or ATTENTION fixedly on an entirely different *Body* (for personal *identification*) than the *current Human Body* "present" *in-session.*

The last one is an interesting point of *fragmentation* only recently added to the list. In this case, we may have a situation of treating the *"wrong body." Ejecting Awareness* from *"the Body"* actually requires the starting point of *being in "the Body"* —and preferably *"the Body"* being used for a *processing session* that keeps directing PCL regarding *"that Body."* In the case of *wrong body*: it may be that an individual's chronic POV is on (or from) a *desired body*, or they have *fixated attention* on a *past body* (previous *body* on the *Backtrack*).

At *Level-8*, a *Seeker/Wizard* no longer *runs "imprint-chains"* in *processing*. The primary *high-level Awareness* methods of *processing* are: *"Spotting"* and *"defragmentation-upon-analytical-inspection."*

This means that basic *"Recall"* and *"Imagine"* techniques still apply, in addition to *identifying "Source," "What Is," &tc.* We don't want to *stick* a *Seeker's attention* on a *Body*, but *ejection* can be difficult if *attention* is already *fixated* on a *Body "elsewhere."* In this instance, more *"descriptive"*-style PCL may need to be *run* in order to "collect" one's *"attention-units"* onto the *current Body.* This sometimes means first getting a *Seeker* to *realize "what" Body/Identity* they *actually* have their *Awareness/Beingness* associated with.

"What Body Would You Like To Have?"

–and/or–

"Describe Your Last Body."

As a preliminary to *Wizard Level-1 Procedure*, a *Seeker* should *defragment* prior *"other-determined" ejections* where *Awareness* may be suspended and/or new *considerations* may have been made about *being "exterior-to"* a *Body.*

This includes, for example: *past deaths, serious illness,* or *injuries*—points when an *Alpha-Spirit* may have temporarily *"gone out"* of the *Body,* or was otherwise *ejected* *"under duress."* [It has been noticed, on the *Backtrack,* that the *Alpha-Spirit* does not "naturally" recover full *attention-Awareness* after such *incidents.*]

There is a phenomenon where a *Seeker*/individual *"goes out"* (*ejects*) and *"goes back in"* (*snaps-in*) so quickly that the *shift* isn't fully *realized* as having happened; but the *"impact"* (of the *"snap-in"*) is *perceived* in some way, which often results in a period of *confusion* (or some other unwanted manifestation). Prior use of *mysticism* or *occultism* (that included *astral travel* or *out-of-body experiences*) may need to be *defragmented.* Previous *processing-sessions,* where a *Seeker* may have suddenly *ejected,* might also require *"repair."*

The main issue is that these events often take place before *Seekers* are properly prepared to handle them. This leaves *residual fragmentation* from the subsequent *"snap-in"* effects thereafter. And any heightened *perception* achieved is generally not very stable. An unprepared *Seeker* may find the experience disorienting—or a disturbance occurs in the *session-environment* while they are operating *"exterior"*—and so they abruptly *snap-back-in,* and "hold on" even tighter to the *Human Condition.*

Early experiments placed particular emphasis on the *"getting out"* part of things. But few of the methods applied directly toward this goal actually produced stable results—or if they were effective in *knowingly ejecting Awareness,* the experience didn't leave a *Seeker* feeling much better, especially if something *caused them* to *snap-back-in.* [This was the case with most traditional applications of *"Astral Projection"* data.]

A.T. realizations include a greater certainty on *being* a *"Spiritual Being"*; *not* a *"Body"* —and that the *Alpha-Spirit* is a *Beingness* that can *consider* itself as *being "anywhere"* and *"anything."* The typical individual (*Alpha-Spirit* + *Human Condition*) generally *considers* that they *need* a *Body*, or that the *Body needs* them, or even that they would be *abandoning* it by *ejecting*.

At *Wizard Level-1* we are primarily concerned with *"ejection"* (and *defragmenting "snap-in"* effects). Our emphasis at this stage is not on vivid *perception*. First we *"get out"*; then we focus on *"looking around."* Upon initially *"getting out,"* a *Seeker* often "loses" the *perception* of *present-time environmental "anchor-points"* in the *Physical Universe*. Their *spiritual perception* is not likely to be "very good" (*clear*) without some kind of *"dimension-points."* This is remedied by practicing *"Creation-Of-Space"* (*PC-5*) and other similar exercises.

Aside from *"other-determined ejections,"* there is not a lot to *process* for *considerations* on the *"getting out"* part. The *Seeker* already desires to *"be out."* That's the natural state and not the point of *fragmentation*. As we know from *incident-running*: we can't *defragment "As-It-Is"* without treating the actual "start" of an *incident*, or finding the earlier "beginning" if necessary. In this case: the earlier beginning of *"being in"* is *"going in."* If one *considers* themselves *"in"* something, they had to *"get in"* in the first place. If an individual is *ejected* at "death," than the *"go in"* would occur at "birth," *&tc*. We often emphasize the *"Heaven Implanting-Incident"* because it is the under-cut to *advanced processing*, being the *entry-point* to the entire *Game* of *this Universe*.

The final part of a *Seeker's* preliminary work for *Wizard Level-1* is *defragmenting "ejection"* and *"snap-in" mechanisms* that may be *imprinted* and/or *automatic*. Otherwise, a *Seeker* is likely to experience additional "push–pull" tension between *Self* and the *Body*. Those that have dealt with this phenomenon often describe it rather like the old children's toy of "a ball attached to a paddle with an elastic string." Knowing this, it is better to take steps to prevent it from occurring, rather than having to *"remedy and repair"* it afterward.

The basic *process* for handling *fragmentation* on *"going in"* is given in *PC Lesson-10* (*"Lifting The Veils"*)—in the section titled: *"Metaspiritual Systemology."* It was also used in some procedures for handling *entities* (*AT#5*). While this previously may have been treated lightly, it becomes more critical to handle for *Level-8.*

As an addition to the instructions/background given (in *PC-10*), if a *Seeker* has access to *Biofeedback-Tech*, the advanced practice for this is to check for *fragmented charge* using a *GSR-Meter*. It will *register* on various *command-wording* (or *"hot buttons"*) associated with *"going in,"* if there is *imprinting*. This is then handled with the *Analytical Recall* technique given there, until no more *charge registers* when that *wording* is *"called"* or *"spotted"* or *"run"* during the *process*. [Use only *circuits* "1," "2" and "3"; then use "0" on your second pass through *Wizard Level-1* material.]

For convenience, the standard list of *keywords/buttons* is: *"Go In"*; *"Put In"*; *"Want To Go In"*; *"Must Get In"*; *"Can't Get In"*; *"Kicked Out"*; *"Be Trapped"*; *"Forced In"*; *"Pulled In"* and *"Pushed In."*

[*New Update* (*for 2024*): As a result of *systematic processing* being in the public hands for several years—in addition to the widespread distribution of other "*New Age*" practices—it has recently been discovered that a *Seeker* may also need to *process-out* those *incidents* where they: "*Tried To Eject, But Didn't/Couldn't.*"]

ADVANCED ABILITY TRAINING ROUTE
(*Wizard Level-1 Procedure*)

Advanced Ability Training (AAT) is not "*ejection processing*"—such a procedure does not exist in *Systemology*. These exercises are not intended to "*induce*" *ejection*; but *ejection* may take place while practicing them. It is true that an ability to handle and direct *ejection* is an intended *end-point* or *end-realization* of this *Wizard-Level*; but it is not what is *processed directly*. [The same AAT route is followed even *after* a *Seeker* "*ejects.*"]

Completing this routine in one single *session* is not required or expected. The "*standard opening procedures*" of a *Formal Session* are not used in *Wizard-Level Training Routines*. At the beginning of each *session*, a *Seeker* must run "*Preventative Fundamentals*" (*PC-9*) as their first *procedure*. This means: checking for *breaks* or *upsets* of "*Flow Factors*" (*PC-7*); making sure *presence* is not on some *problem* elsewhere (*PC-4*); and scanning over any *Harmful-Acts* or *Hold-Backs* that may have our *attention* because "*someone almost found out,*" &tc. (*PC-6*).

When a *Seeker* completes this route/routine, they proceed to the *next* section: "*Wizard Level-1 Stabilization.*" If you find difficulties processing this routine (that are not a result of *entities*, short-cutting previous *processing-levels*, or failing to provide *presence in-session, &tc.*), go directly to "*Wizard Level-1 Stabilization.*" It may be used to: *stabilize* results from *Wizard Level-1* and/or *enable* one to get better results (if necessary).

Wizard Level-1 puts emphasis on getting a *Seeker willing* and *able* to *knowingly eject Awareness* from its *fixation* on the *Body*. *Wizard Level-2* puts emphasis on increasing the *Spiritual Perception* of a *Seeker* once *ejected*. There is, however, no real distinction between the "type" of *systematic techniques* and exercises used for these purposes. They were all originally researched and experimented with during the same phase of work at the *Systemology Society* (2020–2022). They are all collected and codified in this manual for the first time.

Ejection could occur at any point of any exercise (from either *Wizard-Level*); and any of the exercises (from either *Wizard-Level*) may also be used after *ejection* to improve its *stability*, or even increase *perception*. Some of the techniques appeared in previous lessons. A *Seeker* was often instructed to simply "*imagine*" or accept whatever "*vague perception*" they had on them—or an "*advanced version*" may have been listed as optional. At *Level-8*, we are interested in taking up these earlier suggestions and actually improving *Spiritual Ability*.

Training Routines are *systematic* arrangements of various *processes* and *exercises*. Unlike the work done for *Level-7*, or involving *Implant-Platforms*, this *route* is not mimicking or replicating some specific *incident* or *sequence*. There is no real concern about seeing instructions "out of order" or following a different order.

A. <u>DEFRAG-BY-ATTENTION</u>

In this first step, we want to increase a *Seeker's ability* to *"Defrag-by-Attention."* This step also helps protect against so easily being the effect of future *Implants*. *"The Jewel of Knowledge"(AT#3)* is used for this step. A *Seeker* already *processed-out "The Jewel (Part #1-5)"* as an *incident* (for themselves) during *Level-7*.

The goal of this step is to be able to *intentionally* and *knowingly Create (Imagine)* and then *Un-Create (disperse)* each *item-line* of *"The Jewel."* A *Seeker* should focus on *copying* the intensity and sensation of the original (*incident*) item, but *not* as a *"recall action."* [When using *Biofeedback*, if enough significance is put on the *creation*, it will *register* as *"mass."* This is then *dispersed* (*"defragged-by-attention"*) and will cease to *register*.]

A *Seeker* continues this until they feel comfortable doing it easily. They should find it interesting and fun; then be able to see the utter ridiculousness of the *Implant*; then be able to *Create* and *Defrag* any of the *items* from the *Implant* again—*knowingly at will.*

One challenge of *Ascension beyond this Universe*, is that even an *Actualized Seeker* (*Alpha-Spirit*) is likely to hit *"The Jewel"* of *this Universe* and end up right back here (if they have not built up an *"immunity"* to it). Most less-*Aware* individuals do not even make it that far in their *"between-lives period,"* often getting "caught" (as *Alpha-Spirits*) by various *"screens"* or *"Implant-Stations"* (*Heaven Implants, &tc.*) before ending up back here.

This is possible because, while the *Alpha-Spirit* is not *actually located* within *this Physical Universe*, its *fixed Awareness* and *considerations-of-Beingness* very much are —even after they are *released* from a *Body*, whether through *body-death*, or intentional *ejection-of-Awareness*.

Ejecting from the *Body* alone does not put one "outside" or "exterior to" the *Physical Universe*. There are other *postulates, reality-agreements, considerations, entities,* and *fragments,* that also contribute to a confinement to, or *fixation* with, *this Universe*—and which require *total defragmentation* to *master Ascension*.

B. SOURCE-OF-SENSATION

This step is to get *certainty* on *ability* to *create sensation* independent of a *body-perception*.

"*Create (Imagine) 'Heat' Until The Body Seems Warmer.*"

C. SOURCE-OF-LIGHT

This step is to get *certainty* on *ability* to *create* a *light-source* independent of *this Physical Universe*. It is *not* necessary for this *light* to be objectively visible or manifest (perceivable to others) in *this Physical Universe*. Alternate: *Creating (Imagining)* and *Un-Creating (dispersing)* a *light-source*. [This *light-source* should not be "*electrical*" (a lightbulb) or "*nuclear*" (like a sun).]

D. SOURCE-OF-BODY-ACTION

Alternate:

1. "*Move The Body.*"
2. "*Realize Who Is Making It Move.*"

E. UNIVERSE FUNDAMENTALS

Run the "*Preventative Fundamentals*" (*PC-9, &tc.*) on each of the following (separately): SPACE; TIME; ENERGY; and MATTER.

F. SPOTTING-THIS-UNIVERSE

Run "Orientation in Space-Time" (PC-1) outside (in a public place): *"Spotting"* (*looking* at something and *noticing* something about it) each of the following (as a separate *process*): SPACE; TIME; ENERGY; MATTER; AN OBJECT; AN ANIMAL; A PERSON; SELF; THE UNIVERSE; ANOTHER'S PERSONAL UNIVERSE; WHAT YOU ARE DOING NOW; WHAT ANOTHER IS DOING NOW.

G. SPOTTING POINTS-IN-SPACE

This step is practiced comfortably lying down; eyes closed. Alternate:

1. *"Spot One Point In The Room."*

2. *"Spot One Point In The Body."*

When a *Seeker* is comfortable with this (and *perception* of it is no longer *changing, improving, &tc.*), then continue this step using *"Two Points.."*; and finally *"Three Points.."* [Versions of this were introduced in *PC-10* and *PC-12*.]

When a *Seeker* can do this step easily, follow this same progressive procedure; but alternating: *"...Point(s) In The Room"* and *"...Point(s) Outside."* [If necessary, the second part may be clarified as *"...Outside The Room (or Building)."*]

H. CREATING AN ILLUSION

This step is practiced comfortably lying down; *body's eyes* closed. Alternate:

1. *"Create (Imagine)."*

2. *"Intend."*

In the first part: a *Seeker Creates/Imagines* "something" (an *object*, an *energy*, a *condition*, an *illusion*, *&tc.*). The second part is repeated many times, *Intending* various things about the *creation*. The suggested list of *intentions* (for PCL) are: *"Hold It Still"*; *"Conserve It"*; *"Protect It"*; *"Control It"*; *"Keep It From Going Away"*; *"Hide It"*; *"Change It"*; *"Rearrange It"*; *"Duplicate It"* (in its same space); *"Turn It Upside-Down"*; *"Turn It On Its Side"*; *"Move It"* (and *"Move It Back"*); *"Be It"*; *"Not-Be It"*; *"Destroy It"*; *"Create It"* (*Again*) and *"Destroy It"* at will.

I. SPOTTING DISTANCES

This step is usually practiced outside. Alternate:

1. *"Spot (Put Attention On) An Object."*

2. *"Notice The Distance (Space) Between You And It."*

J. PROJECTING ENERGY-BEAMS

This step is usually practiced with a combination of *intention* and *visualization*. This is done outside and/or inside. Note any *realizations*. [Handling *"spiritual energy"* is introduced at *Processing Level-6 (PC-13)*.]

1. *"Spot (Put Attention On) An Object."*

2. *"Place (Put Out) An Energy Beam, Wrapped Around You And It."*

3. *"Pull Yourself Toward It By Shortening (Retracting) The Beam."*

K. RECEIVING (DRAWING OUT) ENERGY

This step is usually practiced with a combination of *intention* and *visualization*. This is done outside and/or inside. Repeat it a dozen times. Note any *realizations*.

1. *"Spot (Put Attention On) An Object."*

2. *"Draw Energy (Out) From It And Into You."*

When a *Seeker* has done this step comfortably on a few objects: practice STEP-I, STEP-J, and STEP-K, on "A CLOUD."

L. LEVEL-7 A.T. STABILIZATION

"The Jewel of Knowledge"(*AT#3*) is used for this step. Refer to the section titled *"Level-7 Stabilization Point."* Complete the steps as given for that procedure (outdoors).

Then practice the procedure indoors; eyes closed. You can *Imagine* (*get a sense*) or use *ZU-Vision* (if possible) to: *"Look Around A City And Spot.."* [Practice it *"mentally/ spiritually"*; but not as a *"recall"* of being outdoors.]

When this step is completed, a *Seeker* continues to the next section.

WIZARD LEVEL-1 STABILIZATION

The following exercises are derived from the original *Systemology Wizard Training Regimen*—many of which were introduced in the *"Pathway" Professional Course (PC)*. For this *stabilization procedure*, a *Seeker* uses the *"advanced version"* (if applicable) of any *processes*. [Apply *"standard opening procedures"* (*Formal Session*) to these *sessions*. Refer to original materials (where indicated) for any additional background or instruction.]

A. TOUCH-AND-LET-GO (*PC-1*)

This step is practiced lying down; eyes closed. Use *advanced version* on:

1. Objects in the room.

2. Specific "spots" in the room.

3. Objects outside (the room).

4. "Spots" outside (the room).

["*Spots*" means "*Spots-in-Space*"—or a small focused area of *Space*—not otherwise defined, or occupied, by *Mass*. A *Seeker* may initially practice using "*specific spots on a (blank) wall*" for "*spots in the room.*"]

B. "THE WALL" (*PC-1*)

This step is practiced lying down; eyes closed. Use *advanced version* to: "*look*" at the *Wall*; "*touch*" the *Wall*; and "*turn around.*" [This is a popular *process* among *Seekers*, often *run* until an actual *ejection* (*Spiritual Perception*) occurs; but that is not its original purpose.]

C. EMOTIONAL FLOWS (*PC-2*)

This step has two parts, each is *run* on various "neutral" *objects* present; then a *Wall*; then with eyes closed (using something the *Seeker* has *Created/Imagined*). This is done by *intention*. But a *Seeker* should continue this until they get a real *sense* of it happening. The following is only an outline. [Use the instructions in *PC-2*.]

1a. Spot an Object/Wall/Creation.

1b. "Feel" various emotions about it.

2a. Spot an Object/Wall/Creation.

2b. Make it "feel" various emotions about you.

D. COMMUNICATION (*PC-3*)

Practice this step of *communication* with an *object*; then a *Wall*; then *parts* of the *Body*. Use *intention* and/or *Imagine* the *communication-and-acknowledgment* cycles—"*Hello,*" "*Thank You,*" *&tc.* [Refer to *PC-3*.]

E. "BELL, BOOK & CANDLE" (*PC-3*)

This step is practiced lying down; eyes closed. Use *advanced version*. [Refer to *PC-3*.]

F. CREATIVENESS PROCESSING (*PC-5*)

This step is practiced with eyes closed. It requires a *Seeker* to be able to *Create/Imagine* and actually *see* or *get a sense* that their *creations* are there. It is sometimes necessary to "*create*" and "*throw away*" a few before one is satisfied with their level of *perception* (or *perfection* of the *creation*).

A *godlike being* should be able to "*create*," "*destroy*" and "*re-create*" *anything*. While operating at *this* level of existence, our best route of exercising this *creative ability* is "*mentally*" or "*imaginatively*." In *PC-5*, the suggestion is for "*acceptance*," "*rejection*" and "*substitutions*" for anything (like "money" or "pain").

In essence, a *Seeker* increases their tolerance to "*take it*" or "*leave it*." It is also useful in *processing*, to "*invent ways to waste it*." [*Update*: also *process-out* "*accepting it under duress*" or "*forced to have it*."]

There is no standard *terminal item-list* of suggested *objects* or *creations* given here. Typically, worksheets and data from earlier *sessions* are used to determine if *residual fragmentation* remains on anything specific. A list could be developed by scanning *terminals* and *concepts* that represent each *Sphere of Existence* (and even the *Arcs of Infinity*). The only challenge here with *Solo-Processing*, is that a *Solo-Pilot* is more likely to *avoid* areas and *terminals* that they "*don't like*" (which defeats the purpose of the exercise).

G. PLACES YOU ARE NOT (*PC-6*)

This step (with eyes open or closed) operates by having a *Seeker* put *attention* on "*exterior*" (or *remote from the body*) *locations* to "check" to see that they "are not there." *Spot* many places. [This is another popular *process* that *Seekers* often *run* until an actual *ejection* occurs.]

"*Spot Places You Are Not.*"

H. HANDLING ORDERS (*PC-7*)

This step is based on the "*advanced processing*" section in *PC-7*. Cycle through these PCL on one *terminal*, getting as many answers as you can, before going to the next one. The *terminals* are: PEOPLE; THINGS; PLACES; GROUPS; GOVERNMENTS; LIFEFORMS; ENERGIES; and SPIRITS.

1. "*Spot Some ___ You Are Not Giving Orders To.*"

2. "*Spot Some ___ That Are Not Giving You Orders.*"

3. "*Spot Some ___ That Are Not Giving Orders To Others.*"

4. "*Spot Some ___ That Are Not Receiving Orders From Others.*"

5. "*Spot Some ___ That Are Not Giving Orders To Themselves.*"

After completing the above to a satisfactory end-point, a *Seeker* takes up the other side of this with the PCL below; for when they *agreed to follow another's orders* for the sake of *having a game*. [Refer to *PC-12* and *AT#2* for what we mean by "*game*."] Rehabilitation of "handling orders" means a *total freedom* of *choice* about *following* or *disagreeing* with "orders" — *not compulsively* one way or the other.

1. "*Spot An Incident When You Chose To Follow Another's Orders (for the sake of having a game).*"

2. "*Notice Some Things About It.*"

Then *Spot* an *earlier incident*, and so on, until you reach the *earliest* one accessible; and *run* that. [The *upper-level* handling of any *turbulence* that does not immediately *disperse-on-realization* (*defrag-by-attention*) is to alternate: "*Spot Something In The Incident; Spot Something In The Room (Environment).*"]

1. "*Spot An Incident Where You Convinced Others To Follow Your Orders (for the sake of having a game).*"

2. "*Notice Some Things About It.*"

Handle *earlier/earliest* as above.

Then practice the other *advanced exercises* for "*Attacking*," "*Hate*," "*Beauty*" and "*Safe To Be*" as given in *PC-7*.

I. (NOT)-KNOWINGNESS (*PC-10*)

Perform this step exactly as given in *PC-10*.

J. ADVANCED EXERCISES (*PC-10*)

Perform this step by completing all *ten* bullet-pointed {"•"} exercises given in the final section of *PC-10*. They are summarized as follows:

1. *Create/Imagine copies* of your (current) *Body*.

2. *Create/Imagine* "ideal" or "healthy" *copies* of your *Body*.

3. *Looking* into a mirror: *something there; nothing there*.

4. "Mentally" (or in *ZU-Vision*) decide *To Be* (as a *viewpoint*) in a *public place*; notice *scenery* and *motion*.

5. Using *Step-4*: *Create/Imagine* and *Uncreate* (*disperse*) *copies* of your *Body being* there *in front* of your *viewpoint*.

6. Using *Step-5*: alternate between *viewpoints*; "inside" and "outside" the *Body*.

7. Using *Step-6*: get a sense of others acknowledging the *Body being* there.

8. Using a *"basic solid shape"* to represent the *Body* for previous exercises.

9. Moving the *"basic solid shape"* around like a playing piece.

10. Performing the exercises using different *Body-Types*.

K. COLLAPSED-SPACE PROCESSING

The *"collapse-of-space"* phenomenon—having *Space "collapse-in"* on one—is *processed* similarly to the *"getting-in"* or *"going-inside" fragmentation* (given in earlier material) that we apply to all *Seekers* (including *entities*). [This *process* should be *added* to all *entity-handling procedures*.]

As with processing *"getting-in,"* this step is also *run* using a list of *keywords/buttons*. In this case, we are treating an even "higher magnitude" of *incident*. In fact, its original development concerned *processing-out* the *loss* of *"Home Universe"* and subsequent *fragmentation* concerning "world-closed-in" type of *incidents*.

Recall data from that far on the *Backtrack* may not be readily accessible to a *Seeker*, so they should do the best they can—and an individual has likely experienced many other *space-collapsing incidents* since then. It is important not to "push" too hard on vivid *recall*, or you may end up "pulling" in *imprinting* from an *entity* that is in close proximity—and misidentifying the *imprint* as your own (and it will persist in restimulation).

The *fragmented charge* on the *keywords* is best determined with *Meter-reads*. The *charge* is *dispersed* by *running "Recall"* on that *item* (using all *circuits*) and *dispersing-by-realization* or *Spotting* (until it no longer *registers* on the *GSR-*

Meter). The list of *keywords/buttons* for this new process are:

1. *World Closed In*
2. *Space Collapsed*
3. *(Your) Energy Collapsed*
4. *Anchor (or Dimension) Points Collapsed*
5. *Anchor (or Dimension) Points Snapped-In*
6. *Everything Fell In (and/or Down)*
7. *Space Was Uncreated (or Dispersed or Un-Space)*
8. *(Your) Energy Was Uncreated (or Dispersed)*
9. *(Your) Frame Of Reference Collapsed*
10. *Caved-In*
11. *Pulled Back*
12. *Withdrew From Everything*
13. *Made It All Unreal*

When this *stabilization point* is completed, a *Seeker* may then return to the top of *Wizard Level-1 Procedure*, if desired (or still left incomplete). If "*entities*" or other *somatic-pings* have become intrusive to personal development, or it seems some "*blockage*" has become active as a result of *Wizard Training*, then a handling of "*entities*" (*&tc.*) may be required.

However, a *Seeker* should not become so immersed in, or enamored by the idea of, treating "*entities*" that there is no *session-time* available for their own *Wizard Training*. There is sometimes a point where you just need to strongly *intend* a *mass-communication* (*to them all*) that "*everyone will get processed in their own turn.*"

Ideally, a *Seeker* will continue onto (and complete) *Wizard*

Level-2 Procedure before treating the material of *"Entities & Fragments"* (*AT#5*) a second time.

Having *"spiritual perception"* is not the determinant factor of *Wizard Level-1* completion; only one's own *certainty* that they have *ejected Awareness "exterior to"* the *Body* is necessary. No matter what one's skill-level or experience, the next set of exercises given for *Wizard Level-2* can enhance the *certainty* that is now there—and the *perception* will follow.

EJECTION, PERCEPTION & BARRIERS
(*Wizard Level-2 Keynote Lecture Excerpts*)

In *Systemology*, we are frequently concerned with *viewpoints*—which is to say *"a point from which to view," "point-of-view"* or *"POV."* In the first two *Wizard-Levels*, the emphasis is specifically on, what are often called, *"remote viewpoints"*—because they are at *"points"* the *Alpha-Spirit* is *"viewing"* (or *perceiving*) from that are *"remote"* (or *"exterior-to"*) the *sensory-perception* and *viewpoints* of a located *Body* (or *genetic vehicle*).

Ejection-of-Awareness is really a matter of one's *considerations* and *certainty* far more than any specific procedure. The same may be said concerning improvement of *Spiritual Perception*. True progress on the *Pathway* is marked by a *Seeker's* increasing ability to actually *change their considerations*—or *"change their minds,"* so to speak. Many individuals are under the delusion that they already maintain this total freedom.

To handle *Spiritual Perception*, a *Wizard* would have to be able to handle *Energy* and *Space*, and of course, *Force*. An individual doesn't do this when operating within the *Human Condition*. There are all kinds of *sensors* and *filters* and *communication relays*—all kinds of various *machinery* —that are in the way of *actually "seeing" this Universe*. When a *Seeker* first *"ejects,"* they are not really expected to have very vivid *perception*.

When we operate within the confines of the *Human Condition*—or more accurately, a *fixed viewpoint* within a *Body* —we are *perceiving* (or *receiving* "signals" and "cues" from) a *Universe* that is really only *"energy-waves," "standing-waves of mass," "particles,"* and various *"forces."* All of this is transmitted and translated by all kinds of *mechanisms* and *machinery* before the *Mind-System* "projects" it on a kind of "screen" for the *Alpha-Spirit* to *"view"* and *perceive* as its own experience. Therefore, an individual is not really in the habit of *perceiving directly*.

Anything that hinders *perception* would be best defined as a *"barrier"*—*"barriers to perception."* Perhaps one of the more fundamental issues is just how many *"barriers"* an individual is *fixated on perceiving*—or is *compulsively* (or *unknowingly*) *"looking through"* in order *to perceive*.

A preoccupation with *barriers* generally defines our *"thoughts"* or *"thinkingness."* When we compare the state of *Knowingness* to levels of *Thinkingness*, all our "thinking" serves to do is handle *barriers*—either avoiding or overcoming them in some way. To be so preoccupied with them, is of course, to be at an *agreement-level* with them, and even at an *effect-level* that is below their mechanics or structure.

The experience of *this Physical Universe* via the *Human Condition* is considered the section of the *"Beta-Awareness*

Scale" that falls between *zero* and *four* on our *Standard Model*. The *Human Condition* being: *Alpha-Spirit* plus a *genetic-vehicle*. But the *Standard Model* extends well beyond the *Human Condition*—it extends from *Infinity* to *Infinity*, and to that which we classify as *Alpha-Awareness* or *Actualized Awareness*.

While our *Standard Model does* systematize upper-level *Actualized Alpha* existence above "*four*," there is also the *low-Awareness* scale that an *Alpha-Spirit* can maintain independent of a *Body*, that extends "out the bottom" *below zero* and *Body Death*. It consists of remorse for a *Body*; the need to protect a *Body*; even not wanting anything to do with a *Body*; but still very much *fixated* on "*bodies*."

When an individual "*ejects*" from a *Body*, by one means or another, there is no guarantee they are going "out the top" of the *Beta-Awareness Scale*; in fact, when individuals return to the *Human Condition* in their next "lifetime" or "incarnation" (after *Body Death*), it would suggest that they do not "*ascend out the top*" automatically (or by default).

Another *sub-zero Awareness-level* is: the use of *bodies* for *hiding in*. The *sensory-functions* of a *Body* allow it to be used by an *Alpha-Spirit* as a personal buffer for handling and *perceiving* the *energy* and *force* of *this Universe*. Over the course of our *fragmented* experience of many *Universes*, we have gotten a bit wise to the fact that these *energy-waves* and *force-fields* are able to be used against us (because we have *considered* such for this *level* of *reality-agreements*) and so we are reluctant to start *confronting* or handling them directly.

As the primary *barrier* an individual has to *getting-out* of their *Body*, or a *Head*, is their own *fixed ideas*: it stands to reason that a *Seeker* may be carrying a lot of *fear*—or some sense of *danger* or *mystery*—concerning what might be *"out there"*; or what they *fear* they might have to handle as a *Spiritual Being* that is free from the *Human Condition*. The result is a *Spiritual Being* that has become *compulsively dependent* on *bodies*—and *this Physical Universe*—for an *"orientation-point"* or *"anchor-point"* to experience its own *Beingness*.

Space is also *perceived* as a *barrier* to *Knowingness*. Although it seems like an *"invisible barrier,"* the layered effect that we perceive at a great *distance* from *Earth* gives us the sense that it is *layers* of *darkness, blackness, unknowingness*, and *mystery*. This better explains our theory behind one of the *Wizard-Level* exercises, where a *Seeker* *"imagines"* many concentric spheres within spheres—or *layers*—of *darkness* or *blackness*, and then practices *"looking through"* these spheres or *layers*. Understanding the basic theory of this *keynote lecture* will help a *Seeker* understand the purpose behind practicing the exercises provided for *Wizard-Levels 1* and *2*.

R.S.V.P– REMOTE SPIRITUAL VIEWPOINTS & PERCEPTION
(*Wizard Level-2 Procedure*)

Wizard Level-2 Procedure is approached similarly to *Wizard Level-1*. In this case, however, there is no change in *routine* if a *Seeker* finds difficulty with the steps. The remedy is simply to start from the top and work through those exercises for which one *does* have *certainty* on before attempting more difficult steps again. This should not be interpreted as a *loss*, because a *Seeker* will likely work through *Wizard Level-2 Procedure* multiple times to increase their handling of *ejection* and *perception.*

Completing this routine in one single *session* is not required or expected. The *"standard opening procedures"* of a *Formal Session* are not used in *Wizard-Level Training Routines.* Instead, at the beginning of each *session*, a *Seeker* runs *"Preventative Fundamentals"* (*PC-9*) as their first *process* (as they did with *Wizard Level-1*). A *Seeker* may also find that using some kind of *"blindfold"* is helpful when practicing some exercises.

A. EJECTION-OF-AWARENESS

At some point during the *Wizard-Level* work, a *Seeker* is likely to come across their preferred or favored *process(es)* or method(s) to "induce" or "assist" *ejection.* This is something that can only be determined after applying the various exercises suggested throughout this manual.

Wizard Level-2 is designed for a *Seeker* that has already achieved an *ejection-of-Awareness*; and is used to further develop that as a *"conscious ability."* Although some exercises are more commonly used than others for *"ejection,"* a direct method is not something we can specifically instruct for STEP-A.

"The Wall," "Places You Are Not," "Back Upper Corner-Points Of The Room," "3 Points In Body; 3 Points In Room," and *"3 Points In Room; 3 Points Outside Of This Universe"* are all popularly used (and some even directly appear in this *routine*). But, this does not rule out the potential for a *Seeker* to make a basic high-power *Intention* (*a Self-made command*) for simply "stepping out" (*ejecting*) at will.

The first time *ejection* is directly implied on the *Pathway,* is in the final exercise of *PC-10*—which is the final lesson of *Processing Level-4* and basic *Beta-Defragmentation Procedure*. [*Processing-Levels 5 & 6* are *Pre-A.T. levels*.] In *PC-10* it describes it as: "...the ability to *conceive of* or *maintain a sense of* "centering" and "focusing" your own *Awareness* as a *viewpoint* (POV) a few feet *behind* the *head* of your current *Body*."

After *ejection*—before a *Seeker* is directed to do anything or go anywhere or look at the *Body*—the first several steps of this *routine* are intended to *stabilize* the *ejected*-state.

B. MAKING COPIES (*PC-2/PC-12*)

The basic PCL for this step are:

1. *"What Are You Looking At?"*

2. *"Make A Copy. (Make Many Copies)."*

With the *body's eyes* closed, post-*ejection*: the *Seeker* "makes" (*Creates/Imagines*) *copies* of whatever they are looking at—whatever they see. No matter what it is—however vague or fuzzy—you just *copy* what is there over and over again.

After you have several copies, you *"push them all together."* The first batch you *"pull the copies in on yourself"*; then the next batch of copies you can *"throw away"* (and continue alternating in this wise). This helps to remedy the *"loss of mass"* feeling after *ejecting* from the *Body*.

[Only *"pull in on yourself"* if you have *knowingly ejected* and are *"exterior to"* a *Body*. Otherwise, as a purely *imaginative exercise*, you would *"push them in on the Body."* Never *"pull-in"* while your *viewpoint* is from *inside the Body*. Get a sense of *"pushing-in"* from the *outside*. This step can be repeated throughout the routine to remedy whenever a *Seeker* feels their "attention thinning" from excessive exercises while *ejected*.]

The *vividness* of *perception*, or the *scenery* altogether, may change several times after treating the *copies*. You just keep *copying* whatever presents itself until there is no longer a change of perception (*e.g.*, vividness or detail isn't improving; scenery isn't shifting around). Then we balance the *somethingness* with the *Nothingness*. A *Seeker* extends or reaches their *Awareness* to "*Spot a Nothingness*" and then *copies* that for a while before going to STEP-C.

C. REACHING & HOLDING

Variations of this exercise appear in "*opening procedures*" of a *Formal Session*; and in "*Creation-Of-Space*" *processes* (*PC-5*). *Locating*, and *holding attention on*, "*corner-points*" of a square room is a form of "*Creation-Of-Space*" (defining "boundaries" or *dimension-points* of perceived *Space*).

Usually only two *corner-points* are used for this exercise —and they are often the "upper-back" *corner-points* of a room (or whatever is *behind* the *Body*), which forces *attention-Awareness* to *reach* in a direction other than what is in front of the *Seeker*.

This exercise can be modified to begin with *one corner-point*; and be extended to use all *four upper-corners* of a room—or even all *eight corner-points* (that form a "cube").

[*Update*: a *Seeker* should always end this exercise by "*letting go*" of any *corner-points* being "*held*."]

D. PLACES YOU ARE NOT (*PC-6*)

This step includes a *process* repeated from *Wizard Level-1*. A *Seeker* puts *attention* on "*remote locations*" to "check" to see that they "are not there."

"Spot A Place You Are Not. (Spot Many Places)."

[*Update*: in *Traditional Piloting*, an effective transition from the previous step is: *"Now, Let Go; and Spot Some Places You Are Not."*]

To effectively practice this step: a *Seeker* doesn't just quickly rattle off a list of arbitrary places. The goal is to actually *look* and *have certainty* from a particular *viewpoint* of *Space*.

E. ABILITY-TO-CONFRONT

This step asks a *Seeker* to *Spot* "things" (with the *body's eyes* closed) that they *consider* comfortable (or "safe") to *look at* (*confront*). This could also apply to "emotions" (or people displaying emotions). This is meant to increase tolerance for handling the *Physical Universe*.

This is not a *creativeness process*. A *Seeker* is not intended to *Create/Imagine* "things" to *look at*—but to actually "go" and *view* them in *this Physical Universe*. The accuracy of the *perception* is not as important as the actual *intention* to "be" at various *viewpoints*.

The basic PCL for this step are:

1. *"Spot Something It Would Be Safe To Look At In This Room."*

2. *"Spot Something It Would Be Safe To Look At Outside This Room."*

F. SHARED-SPACE

Part of the *reality-agreements* and *Implanted-Postulates* for *this Universe* include the *consideration* that *"two things* can't occupy the same *Space."* So long as a *Seeker* has heavy charge on this *consideration*—and the *consideration* that they, themselves, occupy a *Body* with *mass*—much of what an *Alpha-Spirit* is capable of would *seem* like a logical impossibility.

"*What wouldn't you mind sharing the same space with?*"

–or–

"*What wouldn't you mind sharing the same space with you?*"

Not *actually* having a *mass* present in *this Universe*, the *Alpha-Spirit* is very much capable of utilizing a *viewpoint* that does share *Space* with something that has *mass*. This step increases *Awareness* (and tolerance) on *ability* to *change* one's *Beingness*. The *process* is *run* to an *end-realization*, or all answers are exhausted.

G. LOCATIONAL VIEWPOINTS (*PC-5*)

This is based on a *meditation* found in "*eastern spiritual traditions*." A version, treated as an *imaginative exercise*, appears in *PC-5* (and should be reviewed for additional instruction and background).

[In *Traditional Piloting*, a *Co-Pilot* delivers "*locational*" PCL as quickly as a *Seeker* can perform them. This is generally determined by the observed *communication-lag* in responses.]

The PCL-sequence given in *PC-5* is:

1. "*Be Near (or Above) ___.*"

2a. "*Be Inside Of ___.*"

2b. "*Be Outside Of ___.*"

3a. "*Be At The Center Of ___.*"

3b. "*Be Outside Of ___.*"

4a. "*Be On The Surface Of ___.*"

4b. "*Be Above ___.*"

[Note that the PCL-*keyword* (*trigger* or *button*) for POV-

Locational (type) *A.T. processing* is "BE" (not "MOVE TO").
"Motion" between perceived *distances* in *space-time* is not
a *consideration* (or *factor*) of the action.]

The applications for this exercise are unlimited. The
original technique is called *"journeying to other planets"* —
hence the *terminals* that a *Seeker* finds most interesting/
effective for this *process* are *"planets."*

A *systematic* approach would begin with being *"near the
Earth"* or *"in the Sky"* before departing for other *planets*.
Other preferred *terminals* are *"The Moon," "The Sun,"* and
"Mars." It is best to *run* a few cycles of being *"near"* each
of these *target-terminals* (with the first PCL) before *adding*
the next PCL-set (*inside/outside, &tc.*) to the cycle.

A variation of this *"change-of-space"* technique is often
used in *defragmentation processing*. By alternating the
direction of *attention*, a *Seeker* is really *"shifting,"* between
(for example) *"Being In The Incident"* and *"Being In The
Room," &tc.* This gives a *Seeker* certainty that what they're
"holding onto" is really "somewhere else."

A *Seeker* already has too many *Universes* confused with,
or superimposed over, *their own*. One purpose of *A.T.*
exercises is for a *Seeker* to *get a sense* of *"separateness"* —
not *"connectedness"* —with *this Physical Universe*.

H. OWNERSHIP-OF-REALITY (*PC-11*)

With the *body's eyes* open: *select* a certain section of *"wall"*
—like a circular *spot* that is a few feet in diameter. This
can also be done with large (significant, heavy, *&tc.*)
objects that are in view. Alternate (repeatedly):

1. *"Get The Idea That You Are Creating It."*

2. *"Get The Idea That ___ Is Creating It."*

For the second PCL, use each of the following terminals separately (*running* each to a satisfactory *end-point* before going to the next): ANOTHER; SOCIETY; LIFEFORMS; A BODY; (YOUR) {SPIRITUAL} MACHINERY; THE {OBJECT ITSELF}; THE PHYSICAL UNIVERSE; AGREED-UPON MACHINERY; SPIRITS; and (A) GOD.

A *Seeker* may discover that *they* (*themselves*) are *not* the one *creating* everything—although it is in their capability. Most of the time, it will be discovered that "old machinery" is responsible for things persisting.

I. BODY-SYMPATHY

When the *Body* is severely *injured*, or even *dies*, an individual that is *fixedly* "*interior*" will *eject* suddenly— but then quickly "*snap-in*" again. This is because when "*exterior to*" a *Body*, at *low-Awareness* levels, an *Alpha-Spirit* has a *reactive-tendency* to "sympathize" with a *Body*. It "*snaps-in*" to try and "protect" or "heal" or even "reanimate" it.

This *process* is included here because it assists in overcoming the general impulse and tendency, while demonstrating both *interiorizing* and *ejection*. This can be *run* as "*imaginatively*" (or as "*actually*") as one's current *ability/perception* allows for. [The *end-realization* is that actions to "*fix*" (*&tc.*) something are best handled *from* the "*outside*."]

1. "*Look Around The Room And Choose An Object. (Preferably large).*"

2. "*Decide That There Is Something Wrong With It. (Pretend anything).*"

3. "*Feel Sorry For The Object; Sympathize With It; Say, 'Oh, Poor Thing'.*"

4a. *"Imagine Yourself 'Going-In-To' The Object To 'Fix It'."*

4b. *"Decide That You Are 'Inside' The Object; Its Mass Is All Around You."*

5a. *"Look Around 'Inside' The Object."*

5b. *"Realize That 'Inside' Is Not A Good Place To 'Fix It' From; That You Made A Mistake 'Going-In'."*

6a. *"Eject Awareness From The Object; Imagine That You Are Looking Down At It."*

6b. *"Imagine 'Fixing It' From The 'Outside'; Imagine 'Putting' An 'Energy Beam' On It And Say, 'There, That Fixes It'."*

7. *"Let Go Of It. (Select Another Object And Repeat The Process)."*

For your second application (in a separate *session*): *run* the *process* on *"Created/Imagined"* objects rather than the physical ones (in a room).

For your third application: *run* the *process* on "dead bodies" (*Imagined*). For "6b" alternate: *"fixing it successfully from the outside (to resurrect it)"* and *"deciding it isn't worth the trouble and abandoning it."*

[This *process* may also be practiced on the *Body*. You can *perceive "putting out"* or *"projecting" energy beams* on anything; getting the *Universe* to directly respond with a physical *effect* is another matter, and a higher gradient of work.]

J. TRUTH/UNTRUTH

Alternate the PCL:

1. *"Spot 3 Things That Are True."*

2. *"Spot 3 Things That Are Not True."*

3. *"Spot 3 Things That Are True For Someone Else."*

4. *"Spot 3 Things That Are Not True For Someone Else."*

5. *"Spot 3 Things That Are True For Others."*

6. *"Spot 3 Things That Are Not True For Others."*

K. THE RIGHT-TO-BE

This step is often practiced outdoors (in public); but as an *"eyes-closed ZU-Vision" process*, it may also be done alone—indoors or in Nature, *&tc.*

This *process* is an *exercise* in *intention*. It is also a practice of *"permitting freedom"* and *"granting livingness"* (which is important for handling *all beings*; not just *"entities"*). Each PCL is done several times (*with full intention*) on several *"target-terminals"* before going to the next; then repeat the full cycle.

[The emphasis of the *process* is found in the first two PCL.]

1. *"Grant Things/People (Another) The Right To Be There."*

2. *"Grant Things/People (Another) The Right To Do What They're Doing."*

3. *"Imagine Things/People (Another) Giving You The Right To Grant Rights."*

4. *"Grant Others The Right To Grant Rights."*

L. NO-BARRIERS

Alternate the PCL:

1. *"Spot Some Barriers That Are Not In Front Of Your Face."*

2. *"Spot Some Barriers That Are Not Behind You."*

3. *"Spot Some Barriers That Are Not On Your Right Side."*

4. *"Spot Some Barriers That Are Not On Your Left Side."*

5. *"Spot Some Barriers That Are Not Above You."*

6. *"Spot Some Barriers That Are Not Below You."*

M. BLACKNESS (AND MYSTERY)

Run the PCL:

1. *"Look Around The Room And Choose An Object."*

2. *"Create/Imagine a Standing-Wave (or Field) Of Blackness In Front Of It."*

3. *"Alternate A Few Times: Fixing Your Attention On The Blackness; And Taking It Off."*

Continue *running* this *process* until you have no "attraction" to the *"Blackness"* (*Veil of Mystery*); and although you have *intended* for it to be there, you can ignore it and *"look through"* it. [*Disperse* the *"standing-wave"* at the end.]

Then repeat the *process* on another object. Then apply the same *process* to *Created/Imagined* objects. [Certainty on this step is required for the next one.]

N. LAYERS-OF-BLACKNESS

Run the PCL (with eyes closed):

1. *"Create/Imagine Many Layers Of Blackness Around You."*

2. *"Look Through Each Layer (In Turn) To See The Next One."*

O. IN-AND-OUT ON OBJECTS

Run the PCL:

1. *"Look Around The Room And Choose An Object."*

2a. *"Get The Sense Of 'Going-In-To' The Object; And Being It."*

2b. *"Imagine Being The Object, In The Object, As Vividly As You Can."*

3. *"Eject From The Object."*

Repeat several times and on different objects. This may

also be practiced with ZU-Vision: *Spotting* objects outside the *session-room* (in a city, *&tc.*) and *"going-in-and-out"* them. [This exercise is found among some of the most ancient mystical practices and *"Hermetic"* training.]

P. EMOTIONAL-INDEPENDENCE

Run the PCL:

1. *"Decide To Feel An Emotion; And Feel It."*

2. *"Make The Body Feel A Different Emotion."*

[You continue *feeling* the original emotion, while the *Body* experiences another.]

Q. CONSIDERATION-OF-BEINGNESS

Run the PCL:

1. *"What Kind Of Object Can You Be For Certain?"*

2. *"Be It; And Experience It."*

Repeat many times. [Then *run* as: *"What Kind of Energy.."* and *"What Kind Of Space.."*]

R. ENERGY-SOURCES

This *process* is applied only after a *Seeker* has handled the ability to identify *"Sources"* and *"What Is"* (*PC-11*) and understands what *"energy"* means (*PC-13/PC-14*).

The basic PCL for this step is:

"Create (Imagine) An Energy-Source."

–or–

"Create (Imagine) Something To Give You Energy."

Repeat many times with many things. [A *Seeker* can do this with increasing magnitude, beginning with *generators* and *power-stations*, then working up to *sun-stars* and *spiritual machinery*. This *process* is *run* to give a *Seeker* certainty that *they* (*themselves*) are their own *energy-source* for *Creating/Imagining* these *mental images*; and also to loosen *considerations* regarding dependency on "external" *energy-sources*.]

S. TERMINALS

Alternate the PCL:

1. *"Spot Two ___ That You Don't Object To Having Together."*

2. *"Spot Two ___ That You Don't Object To Having Apart."*

Repeat many times on each of the following *terminals* (in turn): PARTICLES; OBJECTS; ANIMALS; PEOPLE; and SPACES.

T. DISAGREEMENT-WITH-GRAVITY

The basic PCL for this step are:

1. *"Get A Sense Of 'Falling Upwards'."*

2. *"Get A Sense Of Other Things 'Falling Upwards'."*

A *Seeker* should stay on one PCL to get a real certainty on their "*sense*" or "*impression*" before alternating.

U. ENERGY AND MACHINERY

Professional Course material for "*Spiritual Energy*" (PC-13) and "*Spiritual Machinery*" (*PC-14*) should be reviewed and all exercises practiced (in their advanced versions, if applicable). Given the progress a *Seeker* has since made, they should have a greater reality on the previous material when revisiting it at *Level-8*.

V. INTERIORIZATION PRACTICE (*PC-5*)

In this step, a *Seeker* practices "going in-to" (*interiorizing*)

and "getting-out of" (*ejecting*) many various *terminals* —
objects, animals, people, buildings, mountains, planets,
suns, galaxies, universes, *&tc.* (to the extent of their
ability and *perception*).

W. SPLITTING

In this step, a *Seeker* "*Imagines*" their *Awareness-of-Being-Oneness* "*splitting*" into two: *being* both "*in the Body*" and
"*exterior-to it*" simultaneously.

APPENDIX: A WIZARD-LEVEL SESSION
(*Basic Script Example*)

0a. "*Start of Session.*"
0b. "*Close your eyes.*"

1a. "*Spot a point in the room.*"
1b. "*Spot a point in your body.*"
1c. "*Find the same point in the room.*"
1d. "*Find the same point in your body.*"
1e. "*The same point in the room.*"
1f. "*The same point in your body.*"
   {*1e* and *1f* repeated several times}

2a. "*Spot two points in the room.*"
2b. "*Spot two points in your body.*"
2c. "*Find the same two points in the room.*"
2d. "*Find the same two points in your body.*"
2e. "*The same two points in the room.*"
2f. "*The same two points in your body.*"
   {*2e* and *2f* repeated several times}

3a. "*Spot three points in the room.*"
3b. "*Spot three points in your body.*"

3c. *"Find the same three points in the room."*

3d. *"Find the same three points in your body."*

3e. *"The same three points in the room."*

3f. *"The same three points in your body."*
   {3e and 3f repeated a dozen times}

4a. *"Three points in the room."*

4b. *"Three points outside the building."*
   {4a and 4b repeated a dozen times}

5a. *"Wherever you are, whatever you are looking at; make a copy of it."*

5b. *"Make another copy of it; exactly like the first."*

5c. *"And make another copy of it."*

5d. *"And another copy."*

5e. *"Take these copies; pull them together; and push them into the Body."*

5f. *"Whatever you are looking at now; make a copy just like it."*

5g. *"Make another copy of it."*

5h. *"And make another copy of it."*

5i. *"And another copy."*

5j. *"Take these copies; pull them together; and push them into the Body."*

6a. *"Wherever you are, reach your attention to locate a Nothingness."*

6b. *"Make a copy of it."*

6c. *"And make another copy of it."*

6d. *"And another copy."*

6e. *"Take these copies; pull them together; and throw them away in the distance."*

7a. *"Spot a point in space where you are certain you are not."*

7b. *"Spot another place you are not."*

7c. *"Spot two places you are certain you are not."*

7d. *"Spot three places you are not."*

7e. *"Spot three houses you are not in."*

7f. *"Spot three schools you do not attend."*

7g. *"Spot three businesses you do not work for."*

7h. *"Spot three groups you do not belong to."*

7i. *"Spot three animals you are not being."*

7j. *"Spot three planets you are not currently on."*

7k. *"Spot three universes you are not currently in."*

8a. *"Spot a calm space in this Universe."*

8b. *"Spot a calm place in the Body."*

{*8a* and *8b* repeated a couple times}

9a. *"Spot the two back upper corner-points in the room."*

9b. *"Reach your attention and just hold onto those two corner-points."*

{*corner-points* held for two minutes}

10a. *"Sense the chair under the Body."*

10b. *"Sense the floor beneath the feet."*

10c. *"End of Session."*

A.T. MANUAL #7
MASTERING
ASCENSION

Keep this reference material accessible:
PC Lesson-1 to 16; Processing-Levels 0 to 6.
AT Manual #1, *"The Secret of Universes"*
AT Manual #2, *"Games, Goals & Purposes"*
AT Manual #3, *"The Jewel of Knowledge"*
AT Manual #4, *"Implanted Universes"*
AT Manual #5, *"Entities & Fragments"*
AT Manual #6, *"Spiritual Perception"*

Review this prerequisite material:
PC Lesson-13, *"Spiritual Energy"*
PC Lesson-16, *"Alpha Thought"*

SELF-DIRECTION & INTENTION

There are many *"New Age"* publications and *"pop-spiritu-ality"* seminars that emphasize various *"secrets of attraction"* and *"powers of intention,"* &tc. This is primarily because all modern *"New Age"* and *"new consciousness"* material is an extension of the *"New Thought"* movement developing in America during the late 1800s and early 1900s—combined with the influence of a *"magical (ma-gickal) revival"* simultaneously occurring in Europe, where *"Will"* became the new *sacred name* for *Self.*

Increasing *"personal horsepower"* behind *"focused inten-tion" is* a critical component for progressive development on the *Pathway* to *Self-Actualizing* as an *"Ascended Master."* It is not, however, the direct emphasis of earlier *pro-cessing-levels*, which focus on more general *defragmenta-tion* of the *Mind-System* and the *Human Condition.* We have specific *systematic* reasons for handling the *Pathway* in this way.

Much like *"Alpha-Thought"* (see *PC-16*), a true and origin-al *"cause-point"* or *"source-point"* of *Intention* is always *"exterior-to,"* *"senior"* to, or otherwise *"beyond"* the level of *Beta-Existence* and even the *Mind-System.* It is plotted at "5" on the *Standard Model* (*ZU-Line*).

At an *Alpha-level, Intention* is a resulting product, expres-sion, or manifestation of *Alpha-Thought*; similar to how *Effort* is a resulting product of *Thought* in *Beta-Existence.* Typically, the *standard-issue Human* is not operating by *direct Intention* in *Beta-Existence*, but instead, *via* (or *through*) a *fragmented Mind-System.*

139

A "*communication*" or "*postulate*" is directed by the *Alpha-Spirit* along the *ZU-Line*. The first "communicable expression" of this—outside one's own *Personal Universe*—is an *Intention*. The *Alpha-Spirit* has already *postulated* that "something" exists (or "*Is*") and can now *intend* "something" about it. This is how things directly operated in earlier *Universes*, before the *condensation* and *solidity* of both a *Mind* and *Existence*.

While operating in *this Universe*, on *Earth*, and with the *Human Condition*, we are not in the habit of *knowingly Self-Directing Intention* toward *bodies* and other *energetic-mass*. In most cases, these *Intentions* are simply "absorbed" by the convoluted *circuitry* and *machinery* of a *Mind-System* (as a *receipt-point* and *relay*).

Once the *communication* of our original *Intention* has "sputtered" around the *considerations* and *reality-agreements* of the *Mind* for a while, it eventually results in (*Self + Body*) experiencing some state of "*Beta-Awareness*" before manifesting as an *effort* (with a *Body*) toward the *action* of using "*force*" in *Beta-Existence*.

A pure *Intention* originates from a *consideration-of-beingness*—or even a *viewpoint*—that is "*exterior-to*" the *Mind-Body* considerations. Anything else and we are not really handling *Intention*; we would be handling *reactive-imagery* and *associative thought* of the programmed, conditioned, and implanted *Mind-System*.

When effectively applied, previous *processing* will have mostly *cleared the way* for *Intention* to be directly *communicated*. This is when a *Seeker/Wizard* can start putting greater emphasis on increasing the "*power*" or "*volume*" of those *Intentions*. Alternating working on this and other *upper-level processing* ("*Implants*" and "*Entities*").

This *Advanced Training* manual (*AT#7*) presents material *Wizard Level-3X*. As of early 2024, this *level* is still in its "experimental stage" (hence the "X")—but it is sufficiently developed for standard release in the "*Keys to the Kingdom*" *A.T. series*.

[As other "higher" (still theoretical) gradients of the *Wizard-Levels* are researched, some material found here may be added to, altered, or altogether reassigned to another *level.*]

INTENTION: DIRECTING THOUGHT
(*Wizard Level-3X Keynote Lecture*)

Having treated "*Entities*" in *A.T. Manual #5*, and "*Ejection*" (*Wizard Level-1*) and "*Perception*" (*Wizard Level-2*) in *A.T. Manual #6*, we arrive at *Wizard Level-3X*: "*Intention.*"

To most effectively progress with *Wizard Level-3X*: a *Seeker* should *alternate* between practicing "*objective*" exercises of "*Intention-On-Mass*" and *processing-sessions* spent *defragmenting* the *considerations* (and other *inhibitors* and *suppressors*) *of* "*Intention.*" The frequency of *alternating*—how often or when—is at a *Seeker's* own discretion to determine for their case.

The basic experimental "*processing routine*" given for *Wizard Level-3X* (in this manual) is fairly *self-guiding* and easily applied by a *Level-8 systemologist*. Therefore, the part we will lead off with for our opening instruction pertains to the potential *systematic* application of other "*objective*" exercises to *standard procedure*.

"INTENTION-ON-MASS" (*WIZ-3X*)

This *"objective exercise"* formula is meant as only *one* part of the complete *Wizard Level-3X* routine. The *other* part is directly *processing-out fragmented considerations* and *postulates*—and other inhibiting factors, such as *Implants* and *Entities*. This cannot be overstated, because a *Seeker* is likely to take a greater interest in, and put more significance on, the *"objective exercises"* right from the start.

The real purpose of *Wizard Level-3X* is to increase certainty on the *ability* to focus and *communicate* a clear *Intention*—which is to say:

1. certainty that a focused *communication*

2. has *arrived* at its *intended "receipt-point"* (or *"effect-point"*)

3. and is *"duplicated"* there, perfectly (accurately) with the "meaning" originally *intended*; for which

4. it is *acknowledged* as having happened.

That is the basic *"communication-cycle"* a *Seeker* should follow when applying *objective exercises*. And it *is* a full *"cycle"* that a *Seeker* should observe. The individual *projects* an *Intention* on a *communication-line* as the *"source-point"* (or *Cause*). They must also be *willing-to-be* the *"receipt-point"* to *perceive* a *"response."*

Our emphasis is on certainty (without question) that a *communicated Intention* is *received*. While this can be *"coached,"* it is not easily *Co-Piloted*. A *Seeker* is typically their own best "judge" on the degree of certainty they have regarding *Intention* and remaining follow-through of the *cycle*.

A *Seeker's* approach to *Wizard Level-3X* must remain *systematic*. We are treating *upper-level* subjects that are too easily *invalidated* by other individuals and the *Physical Universe*. We must keep the aforementioned goals for this *level* in view, rather than invalidating our *gains* and abandoning the *Pathway* simply because *objects* in the room don't just start "*floating all around*" on *command*.

The *Systemology Society* "*research division*" reviewed a tremendous amount of "*New Age*," "*New Thought*" and "*para-psychological*" material pertaining to "*telekinesis*" for the development of *Wizard Level-3X*—little of which was *systematically applicable* to our purposes, but it provided a place to start.

First of all, the "*para-scientific*" fields exploring this previously have misappropriated the "*source-point*" of *Intention* as the *Mind* (such as "*mind over matter*"), when all *spiritual abilities* are those originating with the *Alpha-Spirit* and *Alpha Thought*—not a *Mind*.

Technically speaking: standard *circuitry* (*Implanting, &tc.*) of the *Mind-System* is a *barrier* that an *Alpha-Spirit* must properly *dissolve* or *disperse* in order to get their *Intention* clearly across. *Intention* is an *Alpha*-quality that is roughly equivalent to "*effort*" in *Beta-Existence*, which is why *direct-intention* can mimic the *effects* of *effort* in *this Physical Universe*.

Secondly, by "*telekinetic ability*," we mean affecting the *energetic-mass* of *Beta-Existence* "remotely" by *Intention* (without direct intervention/*effort* applied by a *body*, or some other "physical" means). Indeed, "*levitation*" is one key example of this. And while it *is* contrary to, or in *disagreement* with, *reality-agreements* maintaining *this Physical Universe*, such was not the case for *Alpha-Spirits* in previous *Universes* (versions of *Beta-Existence*).

Thirdly, we considered *mirroring* the "experimental procedures" from various research organizations that study the *telekinetic* phenomenon of "moving things with one's mind." These procedures are similar to what you see in movies with "paranormal investigators." In most cases, an *"ashtray"* is set on a table. It has a "circle" drawn around it and the individual focuses on moving the *ashtray* out of the "circle."

We liked the idea of the *ashtray*; we disliked the activity itself as a *systematic process* or exercise. For one, it limited the idea of practicing with *alternating Intentions*, when about all you could really say to the thing is *"move"* or *"move"* repeatedly. The other concern was the *invalidation issue*—setting up a hidden standard for personal gains where the only achievement of success possible is spontaneous "action-at-a-distance."

The *ashtray*, however, *is* an appropriate *object* for instructing this type of *objective* exercise.

1. It is a *receptacle* by design. For *"consideration"* and *"visualization"* sake, this allows a *Seeker* to more easily conceive of directing *Intention* not only *into* the "substance" of the *object*, but also *"filling"* it, and *permeating* its *Space*.

2. It is of *moderate size* to focus attention on; preferably colored-*glass*, rather than *plastic* or *transparent*.

3. It is *lightweight*, which makes it easy to physically handle during exercises.

Practice of this exercise will not be unusual to an experienced *Seeker*. We previously demonstrated other variations of this technique—for example, when the PCL called for "making objects feel an emotion," *&tc*. However, in previous *processing-levels*, we did not particularly address the *Intention*, or emphasize the "*communication-cycle*" that ensues for the exercise to be truly effective as a *systematic process*.

The following *formula* identifies the "*communication-cycle*." A *Seeker* should work toward developing the highest possible *certainty* on these basic points during their practice:

0. *Forming a clear "Intention" — thinking a 'Thought';*

1. *Directing the Intention toward, inside, and all around, the object;*

2. *Knowing that the Intention (command, communication, &tc.) has been received;*

3. *Perceiving the response, feedback, or effect-action taking place.*

4. *Acknowledging that the response (&tc.) has been received.*

There are two "*intended commands*" directed toward the *object* in this *systematic* version of other methods. They are: "*Rise Up!*" and "*Set Down!*" The *acknowledgment* that is given to end either *cycle* is "*Thank You!*"

To validate that there is *feedback* or *effect* for this exercise: after there is certainty that the directed *Intention* to "*Rise Up*" is received, the *Seeker* physically *lifts* the *object* up; and after "*Set Down*," they *set* it back down.

145

The basic instruction for this exercise is no more complicated than this. To provide variation to the practice, we suggest:

1. commands *intended* out loud;

2. commands *intended* silently; and

3. *Intentions* given with nonsense words.

ADDITIONAL DATA ON LEVITATION

An occurrence of the actual at-a-distance phenomenon of *"telekinesis"* or *"levitation"* is *not* one of the prescribed *Wizard Level-3X* end-goals. This does not exclude the possibility for a *Wizard-Level Seeker* to achieve it; but it is not how we measure personal success for this gradient of *upper-level* work.

Based on our experimental and research data: if and when a *Seeker* experiences this phenomenon, it will occur without any actual *effort* or *strain*—or any other *forced intensity* behind the directed *Intention*—and to accomplish "on command," would require being in perfect *communication* with the *target-object.*

Although we have not yet treated the subject of *"energy"* directly for the *Wizard-Levels*, it can already be determined that the matter of *"levitation"* (*&tc.*) is not a concern of *"having enough energy"* to physically move the *mass.* The *Alpha-Spirit* has unlimited ability to *create "Energy"* at will, which is only hindered by other *considerations* about *"energy-sources"* and *"restrictive uses"* (*&tc.*) that are specific to *this Universe.* In spite of this, for our *practice exercises*, it is still better to work with *mass* that can be easily handled (like an *ashtray*). Working with heavier *masses* may just *"pull-in"* additional *considerations* regarding one's physical abilities.

This all being said: the primary focus of *Wizard Level-3X Procedure* is *processing willingness, reach,* and *responsibility,* to increase clarity of *Intention* and the certainty of *being-at-Cause.*

WIZARD LEVEL-3X PROCEDURE
(*Example–Intention: Levitation*)

Start each *session* by *running "Preventative Fundamentals"* (*PC-9*). Now that we are treating specific subjects or areas at *Level-8,* it might be helpful to also check "*Preventative Fundamentals*" on any accessible *entities* that may get "*restimulated*" or "*intrusively active*" regarding "*Levitation*." This is done by addressing the surrounding area, usually with a *Biofeedback-Device* (after any personal "*Meter-reads*" on the word "*Levitation*" are *defragmented*).

This *upper-level* procedure utilizes virtually all *Systemology processing* theories in a single routine. It is applied to the example for which we have been discussing—"*Intention: Levitation*"—but its formula could be easily modified to *process-out* innumerable other areas as well.

A. ANALYTICAL RECALL

Run the PCL as *Basic (Light) Recall.* Cycle through each set-of-three a few times before going to the next. Since access to the *Backtrack* may be currently limited, if you are unable to directly "*recall*" what is asked for, *consider* the first "*idea*" or "*mental image*" that occurs. If nothing is *resurfacing* or "coming to mind," simply "*Imagine*" a scenario for that *item-line.*

 PCL = "*Recall a time...*"

1a. "*you enjoyed levitating something.*"

1b. *"another enjoyed you levitating something."*
1c. *"another enjoyed others levitating something."*

2a. *"you disliked levitating something."*
2b. *"you disliked another levitating something."*
2c. *"another disliked others levitating something."*

3a. *"you levitated something because you thought it was important."*
3b. *"you felt it was important for another to levitate."*
3c. *"another felt it was important for others to levitate."*

4a. *"you levitated something to create a good effect."*
4b. *"you felt it created a good effect for another to levitate."*
4c. *"another felt it created a good effect for others to levitate."*

5a. *"you could levitate something, but chose not to."*
5b. *"another could levitate something, but chose not to."*
5c. *"others could levitate something, but chose not to."*

6a. *"you levitated something and it improved communication."*
6b. *"another levitated something and it improved communication."*
6c. *"others levitated something and it improved communication."*

7a. *"you levitated something and it made people like you better."*
7b. *"another levitated something and it made people like them better."*
7c. *"others levitated something and it made people like them better."*

B. BASIC CONSIDERATIONS/DECISIONS

Run the PCL:

1. *"Recall some decisions you have made about levitating."*
2. *"Recall some decisions someone else has made about levitating."*

3. *"Recall some decisions others have made about levitating."*
4. *"Write down some bad effects you could create by levitating."*
5. *"Write down some good effects you could create by levitating."*
6. *"Write down some games you would spoil by levitating."*
7. *"Write down some new games you could have by levitating."*

C. HELP

One of the reasons an *Alpha-Spirit* restrains their abilities is because they don't believe that it will *help* others, or it is connected to times when they have *failed-to-help*. We focus on the more positive aspects in this *basic process*, rather than *resurfacing* "trauma." But we still must treat the *considerations* from both sides: *"levitating"* and *"not-levitating."*

1. *"How could you help another by not-levitating?"*
2. *"How could another help you by not-levitating?"*
3. *"How could another help others by not-levitating?"*
4. *"How could another help themselves by not-levitating?"*
5. *"How could you help yourself by not-levitating?"*
6. *"How could you help another by levitating?"*
7. *"How could another help you by levitating?"*
8. *"How could another help others by levitating?"*
9. *"How could another help themselves by levitating?"*
10. *"How could you help yourself by levitating?"*

D. PROBLEMS AND SOLUTIONS

Run the PCL (repeat as needed):

1a. *"Spot a problem that not-levitating would solve."*
1b. *"How would that be a solution?"*

2a. *"Spot a problem that another/others might solve by not-levitating."*

2b. *"How would that be a solution?"*

3a. *"Spot a problem that you might solve by preventing others from levitating."*

3b. *"How would that be a solution?"*

4a. *"Spot a problem that you might solve for others by not-levitating."*

4b. *"How would that be a solution?"*

E. PROBLEMS AND RESISTANCE

This *process* illustrates another angle for addressing *considerations-of-problems*. It follows the theory that an individual must *be resisting against* "the other side" (and therefore feeding it *attention* and *energy*) in order to be *fixated* on a *"problem." Run* the PCL (repeat "b" a number of times to answer "a"):

1a. *"Spot a problem that you could have with levitation."*

1b. *"What would you have to 'resist' (or 'be resisting') to consider that a problem?"*

2a. *"Spot a problem that someone else could have with levitation."*

2b. *"What would they have to 'resist' (or 'be resisting') to consider that a problem?"*

3a. *"Spot a problem that others could have with levitation."*

3b. *"What would they have to 'resist' (or 'be resisting') to consider that a problem?"*

F. CONNECTEDNESS/SEPARATENESS

Alternate the PCL within each set:

1a. *"Spot an object in the room."*

1b. *"Get a sense of being connected with it."*

1c. *"Get a sense of being separate from it."*
        {alternate (1b) and (1c)}

2a. *"Spot objects in the room that you would be willing to connect with."*

2b. *"Spot objects in the room that you would be willing to make connect with you."*

3a. *"Spot objects in the room that you are separate from."*

3b. *"Spot objects in the room that are separate from you."*

G. INVALIDATION

This *process* is *run* like checking *"Preventative Fundamentals"* on a *GSR-Meter* for any *"charge"* that *registers*. For each *Meter-reading-item*, you *"Spot {'What Is'}"* for that item until it *discharges/disperses* on *realization*.

1. *"On 'Levitation'; have you invalidated yourself?"*

2. *"On 'Levitation'; has another/others invalidated themselves?"*

3. *"On 'Levitation'; have you been invalidated by another?"*

4. *"On 'Levitation'; have you invalidated another/others?"*

5. *"On 'Levitation'; has another invalidated others?"*

6. *"On 'Levitation'; have you gotten another/others to invalidate themselves?"*

H. RESISTANCE/WILLINGNESS

This *process* requires directing (putting or placing) a *"thought"* or *"concept"* (*Intention*) into an *object*. Repeat with many *objects*.

1. *"Spot an object in the room."*

2a. *"Put into it 'a resistance to being levitated'."*

2b. *"Put into it 'a willingness to being levitated'."*
        {alternate (2a) and (2b) on *object*}

I. CAUSE/BLAME

This is partly an *"imaginative process."* It requires perceiving (receiving) a *"response"* or *"intention"* (*communication*) from an *object*. [Of course, the whole thing occurs based on your own Intention to *create* (or *Imagine*) and getting the sense of it occurring.] Alternate (2a) and (2b); but *run* one several times before shifting to the other. Repeat with many *objects*.

1. *"Spot an object in the room."*
2a. *"Have it looking up at you with admiration for being Cause."*
2b. *"Have it looking up to blame you."*

J. HARMFUL-ACTS/HOLD-BACKS

Harmful-Acts lead to *Hold-Backs* (see *PC-6*), which are a major contributor to compulsively restraining abilities. Since access to the *Backtrack* may be currently limited, if you are unable to directly *"Spot"* what is asked for, *consider* the first *"idea"* or *"mental image"* that occurs. If nothing is *resurfacing* or "coming to mind," simply *"Imagine"* a scenario for that *item-line*. *Spot* many examples for each:

1. *"Spot an act of harming something by levitating."*
2. *"Spot a harmful-act of preventing others from levitating."*
3. *"Spot times when you regretted having levitated something. If necessary, scan the incident in reverse; Spot the harmful-act 'As-It-Is' and defragment-by-realization."*
4. *"Spot times you had justification for stopping others from levitating. Write down any of these 'justification considerations'. Check for an earlier harmful-act against the terminal (others) or against you (if you do think you were really justified in stopping them)."*

K. VALIDATION-FOR-INABILITY

Often times, if an individual is *not* using an *ability*, it is because they *consider* themselves as getting *more validation* (from others) for *not* using the *ability*. *Run* the PCL for *considerations*:

1. *"How could you validate someone else for not-levitating?"*
2. *"How could someone else validate you for not-levitating?"*
3. *"How could others validate others for not-levitating?"*

L. HARMFUL-ACTS AND SOLUTIONS

In previous *Universes*, *levitation-abilities* allowed for so much "trouble" that we worked very hard at preventing it with the *reality-agreements* of *this Physical Universe*. Much of our own *agreement* to these conditions involves trying to solve the problem of others being able to *levitate* as a means to *harmful-acts*.

1a. *"Write down a harmful-act you could commit against another/others by levitating."*
1b. *"How would that be solved or prevented?"*
2a. *"Write down a harmful-act another/others could commit against you by levitating."*
2b. *"How would that be solved or prevented?"*
3a. *"Write down a harmful-act another could commit against others by levitating."*
3b. *"How would that be solved or prevented?"*
4a. *"Write down a harmful-act you could commit against yourself by levitating."*
4b. *"How would that be solved or prevented?"*

M. MENTAL REACH

This is an *"objective exercising"* break from the previous, more *subjective*, *processes*. Simply *"Spot objects in the room"* and *"mentally reach and let-go (from each one) three times."*

N. <u>ALPHA-THOUGHT/POSTULATES</u>

Alternate the PCL:

1. *"Spot/Recall some postulates you have made about levitation."*
2. *"Spot/Recall some postulates someone else has made about levitating."*
3. *"Spot/Recall some postulates others have made about levitating."*
4. *"Spot/Recall some postulates you have made about another/others levitating."*

O. <u>JUSTIFICATION CONSIDERATIONS</u>

This is a *listing* exercise. If you are using a *Biofeed-back-Device*, then you can check your *listed-items* for *Meter-reads*. Even if there is no significant *fragmented-charge* on all of these PCL-prompted *considerations*: simply use it for *light processing*; *listing* basic *considera-tions*. [Note: all of these PCL are looking to target the *same "justification"* from different angles.]

1a. *"How could you make yourself right by not-levitating?"*
1b. *"How could you make others wrong by not-levitating?"*

2a. *"How could you make yourself right by preventing levitation?"*
2b. *"How could you make others wrong by preventing levitation?"*

If you have difficulty with listing on these, consider the following approach:

> *"How could 'not-levitating' (or 'preventing-levitation') earn you 'sympathy' from others?"*

P. WILLINGNESS

One reason we *hold-back* our *ability* to *levitate* is because we don't want others to do it. On the *Backtrack,* things could easily get "out-of-control" when this *ability* was standard.

With the way our *reality-agreements* and *considerations* for *existence* are structured: we are not going to be *fully willing* to *levitate* unless we are *fully willing* to grant others the right to use that *ability* as well.

The basic PCL for this *process* ("b") must each be alternated with *"willingness-for-Self"* ("a") in order to keep the *process running.*

1a. *"Look around and spot an object you would be willing to move."*

1b. *"Look around and spot an object you would be willing for someone else to move."*

2a. *"Look around and spot an object you would be willing to move."*

2b. *"Look around and spot an object you would be willing for an Alpha-Spirit to move."*

3a. *"Look around and spot an object you would be willing to move."*

3b. *"Look around and spot an object you would be willing for a Bonded-Entity to move."*

4a. *"Look around and spot an object you would be willing to move."*

4b. *"Look around and spot an object you would be willing to have move by itself."*

Q. NEGATIVE-LOCATIONAL

This *process* is *run* to loosen-up *compulsive machinery.*

1. *"Spot some places where you are not."*

2. *"Spot some places where you don't have to levitate."*
3. *"Spot some places where another doesn't have to levitate."*
4. *"Spot some objects you don't have to levitate."*
5. *"Spot some objects another doesn't have to levitate."*
6. *"Spot some people you don't have to stop from levitating things."*
7. *"Spot some people that someone else doesn't have to stop from levitating things."*
8. *"Spot some objects you don't have to hold still."*
9. *"Spot some objects someone else doesn't have to hold still."*

R. "MUST-NOT-TOUCH"

Alternate each PCL-set several times.

1a. *"Spot an object in the room."*
1b. *"As your attention fixes on it, have it say: 'Must Not Touch'."*

2a. *"Spot an object in the room."*
2b. *"As your attention fixes on it, you say to it: 'Must Not Touch'."*

3a. *"Spot an object in the room."*
3b. *"Put an energy-beam on it with your attention, and have the walls say: 'Must Not Touch'."*

4a. *"Spot an object in the room."*
4b. *"Put an energy-beam on it with your attention, and you tell the walls: 'Must Not Touch'."*

S. ACTS/HOLD-BACKS (6TH SPHERE)

Alternate each PCL-set several times.

1a. *"What have you done to an environment?"*
1b. *"What have you held-back from an environment?"*

2a. *"What has someone else done to an environment?"*
2b. *"What has someone else held-back from an environment?"*

3a. *"What have others done to an environment?"*

3b. *"What have others held-back from an environment?"*

T. ACTS/JUSTIFICATION (6TH SPHERE)

Alternate each PCL-set several times.

1a. *"What have you done to objects?"*

1b. *"How have you justified that?"*

2a. *"What have you done to energies?"*

2b. *"How have you justified that?"*

3a. *"What have you done to spaces?"*

3b. *"How have you justified that?"*

4a. *"What have you done to the future of an environment?"*

4b. *"How have you justified that?"*

U. CAUSE/HOLD-BACKS (6TH SPHERE)

Alternate each PCL-set several times.

1a. *"What could you cause to happen to an object?"*

1b. *"What could you hold-back from doing to an object?"*

2a. *"What could someone else cause to happen to an object?"*

2b. *"What could someone else hold-back from doing to an object?"*

3a. *"What could you cause to happen to an energy?"*

3b. *"What could you hold-back from doing to an energy?"*

4a. *"What could someone else cause to happen to an energy?"*

4b. *"What could someone else hold-back from doing to an energy?"*

5a. *"What could you cause to happen to a space?"*

5b. *"What could you hold-back from doing to a space?"*

6a. *"What could someone else cause to happen to a space?"*

6b. *"What could someone else hold-back from doing to a space?"*

7a. *"What could you postulate into an object's future?"*

7b. *"What could you hold-out from postulating into an object's future?"*

8a. *"What could someone else postulate into an object's future?"*

8b. *"What could someone else hold-out from postulating into an object's future?"*

V. <u>CONSEQUENCES</u>

We have discussed *"reality-agreements"* and *"Monitor-Entities"* in previous *A.T. Manuals*. An individual is likely to have a "sense of" the idea that performing something like *levitation* would "break the rules" and one would be in "trouble" with some kind of "super-force," *&tc*. Therefore, a *Seeker* may be holding onto some *highly charged considerations* concerning anticipated consequences to *levitation*.

The first PCL is for *listing*. After writing down answers, see if any *register* on a *GSR-Meter* (or feel as though they have *fragmented charge* attached to them). Continue the *process* with the remaining PCL until you get a sense of *relief*—or greater certainty of *being-at-Cause*—regarding the situation; then return to ("1").

1. *"What horrible thing might happen if you levitated an object?"*

2. *"Create a mental image picture of the horrible thing happening out in front of you."*

3. *"Make it more solid."*

4. *"Copy it many times; make each copy more solid."*

5. *"Make more copies; change the colors and move things around in the scenery."*

6. *"Push some copies into the Body; throw some copies away into the distance."*

W. HIGH-PRESSURE TRAPS

On the *Backtrack*, sometimes *objects* were set up to "explode" or "implode" when you touched them—either as a stand-alone "*trap*," or to reduce one's *Actualized Awareness* during an *Implant*. Alternate each PCL-set several times.

1a. "*Spot an object in the room.*"
1b. "*Put an energy-beam on it with your attention; and imagine the object exploding.*"

2a. "*Spot an object in the room.*"
2b. "*Imagine someone else putting an energy-beam on it; and the object exploding.*"

3a. "*Spot an object in the room.*"
3b. "*Put an energy-beam on it with your attention; and imagine it imploding (pulling at you with a vacuum suction).*"

4a. "*Spot an object in the room.*"
4b. "*Imagine someone else putting an energy-beam on it; and the object imploding (pulling them into the vacuum suction).*"

X. POSITIVE-LOCATIONAL

1. "*From where could you levitate an object?*"
2. "*From where could someone else levitate an object?*"

Y. THOUGHT-BARRIERS

Check the following areas for *fragmented charge*. For each *Meter-reading-item* (or if you sense *turbulence* for an area): "*Spot {'What Is'}*" for that *item* until it *discharges/disperses* on *realization*.

1. "*Getting someone to stop levitating your things by convincing them that only you can levitate the things that you have created.*"

159

2. *"Deciding that: since you can't levitate things, you are going to make certain that no one else can either."*
3. *"Being ordered to levitate something that you don't want to, and avoiding it by demonstrating that you can't really do it."*
4. *"Deciding (or being convinced) that: you shouldn't levitate objects because it sets a bad example for other people with poor control, who would try to do it in foolish ways and mess things up."*

Z. ENERGY (BASIC RECALL)

Before *running* the PCL: check *Preventative Fundamentals* specifically *"On Using Energy"* (both for *Self* and accessible *entities*).

1. *"Recall controlling energy."*
2. *"Recall someone else controlling energy."*
3. *"Recall others controlling energy."*

AA. CONTROLLING ENERGY

This is an *objective exercise*. It is practiced while walking around your home, *&tc*. Practice with "water faucets" that have a visible *flow* (*the water*) before handling "light-switches" or "electrical flows."

1. *"Start and stop energy-flows by turning things 'on' and 'off'."*
2. *"Take notice of the flow when you turn something 'on'; and the no-flow when you turn something 'off'."*

BB. HARMFUL-ACTS/HOLD-BACKS

Run the *processes* for STEP-J; but replace *"levitating"* (or *"levitating something"*) with *"Creating Energy"* (for the PCL).

CC. VALIDATION-FOR-INABILITY

Run the *processes* for STEP-K; but replace *"not-levitating"* with *"not-Creating Energy"* (for the PCL).

DD. HARMFUL-ACTS AND SOLUTIONS

Run the *processes* for STEP-L; but replace *"levitating"* with *"Creating Energy"* (for the PCL).

EE. ENERGY (GENERAL)

1. *"Spot some places where you are not."*
2. *"Spot some places where energy is not."*
3. *"Spot some energy that is not currently hitting you."*
4. *"Spot some places where you are not putting energy."*
5. *"Spot some energy that you could have."*
6. *"Spot some energy that you could permit to remain where it is."*
7. *"Spot some energy that you could permit to disperse."*
8. *"Spot some energy that you could disagree with."*
9. *"Spot some energy that you could agree with if it suddenly appeared."*

FF. OWNERSHIP-OF-ENERGY

1. *"Spot some energies that you could own."*
2. *"Spot some energies that you would be willing for another to own."*
3. *"Spot some energies that you would be willing to give to another."*
4. *"Spot some energies that you would be willing for another to give to you."*
5. *"Spot some energies that you would be willing for another to give to others."*

GG. PUTTING-ENERGY-IN-WALLS

Practices of "putting" (*projecting/directing*) "*thoughts*" and "*concepts*" into *Walls* is a standard method of *processing-out compulsive "machinery.*" However, just putting the "*idea*" of *heat, cold, electricity,* or *radiation,* into *Walls* is not as *systematically* effective as with other applications of this technique.

In *this Physical Universe,* such energetic manifestations are the result of "*particle motion.*" Therefore, when this type of exercise is applied to the concept of *Energy* (*heat, &tc.*), it is important to also add the *creation/imagining* of the "*particles-in-motion*" to that *Energy-type.*

HH. FALLING-UPWARDS (GRAVITY)

The basic PCL for this exercise are:

1. "*Get a sense of falling upwards.*"
2. "*Get a sense of other things falling upwards.*"

A *Seeker* should stay on one PCL to get a real certainty on their "*sense*" or "*impression*" before shifting.

Variations of this exercise include:

1. *Create/Imagine various objects on the ground outdoors, one at a time, at an increasing scale of size (ashtrays, books, boxes, furniture, automobiles, aircrafts, &tc.); then have them "fall upwards" into the sky and outer space.*
2. *Spot objects in the room. For each one in turn: create/imagine a copy of it "falling upwards" through the ceiling, into the sky.*
3. *Eject-Awareness and spot large objects, one at a time, around the planet (buildings, monuments, mountains, &tc.); then Imagine them "falling upwards" into the sky and outer space.*

II. "CAN'T-DO-THAT"

Alternate each PCL-set several times.

1a. *"Spot an object in the room."*
1b. *"Put an energy-beam on it with your attention, and have it say: 'You Can't Do That'."*

2a. *"Spot an object in the room."*
2b. *"Put an energy-beam on it with your attention, and you say to it: 'You Can't Do That'."*

3a. *"Spot an object in the room."*
3b. *"Put an energy-beam on it with your attention, and have the walls, floor, and ceiling, laugh while saying: 'You Can't Do That'."*

4a. *"Spot an object in the room."*
4b. *"Put an energy-beam on it with your attention, and you laugh while telling the walls, floor, and ceiling: 'You Can't Do That'."*

JJ. SPOILING-THE-GAME (TRUST)

Alternate a PCL-set, then shift.

1a. *"Spot an object in the room."*
1b. *"Decide to levitate it because you can; then decide not to because it would spoil-the-game."*

2a. *"Spot some people you could trust with the ability to levitate."*
2b. *"Spot some people who would be safe if you had the ability to levitate."*

KK. INTERIORIZING-EJECTION

Alternate a PCL-set, then shift.

1a. *"Spot an object in the room."*
1b. *"Interiorize into it; then eject out from it."* {repeat several times}

2a. *"Spot an object in the room."*

2b. *"Imagine/visualize other Alpha-Spirits interiorizing into it and ejecting out of it."*

LL. CONCEPTUAL-CERTAINTY

Uncertainty—the *"lack of certainty"*—reduces an individual's *Actualized Awareness* by suspending their *attention* on a perpetual "maybe." This is accomplished (often with *Implanting*) by holding an intense *energetic-charge* on two *opposing considerations* about a specific *concept*. For example, if equally *charged*: *"I can do.."* and *"I can't do.."* would keep an individual in a state of partial *unknowingness* about their abilities.

Alternate the two PCL of a set before going to the next. Make sure that you *really "get a sense"* of what each PCL calls for (rather than a vague idea).

1a. *"Get a certainty that objects can be levitated."*

1b. *"Get a certainty that objects cannot be levitated."*

2a. *"Get a certainty that you can levitate objects."*

2b. *"Get a certainty that you cannot levitate objects."*

3a. *"Get a certainty that others can levitate objects."*

3b. *"Get a certainty that others cannot levitate objects."*

4a. *"Get a certainty that you can generate energetic-force."*

4b. *"Get a certainty that you cannot generate energetic-force."*

5a. *"Get a certainty that others can generate energetic-force."*

5b. *"Get a certainty that others cannot generate energetic-force."*

6a. *"Get a certainty that you must levitate things."*

6b. *"Get a certainty that you must not levitate things."*

MM. INTENTION-ON-PEOPLE

Run this *process* in a public place (where people are visible). If this is not convenient when reaching this step of the procedure: continue to the next step and return to this *process* when it can be completed.

The purpose of this *process* is to loosen one's fixed *postulates* and *reality-agreements*. It is *run* by *postulating* (or *imagining/visualizing*) opposing *"ideas"* (or *Intentions*) and "putting" (*placing/projecting*) them into others. [This is *run* silently by *Intention*.]

1a. *"Postulate 'an inability to levitate' into people."*
1b. *"Postulate 'an ability to levitate' into people."*

2a. *"Grant people 'the right to levitate'."*
2b. *"Imagine people granting you 'the right to levitate'."*

3a. *"Postulate 'a lack of energy' into people."*
3b. *"Postulate 'an abundance of energy' into people."*
3c. *"Postulate 'being a source of energy' into people."*

4a. *"Grant people 'the right to generate energy'."*
4b. *"Imagine people granting you 'the right to generate energy'."*

5a. *"Postulate 'a lack of havingness' into people."*
5b. *"Postulate 'an abundance of havingness' into people."*
5c. *"Postulate 'being a source of havingness' into people."*

6a. *"Grant people 'the right to create mass'."*
6b. *"Imagine people granting you 'the right to create mass'."*

7a. *"Postulate 'a lack of space' (or collapsed space) into people."*
7b. *"Postulate 'an abundance of space' into people."*
7c. *"Postulate 'being a source of space' into people."*

8a. *"Grant people 'the right to generate space'."*
8b. *"Imagine people granting you 'the right to generate space'."*

9a. *"Postulate 'a lack of time' (not enough time) into people."*
9b. *"Postulate 'an abundance of time' into people."*

9c. *"Postulate 'being a source of time' into people."*

10a. *"Grant people 'the right to generate their own independent time'."*

10b. *"Imagine people granting you 'the right to generate your own independent time'."*

NN. <u>MACHINERY AND ENTITIES</u> (*AT#5*)

• Check for any *Programmed Machine Entities* (PME) that are currently:

–*"being levitation machinery"*;
–*"being broken levitation machinery"*; or
–*"being levitation-blocking machinery."*

Use *A.T. Manual #5* to handle each one found (e.g. *Spot being made into a machine; Spot the first time;* run *"Identification Procedure"*). If *Control Entities* (CE) or other types become active (or restimulated) doing this, handle them as well. [This type of *machinery* usually accumulates around the *"Third Eye"* area of the forehead.]

• Check for any PME that are currently:

–*"being machinery that puts out energy-beams"*;
–*"being broken machinery that puts out energy-beams"*; or
–*"being energy-beam-blocking machinery."*

• Check for any *"Watchers"* (*"Monitors"*), *"Bonded-Entities,"* or other CE that might be secretly observing you, and reporting on you—particularly if you do any major *"rule-breaking activities,"* such as *levitation*.

Starting at *Level-8*, a *Seeker/Wizard* becomes increasingly aware of whether or not there is anything "focused in" on them from a distance that might be blocking *levitation, generating energy,* and other *spiritual abilities*.

Another way of handling interference is to *"put an energy-beam on the object with your attention"* and then check with a *GSR-Meter* if there are any *entities* (*&tc.*) opposing, protesting, invalidating, or trying to stop you from *levitating* the *object* in any way. [This is worth checking on for the *ashtray* used in the *"Intention-On-Mass"* exercise—especially before any attempts to practice it "metaphysically."]

OO. REALITY-POSTULATING

This *process* is based on the theory that an individual (*Alpha-Spirit*) is *continuously* and *compulsively* "*creating reality*" on an *automatic* basis. Therefore, what a *Seeker* is doing *unknowingly*, we have them practice doing with *intentional-control*.

This is an *objective exercise* that involves "*putting intentions*" (*postulates*) into *objects* found in the room or environment.

PCL = "*Spot an object in the room and...*"

1. "*postulate solidity into it.*"
2. "*postulate weight into it.*"
3. "*postulate color into it.*"
4. "*postulate temperature into it.*"
5. "*postulate energy into it.*"
6. "*postulate space into it.*"
7. "*postulate thought into it.*"
8. "*postulate mystery into it.*"
9. "*postulate beauty into it.*"
10. "*postulate that it has a past (Backtrack) stretching behind it.*"
11. "*postulate that it has a future (track) ahead of it.*"

PP. TOUCH-AND-GO (COMPONENTS)

This is an extension of the previous *process*. In this step, you select an *object*; then practice "*reaching*" and "*letting-*

go" (with your *attention*) of a single specific *"component-quality"* of the *object* (listed in the previous step), such as *weight* or *color, &tc.*

After working through the list several times: repeat the *process*; but this time *"intensify"* or *"increase"* the *component-quality* before *"letting-go."* A basic PCL-formula for this is:

"Reach for the {component-quality}. Increase (or intensify) it; then let go of it."

QQ. "BELL, BOOK & CANDLE" (*PC-3*)

Perform the "physical" and "advanced" versions. [See *PC-3*.]

RR. "CRYSTAL CLEAR" (*Liber-2B*)

Take up a copy of the book *"Crystal Clear: Handbook for Seekers"* and make a pass through the entire text; *run* all *processes* to *total defragmentation* and "end-cycle" on your use (necessity) of that material.

After *running through* this entire procedure (from STEP "A" to "QQ") at least twice—in addition to at least two hours (total among *sessions*) spent practicing *"Intention-On-Mass"*—the *Seeker/Wizard* may then proceed to apply even more *advanced systematic exercises* (from the next section) to their *Wizard Level-3X* routine.

ADVANCED ABILITY TRAINING– 3X
(*Example–Intention: Levitation*)

For use after completing standard *"Wizard Level-3X Procedure"* (previous section).

3X-A. "INTENTION-ON-MASS"

[See *"Intention: Directing Thought (Wizard Level-3X Keynote)"* for details.]

3X-B. "BEAMS-ON-A-BODY"

The *Alpha-Spirit* is quite out-of-practice with handling *Energy* and *Force* directly. This exercise practices handling the *Body* using *"energy-beams."* Even above other *mass* in the *Universe*, a *Seeker* would have the greatest certainty of *control* with the *Body* they are currently accustomed to using. [Review the material and exercises from *"Spiritual Energy"* (PC-13).]

This exercise is usually practiced after *ejecting-Awareness* and standing "outside of, but near to" the *Body*. When operating in this wise, a *Seeker* can get a sense, however slight, of "operating the *Body from* outside the *Body*." Experience with this can improve *"ejection-stability"* — handling *body-motion* while *"exterior to"* the *Body*, without automatically "snapping-in."

This exercise is similar to *"Intention-On-Mass"* (3X-A). We practice "lifting" and "setting down" a bit of *mass*. However, in this case, the *Intention* includes the *creation* and *control* of an *energy-beam* to conduct the action (rather than a strictly verbal-style *"command-intention"* directed at *mass*).

The basic instruction is: "starting with a single finger, practice using *energy-beams* to lift/move the finger, rather than relying on the *Body's* muscles." {more details below}

You can project an *energy-beam* from "where *you* are" (POV) or from another "remote point." This means an *energy-beam* can be "put out," "projected" or otherwise "postulated" without attaching the other "end" of it to *Self*. For example: a *Seeker* could run *beams* from a spot on the ceiling of a room. A *Seeker* should practice with various approaches to this exercise (as their own personal experiment).

There is a "puppet-master method" of treating *energy-beams* like "wires" or "cables" being handled from "above" (or from the *Alpha-Spirit* while *exterior-to* the *Body*)—and essentially operating the *Body* like a "*marionette-doll.*" A more *systematically* accurate approach would involve the "*lengthening*" and "*shortening*" of an *energy-beam* "*wave*" to control the "tension" or "force"—to either "push" or "pull" on the *beam*.

This exercise begins with a single finger, then works up to a hand, and then an arm. Eventually this can be extended to include all parts of the *Body* simultaneously. When applying *systematic* methods to the *Body*, the best practice is to alternate the side of the *Body* you're working with for each cycle or *session*—"right index finger" then "left index finger," &tc.

From previous exercises, a *Seeker* is used to alternating the "putting on" and "pulling off" of *energy-beams*. This is not standard practice when using the *Body* as an *exercise-target* directly. If you repeatedly "put on" and "pull off" *beams* from the *Body*, they have a tendency to get "sticky." Therefore, once *attention* is fixed on the *beam*, the alternation from "*On*" to "*Off*" should be treated like "*Turning It Off*" rather than "*pulling-it-off.*"

Similarly to how we manually manipulate motion of an *object* for "*Intention-On-Mass*," this exercise is *not* expected to set a *Seeker* up for failure or *invalidation*. You can also use "*creativeness processing*" to practice "*imagined*" versions of any gradient or magnitude that exceeds one's reality. For example: if you make good progress with fingers, but not hands, simply spend time *visualizing* the practice you find difficulty with.

Although handling of *energy-beams* is entirely within the scope of *Level-8*, a *Seeker* can treat the exercise as *imaginatively* as necessary, based on their current reality on it, in order to practice it. As with exercise 3X-A, always leave yourself with a *"win."* [In the end, one way or the other: *postulate* that the *finger will lift, &tc.*]

For each part of the *Body* (*finger, &tc.*), practice the following steps:

1. Lay your hand down flat on the table. [For moving the entire arm, lay down and stretch out the entire arm, *&tc.*]

2. *Eject-Awareness.* Float above that part of the *Body* and fix an *energy-beam* on it with your *attention* (or *by Intention*). Alternate practicing: *"putting the beam on it"*/*"turning it on"* and *"turning it off."*

3. Put the *beam* on the *body-part* and *"lift it up."* Practice: *"putting the beam on it," "lifting it," "moving the body-part very precisely," "putting it down,"* and *"letting-go"* (*"turning off"* the beam).

3X-C. "4TH-DIMENSIONAL THICKNESS"

Creation and *masses* in *this Physical Universe* are composed of *3-Dimensional structures.* However, there is a slight degree of *"fourth-dimensional thickness"* to its substance. If you were to *imagine* a *2-Dimensional "Flatland"* drawn out on a sheet of paper—the *paper* and *ink*, themselves, would have a slight *3-Dimensional thickness.*

When handling *entities*, you may sometimes perceive a

Bonded-Entity as a small *"spark"* disappearing in the distance—and yet it doesn't seem to move off very far, relative to our *3-Dimensional Space*. It is essentially moving off into a *fourth-dimensional direction* that is *"sideways"* of the basic *reality* of *this Physical Universe.*

In our practice of *"Reaching for Nothingness"* (and other exercises involving *"direction"*), we tend to work primarily with the *six directions* of our familiar *3-Dimensions.* They are:

left/right; *front/back*; and *up/down.*

Technically, on *Earth*, we treat these as:

east/west; *north/south*; and *up/down.*

They are measured in "geometry" as:

height (or *length*), *width*, and *depth.*

And as the axis-coordinates:

longitude, latitude, and *altitude.*

By a *Fourth-Dimension*, we do not mean what is *postulated* as *"Time"*; we mean a *fourth "spatial" dimension.* This would, by definition, include two additional *"directions."*

Mathematician and writer, *Charles H. Hinton* (*1853-1907*), coined the term *"tesseract"* to describe a *"four-dimensional cube."* More specifically to our purposes, he appointed names to the two *4-Dimensional directions* (derived from the Greek language):

ANA = "upwards toward"

KATA = "downwards from"

In other explanations: this is also described as *"unfoldment"* and *"folding"*—and sometimes *"expansion"* and *"contraction"*—or even likened to a *"breath."* While it is geometrically demonstrable, it is not necessarily communicable clearly with words and descriptions that are all relative to visible *3-Dimensional* examples.

And this is not altogether different from what is implied in "*Mardukite Zuism*" with its terms (from the *Sumerian* language): *AN* and *KI*. These are the two *directions* indicated on the *Standard Model* by the *ZU-Line*, demonstrating the true "*interdimensional*" quality of *our cabala* that is not so easily depicted on paper. It *can*, however, be conceived of when applying the "*spatial exercises*" of our *Systemology*.

This subject is presented for *Wizard Level-3X* to supplement "*Intention-On-Mass*" exercises involving an *object* (such as the *ashtray*). [Review *PC-5* material on handling "*Space*" and "*Creation-Of-Space*."]

Apply the following procedure to your *Wizard Level-3X objective exercises* with an "*object*." Practice each step until there is certainty on it before proceeding to the next.

A. *Postulate* the "*Space*" around the *object* by *Intention*. Put up *eight corner-points* as a "*cube-of-space*" around the *object*. Keep this *created-space* "in place" for the remaining steps.

B. *Imagine* a *3-Dimensional* coordinate-system with three *axis* composing the "*cube*." This can be *imagined* as a "*matrix*" or a potential "*graph*" (such as you might use in a geometry class, describing an *X*, *Y*, and *Z-axis*). The "mathematics" behind this is unimportant. We described the *six directions* of *3-Dimensional Space* above. [These are what extend from the *three dimensional axis-lines* that are all at "right-angles" or "perpendicular" to one another.] All that is necessary for this step is that they are *realized* for what they are within the *created-space*—because the final part is: *Imagine* a *fourth dimensional axis-line* extending off both ways in *non-physical directions* (ANA and KATA; or AN and KI).

C. *Spot* the "center" of the *object*. Reach your *attention* down one *direction* of this *fourth axis-line*; and find the *object* continuing to *exist* in that *direction* until you reach the "end" of the *object*. Then *spot* the *Nothingness* on the far-side of the *object* in that *direction*. *Spot* the "center-point" (in the *Physical Universe*) of the *object* again. Then repeat this step in the opposite *direction*, finding the "end" of the *object* on the other side and the *Nothingness* extending beyond that.

D. Using the perception achieved from the previous steps: *Spot* a *fourth-dimensional "edge"* of the *object* extending in one of the 4-D *directions*. Alternate: "*reaching*" and "*letting-go*" of that edge with your *attention* (or by *Intention*). Then *spot* the other 4-D "*edge*" and repeat. Then alternate "*reaching*" and "*letting-go*" of *both* "*edges*" simultaneously. It is rather like "holding" (*sensing*) its *fourth-dimensional thickness* with "*spiritual hands*." [Once you have certainty on being able to *locate* and *perceive* its *fourth-dimensional thickness*, maintaining the *active creation* of an *axis-coordinate system* is no longer necessary.]

E. Use *Intention* to put up *eight corner-points* around the physical *object* (fairly close to it). Then, put a second set of *eight anchor-points* in the same place as the first. Take the second set and extend it out into the *fourth-dimension* until it passes beyond one of the 4-D "*edges*" of the *object*, into the *Nothingness* beyond it. Then move it back slightly so that it only encompasses the last bit of 4-D *Space* that the *object* actually occupies. Then do the same with the other "*edge*."

F. *Imagine* that the *eight corner-points* of one *cube* extend to the *eight corner-points* of the 4-D *cube*. [This is the idea behind a 4-D *"hypercube"* — or *cube within a cube* — except one of the *cubes* extends into a *fourth-dimension.*] *Imagine* that the 3-D *object* is actually in each of these *cubes* simultaneously, and also as a "smear" or "spread" stretching between them.

G. By *Intention* (or *imaginative visualization*), *get the sense* of *extending* your *"spiritual hands"* out and grabbing the 4-D *edges* of the *object.* Then alternate the *"Intention-based"* PCL (from the *"Change and Motion" processing* in *PC-4*):

1. *"Keep It From Going Away."*

2. *"Hold It Still."*

3. *"Make It More Solid."*

3X-D. <u>ADVANCED 3X-A</u> {3X-AX}

Refer to *"Intention: Directing Thought (Wizard Level-3X Keynote)"* for background and details on the basic *process.* It is presumed that a *Seeker* will already have practiced the basic version for a number of hours prior to handling this exercise. [Experience with procedure 3X-B and 3X-C is also required.]

3X-D combines elements from each of the three previous exercises. In this *process,* we advance the original 3X-A procedure by incorporating *Energy* along with our *Intention* for an *object* (*ashtray, &tc.*) to *"Rise Up"* — similar to what is practiced in 3X-B. In addition to this, we extend our reach on the *object* into the *fourth-dimension* — as in 3X-C.

Having proficiency with the previous parts of this manual, and the high-level of *Actualized Awareness* applied by a *Seeker/Wizard* (at *Level-8*): a "shadow" of the *object's structure* — like an *"etheric"* or *"akashic"* essence of it — *will* move by applying this procedure. Whether or not the *physical object* automatically "catches up" to where you've shifted its *Beingness* to, is of course, another matter.

The degree to which a *Seeker* is at *Cause* over the *physical object* itself is likely to remain low at the beginning— therefore, we use our physical hands (as in 3X-A) to finish seeing our *intended effect* through to the end. The quotient of certainty—or percentage of *Being-at-Cause*— ebbs and flows (rises and falls) as one repeats the *process*; always end your practice on a *"win"* (when certainty is high).

We can estimate that for an individual to actually get even the smallest response from *energetic-matter* in the *Physical Universe* requires being over 90% *at-Cause* over the object/item. This is challenging to achieve in *this Physical Universe*, because the building-blocks of what is considered *"creativeness"* at a material level require a *Body* to use *effort* and *force* against *already created* (*other-determined*) *Space-Time* and *energetic-matter*. This was much less the case in much earlier (previous) versions of *Beta-Existence*.

A *Human* believes they have to use *effort* and *force* on what is *already here* in order to *do* or *have* anything. The *Space* and *mass* of *this Universe* is generally *"misowned"* by us—and therefore *persists*. Its *"Is-ness"* is really the result of an *other-determined creation*; thus we have difficulty in assuming *total responsibility* and *control* of it as being "ours." So, we go on *altering* what we have been given (*"What Is"*) and making it more and more solid all the time; and ourselves becoming more *solidly fixed* on the *reality-agreements* of *this Game*.

A. Reach into the *object* and spread *"golden energy"* throughout it. Extend this *Energy* out in the *4-Dimensional* directions (see 3X-C) to fill the entire *object* with this *"golden energy"* between its *fourth-dimensional "sides."* Extend even more *Energy* into the *object's* "future" and "past" until the entirety of the *object* is filled with the *"golden energy."* [As you continue with the remaining steps, occasionally "refresh" the *object* with this *Energy*.]

B. *Intend* the *object* to rise upwards. You can apply verbal commands, as in the basic version of 3X-A, or you can direct your *Intention* silently. Then *"See"* (or *Imagine/visualize*) the "etheric shadow" portion of the *object* "rise" up approximately a *foot* (*twelve inches*) above the surface (table) it is set on. If necessary, apply the 3X-C practice of also using your *"spiritual hands"* in the *fourth-dimension*; or you can apply the *"energy-beam"* method of 3X-B to improve your certainty. [Technically, the entire action is accomplished by *Intention* alone.]

C. *Acknowledge* the portion of the *object* that *did* move for having moved.

D. With the *body's hand*, move the rest of the *physical object* up to the position that you are holding the portion that moved. Have the *object "feel relieved for having caught up with itself."* Then *acknowledge* it for completing the *intended* movement.

E. *Intend* the *object* back down to where it was setting. *Acknowledge* the portion that *moves*; then use the *body's hand* to complete the action with the rest of the *physical object*, have it feel *"relieved," acknowledge* it, and *"let go"* of it.

F. Repeat STEP-B through STEP-E until an appropriate end-point.

Extended Version:

G. With eyes closed (and/or *Awareness-ejected*): perform a *"Creation-Of-Space"* (defining it with *eight corner-points, &tc.*) and *Create/Imagine* a *"Copy"* of the *object* in that *Space*. *Intend* the *object* to *"Rise Up"* and *"Set Down"* and have it do so, giving it *acknowledgments*.

H. Have the *object "protesting"*; and you move it anyway.

I. Have the *object "enjoying it"* as you move it.

J. Have the *object "wanting to move somewhere else"*; but you move it to where you want it anyway.

K. Alternate between *running* all of STEP-B through STEP-E and STEP-G through STEP-J repeatedly to an appropriate end-point.

3X-E. <u>BETA-INTERCONNECTEDNESS</u>

One of the *"barriers"* embedded in the *reality-agreements* of *this Physical Universe* is part of what we generally refer to as *"gravity."* The underlying design for *this Universe* is "interconnectedness." By this, we mean that each manifestation or existing part of the *Space-Time Energy-Matter* of *this Universe* also acts to "hold" all the other parts in place. This is the magnitude of what a *Seeker/Wizard* is working to get greater *control* over when applying *Intention* to it—or even *ascend beyond* it (which is actually the entire point behind all of this).

[For written instruction of this exercise: we capitalize the words *"The Object"* when referring to *the object* (*ashtray, &tc.*) that we've been using for the *3X-series* exercises. This is important to distinguish since we will also be referring to other *"objects in the room."*]

A. *"Spot other objects in the room. For each: have (get a sense of) The Object connect with it, and disconnect from it, several times."*

B. *"Spot other objects in the room. For each: have (get a sense of) it connect with, and disconnect from, The Object, several times."*

C. *"Spot other objects in the room. For each: have (get a sense of) The Object agree with it, and disagree with it, several times."*

D. *"Spot other objects in the room. For each: have (get a sense of) it agree with, and disagree with, The Object, several times."*

E. *"Spot other objects in the room. For each: have (get a sense of) The Object communicate with it, and go out-of-communication with it, several times."*

F. *"Spot other objects in the room. For each: have (get a sense of) it communicate with, and go out-of- communication with, The Object, several times."*

G. Repeat STEP-A through F; but instead of *"objects in the room," Spot* things at a distance, including: *"The Center Of The Earth"; "The Center Of The Sun"; "The Sun (As A Mass)"; "The Center Of The Galaxy,"* &tc.

3X-F. UNIVERSE-AS-A-TERMINAL

Practice with *getting a sense* of *The Universe* as a *terminal.* In *systematic* terms: *"gravity"* is the structural-impulse of *objects* in (and the basic design of) *this Physical Universe* to:

"keep each other from going away."

"Inertia" is the structural-impulse to:

"hold objects still."

And various built-in *mechanisms* also:

"make it more solid."

Run this *process, "getting the sense"* of these things to the fullest extent that you can.

A1. *"Have the Universe 'keep The Object from going away';
then have it 'let go'."* (repeat)

A2. *"Have The Object 'keep the Universe from going away';
then have it 'let go'."* (repeat)

B1. *"Have the Universe 'hold The Object completely still';
then have it 'let go and leave it uncontrolled'."* (repeat)

B2. *"Have The Object 'hold the Universe completely still';
then have it 'let go and leave it uncontrolled'."* (repeat)

C1. *"Have the Universe 'make The Object more solid'; then
have it 'let go and leave it uncontrolled'."* (repeat)

C2. *"Have The Object 'make the Universe more solid'; then
have it 'let go and leave it uncontrolled'."* (repeat)

3X-G. <u>TOTAL-RESPONSIBILITY</u>

To take total *command* and *control* of a *"creation"* (*object,
&tc.*)—even a mutually "agreed-upon" *Physical Universe*
"creation" (that is also being *postulated* into being by *others*; or is *other-determined*)—the *secret* is to take *total/full*
responsibility for that *"creation"* and make the *postulate*
that keeps it there your own.

Run this PCL. Keep extending your *"sphere-of-responsibil-
ity"* for the *object* until it completely encompasses the
object—As-It-Is now, was, and *ever will be.*

1. *"What about that object could you be responsible for?"*

(then)

2. *"Postulate total responsibility for that object."*

(then end that *cycle*; and repeat)

Use *concepts* from lines A1, B1, and C1 (above) to:

"Spot the structural-impulse of the Universe to ___."

A. Practice with each—*"Hold The Object Still"*; *"Keep The
Object From Going Away"*; and *"Make The Object More Sol-*

id" —in turn to get a good reality on each.

B. Practice them quickly in succession until you can fully conceive of *all three* within a *single* instantaneous *"spotting"* of *"the combined impulses being intended into the object"* by the *Universe.*

C. Repeat *getting a sense* of this *impulse;* but get it faster and faster. *Consider* it as a *"wave"* that repeats the *Intention* onto the *object* many thousand times per second. You don't have to duplicate each time-per-second individually; you simply *get a sense* of the basic *impulse* with certainty; and then *get the concept* of (or *consider*) it repeating as a super-fast *wave* that produces a *super-high frequency* (but mostly inaudible) *"hum."*

D. Then make the *wave*-frequency just a little faster until it's too fast to produce a *"hum,"* but simply *Is.* [*This* is the *"Universe Postulate"* (Alpha-Thought) of the *"Is"*-factor of the *object.*]

E. *Get a certainty* on the *Universe Postulate* (from STEP-D) and *consider* it as repeating constantly on the *object*, and *re-creating* (*postulating*) it into existence within consecutive *Spaces*, as though it is "carrying" the existence of the *object* "forward" in *Time.*

F. Make the *Universe Postulate* "your own" —as essentially your own *"Alpha-Thought"* or *"Postulate."* [This, itself, is accomplished by your *Intention.*] Accept *total/full responsibility* for the continuous *"re-creation"* and *"location"* of the *object* in *present-time.* Put out the *Intention:* *"I'm Creating It."* And have the *Universe,* "acknowledge" that.

G. *Intend* to move the *object;* and *move it.* [Use the *body's hands* if necessary.]

Scan through the processes and exercises of the *"Wizard*

Level-3X Procedure" and clean up any areas that still have any *fragmentary charge*, or that you think still require significant improvement. Then work through the exercises of this *"Advanced Ability Training–3X"* section again.

This concludes the experimental portion of *Wizard Level-3*. The remainder of this manual pertains to additional research and developments regarding *Implant-Platforms*.

IMPLANTING THE HUMAN CONDITION
(*Prison Planet Implant-Platforms*)

[This discourse presents material that is not necessarily confidential, but is only appropriate for those *Seekers* that have studied (worked through) all previous *A.T. Manuals* of the *"Keys to the Kingdom"* series.]

More recent *Implants* of *this Universe*—and especially *"after Earth"* was intended as a *prison-planet*—are far more complex in their design and configuration than *older Implants* from previous *Universes*.

Since this *older* knowledge is retained by some *universal superpower forces* (*the Implanters*) in *this Universe*, it is not surprising that *older Implants* could be combined together and expanded appropriately for more recent use. What this gives evidence for is the fact that the *"reality systems"* have become so *convoluted* and *condensed* that it has taken far greater lengths than ever before to keep an *Alpha-Spirit* suppressed within a *Universe*, or a *planet*, or the *Human Condition*.

Components of *"The Jewel"* and the original *"Heaven Incident"* during *Entry-Into-This-Universe* are far more basic than when these *Implants* are revised and revisited again later on, in relatively more recent *Implanting-Incidents*. For example: the original *Entry-Incident* uses only *one Jewel*; whereas when the same sequencing is repeated during the *Hellfire Incident* (and other more recent incidents*), there are *three Jewels*.

The *solidarity* and *reality-agreements* of each *descending* (*condensing*) *Universe* continued to be compounded (or superimposed) "on top" of all former ones. The *postulates* and *creations* keep "stacking up" until we are left with something as *solid* and *condensed* as *this Physical Universe*. It also seems to require layer upon layer of more complex *Implants* to keep everything existing in *this Universe* both *created* and under *control*.

What is most accessible for us to continue researching for the *Pathway*—and what is most beneficial for us to handle—is that which is specifically entrapping an *Alpha-Spirit* on *Earth*, and holding them in the *Human Condition*. Curiously, the *Implants* all stem from previous *Universes*; but they have never before been so complexly designed or so intricately interwoven into each other—or used on *Alpha-Spirits* so often.

In this manual (*AT#7*) we will provide additional data concerning *Implant-Platforms* that compose, what we refer to here as, the "*Heaven Implant Series*" (since repeating the phrase "*Prison Planet Implant*" is considered rather *negative*). The *Implants* and *incidents* we treat in our work have no formal names in *human language*; nor has our *systemological data* ever been fully collected and codified within a single paradigm before now.

These new *Platforms* and *Goals-lists* represent an *incident* far more intricate than the original *Entry-Into-Universe*

"*Heaven Incident*" and *that Goals-Sequencing*—therefore, this is *not* part of the original *Incident*, but is only intended to give the illusion of being so (and *restimulate* it). [Our earliest unpublished research on this subject referred to this series as the "*Prison Planet Implant*" so as not to confuse this research with the original "*Heaven Incident.*" We could just as easily refer to this series as the "*Judgment Incident.*"]

It is difficult to "*date*" the "*earliest usage*" of this "*Heaven Implant Series*" with a *GSR-Meter*. The *incident* is intentionally designed to *implant false dates*, just to make it more confusing to remember clearly (*locate* and *spot*) on the *Backtrack*. It is also difficult to determine just how often they are used for an individual's "*between-lives*" period. [To avoid *confusion, restimulation,* or *flying-by unhandled fragmentary charge*: this *Implanting* should only be handled *after* all of *Systemology Level-7* is fully *defragmented.*]

At the very least: research suggests that if an *Alpha-Spirit* is able to get nearly out of *this Solar System* (*between-lives*), there is a "net" or "screen" that seems to catch them and set them up for this *re-implanting.*

Research also indicates: use of this unique arrangement of "*Heaven Implant*" is only approximately 10,000 to 12,000 years old at most. It is specific to the *Human Condition* and *Earth* as a *prison-planet.*

We say "*Heaven Implant,*" but it is really structured like a "*court-sentencing incident.*" It is the "*Judgment*" archetype (in *religion* and the *tarot*) and uses *heavy-dogmatic* symbolism that was once absent from modern religions—like *Christianity*—until its incorporation as a *restimulative control-mechanism* (against the *Human* population) during the *"Dark Ages"* of Earth's more modern history. [Most *Buddhism* seemed to escape the *effects* of this, since it already sought to avoid the *"Heaven-area"* as an *"Implant-Station."* So, our ideas about that are not really a *new consideration.*]

It has also been determined that *Implanting-Incidents* commonly incorporate IPU-*Goals* and *Symbols*, or variations thereof, in order to *restimulate* and *communicate* in an *"archetypal"* language that is universally understood — or at least includes enough recognizable content (*data*) that people will react to. [This is one reason we introduced experimental *Implant Penalty Universe* (IPU) information earlier (than what might be considered absolutely necessary) in *A.T. Manual #4.*]

The experience of actually going through these types of *incidents* is likened to an "escalator" or "treadmill." The *archetypal* scenery, or common environmental conditions, of this *Implanting-Incident* incorporates *"pyramids"* and *"aerial staircases"* and even *"spiral-like descending arrangements of pillars"* with IPU-*Goal terminals* on top of them.

The basic pattern behind the material we are going to address, originates prior to *this Universe* — but complexity has since been added to the *"command-line"* encoding for the *Platform.* The IPU data concerning *restimulative* "Price" and "Survive" *command-items* (given in AT#4) actually pertain to *this "Heaven Implant."*

Just as is the case with the *Hellfire Incident,* there are some individuals occupying *Human-forms* on *Earth* today that emigrated from the *Magic Universe* after the *Prison-Planet Incidents* — or have otherwise been able to side-step or escape much of the standard-issue *Human-Implanting.*

However, most of the other *entities* and *fragments*, which may be affecting your case, *were* here a very long time (and are heavily *Implanted*). Like *"Platforms #1-18"* (*AT#3*), additional *Implants* are researched, in part, for *releasing* more *entities*.

An Advisement on Running Implant-Platforms: a *Seeker* may be encountering difficulties (primarily if working along the *upper-levels* of the *Pathway* without any supervision) when *processing-out Implant-Platforms*, if they are mistakenly *running* all of them the same way they treated *"The Jewel (Parts #1-5)"* in *AT#3*. That is *not* how *they* should be *run*.

Only the original *Entry-Incident "The Jewel"* is common to all *Alpha-Spirits* of *this Universe*. It is *processed-out* completely by fully contacting each of the *command-lines* *until it does* give a *"Meter-read"*; and then duplicating it *"As-It-Is"* until it no longer *registers* any *charge*. *No other Implant-Platform is run that way.*

For all other *Platforms* we have provided: each *item* (*line*) is *"spotted"* and *if it does* *"read,"* then it is *run* until it no longer *registers* a *charge*. If the *line* doesn't *read*, then it isn't *run* any further.

If you are not able to use a *Biofeedback-Device* for your handling of *Wizard-Level* work: review the material found in *PC-11* through *PC-14*, and all *A.T. Manuals*, very thoroughly.

Being how recently this *Implanting-Incident* began being used, it is likely that an individual on *Earth* today would have at least some *fragmented charge* attached to the *Implant*.

INCIDENT SEQUENCE

This is the *incident-sequence* of being *"sentenced to Earth"*:

1. You are captured (somehow). For the original incident: it is possible that most *Humans* were part of a "rebel-fleet" against some kind of "galactic-empire" — therefore, captured *en masse* as "prisoners-of-war."

2. You are hit with *heavy energy-waves*; then told you are a *"convicted criminal"* and are awaiting sentencing for your crime. You are hit with *imprints* depicting you on trial; but you are not told what your crime is. You are told that *"memory of your horrific crime has been erased as part of this criminal rehabilitation process."*

3. Then you are sentenced in court. You are sentenced to make a copy of yourself that will be punished. You are told that after you make a copy to be punished in your place, then you will be set free. A *heavy wave-force* hits you and you sense that you are standing beside yourself. But this is a fake *splitter-incident*; they just put up a *"doll"* that looks like you and then tell you that you have been *divided*.

4. You are told that you are the copy that is to be punished, and that they will set your real-self (the *"doll"*) free if you willingly accept your punishment.

5. You are told that you are being sentenced to *"Hell"* and they take you down into the "basement" of the court-house, which resembles a *"Medieval-style dungeon."*

[In former *Universes*, most of the remaining sequence would have taken place in some kind of *"implant universe"* or *"pocket universe"* — or would have been used in a transition between *Universes*. But, in this case, we know that this particular *incident* is specific to *this Universe*, *Earth*, and *Humans*. It is more likely some kind of exceptionally advanced *electrically-implanted virtual-reality computer-simulation*. It is a *real experience*, but it does not *actually* take place within the *Physical Universe*.]

6. You are standing in the "basement" of some underground facility, at the bottom level of what they told you is "*Hell*." One of the "basement-walls" is missing, and as you look out and down you see an "*Infinite Universe*" with a vast swirling cloud of "*chaos*" suspended in the center.

7. You are told that "*you have become evil*" and that "*you have turned against your creator and therefore are to be thrown into The Chaos and be torn apart as a Spiritual Being*."

8. But then they agree to give you one last chance. They will review your history and show you how you have come to this degraded state. You are told that in doing so, they will "*run time backwards for you so that you may have another chance*." They say: "*Now pay close attention, so that you can learn from your mistakes*."

9. Then you begin to walk backwards—literally going backwards up a staircase; occasionally down, but mostly up—working your way gradually back out of "*Hell*" and through cities and mountainscapes, and eventually going even further and higher, backwards up a "*stairway to Heaven*."

10. As this backwards movement occurs: you are being *Implanted* with *Goals* and *command-items*. The first *Implanted-Goal* (at the bottom, while facing *Chaos*) is: **TO BE ENDED**. You are hit with *300 items* on this one *Goal*, as you slowly back-up the stairway.

The process is *excruciatingly* slow. The same *Platform-pattern* of *300 items* is then applied to the *next Goal* in the *sequence*, as you move a little further backwards up the stairway. This occurs in this wise for approximately *200 Goals*.

At the very top of all the stairways—there may be *six* total—you reach what they call *"Heaven"* and the *Implanted-Goal* is: TO BE CREATED (which takes place before an imprint of *God's Throne In The Clouds*).

11. At the very top, the *imprinted imagery* continues displaying various scenes of *Physical Universe "creation"* and the "creation of Humans"—much of which mirrors symbolism from the ancient *Babylonian Epic of Creation* tablets, and elements of the *Book of Genesis, &tc*. Then they tell you that everything you've seen on this backwards journey is a depiction of how you've lived your *"evil"* existence—but now you have a chance to live again, and having learned from your mistakes, will do better this time.

12. Then they "let you go"—and it's like being shot from a sling or catapult. You fly down all the staircases, getting hit with all the *Goals* and *items* again, but moving in a forward direction (and the *Goals-sequence* is experienced in reverse to how you received them moving backwards (going up). This all happens at an incredibly fast speed. You go all the way back to the "basement" and out the "missing wall" and start falling towards the swirling mass of clouds.

13. They catch you as you are falling. They say (something like): *"Here you've gone and done the same terrible things again. But we will give you one last chance. Now pay closer attention this time!"*

14. Then back up the staircases you go, excruciatingly slowly, getting the same *Implanted-Goals Sequencing* as you move backwards up to the top again—and back down.

15. The full sequence of "backing up the stairways" and "flying down into Chaos" occurs *three times* total. On the final (*third*) time: they allow you to fall into the "*swirling cloud of Chaos.*" Once there, there are probably *millions* of *imprints* (*objects, scenery, &tc.*) that are flying around you like a tornado.

16. Then you spot a "calm area"—an "eye in the center of the hurricane" so to speak—and in the center of that "calm area" you see the *Earth.* You move down to it in order to escape the *Chaos,* and there is an overwhelming sense of *peace* and total *relief* as you go unconscious. After that, you are compelled to *reincarnate* here on *Earth.*

HEAVEN IMPLANTS (PRISON SERIES)
(*Parts #1 to 6*)

The "*Heaven Implant Series*" that occurs during the previously given *Incident-Sequence* is divided into *six* parts or *Platforms.* All *300 item-lines* occur for each *Goal*; and the individual doesn't get to the top of the "*Stairway to Heaven*" except with the top/highest *Goal* in the sequence: "CREATE."

In *this* section, we will provide a *short-form formula* for all *six* parts.

In the *next* section, we will provide the *Goals-list* that is used to fill in the *blank spaces* and complete this pattern-formula of "*items*" for each of the *Goals.*

Each of the *six Platforms* has its own wording-style, grammar, or syntax. We will introduce each *Platform* by explaining how the "wording" (or "tense") of a *Goal* should be modified to fit that *Platform.* That being said:

the wording of the *"item-lines"* will not always sound like a conventional use of language.

<u>PART-1</u>

Goal is inserted {*into the blank space*} in past tense, without "TO" —for example: *"forgotten"* instead of *"to forget"*; *"ended"* instead of *"to be ended," &tc.*

1. ___
2. NOT ___
3. ABSOLUTEABLY ___
4. ABSOLUTEABLY NOT ___
5. PERFECTABLY ___
6. PERFECTABLY NOT ___
7. SUPERIORABLY ___
8. SUPERIORABLY NOT ___
9. INCOMPARABLY ___
10. INCOMPARABLY NOT ___
11. WONDERFULLABLY ___
12. WONDERFULLABLY NOT ___
13. FASCINATABLY ___
14. FASCINATABLY NOT ___
15. BEAUTIFULLABLY ___
16. BEAUTIFULLABLY NOT ___
17. HIGHLY ACCEPTABLY ___
18. HIGHLY ACCEPTABLY NOT ___
19. RECOMMENDABLY ___
20. RECOMMENDABLY NOT ___
21. ACCEPTABLY ___
22. ACCEPTABLY NOT ___
23. ENGROSSABLY ___
24. ENGROSSABLY NOT ___
25. VITALABLY ___
26. VITALABLY NOT ___

27. EAGERABLY ___
28. EAGERABLY NOT ___
29. ENTHUSIASTICABLY ___
30. ENTHUSIASTICABLY NOT ___
31. ENJOYABLY ___
32. ENJOYABLY NOT ___
33. PLEASUREABLY ___
34. PLEASUREABLY NOT ___
35. AGREEABLY ___
36. AGREEABLY NOT ___
37. DEDICATEABLY ___
38. DEDICATEABLY NOT ___
39. COMMENDABLY ___
40. COMMENDABLY NOT ___
41. DESIREABLY ___
42. DESIREABLY NOT ___
43. CREATABLY ___
44. CREATABLY NOT ___
45. WANTABLY ___
46. WANTABLY NOT ___
47. COVETABLY ___
48. COVETABLY NOT ___
49. HOPEFULABLY ___
50. HOPEFULABLY NOT ___
51. POWERFULLABLY ___
52. POWERFULLABLY NOT ___
53. DECIDEABLY ___
54. DECIDEABLY NOT ___
55. CREDITABLY ___
56. CREDITABLY NOT ___
57. DEMANDABLY ___
58. DEMANDABLY NOT ___
59. BOREABLY ___
60. BOREABLY NOT ___

61. UPSETTABLY ___
62. UPSETTABLY NOT ___
63. REGRETTABLY ___
64. REGRETTABLY NOT ___
65. DEJECTABLY ___
66. DEJECTABLY NOT ___
67. COMPULSABLY ___
68. COMPULSABLY NOT ___
69. UNSTOPABLY ___
70. UNSTOPABLY NOT ___
71. DEGRADEABLY ___
72. DEGRADEABLY NOT ___
73. IDIOTABLY ___
74. IDIOTABLY NOT ___
75. LOSEABLY ___
76. LOSEABLY NOT ___
77. BADABLY ___
78. BADABLY NOT ___
79. UNCONFRONTABLY ___
80. UNCONFRONTABLY NOT ___
81. FORGETTABLY ___
82. FORGETTABLY NOT ___
83. UNWANTABLY ___
84. UNWANTABLY NOT ___
85. PLAYABLY ___
86. PLAYABLY NOT ___
87. ABANDONABLY ___
88. ABANDONABLY NOT ___
89. ___ –ING
90. NOT ___ –ING
91. ___ –ERS
92. NOT ___ –ERS
93. ___ –INGNESS
94. NOT ___ –INGNESS

95. ___–ISHNESS
96. NOT ___–ISHNESS
97. ___–ATIVES
98. NOT ___–ATIVES
99. ___–IVITY
100. NOT ___–IVITY

PART-2

Goal is inserted {*into the blank space*} in present tense, with "TO"—for example: "*to forget*"; "*to be ended*," &tc. [Note: some researchers got better "*Meter-reads*" without the "TO" and adding "–ING" (*forgetting, ending, &tc.*) for most of this part. Experiment with both ways to see what "*reads*" best for you.]

101. ___
102. NOT ___
103. ABSOLUTEABLE ___
104. ABSOLUTEABLE NOT ___
105. PERFECTABLE ___
106. PERFECTABLE NOT ___
107. SUPERIORABLE ___
108. SUPERIORABLE NOT ___
109. INCOMPARABLE ___
110. INCOMPARABLE NOT ___
111. WONDERFULLABLE ___
112. WONDERFULLABLE NOT ___
113. FASCINATABLE ___
114. FASCINATABLE NOT ___
115. BEAUTIFULLABLE ___
116. BEAUTIFULLABLE NOT ___
117. HIGHLY ACCEPTABLE ___
118. HIGHLY ACCEPTABLE NOT ___
119. RECOMMENDABLE ___

120. RECOMMENDABLE NOT ___
121. ACCEPTABLE ___
122. ACCEPTABLE NOT ___
123. ENGROSSABLE ___
124. ENGROSSABLE NOT ___
125. VITALABLE ___
126. VITALABLE NOT ___
127. EAGERABLE ___
128. EAGERABLE NOT ___
129. ENTHUSIASTICABLE ___
130. ENTHUSIASTICABLE NOT ___
131. ENJOYABLE ___
132. ENJOYABLE NOT ___
133. PLEASUREABLE ___
134. PLEASUREABLE NOT ___
135. AGREEABLE ___
136. AGREEABLE NOT ___
137. DEDICATEABLE ___
138. DEDICATEABLE NOT ___
139. COMMENDABLE ___
140. COMMENDABLE NOT ___
141. DESIREABLE ___
142. DESIREABLE NOT ___
143. CREATABLE ___
144. CREATABLE NOT ___
145. WANTABLE ___
146. WANTABLE NOT ___
147. COVETABLE ___
148. COVETABLE NOT ___
149. HOPEFULABLE ___
150. HOPEFULABLE NOT ___
151. POWERFULLABLE ___
152. POWERFULLABLE NOT ___
153. DECIDEABLE ___

154. DECIDEABLE NOT ___
155. CREDITABLE ___
156. CREDITABLE NOT ___
157. DEMANDABLE ___
158. DEMANDABLE NOT ___
159. BOREABLE ___
160. BOREABLE NOT ___
161. UPSETTABLE ___
162. UPSETTABLE NOT ___
163. REGRETTABLE ___
164. REGRETTABLE NOT ___
165. DEJECTABLE ___
166. DEJECTABLE NOT ___
167. COMPULSABLE ___
168. COMPULSABLE NOT ___
169. UNSTOPABLE ___
170. UNSTOPABLE NOT ___
171. DEGRADEABLE ___
172. DEGRADEABLE NOT ___
173. IDIOTABLE ___
174. IDIOTABLE NOT ___
175. LOSEABLE ___
176. LOSEABLE NOT ___
177. BADABLE ___
178. BADABLE NOT ___
179. UNCONFRONTABLE ___
180. UNCONFRONTABLE NOT ___
181. FORGETTABLE ___
182. FORGETTABLE NOT ___
183. UNWANTABLE ___
184. UNWANTABLE NOT ___
185. PLAYABLE ___
186. PLAYABLE NOT ___
187. ABANDONABLE ___

188. ABANDONABLE NOT ___
189. (TO) ___ –ING
190. NOT ___ –ING
191. (TO) ___ –ERS
192. NOT ___ –ERS
193. (TO) ___ –INGNESS
194. NOT ___ –INGNESS
195. (TO) ___ –ISHNESS
196. NOT ___ –ISHNESS
197. (TO) ___ –ATIVES
198. NOT ___ –ATIVES
199. (TO) ___ –IVITY
200. NOT ___ –IVITY

PART-3

Goal is inserted {*into the blank space*} in present-tense, without "TO" —for example: "*forget*"; "*being ended*," &tc.

201. ___
202. NOT ___
203. ___ –ING
204. NOT ___ –ING
205. ___ –ERS
206. NOT ___ –ERS
207. ___ –INGNESS
208. NOT ___ –INGNESS
209. ___ –ISHNESS
210. NOT ___ –ISHNESS
211. ___ –ATIVES
212. NOT ___ –ATIVES
213. ___ –IVITY
214. NOT ___ –IVITY

PART-4

Goal is inserted {*into the blank space*} without "TO" and as an "–ING" form; "*to forget*" becomes "*forgetting.*" On the "TO BE" type *Goals,* the "–ING" is added to "BE"; "*to be ended*" becomes "*being ended.*"

215. THOSE WHO ARE ___
216. THOSE WHO ARE NOT ___
217. GOALS THAT LEAD TO ___
218. THOSE WHO HATE ___
219. ACTIVELY ___
220. DOESN'T WANT TO BE ___
221. ADVANTAGES OF ___
222. NO ADVANTAGES OF ___
223. ANY NECESSITY FOR ___
224. NO NECESSITY FOR ___
225. ANY EXISTENCE OF ___
226. SUPPRESSING EXISTENCE OF ___
227. ANY INSTANCE ON ___
228. INVALIDATING ___
229. ANY DEPENDENCE ON ___
230. DENYING ___
231. THOSE WHO ARE CREATING ___
232. THOSE WHO ARE DESTROYING ___
233. ANY ACTIONS OF ___
234. NO ACTIONS OF ___
235. ANY BELIEF IN ___
236. NO BELIEF IN ___
237. PROPONENTS OF ___
238. OPPONENTS OF ___
239. FANTASTIC IMPORTANCE OF ___
240. UNIMPORTANCE OF ___
241. OBSESSIONS FOR ___
242. REPULSIONS FOR ___

243. INTERESTINGNESS OF ___
244. UNINTERESTINGNESS OF ___
245. CONCERNS OF ___
246. NO CONCERNS OF ___
247. UPSETS ABOUT ___
248. NO UPSETS ABOUT ___
249. DESPERATIONS OF ___
250. NO DESPERATIONS OF ___
251. FRENZIEDNESS(ES) OF ___
252. NO FRENZIEDNESS(ES) OF ___
253. PAINFULLNESS OF ___
254. PAINLESSNESS OF ___
255. HOPELESSNESS OF ___
256. HOPEFULLNESS OF ___

PART-5

For the "odd numbered" *items*, the *Goal* continues to be inserted in present-tense without "TO" and as an "–ING" form; "*forgetting*," *&tc.* For "TO BE" type *Goals*, the "–ING" is added to the "BE"; "*to be ended*" becomes "*being ended.*"

The "even numbered" *items* are stated as a *Beingness*. In this case, for the "TO BE" type *Goals*, the "TO BE" is simply dropped; "*to be ended*" becomes "*(an) ended (being).*"

257. THE EXHAUSTIONS OF ___
258. AN EXHAUSTED ___ BEING
259. THE STUPIDITY OF ___
260. A STUPIDIFIED ___ BEING
261. THE EFFORTS OF ___
262. A WEAKENED ___ BEING
263. THE UNREWARDINGNESS OF ___
264. AN UNREWARDED ___ BEING

265. THE COMPLICATIONS OF ___
266. A COMPLICATED ___ BEING
267. THE DEMANDS OF ___
268. A DEMANDING ___ BEING
269. THE DETERMINATIONS OF ___
270. A DETERMINED ___ BEING
271. THE FOOLISHNESS OF ___
272. A FOOLISH ___ BEING
273. THE COMPULSIONS OF ___
274. A COMPULSIVE ___ BEING
275. THE INVALIDATIONS OF ___
276. AN INVALIDATED ___ BEING
277. THE LIMITATIONS OF ___
278. A LIMITED ___ BEING
279. THE DEGRADATIONS OF ___
280. A DEGRADED ___ BEING
281. THE OVERWHELMS OF ___
282. AN OVERWHELMED ___ BEING
283. THE MISERY OF ___
284. A MISERABLE ___ BEING
285. THE UNAWARENESS OF ___
286. AN UNAWARE ___ BEING
287. THE OPPONENTS OF ___
288. AN OPPOSED ___ BEING

<u>PART-6</u>

For the "odd numbered" *items*, the *Goal* continues to be inserted in present-tense without "**TO**" and as an "**–ING**" form; "*forgetting*," *&tc.* For "**TO BE**" type *Goals*, the "**–ING**" is added to the "**BE**"; "*to be ended*" becomes "*being ended.*"

The "even numbered" *items* are stated in the basic "**TO** {**GOAL**}" style; "*to forget*," "*to be ended*," *&tc.*

The last *item-line* links the *Platform* to the *next Goal* in the *sequence*. This last *item-line* is actually a *"negation-item"* (or *"oppositional nix-item"*) of the *next Goal*. It immediately precedes the first *item-line* of PART-1 for the *next Goal*.

[Note that unlike the original *"Heaven Incident"* pageantry of *Goals-Sequencing*, this entire *Implanting-Incident* runs the *sequence-ordering* in each direction (*three times*), and the *"next Goal"* depends on whether you are going "ascending" or "descending" on the *chain*.]

289. THE FORBIDDENNESS OF ___
290. SOMEBODY WHO NEEDS ___
291. A HATRED OF ___
292. SOMEBODY WHO LOVES ___
293. THE INHIBITEDNESS OF ___
294. SOMEBODY WHO DESIRES ___
295. THE ABSENCE OF ___
296. SOMEBODY WHO COMPULSIVELY CREATES ___
297. STOPPED ___
298. SOMEBODY WITH THE GOAL ___
299. ANY IMPOSSIBILITIES OF ___
300. SOMEONE OR SOMETHING WITH THE GOAL ___
301. THE NON-EXISTENCE OF ___
302. THE GOAL ___
303. {*current goal*}
304. NOT {*next goal*}

HEAVEN IMPLANTS (PRISON SERIES)
(*Goal-Sequencing List*)

This is the *Goal-Sequencing List* in the order that it is first encountered in the *Implanting-Incident*.

On your first *run* through the *sequence,* you are working from the "bottom" to the "top." You begin at the "bottom" and walk "up" a *stairway* backwards while perceiving *300 items* for that *Goal.* The remaining *stairway* extends upward *behind* you. The "bottom-level" *Goal* is: TO BE ENDED.

There is usually some type of unique related *imprinted-imagery* that is displayed for each *Goal* while the *items* are *Implanted.* We have very limited data to describe this (given with each *Goal* when available). The scenery from *one Goal* "scrolls" or "blends" into the scenery of whatever is *next* without any "break."

On your second *run* through the *sequence,* you will treat the *Goals-list* in the reverse order of what is printed here. For this, you will work from the "top" and proceed forward going "down" the stairway. The "top-level" *Goal* is: TO BE CREATED.

We have certainty on the actual *Incident-Sequence,* the *first* and *last* primary *Goal* for the *Goal-Sequence,* and an estimated 80-90% of the *Goals* that lie between. Based on our experience, this is apparently sufficient enough *data* to "*Spot*" in order to *defragment* the entire *Platform-series.*

1. TO BE ENDED
   A black pathway through empty space, ending at the swirling spiral of Chaos.

2. TO BE TORTURED
   A dark dungeon; layered down to the "final pit" and a pathway through Nothingness.

3. TO BE INSUBSTANTIAL

4. TO BE FLAYED
   Strapped down to a stretcher; being wheeled into surgery.

5. TO BE NUMB

An ice-cave; crystalline arches at the entrance.

6. TO BE FROZEN

Snow-covered landscape; ice-sculptures (statues) say the items. On Part-6, you are dunked in ice-water on each item.

7. TO BE BURNED

Burning landscape; flames say the items. Repeatedly dropped into a "fiery pit" (on each item).

8. TO BE UNAFFECTED

Surrounded by violent explosions that don't quite hit you.

9. TO BE HORRIFIED

Smokey pits; victims on either side of the stairway; demons say the items.

10. TO BE UNAWARE

11. TO BE IN HELL

Bridges over flames and rivers of fire. Bridges lead to cities; final bridge leads to mountain-cave.

12. TO BE GAMELESS

Gray pathway near mountain-cave; gray clouds; everything is gray (washed-out color).

13. TO BE HAUNTED

Gray landscape.

14. TO BE SELF-PITYING

Rough-rock bridges over ash.

15. TO BE DRAINED

Bleak gray landscape with dark misshapen trees. Spirits hit at you and it feels like they pull away energy.

16. TO BE IGNITED

17. TO BE INTERIORIZED

Snapping into dead bodies, one to another, in a morgue.

18. **TO BE BODILESS**

   Floating over a pile of ashes. Nice things are all around but you can't grab a hold of them.

19. **TO BE BURIED**

20. **TO BE MOURNFUL**

   Walking through a graveyard; tombstones say items.

21. **TO BE NON-EXISTENT**

22. **TO BE DEAD**

23. **TO FAIL**

   Walking through a battlefield with barbed-wire fences. Fence-poles say items.

24. **TO BE WIPED OUT**

   Battlefield; dying soldiers say items.

25. **TO BE APATHETIC**

   Pathway through war-torn battlefield.

26. **TO BE DEFEATED**

   Battlefield. Tanks and planes say "odd-numbered" items; fighting soldiers say "even-numbered" items.

27. **TO BE MURDEROUS**

   Walking along a tall wall overlooking battlefield; exploding bombs say the items.

28. **TO BE HATED**

   In a railroad car, on a track running between barbed-wire fences of battlefield.

29. **TO BE IGNORED**

   On railroad car.

30. **TO BE BLAMED**

   On railroad car; billboards say items.

31. **TO BE UNCARING**

   Elegant railroad car; passing people starving and pleading for help.

32. TO BE POSSESSED (TAKEN OVER)
Railway train shed; loud-speakers say items.

33. TO BE VENGEFUL
Between a train shed and a harbor.

34. TO BE PERSECUTED
Running alongside a harbor near a village, trying to escape townspeople with pitchforks, &tc., who say the items.

35. TO BE PARANOID
Floating in dark waters.

36. TO BE PURPOSELESS
A canal. Poles in water say items.

37. TO BE SELF-CONFLICTING
Canal with cottages along the banks. You try to go in different directions simultaneously. You split/divide on the "odd-numbered" items, and recombine on the "even-numbered" items.

38. TO BE COMBINED
Body is on a pole of the canal near cottages. Copies of yourself come flying out of cottages and snap-in to your body.

39. TO BE DIVIDED
Canal boat. Floating past docks during electrical storm. Copies of yourself are standing at edge of docks, then turn around when you approach and walk away. Lightning bolts say items.

40. TO BE UNCHANGING
Canal.

41. TO BE SICK
Canal; lying sick in boat.

42. TO BE HOPELESS
Canal; sidewalk to either side; statues say items.

43. TO BE SELF-INVALIDATIVE
Canal.

44. TO GIVE UP
Canal through a desert. Pyramids, on either side, say items.

45. TO FEEL MISERABLE
Amusement park ride; inside some kind of box that jerks around.

{might be missing *Goals* here}

46. TO BE UNCONSCIOUS

47. TO BE HURT
In a cart/car; going down a steep mountain; smashing into things.

48. TO BE SELF-DESTRUCTIVE
Pits containing various hazards line both sides of the roadway. The pits say the items. On the "odd-numbered" items, you step off the roadway and fall into a pit. On the "even-numbered" items, you end up back on the roadway.

49. TO BE TRAPPED
Amusement park; carousel; going up and down on a pole; fake horses all around.

50. TO BE LOST
"Spinning plates" (?)

51. TO BE LOCATED
Walking down streets; walking down corridors. Doors (with faces) say items.

52. TO BE DISPERSED
Strapped to a bulls-eye on a flying target; things keep hitting you. On the "odd-numbered" items, pieces of the body fly off in all directions. On the "even-numbered" items, the pieces are pulled back together.

53. TO BE OVERWHELMED
    Amusement park. Contains imagery from other parts of the Implanting-Incident.

54. TO BE PUNISHED
    Amusement park.

55. TO BE DOMINEERING
    Amusement park.

56. TO BE CRIPPLED
    Amusement park.

57. TO BE SPINNING
    Amusement park; spinning pole.

58. TO BE STOPPED
    Amusement park; ride-car keeps stopping in unpleasant places.

59. TO BE DIZZY (?)

60. TO BE UNAFFECTED (?)

61. TO BE UNBALANCED
    Amusement park; "spinning plates" (?)

    {might be missing *Goals* here}

62. TO BE CARELESS

63. TO BE SELF-CONTROLLED

64. TO BE RECKLESS

65. TO BE CONTROLLED (?)

66. TO BE GET WORSE
    Underground cave. Stalagmites say "odd-numbered" items; the floor says "even-numbered" items.

67. TO BE DRUGGED (?)

68. TO BE AGONIZED (?)

69. TO EXPERIENCE NOTHING

70. **TO BE ELECTROCUTED**
Hitting against large round electrified terminals on either side. (Like being in a pinball game.)

{might be missing *Goals* here}

71. **TO BE DISMEMBERED (?)**

72. **TO BE WORRIED (?)**

73. **TO BE UNTHINKING**
In a swamp; on a boat.

74. **TO BE DEPRESSED**
Poling a boat through a muddy swamp.

75. **TO BE INDIFFERENT**
Being dragged through a muddy swamp by snakes (that say the items).

76. **TO BE STUCK**
Hopping through a muddy tar-swamp. You get stuck on the "odd-numbered" items, and lift out on the "even-numbered" items.

77. **TO BE FLEEING**
Wading through muddy swamp in haste.

78. **TO BE INFESTED**
In a marsh, on a raft. Firefly-like bugs enter your body on the "odd-numbered" items. Feeling of being infested with entities.

{might be missing *Goals* here}

79. **TO BE EVIL (?)**
Creatures rise up out of marshy swamp to say items.

80. **TO BE UNIMPORTANT**
Walking through marsh; stakes sticking up out of the water with heads on them, which say the items. There are electric shocks associated with the "odd-numbered" items.

81. **TO BE IMPLANTED**

82. TO BE VISCOUS

On a cliffside, near the sea; stairway leads down into the water.

83. TO BE PURSUED

Running through a forest toward a beach.

84. TO BE NERVOUS

In the forest; trees say the items.

85. TO BE CRIMINAL

Walking down urban streets.

86. TO BE DOCILE

87. TO BE TREATED

Hospital.

88. TO BE INSANE

Hospital.

89. TO BE CONDEMNED

Walking from a courthouse to jail; prisoners say items.

90. TO BE DISHONEST

91. TO BE ACCUSED

Walking between pillars (that say items).

92. TO BE GUILT-RIDDEN

In a forest; faces on trees say items.

93. TO BE TREASONOUS

94. TO BE BLINDED

95. TO BE SPYING

96. TO BE BETRAYED

{might be missing *Goals* here}

97. TO BE VILIFIED (?)

98. TO BE TREACHEROUS (?)

99. TO BE DEGRADED

100. TO BE ASHAMED

101. **TO BE PERVERTED**
   Carnival. (?)

102. **TO HAVE CRAVINGS**
   Carnival market; things on display. (?)

103. **TO BE EMPTY**
   Floating above market or shopping mall.

104. **TO BE GLUTTONOUS**
   Restaurant terrace overlooking market or shopping mall.

105. **TO BE REJECTED**
   A mall-tunnel or concourse.

106. **TO BE DISGUSTING**
   A sewer-like subway station/tunnel.

107. **TO BE TIDY**
   A carpeted hallway.

108. **TO BE MESSY**

109. **TO BE CLUNG-TO**

110. **TO BE ABANDONED**

111. **TO BE DEPENDENT**

112. **TO BE UNFEELING**

113. **TO BE SEXUAL**

114. **TO BE ALONE**

115. **TO BE TOGETHER**

116. **TO BE ISOLATED**

117. **TO BE CORRUPTING**

118. **TO BE CORRUPTED**

119. **TO BE INHIBITED**

120. **TO BE WANTON**

121. **TO BE FRUSTRATED**
   {might be missing a *Goal* here}

122. **TO BE DISINTERESTED**

123. **TO BE DISAPPOINTED**

124. **TO BE HUMAN**

Goal might actually be: To Be Selfish. (Or "To Be Selfish" might need to be inserted as next goal or previous goal.)

{might be missing a *Goal* here}

125. **TO BE ENRAGED**

126. **TO BE DROPPED**

127. **TO BE CARRIED**

On a ski-lift. (?)

128. **TO BE EXHAUSTED**

Trudging up a mountain-slope from a beach; eventually reaching snowy area.

129. **TO BE OVEREXERTED**

{might be missing a *Goal* here}

130. **TO HALLUCINATE**

131. **TO BE TERRIFIED**

132. **TO BE FOOLISH**

133. **TO BE RESPONSIBLE**

Traveling in a car at high speed, down a steep slope.
Light-posts say items as you pass by.

134. **TO BE IRRESPONSIBLE**

135. **TO BE BURDENED**

Trudging through primitive village carrying many things.

136. **TO BE NEGLIGENT**

137. **TO BE CAREFUL**

138. **TO BE CRUSHED**

Industrial factory-like environment; on a conveyer-belt.
Cylinders come down and crush you; walls smash inward from the side.

139. **TO BE INATTENTIVE**

140. TO BE SELF-CRITICAL

  {might be missing *Goals* here}

141. TO BE REGRETFUL

142. TO BE INCOMPETENT

143. TO BE ENSLAVED

144. TO BE CRUEL

145. TO BE IRRITATED (?)

146. TO BE EXPLOITED (?)

147. TO BE RESISTED (?)

148. TO BE MISLED (?)

149. TO BE ASLEEP

Fluffy pillow-like landscape; soft pathway; stuffed-animals, on either side, say the items.

150. TO BE TIRED

  {might be missing *Goals* here}

151. TO BE CRITICAL

152. TO BE CRITICIZED

Broad stairway in the air; statues along either side say the items.

153. TO BE ARROGANT

Roadway in the sky.

154. TO BE WRONG

155. TO BE IMPORTANT

Roadway in the sky. "Pennant-poles" say the items.

156. TO BE BOTHERED

157. TO BE POWERFUL

158. TO BE TROUBLED

159. TO HAVE PICTURES

160. TO BE UNSEEING

161. TO BE REVOLTED

162. TO BE AFFECTED

163. TO BE TOUGH (?)

164. TO BE FRAGILE (?)

165. TO HAVE NOTHING

166. TO BE POSSESSIVE

167. TO BE MASSLESS

Moving through "solid" doors.

168. TO BE SOLID

Walking beneath iron-arches.

169. TO BE ALTERED (?)

170. TO BE INCOMPLETE (?)

171. TO BE BLOCKED (?)

172. TO BE IRRADIATED (?)

173. TO BE DISTRACTED (?)

174. TO FORGET

175. TO REGRET

176. TO LEVITATE

Walking on a transparent bridge in the sky. All of the imagery is of harmful-acts.

177. TO COMPULSIVELY CREATE

Aerial stairway.

178. TO BE CAST OUT

Thrown out of heaven, through its gates.

179. TO BE IN HEAVEN

Pathway through clouds between the gates and the heavenly kingdom.

180. TO BE REBELLIOUS

181. TO BE GOOD

You eventually back up all the way to where "God's Throne" sits at the top of the stairway.

182. TO BE CREATED

The top-most item displays you being created by "God."

HEAVEN IMPLANTS (ETHICS SERIES)
(*Implant-Running Process / Goals-List*)

When an *Alpha-Spirit* first separates from the *Infinity of Nothingness*, it is an incredibly powerful—but also an incredibly innocent and naïve—*Spiritual Being* with a *creative* nature. The one thing we could absolutely say for certain is: the basic nature of the *Alpha-Spirit* is definitely *not* "inherently evil."

There is a long history of attempts to *Implant* individuals to "make them good." Of course, the only reason they do the things they do is because of how *fragmented* they are; and one of the reasons individuals have become so *fragmented*, is the tremendous quantity of accumulated *Implants* they've been subjected to.

Implanting has never once "made someone good." For one thing: an individual doesn't need to be "made to be good." *Ethics* have never been successfully "*enforced*" and "*personally developed*" simultaneously.

An individual either *has* the *Awareness* and *ability-to-confront* what has happened (and *decide* to *change* their course of future *thought* and *action*), or they *don't* have the *Awareness*—in which case, they are not able to see what has happened "*As-It-Is*," and/or their *considerations* are too heavily wrapped up in *justification*. In any case: *Implanting* will not make the individual *more aware*.

There have been many versions of the "*Ethics-Implant*"

pattern, extending back through several *Universes*. In each *Universe*, the *Platform-pattern* tends to become a little more complex, with more *command-lines* added to the existing *Platform* from a prior *Universe*—as is commonly found in later (more recent) *Implants*.

The real purpose behind any *Implant* is to suppress *Alpha-Spirits*, reduce their *Actualized Awareness*, and keep them under some kind of "*other-determined*" (rather than "*Self-determined*") *control*. You can "*condition*" individuals into being quiet, complacent, orderly "*good citizens*"—but this doesn't make them more *ethical*.

An "*Ethics-Implant*" isn't only about making the *Implanted*-individual a more ethical person; it sells them on the idea that "everyone is *bad*" and that this is "what is *wrong* with everyone" (*including* themselves), and that "everyone needs to have *ethics enforced* on them." It gets one to be more tolerant/agreeable to *enforcement*.

We include this as part of the "*Heaven Implants*" because it tends to show up *between-lives* and emphasizes what some might consider "*religious morality*" (although it really serves a more "civic/societal" function). In contrast to many other *Implants*, the "*items*" of an *Ethics-Platform* all seem "positive" or "good things"—such as "*creating goodness*" and "*destroying criminality.*" But, this deceptively just makes the person more agreeable to the general content/message of the *Implant*, which again, is inhibiting "*thinking for one's self.*"

Due to the many variations and versions, critical research-time was not spent in developing full *Platforms* that are each only slightly modified from one another. The *Goals-list* for this *Implant* is also *not* so deeply ingrained or heavily charged that we have to run hundreds of *items* off of a *Goal* in order to *defragment* it.

Therefore, we provide an *"Ethics-Implant Running Procedure."* It is designed to only apply as many details as are necessary to be able to easily *"defrag-by-realization"* (by *Spotting* a few key aspects of the *Platforms*). This procedure only has a dozen steps; and is *run* on each of *20 Goals* (as given in the attached *Goals-list*).

IMPLANT-RUNNING PROCEDURE

A. *Spot* the first *item* of the original *Implant-Platform* as used in the *Symbols Universe*:

TO BE {*Goal*} IS NATIVE STATE

B. *Spot* the first *item* of the *Implant-Platform* as used in a later version:

TO CREATE {*Positive State*} IS NATIVE STATE

C. *Spot* the *item* related to the later *Implant-Platform* from STEP-B:

TO DESTROY {*Negative State*} IS NATIVE STATE

D. Another version uses the entire series of *64 Implanted Penalty-Universe* (IPU) *Goals*; *running* from *"Create"* to *"Endure."* You should only need to *Spot* a few of them. The first two and last two of the series are given below to demonstrate the *pattern*. [Refer to *AT#4* for additional IPU details (if needed).]

TO BE IS TO CREATE {*Positive State*}

TO BE IS TO CAUSE {*Positive State*}

TO BE IS TO EAT/ABSORB {*Positive State*}

TO BE IS TO ENDURE (ANYTHING FOR THE SAKE OF) {*Positive State*}

E. As related to the version from STEP-D: this *Implant-Platform* uses *64 inverted IPU-Goals* in *reverse order*—from *"Endure"* (now inverted as *"Dissipate"*) up to *"Create"* (now inverted as *"Destroy"*). These are run on the *"Negative Goal States"* (as given in the *Goals-list*). You should only need to *Spot* a few of them. The first two and last two of the series are given below to demonstrate the *inverted reverse-order pattern*.

TO BE IS TO DISSIPATE {*Negative State*}

TO BE IS TO REFUSE {*Negative State*}

TO BE IS TO UNDO {*Negative State*}

TO BE IS TO DESTROY {*Negative State*}

F. The earliest versions included a *"splitter-incident."* In this case, you were required to push *fragments* of yourself onto others to "make them follow the rules." [Refer to *AT#5* concerning *"Control Entities"* (CE).]

1. *"Spot pushing fragments of yourself onto others and compelling them to be {positive state}."*

2. *"Spot pushing fragments of yourself onto others and inhibiting them from {negative state}."*

Note: any *fragments* (*split pieces*) you *Spot*, you should *run* the *"Entity Locational Procedure"* (*AT#5*) on them (*"Point to the being you divided from"*).

Also (if necessary or applicable): handle any more recent actions of *"forcing others to be {positive state}"* and/or *"inhibiting others from {negative state}."* [In this case, we don't mean reasonable efforts to help others improve; we mean more heavy-handed scenarios.]

G. *Spot* any *entities* (or *fragments*) that have been pushed onto you (by others) to compel you *"to be {positive state}"* or *"inhibit you from {negative state}."* Handle by having the *entity* "*Spot*" the false data of the *Implant* and/or the *top item* (STEP-A); or else, "*Locational Procedure,*" &tc. [See AT#5.]

H. *Defragment* some of the *tendencies/considerations* laid in by the *Implant.*

1. "*Spot wanting to be compelled by others to be {positive state}.*"

2. "*Spot wanting to be inhibited by others from {negative state}.*"

3. "*Spot the realization that these cravings/tendencies were installed by the Implant.*"

I. *Defragment* some of the *Implanted data.*

"*Spot the false data: that people are basically {negative state}.*"

J. *Defragment* some misconceptions.

"*Spot the misconception: that this Implant is necessary to your well-being, and the well-being of others.*"

K. *Spot* the first *item* of the *IPU-Platform. Spot* this for yourself—and for any partially awake *entities* that haven't *released/dispersed* yet.

TO CREATE IS NATIVE STATE

L. (If necessary) *Spot* the first *item* of the *Agreements Universe-Platform. Spot* this for yourself—and for any partially awake *entities* that haven't *released/dispersed* yet.

TO AGREE IS NATIVE STATE

[Note that if you don't get a sense of relief on the *Goal-item* from this procedure: *spot* any *harmful-acts* on the *Backtrack* regarding your participation in designing the *Implant*; or *Implanting* others; or wanting others *Implanted* with this; or even forcing others to be *Implanted* with this.]

ETHICS-IMPLANT GOAL-LIST

There are 20 *Implanted Goal-items* for this *Platform-pattern*. The basic *Goal* is listed in capital letters. There are also "Create" (*positive state*) and "Destroy" (*negative state*) *Goal-items* listed for each basic *Goal*. Use this data to fill-in {indicated spaces} for the steps of the procedure. You may have to slightly adjust the wording of a *goal-state* to make sense in the *processing command-lines* of the procedure.

1. TO BE ETHICAL
   POS. (to create) ethics
   NEG. (to destroy) criminality

2. TO BE RESOURCEFUL
   POS. (to create) resourcefulness
   NEG. (to destroy) complacency

3. TO BE SYMPATHETIC
   POS. (to create) sympathy
   NEG. (to destroy) callousness

4. TO BE DUTIFUL
   POS. (to create) dutifulness
   NEG. (to destroy) carelessness

5. TO BE RESPONSIBLE
   POS. (to create) responsibility
   NEG. (to destroy) irresponsibility

6. TO BE HONORABLE
   POS. (to create) honor
   NEG. (to destroy) dishonor

7. TO BE LOYAL
   POS. (to create) loyalty
   NEG. (to destroy) disloyalty

8. **TO BE TRUSTWORTHY**
   POS. (to create) trustworthiness
   NEG. (to destroy) betrayal

9. **TO BE INDUSTRIOUS**
   POS. (to create) industriousness
   NEG. (to destroy) laziness

10. **TO BE MERCIFUL**
    POS. (to create) mercifulness
    NEG. (to destroy) vengefulness

11. **TO BE OBEDIENT**
    POS. (to create) obedience
    NEG. (to destroy) disobedience

12. **TO BE PATIENT**
    POS. (to create) patience
    NEG. (to destroy) impatience

13. **TO BE HELPFUL**
    POS. (to create) helpfulness
    NEG. (to destroy) unhelpfulness

14. **TO BE CARING**
    POS. (to create) caring
    NEG. (to destroy) uncaring

15. **TO BE PROTECTIVE**
    POS. (to create) protectiveness
    NEG. (to destroy) unprotectiveness

16. **TO BE THRIFTY**
    POS. (to create) thriftiness
    NEG. (to destroy) wastefulness

17. **TO BE POLITE**
    POS. (to create) politeness
    NEG. (to destroy) rudeness

18. **TO BE RESPECTFUL**
   POS. (to create) respectfullness
   NEG. (to destroy) disrespectfullness

19. **TO BE GOOD**
   POS. (to create) goodness
   NEG. (to destroy) badness

20. **TO BE REVERENT**
   POS. (to create) reverence
   NEG. (to destroy) irreverence

SPIRITUAL-DISABILITY IMPLANT
Experimental Ascension Processing

[This is *experimental* material. It has been researched and developed sufficiently for effective use and therefore is included with *Wizard Level-3* procedures. Slight revisions may occur in the future where noted and/or it may be re-classified for a higher *Wizard-Level*.]

This *Implant-Platform* is *very old*—likely originating in the *"Symbols Universe"* (see *AT#1*) or possibly earlier. Unlike relatively more recently designed *Implants*, the *effectiveness* of this one is not the result of *non-sensical confusion*. It was carefully constructed to *"imitate"*—and be *experienced as*—an individual's *own thoughts.*

When first researched, we referred to this *Implant* as a *"mental-disability"* *Implant* (but such terminology is commonly misunderstood to mean something else regarding the *Human Condition*). We originally labeled it for the *"Mind"* because it *fixes "mental-circuitry" in-place* for many *considerations* that an *Alpha-Spirit* would have otherwise treated (or not) on their own *Self-determination* (*knowingly/consciously* with *Alpha-Thought*).

It covertly installs "foundations" for a *fragmented Mind*— establishing "*circuitry*" (or *associative connections*) with various *concepts, considerations,* and *terminals*; none of which seems, on the surface, as though it is "damaging." But it is; because it reduces *spiritual ability* by *fixing attention* (as *fragmentary charge*) on a lot of *considerations.*

Each *series-run* of the *Implant* is modified by a single basic *Intention* or *Goal.* The *first three series-runs* draw an individual "in" to the content by using "I.." statements. This means it starts by having hundreds of "I.." statements *firing* "internally" as though they were one's own. The remainder of the *series-runs* concern "To (do something)" statements, worded as *associative-knowledge* about basic *Goals.*

At this point in *Advanced Training,* it should already be fairly obvious as to "why" *compulsively* and *unknowingly* maintaining *fragmentary charge* on all of these "*items*" is *spiritually unhealthy* or *debilitating.* Therefore, let us focus on the mechanics of the *Implant* itself, and *defragmenting* the *Platform.*

To illustrate this: let's take up a "*null-example*" (that does not actually appear in the *Implant-Platform*) about "*Eating.*" It probably would be included if this *Implant* were constructed today, but at the time of its origination, "food-intake" *considerations* were not a "standard" part of an *Alpha-Spirit's* existence or reality.

A basic short-form formula for this *Implant-Platform* would only include the main reoccurring "*root*" for each "*item-line.*" In this case:

0.1.X ____ TO EAT
0.2.X ____ TO STARVE

Here you see what appear to be opposing *concepts*. All of the *items* in this *Implant* occur in pairs. Each *series* inserts a different *keyword* or *impulse* at the start of the statement. The first statement is given a "positive" and the second is given a "negative." And in the end, they both will basically mean the same thing. For the first *series-run* of "*I want*"/"*I don't want*," the *command-lines* would be *processed-out* (*discharged/defragged*) as:

0.1.1 (I WANT) TO EAT
0.2.1 (I DON'T WANT) TO STARVE

At first glance, it would seem like there is nothing wrong with these *considerations*. But, what if you had never had them before? What if there was no need to even *consider* them?—but here they are: the formation of a specific "*thought-tendency*" or "*circuit*" about *eating*, *food*, *&tc*. Once the "*wanting*" is installed, it's that much easier to install a "*need*" on that "*circuit*" for the *second series-run*, when the *command-lines* change to:

0.1.2 (I NEED) TO EAT
0.2.2 (I CAN'T BEAR) TO STARVE

By starting at the "top" (earliest point) of the *Implant-Platform*, the heavier laden *charge* can be *dispersed* from the foundations before the additional *series-runs*. Although there were originally over a hundred *series-runs* during the original *Implanting-Incident*, the entire *pattern* is likely to start coming apart and *disperse* after *processing-out* only a few dozen (for a *Wizard Level-3* practitioner) when working from the "top."

After the *first three series-runs*, the remainder of the *Implant* contains many arbitrary *considerations* that add even more "*energetic-mass*" to all those key areas that were just installed. They are really "*equations*" of "*associative thought.*" The *command-items* all relay that "one thing *is* (equal to) another thing"—and this is done thousands of times over the course of the remaining series-runs.

To illustrate how the remaining *series* are *run*, we will apply the "*fourth series-run*" to our example from above. The *series-four list-items* are: "*To Agree*"/"*To Disagree.*"

0.1.4   (TO AGREE) [IS] TO EAT

0.2.4   (TO DISAGREE) [IS] TO STARVE

[Note that for *series-four* (and afterward), you also have to insert an "*is*" between the variable *list-item* and the re-occurring *root* in order to complete each *command-line.* None of this was *Implanted* in *human-language.* Inserting "*is*" helps the *item-line* make more sense in order to properly *contact* and *process-out* its *meaning.*]

[Although it does not appear in the *Implant*, it is possible that we put some *charge* on the above examples during instruction. Your first *processing-action* might be to make sure *they* don't *register* on a *GSR-Meter*; or if you feel anything related to them, *defragment* it by the same methods you have *processed-out* other *items.*]

This *Implant* first occurs on the *Backtrack* many *Universes* ago, when *Implanting* methods were far more "*energetic*" or "*telepathic*"—relative to the heavier "*electronic*" incidents that take place in *this Physical Universe.* But, early on, *Implants* took a lot of *energy*, and required a lot of "*time*," just to get an *Alpha-Spirit* to "budge" even a little bit on their *considerations.*

Of course, *this Implant* is incredibly lengthy; but at the time it first occurs, *Alpha-Spirits* had a far different appreciation of relative "*time-spans*" than we do today. While an individual *Implanting-Incident* was seldom very effective early on, the *Implanting* repeatedly continued on the *Backtrack*. It cumulatively "built-up" upon its own foundations; and other *Platforms* often added to it, by restimulating it, and reducing an individual's *Awareness* enough to accept installation of some new *Implant*.

Data for any original *incident* is limited. The *Implanting-gimmick* used for this is: projecting *energy-waves* at the *Alpha-Spirit* from opposing sides. The early *series-runs* come from *left* and right. Later *series* have them come from *front* and *back*, then eventually *above* and *below*. The "positive" *command-item* of each *pair* comes from a "*golden sphere*"; the "negative" one comes from a "*silver sphere*." There is also a "*dark explosion*" that sends out "*sheets of black energy.*"

Only a "short-form" formula is given for what would otherwise require *35,000 command-lines* to write out fully. [A *Seeker* is *not expected* to have to *run every series* to *disperse* the *Implant* anyways.] However, this is still an experimental *Platform*. We cannot yet instruct with certainty on whether or not a *Seeker* should take *charge* off of the reoccurring "*ending roots*" of the *Platform* prior to *processing-out* the *Implant*.

–It *is*, however, best practices to lightly "*scan*" for, and handle, any "*misunderstood words*" before *running* the *Implant*.

–It *is* also best practices to *discharge* the variable "*list-item*" to be inserted at the top of each *series-run*, as your *first command-line*. For example: "*I Want*" and "*I Don't Want*," and then both of them simultaneously, or as a single line—"*I Want*"/"*I Don't Want*." The *variable item-*

list is included in this manual after the *Platform formula* (below).

–In that same style, although it is not indicated here: it is common to *process-out* each of the *command-lines* in a pair, on their own, and then to *run* a *third command-line* combining them and making sure that no "residual" *registers* on a *GSR-Meter*. A *Seeker* will have noticed this *combined-line* from their previous study/use of some *Implant-Platforms*.

While combining pair-*lines* for a third *is* a common practice, given the current experimental state of this material, we cannot at this time say with certainty if it should be observed here. Further work is still required to perfectly refine *Wizard Level-3*, in addition to completing research and developing additional *Wizard-Levels* (as described in *AT#8*).

SPIRITUAL-DISABILITY PLATFORM

1.1.X ___ TO ESCAPE
1.2.X ___ TO BE CAPTURED

2.1.X ___ TO START
2.2.X ___ TO STOP

3.1.X ___ TO GO FORWARD
3.2.X ___ TO GO BACK

4.1.X ___ TO BE AWAKE
4.2.X ___ TO BE ASLEEP

5.1.X ___ TO BE COMPETENT
5.2.X ___ TO BE INCOMPETENT

6.1.X ___ TO REMEMBER
6.2.X ___ TO FORGET

7.1.X ___ TO BE LIGHT
7.2.X ___ TO BE HEAVY

8.1.X ___ TO BE TREATED HONESTLY
8.2.X ___ TO BE FOOLED

9.1.X ___ TO BE ALLOWED TO REMAIN
9.2.X ___ TO BE DRIVEN AWAY

10.1.X ___ TO BE AWARE
10.2.X ___ TO GO UNCONSCIOUS

11.1.X ___ TO BE ABLE TO STOP
11.2.X ___ TO BE MADE TO CONTINUE

12.1.X ___ TO BE FINISHED WITH THIS IMPLANT
12.2.X ___ TO BEGIN THIS IMPLANT

13.1.X ___ TO BE UNSPINNING
13.2.X ___ TO BE DIZZY

14.1.X ___ TO BE ABLE TO FIND OUT
14.2.X ___ TO BE UNABLE TO FIND OUT

15.1.X ___ TO BE PERCEPTIVE
15.2.X ___ TO BE BLIND

16.1.X ___ TO BE REPLENISHED
16.2.X ___ TO BE DRAINED

17.1.X ___ TO BE ENERGETIC
17.2.X ___ TO BE TIRED

18.1.X ___ TO BE LIVELY
18.2.X ___ TO BE IN A STUPOR

19.1.X ___ TO WAKE UP
19.2.X ___ TO BE KNOCKED OUT

20.1.X ___ TO BE BLESSED
20.2.X ___ TO BE CURSED

21.1.X ___ TO KEEP TRACK OF THINGS
21.2.X ___ TO LOSE TRACK OF THINGS

22.1.X ___ TO FOCUS ATTENTION
22.2.X ___ TO BE DISTRACTED

23.1.X ___ TO GET MOVING

23.2.X ___ TO GET STUCK

24.1.X ___ TO BE FORGIVEN

24.2.X ___ TO BE BLAMED

25.1.X ___ TO DO WHAT I'M DOING

25.2.X ___ TO DO SOMETHING ELSE

26.1.X ___ TO DO WELL

26.2.X ___ TO DO POORLY

27.1.X ___ TO FEEL PLEASURE

27.2.X ___ TO FEEL PAIN

28.1.X ___ TO BE CONFORTED

28.2.X ___ TO BE TORTURED

29.1.X ___ TO BE HEALTHY

29.2.X ___ TO BE SICK

30.1.X ___ TO BE CREATED

30.2.X ___ TO BE DESTROYED

31.1.X ___ TO BE UNTOUCHED

31.2.X ___ TO BE IMPACTED

32.1.X ___ TO BE ORIENTED

32.2.X ___ TO BE DISORIENTED

33.1.X ___ TO BE CAPABLE OF THINKING

33.2.X ___ TO BE INCAPABLE OF THINKING

34.1.X ___ TO DO ENOUGH

34.2.X ___ TO DO TOO LITTLE

35.1.X ___ TO FIND THINGS

35.2.X ___ TO LOSE THINGS

36.1.X ___ TO BE HARD TO FOOL

36.2.X ___ TO BE EASY TO FOOL

37.1.X ___ TO BE REWARDED

37.2.X ___ TO BE PUNISHED

38.1.X ___ TO BE PLEASED

38.2.X ___ TO BE DISAPPOINTED

39.1.X ___ TO BE FREE
39.2.X ___ TO BE TRAPPED
40.1.X ___ TO BE REFRESHED
40.2.X ___ TO BE WORN DOWN
41.1.X ___ TO BE PATIENT
41.2.X ___ TO BE IMPATIENT
42.1.X ___ TO ACCEPT THINGS
42.2.X ___ TO BE ANXIOUS ABOUT THINGS
43.1.X ___ TO HAVE CONFIDENCE
43.2.X ___ TO HAVE DOUBTS
44.1.X ___ TO BE TROUBLE-FREE
44.2.X ___ TO HAVE TROUBLE
45.1.X ___ TO BE MANIFESTED (*made*)
45.2.X ___ TO BE UNMANIFESTED (*unmade*)
46.1.X ___ TO HAVE AN IDENTITY
46.2.X ___ TO BE NOBODY
47.1.X ___ TO BE AN INDIVIDUAL
47.2.X ___ TO BE PART OF A COMPOSITE
48.1.X ___ TO HAVE FREE WILL
48.2.X ___ TO BE CONTROLLED
49.1.X ___ TO BE JUSTIFIED
49.2.X ___ TO BE UNJUSTIFIED
50.1.X ___ TO BE PROPER
50.2.X ___ TO BE SCANDALOUS
51.1.X ___ TO HAVE PRIDE
51.2.X ___ TO BE ASHAMED
52.1.X ___ TO BE EARLY
52.2.X ___ TO BE LATE
53.1.X ___ TO BE RELAXED
53.2.X ___ TO BE NERVOUS
54.1.X ___ TO PAY ATTENTION

54.2.X ___ TO IGNORE THINGS

55.1.X ___ TO BE CERTAIN
55.2.X ___ TO BE CONFUSED

56.1.X ___ TO HAVE A FUTURE
56.2.X ___ TO BE DOOMED

57.1.X ___ TO HAVE PLEASANT SENSATIONS
57.2.X ___ TO HAVE DISTURBING SENSATIONS

58.1.X ___ TO BE AGREED WITH
58.2.X ___ TO HAVE ARGUMENTS

59.1.X ___ TO HAVE FEELING
59.2.X ___ TO FEEL NUMB

60.1.X ___ TO HOLD TOGETHER
60.2.X ___ TO FALL APART

61.1.X ___ TO BE ETHICAL
61.2.X ___ TO BE IMMORAL

62.1.X ___ TO BE NICE
62.2.X ___ TO BE NASTY

63.1.X ___ TO BE GIVEN THINGS
63.2.X ___ TO BE DEPRIVED OF THINGS

64.1.X ___ TO FEEL COMFORTABLE
64.2.X ___ TO FEEL STRAINED

65.1.X ___ TO BE WHOLESOME
65.2.X ___ TO BE INFECTED

66.1.X ___ TO BE ALLOWED TO CONTINUE
66.2.X ___ TO BE INTERFERED WITH

67.1.X ___ TO BE SPECIAL
67.2.X ___ TO BE MUNDANE

68.1.X ___ TO CONCENTRATE
68.2.X ___ TO BE DISPERSED

69.1.X ___ TO BE WILLING
69.2.X ___ TO BE UNWILLING

70.1.X ___ TO BE SUPERIOR
70.2.X ___ TO BE INFERIOR

71.1.X ___ TO BE CLEAN
71.2.X ___ TO BE INFESTED

72.1.X ___ TO BE SPACIOUS
72.2.X ___ TO BE SOLID

73.1.X ___ TO BE COOL
73.2.X ___ TO BURN

74.1.X ___ TO BE WARM
74.2.X ___ TO FREEZE

75.1.X ___ TO FEEL SAFE
75.2.X ___ TO BE AFRAID

76.1.X ___ TO PROTECT MYSELF
76.2.X ___ TO RUIN MYSELF

77.1.X ___ TO BE NOBLE
77.2.X ___ TO BE DEGRADED

78.1.X ___ TO FEEL COMPLACENT
78.2.X ___ TO FEEL WORRIED

79.1.X ___ TO AVOID GRIEF
79.2.X ___ TO BE GRIEF-STRICKEN

80.1.X ___ TO FEEL RELIEF
80.2.X ___ TO FEEL PRESSURE

81.1.X ___ TO BE SETTLED
81.2.X ___ TO BE HYPER-ACTIVE

82.1.X ___ TO BE RESTED
82.2.X ___ TO BE UNABLE TO REST

83.1.X ___ TO BE ACCURATE
83.2.X ___ TO MAKE MISTAKES

84.1.X ___ TO BE KNOWING
84.2.X ___ TO BE UNKNOWING

85.1.X ___ TO SEE THINGS CLEARLY

85.2.X ___ TO HAVE DISTORTED PERCEPTIONS

86.1.X ___ TO BE LUCKY
86.2.X ___ TO BE UNLUCKY

87.1.X ___ TO AVOID ACCIDENTS
87.2.X ___ TO HAVE ACCIDENTS

88.1.X ___ TO BE FAVORED
88.2.X ___ TO BE PICKED ON

89.1.X ___ TO BE SMART
89.2.X ___ TO BE DUMB

90.1.X ___ TO HAVE PURPOSE
90.2.X ___ TO BE PURPOSELESS

91.1.X ___ TO BE A PART OF THINGS
91.2.X ___ TO BE DETACHED

92.1.X ___ TO HAVE INTERESTS
92.2.X ___ TO BE UNINTERESTED

93.1.X ___ TO DO THE RIGHT AMOUNT
93.2.X ___ TO DO TOO MUCH

94.1.X ___ TO BE GUIDED
94.2.X ___ TO BE MISLED

95.1.X ___ TO BE BLOCKED
95.2.X ___ TO BE UNBLOCKED

96.1.X ___ TO HAVE OPEN PERCEPTIONS
96.2.X ___ TO BE COVERED IN BLACKNESS

97.1.X ___ TO BE RATIONAL
97.2.X ___ TO BE IRRATIONAL

98.1.X ___ TO HAVE CORRECT RECOLLECTIONS
98.2.X ___ TO MISREMEMBER

99.1.X ___ TO BE UNBOTHERED
99.2.X ___ TO BE RESTIMULATED

100.1.X ___ TO DO WHAT IS NEEDED
100.2.X ___ TO OMIT THINGS

101.1.X ___ TO BE CAREFUL
101.2.X ___ TO BE CARELESS

102.1.X ___ TO BE ABLE
102.2.X ___ TO BE INCAPABLE

103.1.X ___ TO REACH
103.2.X ___ TO WITHDRAW

104.1.X ___ TO KNOW WHO I AM
104.2.X ___ TO BECOME CONFUSED ABOUT IDENTITY

105.1.X ___ TO TAKE CARE OF MYSELF
105.2.X ___ TO BE HELPLESS

106.1.X ___ TO BE INDUSTRIOUS
106.2.X ___ TO BE LAZY

107.1.X ___ TO BE INCLUDED IN THINGS
107.2.X ___ TO MISS OUT ON THINGS

108.1.X ___ TO BE VALIDATED (*praised*)
108.2.X ___ TO BE INVALIDATED

109.1.X ___ TO BE ADMIRED
109.2.X ___ TO BE ABHORRED

110.1.X ___ TO BE BEAUTIFUL
110.2.X ___ TO BE UGLY

111.1.X ___ TO BE BIG
111.2.X ___ TO BE SMALL

112.1.X ___ TO COMMUNICATE
112.2.X ___ TO BE UNABLE TO COMMUNICATE

113.1.X ___ TO BE COMMUNICATED WITH
113.2.X ___ TO BE IGNORED

114.1.X ___ TO CONSERVE THINGS
114.2.X ___ TO WASTE THINGS

115.1.X ___ TO PERCEIVE TRULY
115.2.X ___ TO BE DELUDED

116.1.X ___ TO BE LOCATED
116.2.X ___ TO BE LOST

117.1.X ___ TO THINK CLEARLY
117.2.X ___ TO HAVE MUDDLED THINKING

118.1.X ___ FOR EVERYTHING TO BE OBVIOUS
118.2.X ___ FOR EVERYTHING TO BE OBSCURE

119.1.X ___ TO BE ENCOURAGED
119.2.X ___ TO BE DISCOURAGED

120.1.X ___ TO BE ACCEPTED
120.2.X ___ TO BE SHUNNED

121.1.X ___ TO BE SUPPORTED
121.2.X ___ TO BE PERSECUTED

122.1.X ___ TO ESTIMATE CORRECTLY
122.2.X ___ TO MIS-ESTIMATE

123.1.X ___ TO BE COMPLETE
123.2.X ___ TO BE INCOMPLETE

124.1.X ___ TO BE ENTHUSIASTIC
124.2.X ___ TO BE DESPONDENT

125.1.X ___ TO GET THINGS RIGHT
125.2.X ___ TO GET THINGS MIXED UP

126.1.X ___ TO GET THINGS CORRECT
126.2.X ___ TO MISS THINGS

127.1.X ___ TO HAVE THINGS IN SEQUENCE
127.2.X ___ TO HAVE THINGS OUT-OF-SEQUENCE

128.1.X ___ TO IDENTIFY THINGS CORRECTLY
128.2.X ___ TO CONFUSE ONE THING WITH ANOTHER

129.1.X ___ TO DIFFERENTIATE THINGS
129.2.X ___ TO THINK THAT EVERYTHING IS THE SAME

130.1.X ___ TO BE ABLE TO KEEP THINGS TOGETHER

130.2.X ___ TO HAVE EVERYTHING FALL APART

131.1.X ___ TO BE TREATED RIGHTLY
131.2.X ___ TO BE TREATED WRONGLY

132.1.X ___ TO BE LOGICAL
132.2.X ___ TO BE ILLOGICAL

133.1.X ___ TO BE IMAGINATIVE
133.2.X ___ TO BE DULL

134.1.X ___ TO FEEL PLEASANT
134.2.X ___ TO FEEL HORRIBLE

135.1.X ___ TO BE ACCEPTING OF THINGS
135.2.X ___ TO BE REVOLTED BY THINGS

136.1.X ___ TO BE RESPONSIBLE
136.2.X ___ TO BE IRRESPONSIBLE

137.1.X ___ TO SEE REALITY
137.2.X ___ TO SEE DELUSIONS

138.1.X ___ TO BE COMPLACENT
138.2.X ___ TO BE DESPERATE

139.1.X ___ TO BE FAST
139.2.X ___ TO BE SLOW

140.1.X ___ TO BE REASONABLE
140.2.X ___ TO BE FANATICAL

141.1.X ___ TO BE RIGHT
141.2.X ___ TO BE WRONG

142.1.X ___ TO BE RICH
142.2.X ___ TO BE POOR

143.1.X ___ TO BE DECISIVE
143.2.X ___ TO BE UNABLE TO MAKE UP MY MIND

144.1.X ___ TO BE WHOLE
144.2.X ___ TO BE DIVIDED AGAINST MYSELF

145.1.X ___ TO BE CONTENTED
145.2.X ___ TO BE BOTHERED

146.1.X ___ TO BE STRONG
146.2.X ___ TO BE WEAK

147.1.X ___ TO BE ENDURING
147.2.X ___ TO BE TRANSIENT

148.1.X ___ TO BE CALM
148.2.X ___ TO BE UPSET

149.1.X ___ TO BE CAREFREE
149.2.X ___ TO BE WEIGHED DOWN

150.1.X ___ TO BE EFFECTIVE
150.2.X ___ TO BE INEFFECTIVE

151.1.X ___ TO PUT THINGS IN THE RIGHT PLACE
151.2.X ___ TO PUT THINGS IN THE WRONG PLACE

152.1.X ___ TO KNOW WHERE THINGS BELONG
152.2.X ___ TO NOT KNOW WHERE THINGS BELONG

153.1.X ___ TO KNOW WHERE THINGS ARE
153.2.X ___ TO NOT KNOW WHERE THINGS ARE

154.1.X ___ TO PUT THINGS THE RIGHT WAY
AROUND
154.2.X ___ TO PUT THINGS BACKWARDS

155.1.X ___ TO BE HAPPY
155.2.X ___ TO BE SAD

156.1.X ___ TO HAVE THE WILL TO LIVE
156.2.X ___ TO BE UNWILLING TO LIVE

157.1.X ___ TO HAVE VARIETY
157.2.X ___ TO BE BORED

158.1.X ___ TO KNOW TRUTH
158.2.X ___ TO BELIEVE IN LIES

159.1.X ___ TO BE TOLD TRUTH
159.2.X ___ TO BE GIVEN FALSE DATA

160.1.X ___ TO KNOW WHAT IS REAL
160.2.X ___ TO BE UNSURE OF WHAT IS REAL

161.1.X ___ TO KNOW WHAT IS THERE

161.2.X ___ TO IMAGINE THINGS THAT AREN'T THERE

162.1.X ___ TO BE COMPLEMENTED

162.2.X ___ TO BE CRITICIZED

163.1.X ___ TO BE LOVED

163.2.X ___ TO BE HATED

164.1.X ___ TO HAVE FRIENDS

164.2.X ___ TO HAVE ENEMIES

165.1.X ___ TO HAVE ALLIES

165.2.X ___ TO HAVE OPPONENTS

166.1.X ___ TO BE LOOSE

166.2.X ___ TO BE RESTRAINED

167.1.X ___ TO HAVE CHOICES

167.2.X ___ TO HAVE NO CHOICE

168.1.X ___ TO BE ALLOWED TO PROCEED

168.2.X ___ TO BE HEMMED IN

169.1.X ___ TO BE CAUSATIVE

169.2.X ___ TO BE AT EFFECT

170.1.X ___ TO REACH THINGS

170.2.X ___ TO BE UNABLE TO REACH THINGS

171.1.X ___ TO CONTROL THINGS

171.2.X ___ TO BE UNABLE TO CONTROL THINGS

172.1.X ___ TO HAVE GAMES

172.2.X ___ TO HAVE NO GAME

173.1.X ___ TO BE SATISFIED

173.2.X ___ TO BE UNSATISFIED

174.1.X ___ TO HAVE WHAT YOU NEED

174.2.X ___ TO SUFFER FROM CRAVINGS

175.1.X ___ TO HAVE NO REGRETS

175.2.X ___ TO BE REGRETFUL

176.1.X ___ TO BE OPEN
176.2.X ___ TO BE CLOSED IN

177.1.X ___ TO ARRANGE THINGS CORRECTLY
177.2.X ___ TO MESS THINGS UP

178.1.X ___ TO SEE ACCEPTABLE THINGS
178.2.X ___ TO BE DAZZLED

179.1.X ___ TO RECEIVE SYMPATHY
179.2.X ___ TO GET NO SYMPATHY

180.1.X ___ TO GET AWAY WITH THINGS
180.2.X ___ TO BE ACCUSED

181.1.X ___ TO BE AQUITTED
181.2.X ___ TO BE CONDEMNED

182.1.X ___ TO BE LET GO
182.2.X ___ TO BE HUNTED

183.1.X ___ TO ESCAPE THE CONSEQUENCES
183.2.X ___ TO SUFFER THE CONSEQUENCES

184.1.X ___ TO AVOID BEING IMPLANTED
184.2.X ___ TO WANT TO BE IMPLANTED

185.1.X ___ TO PLEASE PEOPLE
185.2.X ___ TO UPSET PEOPLE

186.1.X ___ TO OBEY THE RULES
186.2.X ___ TO BREAK THE RULES

187.1.X ___ TO BE GOOD
187.2.X ___ TO BE EVIL

188.1.X ___ TO HELP OTHERS
188.2.X ___ TO HARM OTHERS

189.1.X ___ TO REASSURE PEOPLE
189.2.X ___ TO SHOCK PEOPLE

190.1.X ___ TO MAKE OTHERS FEEL SAFE
190.2.X ___ TO TERRORIZE OTHERS

191.1.X ___ TO HAVE NORMAL DESIRES

191.2.X ___ TO BE OBSESSED

192.1.X ___ TO BE SANE
192.2.X ___ TO BE INSANE

193.1.X ___ TO TAKE ENOUGH TIME
193.2.X ___ TO TAKE TOO LONG

194.1.X ___ TO BE INDEPENDENT
194.2.X ___ TO BE DEPENDENT

195.1.X ___ TO BE SATISFIED
195.2.X ___ TO HAVE LONGINGS

196.1.X ___ TO KNOW WHAT'S GOING ON
196.2.X ___ TO BE PUZZLED BY EVENTS

197.1.X ___ TO KNOW WHAT'S GOING TO HAPPEN
197.2.X ___ TO BE TAKEN BY SURPRISE

198.1.X ___ TO KNOW THE CONSEQUENCES
198.2.X ___ TO BE CAUGHT UNAWARE

199.1.X ___ TO BE ABLE TO ADAPT
199.2.X ___ TO BE UNABLE TO CHANGE

200.1.X ___ TO BE FLEXIBLE
200.2.X ___ TO BE RIGID

201.1.X ___ TO BE ON TIME
201.2.X ___ TO BE TOO LATE

202.1.X ___ TO BE PARTICIPATING
202.2.X ___ TO BE ALONE

203.1.X ___ TO LIKE WHAT IS GOING ON
203.2.X ___ TO DISLIKE EVERYTHING

204.1.X ___ TO BE ABLE TO PROTEST
204.2.X ___ TO HAVE TO PUT UP WITH EVERYTHING

205.1.X ___ TO BE ABLE TO CHANGE CONDITIONS
205.2.X ___ TO BE STUCK WITH THINGS AS THEY ARE

206.1.X ___ TO BE STABLE

206.2.X ___ TO BE PUSHED AROUND

207.1.X ___ TO BE ABLE TO DECIDE NOT TO DO
SOMETHING

207.2.X ___ TO BE FORCED TO DO THINGS

208.1.X ___ TO BE AT THE RIGHT DISTANCE

208.2.X ___ TO BE TOO CLOSE

209.1.X ___ TO HAVE HOPE

209.2.X ___ TO BE HOPELESS

210.1.X ___ TO UNDERSTAND THINGS

210.2.X ___ TO MISUNDERSTAND THINGS

211.1.X ___ TO RECEIVE HELP

211.2.X ___ TO GET NO HELP

212.1.X ___ TO BE FAIR

212.2.X ___ TO BE UNFAIR

213.1.X ___ TO BE SHARING

213.2.X ___ TO BE SELFISH

214.1.X ___ TO HAVE THE RIGHT AMOUNT

214.2.X ___ TO HAVE TOO MUCH

215.1.X ___ TO FEEL FULL

215.2.X ___ TO FEEL EMPTY

216.1.X ___ TO BE AT THE RIGHT TIME

216.2.X ___ TO BE EARLY

217.1.X ___ TO BE IN THE RIGHT SPACE

217.2.X ___ TO BE IN THE WRONG SPACE (*place*)

218.1.X ___ TO BE KIND

218.2.X ___ TO BE CRUEL

219.1.X ___ TO BE HUMAN(E)

219.2.X ___ TO BE A MONSTER

220.1.X ___ TO BE WHERE YOU SHOULD BE

220.2.X ___ TO BE TOO FAR AWAY

221.1.X ___ TO BE SUCCESSFUL

221.2.X ___ TO BE A FAILURE

222.1.X ___ TO WIN

222.2.X ___ TO LOSE

223.1.X ___ TO FEEL RELIEVED

223.2.X ___ TO FEEL CRUSHED

224.1.X ___ TO BE DEFENDED

224.2.X ___ TO BE ATTACKED

225.1.X ___ TO BE TOUGH

225.2.X ___ TO BE OVERWHELMED

226.1.X ___ TO BE DETERMINED

226.2.X ___ TO GIVE UP

227.1.X ___ TO BE A GOOD CITIZEN

227.2.X ___ TO BE A CRIMINAL

228.1.X ___ TO BE A MEMBER OF SOCIETY

228.2.X ___ TO BE AN OUTCAST

229.1.X ___ TO SUPPORT SOCIETY

229.2.X ___ TO OVERTHROW SOCIETY

230.1.X ___ TO ADVANCE

230.2.X ___ TO BE HELD BACK

231.1.X ___ TO HAVE NICE THINGS

231.2.X ___ TO HAVE NOTHING

232.1.X ___ TO HAVE ENOUGH SPACE

232.2.X ___ TO HAVE TOO LITTLE SPACE

233.1.X ___ TO BE ALLOWED TO REMAIN

233.2.X ___ TO BE KICKED-OUT OF SPACES

234.1.X ___ TO BE WISE

234.2.X ___ TO BE FOOLISH

235.1.X ___ TO DO THINGS AT THE RIGHT TIME

235.2.X ___ TO DO THINGS AT THE WRONG TIME

236.1.X ___ TO HAVE ENOUGH TIME

236.2.X ___ TO RUN OUT OF TIME

237.1.X ___ TO RISE
237.2.X ___ TO FALL

238.1.X ___ TO GROW
238.2.X ___ TO SHRINK

239.1.X ___ TO GET BETTER
239.2.X ___ TO GET WORSE

240.1.X ___ TO BECOME MORE SUBSTANTIAL
240.2.X ___ TO GET THINNER

241.1.X ___ TO KNOW WHAT TIME IT IS
241.2.X ___ TO NOT-KNOW WHAT TIME IT IS

242.1.X ___ TO KNOW WHAT SPACE I'M IN
242.2.X ___ TO NOT-KNOW WHAT SPACE I'M IN

243.1.X ___ TO ESTIMATE TIME CORRECTLY
243.2.X ___ TO MIS-ESTIMATE TIME

244.1.X ___ TO ESTIMATE DISTANCE CORRECTLY
244.2.X ___ TO MIS-ESTIMATE DISTANCE

245.1.X ___ TO HAVE FAITH
245.2.X ___ TO HAVE DISBELIEF

246.1.X ___ TO BE ENLIGHTENED
246.2.X ___ TO BE MYSTIFIED

247.1.X ___ TO SPOT THE SOURCE OF THINGS
247.2.X ___ TO SPOT THE WRONG SOURCE

248.1.X ___ TO PLEASE 'GOD'
248.2.X ___ TO DISPLEASE 'GOD'

249.1.X ___ TO OBEY 'GOD'
249.2.X ___ TO DEFY 'GOD'

250.1.X ___ TO BE SAVED
250.2.X ___ TO BE DAMNED

251.1.X ___ TO BE IN HEAVEN
251.2.X ___ TO BE IN HELL

252.1.X ___ TO BE ALIVE

252.2.X ___ TO BE DEAD

253.1.X ___ TO BE IN PARADISE FOREVER

253.2.X ___ TO BURN IN HELL FOREVER

254.1.X ___ TO CREATE

254.2.X ___ TO DESTROY

255.1.X ___ TO HAVE REALITY

255.2.X ___ TO FEEL UNREAL

256.1.X ___ TO HAVE THE RIGHT TIME

256.2.X ___ TO HAVE THE WRONG TIME

257.1.X ___ TO HAVE THE RIGHT SPACE

257.2.X ___ TO HAVE THE WRONG SPACE

258.1.X ___ TO HAVE THE RIGHT ENERGY

258.2.X ___ TO HAVE THE WRONG ENERGY

259.1.X ___ TO HAVE THE RIGHT MASS

259.2.X ___ TO HAVE THE WRONG MASS

260.1.X ___ TO BE REAL

260.2.X ___ TO BE UNREAL

261.1.X ___ TO BE RIGHT ABOUT TIME

261.2.X ___ TO BE WRONG ABOUT TIME

262.1.X ___ TO BE RIGHT ABOUT SPACE

262.2.X ___ TO BE WRONG ABOUT SPACE

263.1.X ___ TO BE RIGHT ABOUT ENERGY

263.2.X ___ TO BE WRONG ABOUT ENERGY

264.1.X ___ TO BE RIGHT ABOUT MASS

264.2.X ___ TO BE WRONG ABOUT MASS

265.1.X ___ TO BE RIGHT ABOUT EXISTENCE

265.2.X ___ TO BE WRONG ABOUT EXISTENCE

266.1.X ___ TO HAVE MASS

266.2.X ___ TO HAVE NO MASS

267.1.X ___ TO HAVE ENERGY

267.2.X ___ TO HAVE NO ENERGY

```
268.1.X ___ TO HAVE SPACE
268.2.X ___ TO HAVE NO SPACE
269.1.X ___ TO HAVE TIME
269.2.X ___ TO HAVE NO TIME
270.1.X ___ TO HAVE A UNIVERSE
270.2.X ___ TO HAVE NO UNIVERSE
271.1.X ___ TO HAVE EXISTENCE
271.2.X ___ TO HAVE NO EXISTENCE
```

[*Research Notes*: There may or may not be missing *command-lines* around *pair-61* and *pair-62*, regarding dichotomies of *"Immortal"/"Age"* and *"Young"/"Old"*; but this is not certain. This *Platform* has proven quite effective as-is, though more experimental testing is still required for its standardization.]

VARIABLE LIST-ITEMS MASTER-LIST

Each of the following lines is an entire *series-run* of the previous *Implant-pattern*. By combining the two, you have the content for the entire *Platform*. Refer to the earlier instructions for details on inserting the variable *list-items* from this *master-list*. For example: the *first command-lines* for the *first series-run* are:

```
1.1.1 I WANT TO ESCAPE
1.2.1 I DON'T WANT TO BE CAPTURED
```

The same *"I Want"/"I Don't Want"* item is then applied to each of the 271 dichotomy-pairs to complete the *first series-run*. Then proceed to the top of the *Implant-pattern* and insert the next set of *list-items*, and so on.

This *master-list* is effective as given. However, our A.T. researchers would *usually* end up *defragging* the whole *Platform* after *running* a few dozen *series*, leaving the remainder to be plotted out mainly by *assessment* and *research-actions* (see *AT#8*). Further into the *master-list* (beyond *item-31*), it is possible that some of the *items* are incorrect, improperly ordered, or altogether missing. More experimental testing is needed for standardization.

[Note that on specifically the *third series-run*, when inserting the negative "*I must not*" on the second item of each pair in the *pattern*, you will have to remove the word "*to*" from the *pattern-line*.]

BEINGNESS CONDITIONS (SERIES-RUNS)
 1. I want / I don't want
 2. I need / I can't bear
 3. I have / I must not

REALITY PERCEPTION (SERIES-RUNS)
 4. To agree / To disagree
 5. To obey / To disobey
 6. To do nothing with the mind / To do anything with the mind
 7. To be unaware of this / To be aware of this
 8. To not figure this out / To figure this out
 9. To resist change / To try to change
 10. To be in a body / To be outside a body
 11. To interiorize (*go inside*) / To exteriorize (*eject*)
 12. To keep this implant / To undo this implant
 13. To generalize / To identify
 14. To associate / To disassociate
 15. To not look / To look
 16. To not scan / To scan
 17. To synchronize with reality / To desynchronize from reality
 18. To fixate on physical reality / To shift in reality
 19. To limit myself to three dimensions / To extend beyond three dimensions

20. To be aware of only three dimensions / To be aware of more than three dimensions

FRAGMENT / DEFRAGMENT (SERIES-RUNS)

21. To not heal / To heal
22. To not cure / To cure
23. To entrap others / To release others
24. To enturbulate others / To unenturbulate others
25. To aberrate / To deaberrate
26. To block others / To unblock others
27. To inhibit others / To uninhibit others
28. To not process-out / To process-out
29. To not clear / To clear
   (*or*) To not defragment / To defragment
30. To not restore / To restore

REALITY-STRUCTURING (SERIES-RUNS)

31. To create physical reality / To not create physical reality
32. To not duplicate / To duplicate
33. To not replicate / To replicate
34. To cross-copy / To not cross-copy
35. To not program thoughts / To program thoughts
36. To respond to programmed thoughts / To ignore programmed thoughts
37. To be unaware of machinery / To be aware of machinery
38. To not create machinery / To create machinery
39. To ignore mental machinery / To control mental machinery
40. To be the effect of mental machinery / To be unaffected by mental machinery
41. To obey universe machinery / To disobey universe machinery
42. To hide universe machinery / To notice universe machinery

LOCATED-BEINGNESS (SERIES-RUNS)

43. To be in one place / To be in many places
44. To not see the structure of things / To see the structure of things
45. To not see through things / To see through things
46. To not look within things / To look within things
47. To not-know / To know
48. To not see remotely / To see remotely
49. To not locate / To locate
50. To not pervade / To pervade
51. To not permeate / To permeate
52. To not dimensionalize / To dimensionalize
53. To see it-as-not / To see as-it-is

TIME-STRUCTURING (SERIES-RUNS)

54. To agree with the time-stream / To leave the time-stream
55. To be wrong about time / To spot the correct time
56. To have a time-track / To have no time-track
57. To take time / To bypass time
58. To be the effect of time / To ignore time
59. To maintain the present / To change the past

ENTITY-FRAGMENTS (SERIES-RUNS)

60. To be the effect of entities / To not be the effect of entities
61. To hold on to entities / To let go of entities
62. To obey entities / To disobey entities
63. To block entities from view / To see entities
64. To be infested / To be clean
65. To infest others / To clean others
66. To be divided against myself / To be whole
67. To fragment / To integrate

SOLIDIFICATION (SERIES-RUNS)

68. To not orient anchor-points / To orient anchor-points

69. To not determinate objects / To determinate objects
70. To leave the structure of things alone / To manipulate (*change*) the structure of things
71. To not make things materialize / To make things materialize
72. To not dematerialize / To dematerialize
73. To make solids impenetrable / To make solids penetrable
74. To not infinitize / To infinitize
75. To not actualize / To actualize
76. To perpetuate reality / To violate reality
77. To leave random / To unrandomize
78. To not read minds / To read minds
79. To not take over other's minds / To take over other's minds
80. To not alter other's minds / To alter other's minds
81. To not implode other's pictures / To implode other's pictures
82. To not swap thoughts / To swap thoughts
83. To not project thoughts / To project thoughts
84. To not endow life / To endow life
85. To not manipulate life-force / To manipulate life-force
86. To not drain life-force / To drain life-force

ABILITY-SUPPRESSION (SERIES-RUNS)
87. To not intend / To intend
88. To not postulate / To postulate
89. To not levitate / To levitate
90. To not teleport / To teleport
91. To not manipulate energy / To manipulate energy
92. To not create energy / To create energy
93. To propagate flows / To dampen flows
94. To not glare (*stare down*) / To glare (*stare down*)
95. To not beam / To beam
96. To not blanket / To blanket

97. To not zap / To zap
98. To not nip / To nip
99. To not manifest / To manifest
100. To not spaceate / To spaceate
101. To not energize / To energize
102. To not historicize / To historicize (?)
103. To maintain a single viewpoint / To maintain multiple viewpoints
104. To need mass / To do without mass
105. To need energy / To do without energy
106. To need time / To do without time
107. To need space / To do without space (?)
108. To fill space / To have space (?)
109. To be located / To not be located
110. To gain mass / To lose mass
111. To be affected by energy / To ignore energy
112. To deteriorate / To improve
113. To follow the laws of energy / To violate the laws of energy
114. To follow the laws of space / To violate the laws of space
115. To follow the laws of time / To violate the laws of time
116. To follow the laws of matter / To violate the laws of matter
117. To not predict / To predict
118. To not predetermine / To predetermine
119. To not find out / To find out
120. To perceive as a body / To perceive as a spirit
121. To operate as a body / To operate as a spirit
122. To be a body / To be a spirit
123. To be "human" / To be god-like
124. To be in this universe / To leave this universe

A.T. MANUAL #8
ADVANCING
SYSTEMOLOGY

Keep this reference material accessible:
PC Lesson-1 to 16; Processing-Levels 0 to 6
AT Manual #1, "The Secret of Universes"
AT Manual #5, "Games, Goals & Purposes"
AT Manual #5, "The Jewel of Knowledge"
AT Manual #5, "Implanted Universes"
AT Manual #5, "Entities & Fragments"
AT Manual #6, "Spiritual Perception"
AT Manual #7, "Mastering Ascension"

NEW STANDARD SYSTEMOLOGY
–A New Dawn of Crystal Clarity–

This is the final training volume of *Systemology Level-8* and the entry-point to the *Infinity Grade* by which one might attain *certainty-of-Beingness* as an *Ascended Master* of *this Physical Universe.* This manual presents qualifying experimental *Wizard-Level 4* to 7 material. Use of this manual also requires applying *systematic processing* as a *research-action,* which will be explained throughout the text.

We are reaching an end-cycle on this instructional communication—part of which includes a concise clarification of terms regarding the *levels* and *gradients* of material that have brought us this far. In brief—the *New Standard Systemology* used by the *Systemology Society* is represented with:

Fundamentals of Systemology
  (Basic Course – *6 Lessons*)

The Pathway to Ascension
  Processing-Levels 0 to 6
  (Professional Course – *16 Lessons*)

Keys to the Kingdom
  Processing-Levels 7 to 8
  Wizard-Levels/Infinity-Grade
  (Advanced Training – *8 Manuals*)
  (Training Supplements – *3 Manuals*)

All *Systemology* publications not included in the list (above) are considered part of the *Systemology Core Research Library*—retained for additional *Pilot Training* and posterity as a detailed chronicle of the developments leading up to this newly refined *standard*. For the *Systemology Society*: the indicated *processing-levels* are treated *independent* of any *Mardukite Academy "Grade"* classification.

The *Mardukite Academy* provides *Systemology* instruction in addition to many other subjects—it has many other "gradients" to reflect that. From an *Academy* viewpoint: *"The Pathway to Ascension"* is *Grade-VI*; and *"Keys to the Kingdom"* represents *Grade-VII*. The only real parallel is the concept of an *"Infinity Grade"* for *8*.

<u>*Mardukite Esoteric Research Library*</u>
(Subject: Systemology – 16 Volumes)

Liber-8 : *Keys to the Kingdom: Vol. II*
Liber-7 : *Keys to the Kingdom: Vol. I*
Liber-6 (5B) : *Pathway/Ascension: Vol. II*
Liber-5 (5A) : *Pathway/Ascension: Vol. I*
Liber-4 : *Systemology: Backtrack*
Liber-180 : *Systemology-180*
Liber-3 (3E) : *The Way of the Wizard*
Liber-3D : *Imaginomicon*
Liber-2D : *Metahuman Destinations: Vol. II*
Liber-2C : *Metahuman Destinations: Vol. I*
Liber-2B : *Crystal Clear*
Liber-One : *Tablets of Destiny Revelation*
Liber-S1Z : *The Power of Zu (Lectures)*
Liber-S1X : *Systemology: Original Thesis*
Liber-S1W : *The Way Into The Future*
Liber-S1A : *Fundamentals of Systemology*

Effectively advancing *Systemology* research has specific requirements. Although the target-goal is always to develop a stable standard for *defragmenting* with certainty, the means by which this data is achieved is not always a very "therapeutic" activity—often "stirring things up" (*resurfacing*) in order to document them, without always having a safety-net. Fortunately, we have *now* reached a level of refinement to our research-methods (communicated in this manual) that will help a *Seeker* avoid the same *pitfalls* of our earlier efforts.

To make "advancements" in any subject requires an actual understanding of the subject you're trying to advance; *e.g. Systemology*. For our purposes, in addition to the *New Standard* courses, this might include examining all of the *Systemology Core Research Volumes.*

To push forth in a subject such as this really requires a strong dedication and passion to the pursuit of *Spiritual Ascension* and accessing the *Magic Kingdom*—which is, of course, the *Holy Grail* we have been after.

An advanced researcher needs to have handled their *"own case"*—or at least be able to get *"exterior to"* it—and also be able to see beyond any "mundane goal" attached to this work, such as fame or fortune. More than just "reading" the books, or "intellectually knowing" the material, a *systemologists* should be able to *apply* the spiritual technology to their lives, using the entire *Universe* as their *"laboratory."*

Although there are obviously "unique" aspects of one's personal *Backtrack* that require "cleaning up," the target-focus of our *New Standard Systemology* are those major elements and specific *incidents* that are more "common" to all cases of the *earthbound "Human Condition"*— and particularly critical to keeping an *Alpha-Spirit "in"* that *condition*. Such data is easier to "test" and also support "systematically" with any certainty.

Most of our research is systematically developed utilizing *Biofeedback-Devices*. This provides greater accuracy when conducting *"Assessments"* (with existing *data-lists*) and *"Listing-Actions"* (to find data; to find a *correct item*). In most cases, this means *Solo-Piloting* with a *GSR-Meter*; or sometimes *Co-Piloting* with an experienced research assistant.

Even when something just "seems right" (or "clicks into place"), to be a *systematic research-action* requires checking/verifying if "what seems right" actually prompts *Meter-reads*. For example: is it a *charged "item-line"* of a *Platform*, or does it just "sound good." Just like when a *Seeker* first *"contacts"* an *incident* with their *Awareness*, sometimes this work requires a bit of "feeling around" until something *registers* definitively.

The most important part of the *research-action* is: *Spotting "What Is"*—or realizing a lot of *"It is __ ,"* without a lot of questions (unknowns), other associations, and freewheeling thought. *"Spot 'What Is'"* with certainty, rather than focusing on what is still out of view, blocked, or heavily *fragmented*. If something is hidden, but not currently *restimulated*, approach it from angles where you have certainty.

When dealing with uncharted areas—particularly concerning *heavy incidents* and *Implant-Platforms*—there are several common ways mistakes can be made, including: missing *reads* (and *items*); putting *items* out-of-sequence;

putting in *items* that aren't supposed to be there; and attributing *reading-items* to one part of an *incident*, when they really apply somewhere else, or even to a completely different *incident* or *Platform*.

Mistakes affect a researcher, just as they do a *Seeker*. When *turbulent charge* or *fragmentation* is missed or "flown by" without handling it, or a *Seeker runs* the "wrong" *item*, their case does not improve. Worse than that, one might become quite ill, or get feelings of "overwhelm" and "invalidation" that stalls or hinders progress. Technically *all systemologists* are "researchers" of their own *Backtrack*; but we don't directly encourage taking a "plunge" into unknown depths until certainty is had on what *is* known and accessible.

When hitting a research-block, or a point where a specific *item* just can't be reached, it is often a good idea to take a short break and let things cool down. You can leave your *session* set up and come back to it. You *don't* want to be sitting in *session*, repeatedly chanting *"What is it!? What is it!?"* to yourself. *Research-actions* can cause *attention* to get *fixed*, frustrations can inhibit clarity, and underlying *restimulation* from unrecognized sources can affect progress. Make sure to check your "preventative fundamentals" at the start of each session.

To fully charge ahead *Self-honestly*, one must be *willing to be wrong*, while still maintaining cautious optimism and tolerance for confusion. Researching with a *GSR-Meter* requires *"unbiased objectivity"*—rather than trying to "steer" results to validate some preferred (personal) theory, *&tc*. And like any other *scientific research*: discoveries must be communicable and demonstrable to others; its methods should be able to be repeated by others—and

257

hence our emphasis on that which is "common" to others, and *registers* as such.

To be a part of this progressive movement requires a *willingness to share knowledge* that will *help*, not *entrap*, your fellow *Seekers*. This means when these *"trap-mechanisms"* are discovered, they are shared with others so they can *realize* things as they are. This knowledge is really only dangerous when it is kept secret, used for the personal gain of a few, or further control of the population, rather than as a means of *spiritual liberation*.

We have been faithfully honest in our relay of the *upper-level* work—where an *item* may be wrong, or a *Goal* is out-of-sequence; these things, when already sensed, have been indicated in the text. Areas that require additional details or data refinement are plainly noted. This is not a shortcoming on our part—for we have already advanced this material to a *New Standard* that has never been reached in the *"New Thought"* before. But the time has come to push this out from the shadows, making it available for other *Seekers* of the *Grail*.

Our *Systemology* is still relatively *"young"* compared to what can evolve from it. And an *Ascension "out"* of *this Universe* is not its only application. If more individuals became *"Seekers,"* we might just be able to *realize* a *"heaven-on-earth"* right where we are. At the very least, we can complete this *Map* for one another, and meet up again in the *Magic Kingdom*, once we've resolved all of our "stuff" down here.

Rather than spend a lot of time on theoretical philosophy, this manual will focus on *upper-level* areas that a *Seeker* will already be familiar with from previous manuals and lessons, but of which are still worthy of greater expansion and refinement. They are all developed enough to present here as launch-points for reaching further; and they all reflect critical points that remain unhandled, at least in part.

THE JEWEL OF KNOWLEDGE
(*Experimental Research*)

[The basic description and background information for *The Jewel of Knowledge* is found in *"The Secret of Universes"* (*AT#1*). This is supplemented by information concerning *False Jewels* in *"The Jewel of Knowledge"* (*AT#3*). The data provided in this current section is incomplete; therefore not included in former manuals.]

The Jewel, in any of its forms, is of popular interest among *A.T. Systemologists* and researchers. The "original" *Jewel of Knowledge* is not necessarily difficult to *"contact,"* but it is particularly challenging to fully *process-out* when *perceptions* are heavily *fragmented*. It remains the most "obscure" of all incidents that an *Alpha-Spirit* has experienced.

The *original Jewel of Knowledge* is incredibly (and deceptively) basic—almost simpleminded. It would probably have little effect on an "experienced" *Alpha-Spirit*; but for an *innocent being* (with no former *"conception of existence"*) freshly separated from the *Infinite*, it was sufficiently powerful in laying in the pattern of reality that is accounted for in *AT#1*.

When "scouting" for *experimental data*, it sometimes requires "feeling around" a bit, or "scanning through" what is known with certainty—and then seeing if any *perceptions*, or even vague impressions, occur. For example: "*they probably told us about how to perceive things.*" This is then checked with *Biofeedback* to see if anything *registers*. Once something is giving definitive *Meter-reads*, it is possible to check other things about it. Then, with more *certainties* to "*scan*" over, more details can emerge.

It is important to note that *intensive research-phases* were once critically necessary for producing material such as "*The Secret of Universes*" (*AT#1*)—or uncovering the nature of a particular *incident*. However, the initial *research-actions*, themselves, undertaken by various pioneers contributing to this work, seldom provided actual *gain* or personal *progress*. Any *relief* only seemed to occur after a particular *process* or *Platform* was at least 99% correct and fully developed for *systematic application*.

GSR-Meter assessments were used to generate most of the additional *experimental data* included here. Even the material here has only been partially *processed-out* by our researchers—which still leaves us with only a partial view of the whole picture. Only some of the *facet-chambers* of the original *Jewel of Knowledge* have been explored directly—leaving much missing-data to still recover. However, there is still much given here.

1. First Split-Viewpoint

Data: You see a *line* and feel as though there is more out of sight. You keep shifting around and seeing different *lines*. There is a sense that there is something greater present here, but you only see one *line* of it at a time. You decide that if you can view two different *lines* simultaneously, that you might *Know* something. So you hold your *attention* on one line, while trying to look at another line, which splits your *viewpoint*.

Now you see through two different *viewpoints*; and by holding them simultaneously, you are able to perceive a "plane" (*planar surface*). Usually it resembles a "square"; but if you shift your *viewpoints* around, it appears otherwise, such as a "triangle." You still feel like there is *more* to *Know*. So, you steady your *attention* on the "plane" while pulling yourself back to "see more"—which splits another *viewpoint* and allows you to see a *three-dimensional* object; usually a "cube"; but again, as you shift your *viewpoints*, you can see that you are looking at different shapes.

The same splitting and perception occurs for *4-D* and *5-D space/objects*; and you "feel good" about this. The *object* being displayed is really a *5-D* object with a *6-D* thickness. When you try splitting further into *six*, the *object* holds steady, and you see some additional thickness to it, but nothing really more. In fact, it starts to appear somewhat ghostly and unreal from that view, which makes you "feel sad" about it.

So, you decide to forget about the *sixth-dimension* and *pretend* the object is *real* enough from before. You go back to admiring it how it was when you "felt good" about it; and decide there is nothing more to *Know*. That's when the experience of this *facet-chamber* ends, and you shift into the next *facet* in the sequence.

2. Need For Agreement

Data: Experience of the next *facet* begins with only a *white-nothingness* or *white-void*. You reach your *Awareness* for something to see but there is nothing. Eventually, you sense the presence of another *being*. You shift your *attention* around until you are able to feel the nearness of one of their *viewpoints*. When you shift your own *viewpoint* to their *viewpoint*, you are able to perceive a *curved-line*.

At first you only see the *curved-line*, but you get a sense that the other *being* is looking at a full *5-D object*. You split your *viewpoint* into *five* to try and see it, but you still only perceive a *curved-line*. You realize that this is because only *one* of your *viewpoints* is matching theirs. When you match all *five viewpoints* to theirs, a *5-D sphere* appears, and you "feel good" about this because it is interesting and permits something greater to *have* a perception of.

You experiment by shifting a *viewpoint* off of theirs, and this causes the *sphere* to "lose" a *dimension* and seem more hollow, which gives a sense of less "*havingness*" and "*loss*"—and makes you "feel bad" about it. When you shift your *viewpoint* back into *agreement* with the *other being*, you "feel better" about it—and decide that *agreement* is a necessary factor. [Then you shift to the *next facet*.]

3. Duplicating Others

Data: You sense another *being*. They manifest/create a "*point*" and extend a *line* from that *point*; then encourage you to do the same. When you eventually do this, you have a *line*. But, since you don't locate it within the same *Space* as theirs, you lose track of their *line* while making yours. After realizing this, you decide to manifest/create your *line* in the same *Space* as theirs, and now you *have* two *lines* to perceive.

Eventually, the other *being* splits their viewpoints to make a square (plane) and invites you to do the same. This is repeated with *3-D* and *4-D cubes*. Each time you get a sense of increased "*havingness*" by making these more interesting objects in agreement with another's creation. You realize the need for following directions and duplicating others.

4. Need For Games

Data: This *facet-chamber* is experienced within a *thirteen-dimensional space*. There are many "*cubes*" with white and black sides. They resemble modern "*dice*" in that the "quantities" shown on their faces/sides are represented by "dots" rather than "symbols." Moving them around at random is uninteresting. Eventually, you find that sorting and arranging them in "sequences" (*&tc.*) is far more interesting and fun.

5. Need For Opponents

Data: There are a series of cubes (as in FACET 4); but this time there are two sets (one white and one black) and a sense that there is another *being* present. The two sets are not identical and the quantities represented on their faces are "random" (non-sequential, with missing numbers). You each take a set and have a "race" to see who can get them in "order" first. You find this more interesting and fun than arranging them alone.

6. Need To Ensure An Opponent

Data: Similar to FACET 5; but when the opponent "weakens," the game becomes less fun. So you encourage and try to help them.

7. Need To Create An Opponent

Data: Set up like earlier *facets*; but this time there is no opponent. You decide to *divide*—and part of you serves to act as the opponent. You realize the necessity of this in order to have a *game.*

8. Need For Barriers

Data: There is a *7-D cube* with variously-shaped holes and slots. There are different *objects* around that can be fitted into them. You can perceive another *being* doing this and it looks interesting. When it's your turn, the *ob-*

jects just drift through the *cube-walls* and each other, and it's not very fun or challenging. You decide that it is only fun when you make the *objects* solid and the *walls* more solid to block things.

9. Encouraging Agreement

Data: You perceive there are four other *beings* in the space. You each share in manifesting/creating a *5-D cube*. This provides a "pleasant feeling" (*havingness*). When one of the others goes out-of-agreement, the *cube* goes hollow. Eventually, some of the others encourage them to get back into-agreement and the *cube* is solid again and "nicer."

Then it happens again where someone goes out-of-agreement, and this time you encourage them to come back into-agreement (and the *cube* is solid again).

Then you decide to go out-of-agreement and leave the "group" and can only see a *line*. You sense the encouragement of others to come back into-agreement (and the *cube* is solid again). Then you all admire the solid *cube* for a while and it is "pleasant." You decide it is necessary to encourage the agreement of others.

10. Need To Agree On Barriers

Data: Similar to FACET 8; but the large object is a *5-D pyramid*, and there are many other *beings* playing, all racing to put their *objects* into the *holes* and *slots*. But everything starts quite transparent and isn't much fun. So, you learn how to make each other's *objects* more solid in order to *have* a *game*.

11. Need To Enforce Agreement

Data: This occurs in a *many-dimensional* space. There are specifically 14 dimensions that are not properly aligned (in right-angles to each other) and 14 different *beings* present. Each different *being* is manifesting/creating a "*dimension point*" that is *anchoring* each single dimensional-space. You are each trying to align two *4-D objects* and get them onto the same axis until everyone can get in-to-agreement on dimensional-space.

No one is making any progress. You finally *agree* with another to share your *anchor-points*. Now the two of you have more in alignment than the others who insist on be-ing individualistic. You, and the other one agreeing with you, decide to *Implant* each of the others with the inten-tion to "go into-agreement." This is accomplished by taking a *being* and "holding" them in the *object* until they *choose to agree* with it.

Since you are "blocking" their *dimension-points* (percep-tions) while you do this, they eventually agree. And since your "side" always outnumbers any individual, you nev-er fail in this task. In fact, it gets much easier as more are added to the group. When everyone is in agreement, the *spatial-dimensions collapse* into a *single reality-frequency* that is pleasing to everyone. And from this, you see the necessity of forcing others into-agreement.

12. Sensation

Data: You see a *4-D object* in front of you. It has *13* differ-ent *3-D* "*sides*"—each of which is a *3-D object* (a *square-based pyramid*). *Ten* of the *3-D pyramids* are solid and *three* are hollow. You receive an *intention/impression* that this is "your form" and you sense an encouragement in becom-ing it. So, you *choose to be the object* (the *multi-pyramid form*) just to see what happens.

Then a *4-D energy-beam* comes in and starts bouncing in and out of your new form. It enters via a *hollow pyramid* and then ricochets off the *solid pyramids* before going out one of the *hollow* ones. Since there are only *three hollow pyramids*, the activity of the *energy-beam* seems unbalanced and you get a sense of incompleteness.

Then another *being* with a similar form as yours is present. The two of you align your *hollow* areas, share the *energy-beams* with one another; and everything is pleasant, harmonic, and you get the sense of this being "*pleasure*." Then the other *being* turns away from you (out-of-alignment), and the *energy-beams* are now all jagged and disorganized. It is not enjoyable, and you get the impression that this is "*pain*."

13. Pleasure Is At Other's Expense
Data: You follow the *being* from the previous *facet* into this chamber, where you find yourselves among a total of 14 *beings* all using the "*multi-pyramid bodies*." There are *energy-beams* bouncing all around the *Space*, and you participate in the exchange of them—but the *beams* are out-of-alignment (feel mildly unpleasant).

Two of the *beings* get into good alignment with each other and begin to experience "*pleasure*" (as described in FACET 12. But this throws everyone else's *beams* into a worse alignment—and you feel "*pain*." So, everyone pushes the *two* out-of-alignment with each other.

Then you have the chance to be in-alignment with another, and do so. It is "*pleasant*," but you notice that everyone else is in "*pain*" again, so you allow them to push you apart. Everyone, including yourself, goes back to feeling only the "*mildly unpleasant*" pattern (as in the beginning).

14. Need For Rules
Data: You watch *three beings* operating in a *7-D space*. *Two* of them create an elaborate *game* with what appears to be various spirals, rods, cones, energies, and balls bouncing

around. You can see that they are interested and enjoying their *game*.

Then the *third being* joins them and wants to play too. But they don't know the *rules* of the *game*, so they invent their own and start playing differently. The first *two* get frustrated and start modifying the *rules* in order to accommodate the new player, but the *game* becomes too chaotic and falls apart. The players break off and examine the results and are "unhappy."

They get back together again; but this time they define clear *rules* for each of the aspects of the *game*, and even *create* something that puts the *rules on display*. But it does more than display them; it *Implants* them. So, when a *fourth being* arrives, they are *Implanted* with the *rules* before they are allowed to *play*. Now things can proceed well and everyone is mostly "satisfied" with the results.

When it comes time for you to come and join the *game*, you have already witnessed the "*need for rules*," and so you *agree to being Implanted* for the sake of sharing in the *game*.

15. Need For Players

Data: A "*multi-dimensional sphere*" is being bounced back and forth between two "teams" (comprised of maybe *eight beings* on each side). Participating in the *game* provides a "*pleasant*" sensation. Then, one of the other players wanders off and the *game* is a little less fun. This causes more to wander off, and there is eventually no one else left but you. For a while, you sit alone and bored.

Then another group arrives and you all play together. When one of the players tries to leave, the others "hold" them and "force" them back into the *game*. Then the *game* remains "*pleasant*." When you have fully realized a necessity to force others to remain in a game, you shift to the *next facet*.

Other facet-chambers requiring research:
16. Need For Duplication
17. Need For Imperfect Duplication
18. Need For Persistence
19. Need For Admiration
20. Need For Acknowledgment
21. Need To Divide
22. Only One Will Survive (Win)
23. {the idea that if two terminals connect to communicate, one will be submissive and the other will be dominant}
24. {the idea that if you communicate too freely, you will connect to terminals that will dominate you}

THE FALSE JEWEL OF KNOWLEDGE
(*Experimental Research*)

Although there have been many *False Jewels* (such as *Entry-Into-This-Universe*), this *Implant* appears relatively early on the *Backtrack*—between the "*Games Universe*" and the "*Symbols Universe*"—and is considered the *earliest* "*False Jewel*."

By the point of this *incident*, an *Alpha-Spirit* had already experienced the *Implant Penalty-Universes* (IPU) and maintained some *fragmented considerations* from the *Games Universe*. But visibly, this only affected what we tended to *create* (*manifest*) or *dramatize*. There was no conception that: to *Implant* caused *fragmentation* that affected us as *beings*. The intention was to simply suppress or limit the interactions in a *Shared-Reality*; but our *Actualized*

268

Awareness and *spiritual abilities* were being *fragmented* in the process.

During the phase of existence that this *Implant* occurred, an *Alpha-Spirit* was still unaffected by *force* or any *energy* directly. Also, we had not yet experienced a heavy "*Splitter-Incident*" that would *actually divide* our *Awareness* into "*split-viewpoints*" (that could individually get *Implanted* without our being conscious of it). At this stage, we were still able to "*collect ourselves*" after an *Implanting-Incident*; such as seems to have been the case after the original IPU experiences. But an individual could still be tricked into limiting themselves.

Although the original *Jewel* had been lost to a fog of *fragmented-time*, it was still treated with a religious-like veneration. Pale *facsimiles* of it were used to make IPU more impactful; but there was no specific emphasis on using them for *Implanting* at that time. Here, the *re-creation* or *facsimile* of *The Jewel* is intentionally used to install *false data* and *fragmented reasoning*—therefore, we refer to it as the *earliest* "*False Jewel.*" Of course, all *Implants* install "*false data,*" but here we concentrate on one *incident* where that is *the* focus.

This *False Jewel* is awarded as a "*prize*" for winning some *game*. The *game* is actually designed for the individual to "*win,*" but they get a sense of earning something valuable. The *Implant* also impresses the individual to trick others into being victim to the *False Jewel* (by promoting how "wonderful" it is to have).

At the start of the *Implant*: *The False Jewel* moves "*into*" the individual's "*center of Beingness.*" *The Jewel* "*flashes*" with each *item*. It is a kind of *radioactive-light* (that accompanies an *electric-crackle*) and spreads completely throughout the individual. The *Platform* begins with a series of *command-items* (all of which are included below).

In *3-D perception, The Jewel* resembles a *"diamond"* — an *eight-sided solid*, or *two pyramids* (one pointing up; one pointing down) sharing a base. As a *"higher-dimensional construct,"* it actually has *64 sides* or *"facets."*

The second part of the incident uses *graphic imagery (symbolism)* to install *64 fragmented agreements* (that follow the *basic* IPU-*sequence*). *The Jewel* "turns" to present *one* of its *64* different *"facets."* During this part, the *"radioactive flashes"* emit a brief *"motion picture"* (rather than a *"command-line"*).

Each of the *64 facets* present a different *"motion picture"* that is only loosely connected to the literal IPU and seldom includes any of the major *"terminals."* Each of these *facets* relay a "basic truth" about existence — but, of course, it is all *fragmented false-data (lies)*.

Each *"motion picture"* is sensed as a "heavy flow" — but it is not so much an "energy" as it is an *internally generated* sense of "overwhelm" or "dread" at the sudden *flash-realization* of the (false) truth. This produces an intensely receptive "haze" (or "daze") of *Awareness*. Such *"flash-insights"* might otherwise be "shrugged off" and ignored with a few moments of *analytic thought*; but in this particular state of "shock," we *agree* that we *believe* them.

After receiving the *"(false)-truth"* from a *facet*: we *agree* to it; then *The Jewel* gets us to *agree-to-forget* it — and hide that *agreement* (with the *false-truth*) from ourselves — because the "truth is too terrible" and would drive us "insane" if we *knew, &tc. The Jewel* then turns to its next *facet* and emits the next *motion-picture* and *false-truth*. The information from one "truth" tends to contradict another; but since each one is forgotten before the next, this doesn't seem to get noticed during the *incident*.

This is a particularly significant area of advanced research, because the *Platform* for this "original" *False Jewel* was likely copied and reused (or added to) many times in subsequent *Universes* on the *Backtrack*. "Spotting" the top of the original *False Jewel* (*Platform*) aids in releasing "*Control Entities*" (C.E.) [AT#5], so there is certainly some validity to what we have already uncovered. However, the research on the *64 facets* is still incomplete.

(ORIGINAL) FALSE JEWEL PLATFORM

A. {*Winning the game.*}

B. {*Being given The Jewel and agreeing to accept it.*}

C. {*The Jewel flows into you.*}

D. {*The Jewel flashes in the center of your being on each of the following command-items.*}

1. TO ACCEPT THE JEWEL IS NATIVE STATE
2. TO ACCEPT THE JEWEL IS TO BE THE STATIC (ALPHA)
3. TO ACCEPT THE JEWEL IS TO FULFILL THE URGE FOR SOMETHINGNESS
4. THE JEWEL IS THE BASIS FOR ALL URGES
5. THE JEWEL IS THE BASIS FOR ALL RELIEF
6. THE JEWEL IS THE ONLY REASON WHY
7. THE JEWEL IS THE BASIS FOR ALL ACTION
8. IN THE BEGINNING, NOW, AND FOREVER, IS THE DECISION; AND THE DECISION IS TO ACCEPT THE JEWEL
9. THE JEWEL CONTAINS ALL REAL DECISIONS
10. THE JEWEL CONTAINS ALL REAL POSTULATES

11. THE JEWEL CONTAINS ALL REAL AGREEMENTS
12. THE JEWEL IS THE ONLY SOURCE OF TIME
13. THE JEWEL IS THE ONLY SOURCE OF SPACE
14. THE JEWEL IS THE ONLY SOURCE OF ENERGY
15. THE JEWEL IS THE ONLY SOURCE OF MATTER
16. THE JEWEL CONTAINS ALL LOVE
17. THE JEWEL CONTAINS ALL EMOTION
18. THE JEWEL CONTAINS ALL THOUGHT
19. THE JEWEL CONTAINS ALL EFFORT
20. THE JEWEL CONTAINS ALL KNOWLEDGE
21. THE JEWEL CONTAINS ALL UNDERSTANDING
22. THE JEWEL IS THE SOURCE OF ALL REALITY
23. THE JEWEL IS THE SOURCE OF ALL MEANING
24. THE JEWEL IS THE SOURCE OF ALL TRUTH
25. THE JEWEL IS THE SOURCE OF ALL BEAUTY
26. THE JEWEL IS THE SOURCE OF ALL VALUE
27. THE JEWEL IS THE SOURCE OF ALL HAVING(NESS)
28. THE JEWEL IS THE SOURCE OF ALL EXISTENCE
29. THE JEWEL IS THE SOURCE OF ALL ENLIGHTENMENT
30. TO ACCEPT THE JEWEL IS TO REACH TOTAL KNOWINGNESS
31. TO ACCEPT THE JEWEL IS TO LEARN THE HIDDEN MEANINGS BEHIND ALL EXISTENCE
32. TO ACCEPT THE JEWEL IS TO KNOW THE TRUE REASON FOR EVERYTHING

E. {*The Jewel turns to its first facet. Motion-picture. False-data. Agreements.*}

"FALSE JEWEL" FRAGMENTED-DATA

Each *facet* of *The Jewel* presents *false-data* using elements of one of the IPU *and* its "inversion" (a negative quality or opposition for each IPU). Some of the existing research on this *false-data* is listed below along with its corresponding IPU. [The entire subject of IPU is still under development and refinement.]

One challenge of this research concerns how many times a *"False Jewel"* has been used with different content. Our target-data here pertained to the *Original "False Jewel."* When other related data was found, but determined to apply only to a *later* (more recent) version of the *"False Jewel,"* it is indicated as such.

[*Advisement:* the *false-data* discovered and provided here IS *false-data.* It sometimes sounds "right" to make it more acceptable—and has become a part of many basic *reality-agreements.* But it is not, itself, truth. It is full of half-truths, inaccurate evaluations, and the resulting considerations. The research discoveries are included here for *processing-out;* not to be mistaken as real "wisdom." *The Jewel,* in all of its forms, always provides *"False Enlightenment"*—but it is also the *only "enlightenment"* that most individuals ever find.]

[The *"Hellfire Incident Location"* is only used *later* in this manual. It is given here to avoid having to print the *Goals-list* twice in the same volume.]

[16. CREATION (*Arc 8*)]

1. "TO CREATE" {*statue*}
   (–) "TO DESTROY" {*devil statue*}
False-Data: 'God' created everything and we just keep messing it up. So you agree that you must never create or destroy anything because it's all really God's *Universe,* not yours.
   [*Hellfire Inc. (loc)*—St. John, Canada]

2. "TO CAUSE" {*old man god*}
   (–) "TO PUT AT EFFECT" {*devil*}

False-Data: When you manifest/create/cause things, they cease to be under your control. So you agree that it is dangerous to manifest anything.

—*Later*: If you could manifest real things in this *Universe*, the ability would go out of control; and you'd manifest things that you are afraid of, which would attack you. So you agree to keep your manifestations from becoming real.

[*Hellfire Inc. (loc)*—Rome]

3. "TO DUPLICATE" {*computer*}
     (or "TO INTENSIFY")
   (–) "TO UNMANIFEST" {*black computer*}
       (or "TO DRAIN") {*black vortex*}

False-Data: When you fight back against something, it is intensified by your efforts to resist it. So you agree not to fight back.

—*Later*: If you think of something, it will get stronger and gain power over you. So you agree not to think about anything outside of normal reality.

[*Hellfire Inc. (loc)*—Washington, DC]

4. "TO IMAGINE" {*cartoon*}
   (–) "TO DISILLUSION" {*vampyre*}

False-Data: There are horrific things beyond the *third-dimension* that don't want you to see them, and will attack you if you do. So you agree not to *imagine* anything beyond the *third-dimension*.

—*Later*: If your *imagination* goes out-of-control, you will *imagine* your worst fears. So you agree not to *imagine* anything.

[*Hellfire Inc. (loc)*—Florida or Brazil]

[15. **KNOWINGNESS** (*Arc 7*)]

5. "TO KNOW" {*2-headed dodo*}
   (–) "TO MISLEAD" {*gorilla-people*}

False-Data: When you knew the real truth, you chose to forget it for good reasons. So you agree not to try to know the real truth.

—*Later*: If the people knew the truth, it would destroy them. So you agree that you must prevent any attempts to reveal the truth.

[*Hellfire Inc. (loc)*—S. Argentina]

6. "TO UNDERSTAND" {*chipmunk*}

  (–) "TO MISUNDERSTAND" {*disabled*}

False-Data: If something *could* be understood, you *would* understand it *already*. The only things worth understanding belong to 'God' and are not to be understood by you. So you agree not to try and understand anything because it would be a worthless effort.

[*Hellfire Inc. (loc)*—Vermont]

7. "TO ABSORB" {*epic hero*}

  (–) "TO DISCARD" {*amazonian*}

False-Data: Beings (entities) are the coin (currency) of the *Universe*; and you can only gain strength and power by absorbing them.

[*Hellfire Inc. (loc)*—Mt. Olympus]

8. "TO LEARN" {*gnome*}

  (–) "TO FORGET" {*troll*}

False-Data: If you learned the truth, it would destroy the *Game*. So you agree to forget this (*The Jewel*) forever.

[*Hellfire Inc. (loc)*—Heidelberg, Germany]

[14. **GAMES** (*Arc 6*)]

9. "TO PLAY" {*child*}

  (–) "TO FOOL" {*joker*}

False-Data: Life is only a *game* and you exist here only as a playing-piece. So you agree that it doesn't matter what you do, or what happens, since there is no higher purpose anyway.

—*Later*: We are all one, so that when you lose to someone else, you have really won, because you are them too. So you agree to lose often, to help yourself win elsewhere.

[*Hellfire Inc. (loc)*—Shanghai, China]

10. "TO COMPETE" {*coach*}
   (–) "TO CHEAT" {*skeleton*}
False-Data: If people compete, only one can win, and many must lose. So you agree to lose the majority of the time.

—*Later*: If you were strong, you would be selfish and evil forever. So you agree to stay weak.

[*Hellfire Inc. (loc)*—Toronto, Canada]

11. "TO MANIPULATE" {*penguin banker*}
   (–) "TO RUIN" {*dragon*}
False-Data: The 'Fates' secretly manipulate your behavior, and you can't do anything about it. So you agree not to take responsibility for anything, because none of it is your fault.

—*Later*: There are evil people who would manipulate society for their own gain and bring harm to others. So you agree to block anyone who tries to manipulate society.

[*Hellfire Inc. (loc)*—Zurich, Switzerland]

12. "TO EXCHANGE" {*spirit-broker*}
   (–) "TO STEAL" {*raccoon*}
False-Data: You gave up your right to disagree in exchange for the chance to 'play' in this *Game*. So you agree not to disagree with the 'rules' of the *Universe*.

—*Later*: You promised 'God' service in exchange for life. So you agree to serve 'God' always and obey the rules of 'his' *Universe* (and not question anything).

[*Hellfire Inc. (loc)*—Hong Kong, China]

[13. **CHANGE** (*Arc 5*)]

13. "TO SHAPE" {*clay people*}

   (–) "TO DISTORT" {*walrus*}

False-Data: You were shaped (made/created) from the postulates of others. So you agree that other's postulates should affect you.

   [*Hellfire Inc. (loc)*—Crete, Greece]

14. "TO CHANGE" {*magician*}

   (–) "TO IMPLODE" {*sorceress*}

False-Data: This *Universe* is a constructed picture, and you are only a figure painted in it by the 'Master-Painter'—moving and acting as is needed to compose the painting. So you agree that you can affect nothing, and cannot change (you must be as you are).

   [*Hellfire Inc. (loc)*—Tunisia, N. Africa]

15. "TO COMBINE" {*conjoined twins*}

   (–) "TO FRAGMENT" {*worms*}

False-Data: Reality can only be manifested/created or affected by group postulation. If you are alone, then you will have no *Universe*. So you agree to combine with other beings and stick to them.

   [*Hellfire Inc. (loc)*—Rangoon, Yangon]

16. "TO (BRING) ORDER" {*gorilla people*}

      (or "TO ALIGN") {*bear-people*}

   (–) "TO (BRING) CHAOS"

      (or "TO REVOLT") {*panther*}

False-Data: Our attempts to be individuals, and go our own way, brings us to a sorry state. So you agree to align with 'God' and follow 'his' desires, and put aside you own wants and needs.

   [*Hellfire Inc. (loc)*—St. Petersburg, Russia]

[12. **REASON** (*Arc 4*)]

17. "TO REASON" {*clown*}

(–) "TO DISCOMBOBULATE" {*one-man band*}

False-Data: The real reason for existence is to feed your 'soul' to 'God'. So you agree to allow yourself to be eaten when the time comes.

[*Hellfire Inc. (loc)*—Manhattan, N.Y.]

18. "TO ORIENT" {*wire man*}

(–) "TO DISORIENT" {*spinning top*}

False-Data: If you were truly 'oriented', you would see that this is all a sham and an illusion and all your 'havingness' would be lost. So you agree to remain disoriented forever.

[*Hellfire Inc. (loc)*—Polar Orbit]

19. "TO GUIDE" {*pilot*}

(–) "TO MISDIRECT" {*scarecrow*}

False-Data: You were once a god and supposed to guide everyone, but you failed and it's your fault that everyone is stuck here now. So you agree to remain here and suffer with everyone else because it's all your fault.

[*Hellfire Inc. (loc)*—Indianapolis]

20. "TO COMPUTE" {*toy bodies*}

(–) "TO CONFUSE" {*zombie*}

False-Data: You must use a 'brain' to think and perceive. So you agree to be 'unconscious' whenever you are out of the 'body'.

[*Hellfire Inc. (loc)*—North Pole]

[11. **CONSTRUCTION** (*Arc 3*)]

21. "TO CONSTRUCT" {*beavers*}

(–) "TO TEAR DOWN" {*wrecking crane*}

False-Data: Everything 'new' is constructed from the remains of older masses and energies. So you agree that nothing can be truly created or destroyed.

[*Hellfire Inc. (loc)* — Bangor, Maine]

22. "TO ENGINEER" {*lobsters*}
    (or "TO ARRANGE")
   (–) "TO UNSTABILIZE" {*goon*}
False-Data: The 'body' was engineered to be a 'spirit-trap' and you can't get out of it until you die. So you agree to accept death and to die as soon as possible to get out of the 'trap'.

[*Hellfire Inc. (loc)* — S. African lake]

23. "TO BUILD" {*snake people*}
   (–) "TO WRECK" {*raging bull*}
False-Data: Matter was built by many beings working in conjunction. So you agree that your postulates alone are not capable of affecting matter.

[*Hellfire Inc. (loc)* — In orbit; and Alaska]

24. "TO STRUCTURE" {*crystals*}
   (–) "TO SHATTER" {*bat-man*}
False-Data: The *Universe* is structured so that objects are 'real', and thoughts are 'unreal'. So you agree that your thoughts cannot really affect anything.

[*Hellfire Inc. (loc)* — Great Salt Lake, UT]

[10. AESTHETICS (*Arc 2*)]

25. "TO INVENT" {*worker gnomes*}
   (–) "TO DIVEST" {*troll*}
False-Data: You are the only real person and you invented everyone else. So you agree to divide and put out frag- mented-pieces of yourself on everyone else to keep them (?) {manifested, under control, in a body..?}

[*Hellfire Inc. (loc)* — Bavaria (Germany)]

26. "TO ENHANCE" {*ghost people*}
  (–) "TO DEGRADE" {*demon*}
        (or "TO WORSEN")

False-Data: The *Universe* was created to 'teach' you a lesson that you desperately need (for enhancement). So you agree to go along with it, and try to learn from it, and not protest or rebel against what happens to you.

[*Hellfire Inc. (loc)*—Copenhagen, Denmark]

27. "TO INSPIRE" {*muses*}
  (–) "TO OCCLUDE" {*mesmerist*}
        (or "TO CONCEAL/BLOCK")

False-Data: Only 'divine inspiration' can bring about 'beauty' (aesthetic art). The whispered inspiration that artists and creators receive comes from 'God'. So you agree to 'listen' for it and obey any whispers (impressions) that appear in your 'mind', because they are 'divine inspiration'.

[*Hellfire Inc. (loc)*—Florence, Italy]

28. "TO BEAUTIFY" {*fairy godmother*}
  (–) "TO MAKE UGLY" {*old witch*}

False-Data: All 'beauty' comes from 'God'. So you agree that anything you create on your own must be ugly.

[*Hellfire Inc. (loc)*—Babylon]

[9. ETHICS (*Arc 1*)]

29. "TO PURIFY" {*fire people*}
  (–) "TO PERVERT" {*satyr*}

False-Data: All your own 'desire' is impure and stems from some 'deep-seeded animal nature'. So you agree to suppress all urges, desires, and goals, in order to 'purify' your 'soul'.

[*Hellfire Inc. (loc)*—Lima, Peru]

30. "TO JUDGE" {*minotaur*}
  (–) "TO DISAGREE" {*snake*}

False-Data: We are all in an *Implant* right now, and existence is just an *'item'*—so you agree that you cannot disagree with, or alter, reality because it's... {not there to be altered (?)}

[*Hellfire Inc. (loc)*—Crete, Greece]

31. "TO DEFEND" {*little green men*}

(–) "TO ATTACK" {*gorilla soldier*}

False-Data: The only real being is 'society'—which is 'God'. We are only 'cells' of its 'body'. So you agree to defend 'society' from {certain type?} individuals who work against it.

[*Hellfire Inc. (loc)*—Japan]

32. "TO STRENGTHEN" {*energy ball*}
    (or "TO PROTECT")

(–) "TO HURT" {*silver ball*}

False-Data: There are 'higher-beings' ('celestial police', 'angels', *&tc.*) who are protecting you from extreme harm. So you agree to give them your loyalty and never question their methods.

[*Hellfire Inc. (loc)*— (?)]

[8. DIVINITY (*Sphere 8*)]

33. "TO ENLIGHTEN" {*rabbit preacher*}

(–) "TO OBSCURE" {*smog monster*}

False-Data: The real truth is so terrible or horrific that if you were to know it, it would you drive you insane. So you agree that you must forget it.

[*Hellfire Inc. (loc)*—Libya or Jerusalem]

34. "TO CONVERT" {*fish man*}

(–) "TO DISABUSE" {*jackal*}

False-Data: People will kill anyone that tries to help them. So you agree not to try to help others.

[*Hellfire Inc. (loc)*—Jakarta, Indonesia]

35. "TO COMMUNE" {*feminine angel*}
    (or "TO CONNECT")

(–) "TO DISCONNECT" {*spider-woman*}

False-Data: We are all fragmented-pieces of a Devil/Satan —a being that rebelled against 'God', looked at 'The Jewel of Knowledge' (which was forbidden), and was punished by being fragmented and sent here. So you agree that we all deserve to be punished and should suffer here complacently.

[*Hellfire Inc. (loc)*—Los Angeles, CA]

36. "TO WORSHIP" {*holy knights*}

(–) "TO PROFANE" {*monk*}

False-Data: We were created for the sole purpose of worshiping 'God'—and that worship consists of taking on 'his' suffering. So you agree to devote yourself to suffering for 'God' and accept it without protest.

[*Hellfire Inc. (loc)*—England]

[7. SPIRITUAL (*Sphere 7*)]

37. "TO PREDICT" {*soothsayer*}
       (or "TO PREDETERMINE")

(–) "TO RANDOMIZE" {*3-headed griffin*}

False-Data: The entire history (track) of the *Universe* was predetermined at its inception (creation). So you agree to follow the course laid out for you and not to try to change anything.

[*Hellfire Inc. (loc)*—Turkey]

38. "TO INFLUENCE" {*cupid/cherub*}

(–) "TO CORRUPT" {*hunchback*}

False-Data: When left uncontrolled, people will work against each other. So you agree to push fragmented-pieces of yourself onto others to influence them to work together.

[*Hellfire Inc. (loc)*—Jacksonville, FL]

39. "TO COLLECT" {*elves/fairies*}

(–) "TO REJECT" {*wolf-man*}

False-Data: We all sprang from the same 'eternal source' and must become 'one' again. So you agree to stick to other beings and try to merge with them.

[*Hellfire Inc. (loc)*—Bombay, India]

40. "TO EMBODY" {*satyr*}
    (or "TO PERMEATE")
(–) "TO DISSOLVE" {*amoeba*}

False-Data: The 'divine light' permeates everything and is the only true source of energy. So you agree that you cannot (internally/personally) create any energy and must be dependent on an outside/external source.

[*Hellfire Inc. (loc)*—Catalina Island]

40X. "TO SOLIDIFY" {*satyr*}
(–) "TO MAKE IT NOT-IS" {*invisible man*}

False-Data: All matter consists of decayed beings. So you agree that matter can affect you.

[6. UNIVERSE (*Sphere 6*)]

41. "TO DISCOVER" {*centaurs*}
(–) "TO HIDE" {*slime monster*}

False-Data: This is the only *Universe* there is. So you agree that discovering anything 'outside' of this *Universe* must be a hallucination.

[*Hellfire Inc. (loc)*—New Zealand]

42. "TO LOCATE" {*leprechaun*}
(–) "TO MISPLACE" {*cricket*}

False-Data: Each being has a unique 'location'—a 'viewpoint'—bestowed by 'God'. This locational viewpoint is where you do all your perceiving and thinking from. [Two separate locations would be two separate individuals.] So you agree that you cannot be in two places at once.

[*Hellfire Inc. (loc)* — In orbit (space-station)]

43. "TO GATHER" {*spacesuit body*}
   (–) "TO ABANDON" {*hobo/tramp*}

False-Data: Our 'souls' are all gathered up by 'God' when we die. So you agree to give up all 'Identity' when you lose the 'body'.

[*Hellfire Inc. (loc)* — Nepal, Asia]

44. "TO OWN" {*fox people*}
         (or "TO PERMEATE")
   (–) "TO BURN DOWN" {*fire-people*}

False-Data: (?)

[*Hellfire Inc. (loc)* — Rio de Jenero, Brazil]

[5. LIFEFORMS (*Sphere 5*)]

45. "TO GROW" {*genetic entity*}
   (–) "TO ROT" {*fungus creature*}

False-Data: (?)

[*Hellfire Inc. (loc)* — Tahiti Island]

46. "TO LIVE" {*dinosaur*}
         (or "TO ENERGIZE") { ? }
   (–) "TO DIE" {*spectre*}
         (or "TO SHOCK") {*electric man*}

False-Data: The 'soul' can only be 'energized' by self-sacrifice. So you agree to sacrifice parts of yourself for the 'common good'.

[*Hellfire Inc. (loc)* — the southern aurora]

47. "TO HEAL" {*tree man*}
   (–) "TO INFECT" {*germ colony*}

False-Data: (?)

[*Hellfire Inc. (loc)* — Prague, Czech Rep.]

48. "TO ADAPT" {*thread man*}
   (–) "TO PROTEST" {*snake*}

False-Data: (?)

[Hellfire Inc. (loc)—Northern Siberia]

[4. SOCIETY *(Sphere 4)*]

49. "TO ESTABLISH" {*3-eyed giants*}
   (–) "TO UNDERMINE" {*3-eyed robot*}
False-Data: 'Society' is a conscious entity—individuals are only cells in that consciousness, and therefore unimportant. So you agree that you must control others for the sake of society.

[Hellfire Inc. (loc)—Philadelphia, PA]

50. "TO SHARE" {*dolphins*}
   (–) "TO POSSESS" {*sea monster*}
False-Data: A 'copy' is always less than the 'original'. We are all the result of a long string of 'copies'. So you agree that you will always be a 'flawed copy' without the original's abilities.
[Some of this data might really apply to another *facet* instead. (?)]

[Hellfire Inc. (loc)—near Hawaii]

51. "TO CONTROL" {*frog king*}
   (–) "TO REBEL" {*gargoyle*}
False-Data: If people were left uncontrolled, everything would fall apart (be destroyed). So you agree that you must control others for their own good.

[Hellfire Inc. (loc)—Caspian Sea]

52. "TO UNITE" {*dog soldiers*}
   (–) "TO CONQUER" {*war eagles*}
False-Data: 'God' has 'died of a broken heart' because we wouldn't stop fighting. So you agree to be afraid to fight.

[Hellfire Inc. (loc)—Frankfort, Germany]

[3. GROUPS *(Sphere 3)*]

53. "TO ORGANIZE" {*file clerk*}
   (–) "TO DISORGANIZE" {*super-villain*}

False-Data: If everyone's postulates were 'equal', all would be chaos. So you agree that the postulates of a 'group' are senior (superior) to the postulates of any one individual.

[*Hellfire Inc. (loc)*—London, England]

54. "TO COOPERATE" {*robots*}
  (–) "TO INDIVIDUATE" {*train-engine*}
False-Data: (?)

[*Hellfire Inc. (loc)*—in orbit]

55. "TO PARTICIPATE" {*merfolk*}
  (–) "TO DEBASE" {*elephant-girl*}
        (or "TO WITHDRAW")
False-Data: We only 'think' that we are living life when really we are all living in a mass-*Implant*, and the next *'item'* is always coming at us. So you agree that you cannot do anything about it (or affect reality).

[*Hellfire Inc. (loc)*—Capetown, S. Africa]

56. "TO EXPAND" {*mouse railroad engineer*}
  (–) "TO CONTRACT" {*maniac/psycho*}
False-Data: (?)

[*Hellfire Inc. (loc)*—Edinburgh, Scotland]

[2. **HOME** (*Sphere 2*)]

57. "TO JOIN" {*cat people*}
  (–) "TO SEPARATE" {*black-cat*}
False-Data: We all join together in agreement to bring about reality. If any one of us really broke that agreement, then the whole thing would fall apart. So you agree that you must keep all agreements made.

[*Hellfire Inc. (loc)*—Orleans, France]

58. "TO REPRODUCE" {*insect invader*}
  (–) "TO INFEST" {*insects*}
        (or "BLANKET")

False-Data: Whenever someone 'reproduces', they are lessened by it. If this were not the case, the *Universe* would be filled up and there would be nothing left. So you agree to be 'less' whenever you reproduce (or 'divide').

[*Hellfire Inc. (loc)*—Calcutta, India]

59. "TO SATISFY" {*cavemen*}
   (–) "TO RIDICULE" {*moron*}

False-Data: Only 'God' is 'absolute'; and the *Universe* is the 'transient state'. So you agree that the *Universe*, itself, is 'unsatisfying'—and only *The Jewel* and spreading *The Jewel* is satisfying.

[*Hellfire Inc. (loc)*—Peking (Beijing), China]

60. "TO CARE (FOR)" {*bird girl*}
   (–) "TO TORTURE" {*devil-pincers*}

False-Data: The only thing that will truly make people happy is to merge with 'God'. So you agree to care for others and help them to accept 'God' (and not rebel no matter how much they suffer).

[*Hellfire Inc. (loc)*—Acapulco, Mexico]

[1. SELF/BODY (*Sphere 1*)]

61. "TO EXPERIENCE" {*bear*}
       (or "TO FEEL")
   (–) "TO DEADEN" {*death-goddess*}

False-Data: (?)

[*Hellfire Inc. (loc)*—Canton, China]

62. "TO REPLENISH" {*a Sumerian*}
   (–) "TO AGE" {*father-time*}

False-Data: Everything that exists follows a cycle of 'create–survive–destroy', and things can only be replenished for so long. So you agree to age and die.

[*Hellfire Inc. (loc)*—Jerusalem]

63. "TO EAT" {*tiger*}

(–) "TO POISON" {*spider*}

False-Data: When you eat something, you gain energy from the spirit of what you've eaten. So you agree that you are infested by spirits.

[*Hellfire Inc. (loc)*—Kenya, Africa]

64. "TO ENDURE" {*pyramid*}

(–) "TO DISSIPATE" {*mummy*}

False-Data: Only 'God' persists; the *Universe* does not persist. So you agree that the only way you can 'endure' is to become 'one' with 'God'—aiding in 'his' purpose to conquer and permeate all beings.

[*Hellfire Inc. (loc)*—Egypt]

"BLACK-BOX" CONTROL-IMPLANTS
(*Experimental Research*)

The "*New Thought*" movement emerged strongly at the beginning of the *20th Century*. Then, waves of "*World War*" slowed its progress, and the spread of its information. But, in the aftermath of *WWII*, in the wake of *Roswell*, and in the shadows of *Atomic* and *Nuclear bombs*, the "*New Thought*" experienced a fierce resurgence in the early 1950s—hoping to provide a solution to a troubled planet, and a cure for the heavily *fragmented Human Condition*.

The "*Black-Box Control Implant*" was the first *spiritual implant* discovered by experimental *New Thought* practitioners. But, it was an entirely new *concept*, for which there was little reference. Anything about the subject spreading up from the underground usually became misunderstood as being part of an even more materialisttype of "alien-implanting" that pertained to tiny *mechanical-devices* inserted in the *physical body*.

In spite of how long *spiritual implanting* has been suspected as being a part of the *Human Condition*, the type of *systematic* approach that we might take today to handle this knowledge was simply not available at that time. The idea of "command-lines" or "processing-out" was not a part of that understanding. So, while this may be the *first Implant* discovered, surprisingly little was known about it directly until relatively recently.

This *Implant* has been used by various "alien-forces" for the sole purpose of "controlling earthbound Human populations"—while at the same time, typically setting themselves up as "gods." Portable devices were even given to ancient "priests" (those selected to propagate the "will of the gods" on *Earth*) to set up in the "temples" and use on other *Humans*. And while an individual is likely to think of "historical" *Mesopotamia*, *Greece*, or the ancient *Far East*: the nature of this *Implant* extends further on the *Backtrack of Earth* to much earlier civilizations that have long since disappeared—like *Atlantis* and *Lemuria* and even earlier than that.

The *Implanting-gimmick* involves *energy-waves* that induce *pain* on the *items* "they" don't want you to do; *pleasure* on the *items* "they" want you to do. As opposed to other earlier *Implanting-Incidents* on the *Backtrack*, this one is more "physical" in its construction and simple in design. It was meant to be easily distributable. Though operating "cheaper portable" ones often resulted in a "backfire" (by design) on the individual that was doing the *Implanting*, so that they would also receive some of its effects.

Based on how it has been perceived: the *waves* are projected from a *"black-box"* on a tripod. This *"black-box"* had a "crank" on it, like a *grinder* or *sifter*, which was turned in one direction or another to generate the *wave*. In some ways, it also resembles an old-style *camera*—and the *beam* of the *wave* may be focused on one area; in this case, a specific part of the *Body*. A person operating it would appear very much like an old-time *"organ-grinder."*

During the *incident*: the following *Platform* (series of command-items) is projected (as *"pleasure"* or *"pain"* energy-waves) at each of the following areas of the *Body*:

1. *Forehead* (*third eye/pineal gland*); 2. *Left Eye*; 3. *Right Eye*; 4. *Mouth*; 5. *Left Shoulder*; 6. *Right Shoulder*; 7. *Chest*; 8. *Stomach*; 9. *Genitals*.

To *process-out* the *Implant*, a *Seeker* "*Spots*" the intense *sensation-wave* (*pain* or *pleasure*) hitting them (in an area of the *Body*) along with the *line-item*. A *Seeker* uses their *attention* to "contact" the *item/wave* impression (similar to "recall") until it no longer *registers* on a *GSR-Meter* (*biofeedback device*).

[Start with *"Forehead"* and *run* each of the following *items* on it, one at a time, making sure each one is completely *defragmented* of *turbulent charge*.]

PLEASURE-PAIN IMPLANT-PLATFORM

1.1.X {*pain*} TO BE EVERYTHING
1.2.X {*pleasure*} TO BE NOTHING

2.1.X {*pain*} TO KNOW
2.2.X {*pleasure*} TO NOT-KNOW

3.1.X {*pain*} TO BE ORIENTED
3.2.X {*pleasure*} TO BE DISORIENTED

4.1.X {*pain*} TO BE CAUSE
4.2.X {*pleasure*} TO BE EFFECT

5.1.X {*pain*} TO BE POWERFUL
5.2.X {*pleasure*} TO BE WEAK

6.1.X {*pain*} TO BE INDEPENDENT
6.2.X {*pleasure*} TO BE OBEDIENT

7.1.X {*pain*} TO PROJECT ENERGY
7.2.X {*pleasure*} TO PUT OUT NO ENERGY

8.1.X {*pain*} TO OPERATE AT A DISTANCE
8.2.X {*pleasure*} TO NOT OPERATE AT A DISTANCE

9.1.X {*pain*} TO INFLUENCE REMOTELY
9.2.X {*pleasure*} TO NOT INFLUENCE REMOTELY

10.1.X {*pain*} TO PERCEIVE AT A DISTANCE
10.2.X {*pleasure*} TO NOT PERCEIVE AT A DISTANCE

11.1.X {*pain*} TO DO THINGS WITH THE MIND
11.2.X {*pleasure*} TO DO NOTHING WITH THE MIND

12.1.X {*pain*} TO BE FREE
12.2.X {*pleasure*} TO BE RESTRAINED

13.1.X {*pain*} TO FIND OUT
13.2.X {*pleasure*} TO NEVER FIND OUT

14.1.X {*pain*} TO REVEAL THIS
14.2.X {*pleasure*} TO NEVER REVEAL THIS

15.1.X {*pain*} TO DISAGREE WITH THIS IMPLANT
15.2.X {*pleasure*} TO AGREE WITH THIS IMPLANT

16.1.X {*pain*} TO REMEMBER THIS IMPLANT
16.2.X {*pleasure*} TO FORGET THIS IMPLANT

17.1.X {*pain*} TO NEVER IMPLANT OTHERS
17.2.X {*pleasure*} TO GIVE THIS IMPLANT TO OTHERS

18.1.X {*pain*} TO NEVER BE IMPLANTED AGAIN
18.2.X {*pleasure*} TO WANT THIS IMPLANT AGAIN

INDIVIDUATION IMPLANT-PLATFORM

The following *Platform* is not a part of the former *incident*, but may likely involve some kind of *"Black-Box"* as it was located on the *Backtrack* almost simultaneously with the *"first Implant"* —but again little was known about it (*"command-lines,"* &tc.).

Although it is considered an *"alien-implant"* (used by technologically advanced societies in *this Universe*), it is unclear if it is used on *Earth,* or only among the more advanced *"space races"* (on *"starships,"* &tc.). Again, little is known about it, except that it is used on "prisoners-of-war" before returning them to their homes; or as a way of making prisoners an *"anti-social spy"* before releasing them back to their own side.

Here, we simply have some *command-lines* that can be *defragmented.*

1. TO SEPARATE
2. TO BE AN INDIVIDUAL
3. TO BE THE ONLY ONE
4. ONLY YOU CAN BE GOD
5. ONLY YOU CAN CREATE
6. ONLY YOU CAN BE CAUSE
7. ONLY YOU CAN KNOW
8. ONLY YOU CAN WIN
9. ONLY YOU CAN CHANGE
10. ONLY YOU CAN REASON
11. ONLY YOU CAN CONSTRUCT
12. ONLY YOU CAN BE BEAUTIFUL
13. ONLY YOU CAN RULE
14. ONLY YOU CAN ENLIGHTEN
15. ONLY YOU CAN INFLUENCE
16. ONLY YOU CAN OWN (HAVE)

17. ONLY YOU CAN BE ALIVE

18. ONLY YOU CAN CONTROL

19. ONLY YOU CAN ORGANIZE

20. ONLY YOU CAN BE ADMIRED

21. ONLY YOU CAN ENDURE

22. ONLY YOU CAN BE AN INDIVIDUAL

23. YOU ARE THE ONLY ONE

RESEARCHING PENALTY-UNIVERSES
(*Advanced Technical Research*)

Understanding *"Implanted Penalty-Universes"* (IPU) is a critical component to upper-level *Systemology* and the *Ascension Path.* Our *Systemology* is currently the only *"New Thought"* tradition that works with this data. The following describes research-methods used to discover this information. The original *research-actions* tended to "stir up" as much as they *defragmented*; but this was necessary for collecting additional details.

[IPU are introduced in *AT#4*, along with *basic processing* instructions. That information will be necessary for applying this section. You will also need to refer to the list of *basic* IPU-*Goals* and *negative* IPU-*Goals* given previously in this current manual. This more recently refined procedure is appropriate for *New Standard A.T.* (*Keys to the Kingdom*) as both *defrag-processing* and a *research-action.* However, it is entirely dependent on having access to that existing data collected for IPU (and all other course lessons and manuals).]

Total Defragmentation of the IPU is too steep of a gradient for any *Seeker* to approach all at once. The original intention for focusing research-efforts on IPU emerged only after realizing how much of their *systematic structure* and *symbolism* kept reemerging in *later* (more recent) *Implants* and *incidents*. Then, as more *archetypes* and significant "themes" continued to resurface, it became a research-area of increasing interest. It is also an incredibly *advanced* area to fully handle and investigate.

There are two *classes* (or *groups*) of *processes* applied in this *procedure*. "*Class-2*" requires having *run* all of "*Class-1.*" You will be handling the basic *64* IPU-*Goals*, and their *64* "*inversions*"—the *negative-goals* listed in the previous section titled: "*The False Jewel of Knowledge.*" You will also need to use IPU-*Platforms #1* and *#2* provided in *AT#4*.

You start by lightly *processing* the basic *Goals* (similar to what is described in *AT#4*). As you start *running* deeper into the IPU-content, more of "*What Is*" becomes accessible. Then you start adding *Class-1 processing-actions* gradually until you are *running* all of the steps on each of the basic *Goals*. After you are getting comfortable handling basic *Goals*, you can start to treat the *negative Goals* using a different method (the "*Treadmill Platform*" given later in this manual). [For *Class-2*, see the later section "*Actual Goals & Basic Purposes*" (and steps of the *Standard Procedure for IPU* given in *AT#4*).]

Similar to what is experienced with other *Implant-Platforms*: initially encountering hundreds of *items* can be slow-going. When you first approach a new *pattern*, you'll find that you have to be much more diligent and meticulous in *processing-out* each individual *item*. Eventually, you can *defragment* whole groups of *items*, just by "*Spotting*" the first one in a set. Then it starts to get much faster; where you *contact* the very first *item* of a *pattern*,

Spot various *Goals,* and completely *disperse* an IPU-*terminal* from your *reality-machinery* with only a minute or two of *processing-time.*

Processing-time at *Systemology Level-8* usually consists of approximately equal amounts of: handling *entities*; increasing *spiritual ability* (with *Wizard Level* exercises); and, *research-actions.* This might not always apply to one single *session*; but an *upper-level Seeker* should make sure that they are balancing actual *personal development* with other work. *Defragmenting* IPU *terminals/symbolism* "frees up" a lot of entangled *energetic-mass.* To avoid feeling a *"loss of having something,"* it is important to exercise certainty on *"creative abilities."*

A *Seeker* typically selects which *Goal* (IPU) to *run* based on an *assessment* of the *16 Dynamic Systems.* One of the *Dynamic Systems* will *register* strongest; then you *assess* from the *4 Goals* listed under that *system.* The exact sequence that an individual experienced various original IPU is not likely the same as someone else. However, *later* (more recent) *Implants* did *restimulate* them in specific sequences. The common ones are:

- The natural sequence of the *Dynamic Systems*: from *16* to *1* (*Create* down to *Endure*)—or the reverse: from *1* to *16.* If the inversions are involved, the *negative Goals* are *alternated* with the *positive Goals* (such as with the *incident* that originally established the *negative-items*).

- The natural sequence, like above; but all *64* basic *Goals* come first (*Create* down to *Endure*), *followed by* the *64 negative Goals* in their reverse dynamic order— *Dissipate* (for *Dynamic System 1*) to *Destroy* (*System 16*).

- The *Dynamic Systems* sequence occur in pairs: the upper *Arc* collapsing into the corresponding lower

Sphere. These are: *16* and *8*; *15* and *7*; *14* and *6*; *13* and *5*; *12* and *4*; *11* and *3*; *10* and *2*; then *9* and *1*. Or, the same pattern may occur in an ascending sequence (from *1* to *16*). And again, if inversions are involved, they might either *alternate* with the basic *Goals*, or *follow* after them (in a reverse sequence).

CLASS–1 IPU PROCEDURE

A. IPU-PLATFORM #1. [*AT#4*] The starting point of all IPU procedures. Once the IPU is contacted, *all items* should either be *registering* as *charged*, or they should be completely clear from previous processing. If a particular *item* doesn't give a *Meter-read*: pause and *imagine/create* exactly what the *item* means, then try to *Spot* the actual *item* in the incident again. If unresolved: continue with some of the steps below and return to this one.

B. Check for any *Harmful-Acts* and/or *hold-backs/hold-outs* (*&tc.*) connected with "doing" this *Goal. Spot* these and any associated *justifications.*

C. "*Spot the Hellfire Incident Location*" (on *Earth*); notice the false manifestation of the IPU that was placed there during the *incident.* The *incident*, itself, is introduced in *AT#5*; but the locations needed here are listed previously in *this* manual (along with the *negative-goals*) in the section titled "*The False Jewel of Knowledge.*"

D. "*Spot the Pyramid Location*" (from a mass-*Implant* taking place on *Earth* in a prior *Universe*); and *Spot* the "face" of the *Goal-terminal* (a "beingness" that represents the *Goal*) within the *Pyramid.* [*AT#4*]

E. "*Spot the {Goal-terminal} Saying {the 'Price' of the Goal}.*" [*AT#4*] For the *negative Goals*: spot the *inverted Terminal* saying, "*This means an end to..*"

F. *"Spot Places Where {Goal-terminal} Is Not."* Then: *"Spot Places In The Penalty-Universe Where You Are Not."*

G. IPU-PLATFORM #2. *[AT#4] Spot* IPU-*Symbol items.* There are a few listed in the *AT#4-directory.* Others can be *Spotted* and *defragged-by-realization.* This *Platform* is only used on basic (*positive*) *Goals.*

H. *Scan* researched IPU *details. [AT#4]*

I. Handle any current *Backtrack* restimulation. *Spot "What Is,"* and *defrag-by-realization.*

J. Check for any *Programmed Machine-Entities* (PME) that are currently *being machinery* related to the *Goal. [AT#5]* Note that a *Seeker* should have already *defragged* the more troublesome *machinery,* and should be able to handle this step using the *"Short Version"* of PME-procedure, having each: *spot being made into a machine; spot the first time; spot making others into a machine; spot the top of IPU-Platform #1; identification cleanup (who are you?).*

K. *Run* a *"creativeness" repair-action* of *machinery* related to the *Goal.* This means starting with *creating/imagining* "broken" or "decrepit" versions of the *machinery* and working your way up to "fine-quality" *machinery;* throwing some *copies* away, pushing some in from the outside, *&tc.*

L. *"Spot Something You Must Not {Goal}."* Repeat to a *release-point* for that area.

M. *"Spot People, Groups (&tc.) That You Would Permit To {Goal}."* Repeat to a *release-point* (total willingness to have others doing this *Goal*).

N. *"Spot Places Where {Goal-terminal} Would Be Safe."* Repeat to a *release-point* (total willingness to have it anywhere, or not have it anywhere, by choice).

O. *"Spot Things That The {Goal-terminal} Does Not Own."*

P. *Create/Imagine* battered and beaten versions of the *Goal-terminal* in various places, and say: *"Oh, the poor thing; see how it needs me?"*

Q. *Spot* the top of the *Failure-Implant*. They would tell you to do the *Goal* to some object and then prove how you failed. The *command-item* is: "You failed to *{Goal}*; so you must depend on others to *{Goal}* for you."

R. *Spot* any *"between-lives scene"* for the *Goal* (if known). [This may not be determined accurately until more of the *fragmentation* is *dispersed.*]

S. *Realization*: the collapse of the basic *Goal* becomes the perceived *justification* for (doing) the *negative Goal.*

T. *"Spot The {Goal-terminal} Saying, 'Do You Want To Achieve The Power {To Goal}'."* This occurs during a *"between-lives sequence."* There is a false promise made to you about the *Goal* that pulls you deeper into it.

U. *"Spot The Desire To Shift To The Negative-Goal, So As To Be Rid Of This Penalty-Universe."*

V. *Run "creativeness"* (*imagining copies*: throwing away; pushing in, *&tc.*) on any objects or interesting things used in the IPU. [*Running "creativeness"* at *Wizard-Levels* increases *certainty* on the *ability-to-have* without *compulsively creating* or remaining attached to anything *unknowingly.*]

W. Check for any other *entities* "stirred-up" (or awakened) by this procedure.

X. *Spot* the first few lines of IPU-PLATFORM #1 again.

BETWEEN-LIVES "JUST-CONS"

There are *"Justification Considerations"* that are *Implanted* during *between-lives periods.* This is likely to have occurred earlier on the *Backtrack.* The *definitions* and *symbols* come from the first *Agreements-Universe,* though there is some relationship to the IPU. This *Implant* leads to *considering* "undesirable things" in order to make IPU-*terminals* (others) wrong.

[This advanced research may apply to *"between-lives scenery"* for IPU-handling (above). Note that there may be minor errors on this list. More research-testing is still needed.]

The top of the *Platform* is:

TO BE RIGHT IS NATIVE STATE.

The following *items* will easily *defrag-on-realization.*

1. The agreeing dog says: *"They're wrong because they disagree with everything."*
2. The good bear says: *"They're wrong because they're nasty."*
3. The causative salesman says: *"They're wrong because they chose to be affected."*
4. The free horse says: *"They're wrong because they let themselves be enslaved."*
5. The beautiful cherub says: *"They're wrong because they're ugly."*
6. The logical alligator says: *"They're wrong because they're illogical."*
7. The winning seagull says: *"They're wrong because they're losers."*
8. The healthy flamingo says: *"They're wrong because they're sick."*

9. The enduring dinosaur says: *"They're wrong because they lack persistence."*

10. The skillful bee says: *"They're wrong because they're incompetent."*

11. The interested fish says: *"They're wrong because they have no interest in anything."*

12. The moving rock says: *"They're wrong because they wouldn't move."*

13. The certain computer says: *"They're wrong because they're always confused."*

14. The pleasurable ostrich says: *"They're wrong because they hurt people."*

15. The cube who is right says *"They're wrong because they were made to be wrong to begin with."*

16. The giant who sees truly says: *"They're wrong because they imagine everything."*

17. The visible statue says: *"They're wrong because they keep everything hidden."*

18. The present jellyfish says: *"They're wrong because they're never there when they should be."*

19. The smart ibis-bird says: *"They're wrong because they're stupid."*

20. The just flame says: *"They're wrong because they're unjust."*

21. The stork who brings order says: *"They're wrong because they make everything chaotic."*

22. The wakeful whale says: *"They're wrong because they're always asleep."*

23. The humorous seal says: *"They're wrong because they're too serious."*

24. The squirrel who plans says: *"They're wrong because they leave everything to chance."*

25. The mechanical man who is whole says: *"They're wrong because they keep falling apart and fragmenting."*

26. The strong robot says: *"They're wrong because they're weak."*
27. The real peacock says: *"They're wrong because they're unreal."*
28. The independent monkey says: *"They're wrong because they let themselves be owned."*
29. The infinite spirit says: *"They're wrong because they're located."*
30. The courageous lion says: *"They're wrong because they're cowards."*
31. The knowing owl says: *"They're wrong because they don't know anything."*
32. The sharing raccoon says: *"They're wrong because they're greedy."*
33. The calm deer says: *"They're wrong because they're nervous."*
34. The sea urchin who is different says: *"They're wrong because they're all the same."*
35. The outgoing turtle says: *"They're wrong because they're withdrawn."*
36. The oriented wooden man says: *"They're wrong because they're disoriented."*
37. The silent cat says: *"They're wrong because they're noisy."*
38. The started snail says: *"They're wrong because they let themselves be stopped."*
39. The ethical octopus says: *"They're wrong because they're all criminals."*
40. The reasonable knight says: *"They're wrong because they're arbitrary and have no reason for what they do."*
41. The responsible possum says: *"They're wrong because they're irresponsible."*
42. The independent corn-man says: *"They're wrong because they follow the crowd and wouldn't act*

independently."

43. The helpful caterpillar says: *"They're wrong because they harm everything."*

44. The alive raggedy doll says: *"They're wrong because they're dead."*

45. The timeless mountain says: *"They're wrong because they cannot endure."*

46. The social potato man says: *"They're wrong because they're all anti-social."*

47. The trusting rabbit says: *"They're wrong because they distrust everything."*

48. The remembering elephant says: *"They're wrong because they forget everything."*

49. The young gorilla says: *"They're wrong because they're old."*

50. The perceptive mouse says: *"They're wrong because they're blind."*

51. The loving flower says: *"They're wrong because they hate."*

52. The serene swan says: *"They're wrong because they're always getting upset."*

53. The big ant says: *"They're wrong because they're small."*

54. The fast horse girl says: *"They're wrong because they're slow."*

55. The industrious donkey says: *"They're wrong because they're lazy."*

56. The truthful walrus says: *"They're wrong because they lie."*

57. The pleasant eagle says: *"They're wrong because they act horribly."*

58. The harmonious angel says: *"They're wrong because they create discord."*

59. The participating kangaroo says: *"They're wrong because they wouldn't participate."*

60. The wise alligator person says: *"They're wrong because they're all fools."*

61. The unicorn who has faith says: *"They're wrong because they're distrustful."*

62. The good snake says: *"They're wrong because they're all evil."*

63. The feeling porcupine says: *"They're wrong because they have no feeling."*

64. The creative fool says: *"They're wrong because they're destructive."*

THE "AGREEMENTS UNIVERSE"
(*Advanced Technical Research*)

The *"Agreements-Universe Implant"* is that *entry-point incident* through which we arrived at the *Agreements Universe* (see *AT#1*)—which began as a simple *agreed-upon Space* in which to *Create* "things" and "play" *Games*. The original *Jewel of Knowledge* impressed upon us the need to enforce a common set of *shared-agreements* in order to operate within the same frame-of-reference or *Universe*.

This *Implant* is unique in that we all went through it by choice, rather than being forced. We "solved" an era of individualized misaligned *Spaces* by constructing an *Implant* that installed a common set of definitions and *reality-agreements*. We rushed to throw ourselves into it and came out into the first *agreed-upon Space*.

As described in *AT#1*: *Alpha-Spirits* divided up into teams, with each working on one "sub-universe" of the *Implant*. Then they were all combined together, and the result became the *Agreements-Universe*. But, of course, each individual was only really aware of the one part that they contributed to working on. The full "set" was not known to anyone until we experienced the *incident*.

Creating components of *reality* without knowing the others meant some things didn't line up or correspond properly to one another—and this obviously led to some problems. It is probably the most *basic* of all the trouble we have since gotten into.

But, notice here that this was not *enforced* on an *Alpha-Spirit*, it was done by choice; and an individual is not likely to fully "drop" these *agreements* (even during *processing*) unless they are completely willing to "drop" contact and communication with *everyone else* that also went into this trap.

Therefore, the best we can hope from the current research is to *defrag* some of the *turbulence* from the *incident* and increase *Awareness* on the wide-view of the exact nature of the *Game* that is actually going on. We can't use *processing* to pull out of the *Universe-Laws* and *agreements* all at once—since such would simply result in chaos anyways—but we can follow a gradient *Pathway* of increasing *freedom* and lessening *barriers*.

Eventually, we might reach a point where we can all get together and go back to change the basic-level *reality-agreements* around a bit so that we can have a better game. But, in the meantime, we also have the IPU to *process-out*, and those really act as a *basic* foundation to our *fragmentation*—since they *were enforced*. But, that doesn't mean we cannot gain benefit now from delving further on the *Backtrack* to see the *agreements*.

The *Agreements-Universe Implant* (AUI) isn't full of hidden implications and subtle meanings. It simply puts up quite a "stack" of simpleminded conceptual definitions, such as you would display for children's educational programs. As such, the definitions are not in "*words*" or "*commands.*"

The definitions present dividing lines that separate a concept into two classes—or else a dichotomy of opposites, such as "*Good*" and "*Bad.*" But, if you are imagining a clean "line" running down a sheet of paper dividing these things, you'd be wrong. The definitions on one "sheet" do not necessarily align with those in the remainder of the "stack." For example, there is another appearance of "*Good*" on the agreements-list that means "*Holy*" as opposed to the one above that means "*Nice.*"

The incident begins with being a part of a crowd and "rushing to get into agreement." Then you pass through an *inverted golden-triangle*, which is the symbol of the *Agreements-Universe*: representing all things focusing down to a single point of *agreement*. Then you get the first "*item-line*" of the *Platform*.

The AUI-*Platform* starts identical to the first several *item-lines* of IPU-*Platform #1* (see *AT#4*); but instead of a "*goal*," the word "AGREE" is inserted. The top of the *Platform* (1.1.1) is then:

TO AGREE IS NATIVE STATE.

The basic sequence of the AUI is:

1. An introduction; like IPU-*Platform #1*.

2. A series of definition sub-universes.

3. A period where you make various *agreements* (after being shown the need for each, you *agree* to it).

The top of the AUI can be *run* this way:

A. *"Spot 'rushing to get into agreement'."*

B. *"Spot 'going through the inverted golden-triangle'."*

C. *"Spot:* **TO AGREE IS NATIVE STATE."**

D. *"Look prior to this; Spot 'deciding that you need to agree'."*

E. (If necessary) *"Spot 'getting others to decide to agree'."*

F. (If necessary) *"Spot 'working on building the Agreements-Universe'."*

The *Platform* then runs just like IPU-*Platform #1*, down through *line-item-*1.6.3:

TO AGREE IS THE BASIS FOR ALL DECISIONS.

The next six *line-items* are:

TO AGREE IS TO ACHIEVE ___.

And the keywords are: *Knowledge, Power, Wisdom, Affinity (or Likingness), Reality,* and *Communication.*

The next *item*:

TO AGREE IS TO PLAY THE GAME.

Then all *64* of the IPU-*Goals* are each given in the form of:

TO AGREE IS TO {*Goal***}.**

Note: this may actually be the first origination of the IPU-*Goals* and the *Dynamic Systems.*

Then: **TO AGREE IS TO KNOW THE MEANING OF THINGS.**

And then the definitions come. For each one you enter a kind of cathedral-looking building through an archway (or maybe it's another *inverted triangle*). The first *item-lines* of each is:

TO AGREE IS TO KNOW THE MEANING OF ___.

The dichotomy would be inserted for the *item*—such as

"*goodness and badness*" — followed by a pair of scenes (one to represent each side of the definition) for each of the *16 Dynamic Systems.* These "scenes" have not yet really been researched. One of the early ones shows a "*Good Bear*" building things and then a "*Bad Bear*" comes and kicks them down. Basic, simple, imagery of this nature. One of the challenges is that later (more recent) *incidents* have added more layers of *fragmentation* over these definitions and *agreements*, which requires clearing out before we can see more.

The following AUI-*list* was compiled by *assessment* rather than our researchers *running* each one. This is still a tentative sequence; but since it does *run* well, it's become as close to a standard as we currently have. [It is possible this should also include "*Serene/Upset*" somewhere in it.]

1. Agreeing / Disagreeing
2. Good (Nice) / Bad {*bears*}
3. Causative / Effected
4. Winning / Losing {*seagull*}
5. Logical / Illogical {*alligator*}
6. Beautiful / Ugly
7. Strong / Weak
8. Interested / Disinterested
9. Certain / Confused
10. Healthy / Sick
11. Sane / Crazy (Truth / Hallucination)
12. Free / Enslaved
13. Enduring / Transient
14. Fast / Slow
15. Right / Wrong
16. Present / Absent (Always / Never)
17. Moving / Stopped (Motion / No-Motion)
        (Changing / Fixed)
18. Seen / Invisible

19. Gives Pleasure / Gives Pain
20. Humorous / Sullen
21. Smart / Dumb {*birds*}
22. Brings Order / Brings Chaos
23. Awake / Unconscious (Asleep) {*dogs*}
24. Just / Unjust
25. Divided / Combined
26. Real / Unreal
27. Courageous / Cowardly {*lion*}
28. Located / Infinite
29. Knowing / Ignorant
30. Owned / Available
31. Volitional / Controlled
32. Older / Younger
33. Wise / Foolish
34. Same / Different
35. Rigid / Fluid
36. Oriented / Disoriented
37. Connected / Withdrawn
38. Truthful / Deceitful
39. Ethical / Criminal
40. Skillful / Incompetent
41. Started / Stopped
42. Responsible / Irresponsible
43. Happy / Sad
44. Singularly Owned / Shared
45. Helpful / Harmful
46. Playful / Serious
47. Trusting / Distrusting
48. Alive / Dead {*raggedy doll*}
49. Loving / Hating {*flowers*}
50. Perceptive / Blind {*mice*}
51. Flexible / Fixed
52. Social / Anti-Social
53. Aware / Unaware
54. Big / Small

55. Reasonable / Arbitrary

56. Industrious / Lazy

57. Quiet / Noisy

58. Numb / Feeling

59. Harmony / Discord

60. Participating / Separated Out

61. Greedy / Sharing

62. Faith / Disbelief

63. Good (Holy) / Evil

64. Remembering / Forgetful

65. Created / Destroyed

ACTUAL GOALS & BASIC PURPOSES
(*Advanced Technical Research*)

One *Implant* that really *fragmented* our *goals* and *purposes* early on the *Backtrack*, is referred to simply as "*The Tread-mill.*" It was constructed in the original "*Games Universe.*" It is unclear whether it was only used as general punishment *there*, or whether it was also part of the *sentencing-incident* where an individual is sent down to the "*next lower*" *Universe.*

A simplified version of each IPU and its *Goals* were used for this *Implant*. A sub-universe dramatizing a related *negative-Goal* was attached to the end of each one. The IPU-version establishes the *negative-Goal* by collapsing the basic (*positive*) *Goal* down to *zero*—to a point of complete apathy, overwhelm, and solidity. Then it is dramatized to essentially "*un-manifest*" everything until you "go out the bottom" of the *Alpha-Awareness* scale.

At the end, you've basically destroyed everything so that there is no "*universe*" left. This leaves you with a false "*native state*" (which is a consideration of one's *basic original nature*) that is made to equal the "*native state*" at the top of the *next* basic (*positive*) *Goal*. This ongoing "scrolling quality" of the *Implant* is the only reason we call it "*The Treadmill*."

One can almost liken this to an old-time cartoon, where the individual remains mostly stationary, while the background scenery "scrolls" to give an illusion of movement and travel. The bottom of the final *negative-Goal* was connected to the top of the first basic (*positive*) *Goal* again, which just kept one moving through all *128* total *Goals*. Once the *Implanting* really starts to take hold, the *Alpha-Spirit* gets a "spinning" sensation.

The basic *Platform* for "*The Treadmill*" begins just like the original IPU (*Platform #1*). [See *AT#4*] However the "*Symbols*" part (*Platform #2, &tc.*) is not used. Instead, the *Implant* goes straight to this *item*:

TO {*goal*} IS TO POSTULATE BEING THE {*terminal*}.

Then a handful of *items* duplicating the IPU scenery occur. But the basic (*positive*) *Goals* end differently. Once the *terminal's body* dies, you are able to "*exteriorize*" from the grave. Once you are floating above the grave, then the *items* from the "*Treadmill Crossover Platform*" begin. This has you abandon the basic *Goal*, then shifts you into *negative-Goal*.

The *fourth item* of the *Crossover Platform* [STEP-D of the sequence (below)] is the end of the basic (*positive*) *Goal*. When *running* it, you should spot the top of the basic *Goal* ("*native state*" item) at this point, because some B.E. and *Fused-Groups* (*AT#5*) are stuck holding on this point, trying to avoid the start of the *negative-Goal*. Use the above information and the IPU details given in *AT#4* for *running* basic *Goals*. The following *Crossover Platform* is *only* used for *negative-Goals* in this *incident.*

<u>TREADMILL CROSSOVER PLATFORM</u>

The *Crossover Platform* begins at the point of the *incident* when you are floating about the grave of the dead IPU-*terminal*. This *Platform* is used for the *negative-Goals* as they appear in *"The Treadmill"*; but this is also the experimental procedure used for handling specifically *negative* IPU-*Goals* wherever they appear in an *Implant* (such as the original *"False Jewel"* given earlier in this manual).

This is the sequence:

A. TO {*positive goal*} IS TO REGRET EVER HAVING {*positive goal-ed*}.

B. TO {*positive goal*} IS TO ABANDON THE GOAL OF {*positive goal*}.

C. TO ABANDON {*positive goal*} IS TO SURVIVE.

D. TO ABANDON {*positive goal*} IS TO FORGET EVER HAVING {*positive goal-ed*}.

   (*"Spot the 'native state' item at the top of Platform #1."*)

E. {You begin to hate.}

F. {You decide to get even.}

G. {You choose a new goal.}

H. {You choose to (*negative goal*).}

I. IN THE BEGINNING, NOW, AND FOREVER, IS THE DECISION; AND THE DECISION IS TO {*negative goal*}.

J. TO {*negative goal*} IS THE ULTIMATE PURPOSE.

K. TO {*negative goal*} IS TO ACHIEVE ___.
   (The *keywords/items* are: *Freedom, Success, Enlightenment, Truth, Beauty, Knowledge, Power, Control, Respect, &tc.* Usually you only have to lightly

spot a few of these to contact the next *item* below.)

L. **TO** {*negative goal*} **IS TO BE THE** {*negative terminal*}.
(At this point of the incident, the *negative-Goal terminal* appears.)

When *processing-out negative-Goals*:
Spot the following data (*where available*).

1. The "*inversion scene*" (used in later *Implants*).
2. This *Implant* making you abandon the basic (*positive*) *Goal*.
3. The top of the basic *Goal* ("*native state*" *item*).
4. The action of the *negative-terminal* in doing *Goal*.
5. The *Hellfire Incident* location.
6. The *Pyramid* location.
7. "*This Means An End To* ___" statement said by the *negative-terminal*.
8. The "*Survive*" statement said by the *negative-terminal*.

OPPOSITIONAL FRAGMENTATION

Games, *Goals*, and *Purposes*, are critical components of our *Systemology*, because they are key to fully understanding the thoughts and behaviors inherent in the *Human Condition*. This is an area that is often more challenging to *confront*, because an individual is likely keeping "one eye" on any signs, or validation, of whatever their own *Goals* and *Purposes* were before they were all *fragmented*. Of course, such is not really within view until the layers of *fragmentation* have been stripped off of whatever we were once interested in.

Developing experimental material for researching the original "*Oppositional-Goals-Problem Implant*" was among the more difficult research-efforts (perhaps second only to the "*Big Splitter Incident*" that is covered in the next section). One of the reasons is that early on, while some gains were made, these areas often stirred-up a lot of trouble for researchers. [Review relevant data in *AT#1* and *AT#2* before handling this section.]

This *Implanting-Incident* occurs while going down a long *"ringed-tube"* as a *transfer-shift* between the *"Thought-Energy Universe"* and what became the *"Conflict Universe."* Each of the "rings" installs another *"oppositional-goal-problem"* as you pass it. It is structured after the IPU-*Goals*. [After this transition, an *Alpha-Spirit* ceases to maintain a *Beingness* as an *energy-sphere-type "body"* and starts to *Identify* with a more material structure.]

The *Implant* installs each *Goal* with *imprints* of 5 different *Identity-phases*. They are:

1. *Goal-terminal*
2. *Oppositional-terminal* (who becomes the "target" of *harmful-acts*)
3. *Encouraging-terminal* (who wants *Goal*, enforces *Goal*; acts as a third party)
4. *Discouraging-terminal* (who doesn't want *Goal*, inhibits *Goal*; you are constantly *justifying* the *Goal* and your *harmful-acts* to this person, which makes the *considerations* "stick")
5. *A Victim* (who unjustly suffers from your *harmful-acts*; this *imprints* you with *regret*)

The experience of each *Goal* is only a short *Platform* of *"This Means __"* *symbols*, which explain the 5 different *Identity-phases* (or *"personas"*) and what's *supposed* to be *expected* from the "scenery." Then the *Implant-Platform* installs a few *"splitter-items"* while an energy-wave is emitted to *enforce* a *5-way split*.

At this point, your *Awareness/Beingness* "splits" into 5

313

fragments, so that *you* actually become *all 5 phases*, but compartmented (hidden) from yourself. Now you are all ready for the "scenery" to begin—but it doesn't; instead you find yourself at the next "ring" of the "tube" and getting the next *Goal* in the sequence. Each time, you are expecting some *pocket-universe drama* to unfold; but you just end up at the next "ring."

After the *Implanting-Incident* ends with the final *Goal*, you end up in the *Conflict-Universe*. There is no "imaginary scenery" or "pocket-universe" where you play things out. All of that *fragmented charge* that is accumulated from experiencing all *64 Goals* (multiplied by *splitting* into *5 phases* for each) of the *Implant* is brought down to the *Conflict-Universe* and dramatized there—in an *actual Shared-Universe*. It is *you* that ends up enacting all the actual events in "real life"—but by following the *implanted* "pattern-of-action."

Your primary activity in the *Conflict-Universe* was running around unbeknownst to *5 split-Identities*, and then trying to *align* with the other four connected to the same *Goal*. You try to be the basic *Goal-terminal*, but your *viewpoint* is really from any of the *5*, depending on the circumstances. *Systematically*: while this is occurring, you have a *sub-identity* attached to (or "in") each of the other *4 phases*; and you, in turn, also are infected by a *sub-identity* of each of the others. This holds you in a specific *phase* and contributes to events. Early on, in the *Conflict-Universe*, this activity all played out with great precision. Later, it became quite convoluted, and none of the activities or *phases* properly aligned with each other. Yet, we still had *5 hidden viewpoints* (*per Goal*) running around and causing trouble in attempts to keep the *implanted-drama* going.

The fact remains that we really *are creating* our own *opposition*, even if *unknowingly*; and most of our *Awareness* or *spiritual power* (or ZU) is still entangled in doing this in present-time. Things are so out-of-alignment in *this Physical Universe*, and in such a way that, with hundreds of these *split-fragments* all working at cross-purposes, the end result is a balance of forces that keeps things fairly "solid" and difficult to change purely by *Alpha-Thought* (*postulate*).

When *running* the *Imprinting-Incident*, the "*This Means ___*" items are accompanied by 3-D *images* (*Imprints*) similar to the IPU-*symbols* (except with different content). But this *restimulates* the "top" of the IPU—whereas most *Implants* stir-up the "bottom." The result is a *being* that is a *super-charged maniac* ready to enthusiastically dive full into the *Goal*.

It is best to work from an established *Platform* when actually *processing-out Implant-fragmentation* (such as what a *Seeker* has been using for their *upper-level* work). However, having this data requires researching it. This area is not included in former manuals because it is still in a "*research-phase.*" To *run* it fully would require researching specific data on each one of the *imprint-picture items* for all *64 Goals*. And "skipping" the *Imprints* for a *Goal* seems to have a tendency to turn on "depressive fatigue" until they *are* found and *run*.

Basic research to establish an experimental procedure (*Platform*) for *oppositional-goals-problems* (OGP) handling occurred in two stages and hit many obstacles. These were easily overcome once we started applying the "*Locational Procedure*" ("*Point To The Being You Divided From*") after each of *item-lines 10* through *14*. This was not available for handling the "*splitting items*" when research first began. It is not indicated in the Platform, but it really is the key to using this for *defragmentation*. The *first item* is the actual *oppositional-goals-problem* (OGP) stated as a personal *consideration*. [Most, if not all, *fragmentation* will usually *disperse* by *item-line 15*.]

1. TO {goal} {target} AND {desired effect on others} OR I WILL {harmful-act}
2. THIS MEANS (to do goal)
3. THIS MEANS (desired effect)
4. THIS MEANS (harmful-act) {picture imprints it being done to the *oppositional-terminal*}
5. THIS MEANS ENCOURAGEMENT {picture imprints *encouraging-terminal*}
6. THIS MEANS DISCOURAGEMENT {picture imprints *discouraging-terminal*}
7. THIS MEANS OPPOSITION {imprint of *oppositional-terminal*}
8. THIS MEANS REGRET {picture imprints you doing the harmful-act to the *victim*}
9. THIS MEANS YOU {imprint of *basic Goal-terminal*}
10. TO {goal} IS TO BE THE {discouraging-terminal} AND DISCOURAGE MYSELF FROM {harmful-act} AND NEVER LET MYSELF KNOW THAT I AM DOING THIS.
11. TO {goal} IS TO BE THE {encouraging-terminal} AND ENCOURAGE MYSELF TO {harmful-act} AND NEVER LET MYSELF KNOW THAT I AM DOING THIS.
12. TO {goal} IS TO BE THE {oppositional-terminal} AND OPPOSE MYSELF FROM {goal-ing} AND NEVER LET MYSELF KNOW THAT I AM DOING THIS.
13. TO {goal} IS TO BE THE {victim} AND SUFFER UNJUSTLY AND NEVER LET MYSELF KNOW THAT I AM DOING THIS.
14. TO {goal} IS TO BE THE {basic-terminal} AND {do goal} AND NEVER LET MYSELF KNOW THAT I AM DOING THIS.

The next *command-lines* are *Implanted* simultaneously in *5 locations*; one for each *split-identity phase*. Rather than going immediately to *item-15*, better *defrag*-results have been achieved by taking each *phase* in turn and *spotting* the other *4 phases* from that viewpoint. For example: conceiving yourself as being the *basic-terminal*, and *spotting* each of the other *phases*; then taking up being the *oppositional-terminal*, and *spotting* each of the other *phases, &tc.*

[A "cloud" of B.E. might suddenly be perceived as active during one of these "*spottings.*" If so, hold the *viewpoint* for the *phase* you're on, and start *dispersing* the *entities* by *acknowledgment, &tc.* You can even run through the above mentioned *spotting-steps* a second time if you find a lot of this happening.]

After using all *5 viewpoints* to *spot* each other (as described above), you should be able to *spot item-15* in all *5 locations* simultaneously; and if so, this is usually enough to *defragment* the remaining *Implant-Platform*.

At whatever point in the *Platform* that the whole "*oppositional-goals-problem*" (OGP) *disperses*, skip to the end. Note that the *5 locations* are likened to "blades" of a *5-bladed fan* that are propelling around a center *location* that your *Awareness* can't occupy.

15. TO {*Goal*} IS TO BE ALL THESE 5 OTHERS AND HIDE FROM MYSELF FOREVER
16. TO {*Goal*} IS TO BE ALL THESE 5 OTHERS AND INSPIRE MYSELF FOREVER
17. TO {*Goal*} IS TO BE ALL THESE 5 OTHERS AND COMPEL MYSELF TO RE-ENACT THIS FOREVER
18. TO {*Goal*} IS TO BE ALL THESE 5 OTHERS AND GO AROUND UNKNOWN TO MYSELF
18x. TO {*Goal*} IS TO BE ALL THESE 5 OTHERS AND COMPEL OTHERS TO RE-ENACT THIS WITH ME

[You are hit by an *energetic-mass* containing the emotion of distrust along with the *next item*.]

19. TO {*Goal*} IS TO BE ALL THESE 5 OTHERS AND AS EACH ONE, DETEST BEING ALL THE OTHERS

20. TO {*Goal*} IS TO BE ALL THESE 5 OTHERS AND AS EACH ONE, KNOW THAT MY VIEWPOINT IS THE BEST (compared to the others)

21. TO {*Goal*} IS TO BE ALL THESE 5 OTHERS AND DENY RESPONSIBILITY FOR DOING THIS, FOREVER

22. TO {*Goal*} IS TO BE SPLIT INTO 5 PARTS AND NEVER LET MYSELF KNOW WHAT I AM DOING

[You are impacted by a *"splitter" energy-beam. (Spot the impact.)*]

23. TO {*Goal*} IS TO BE DIVIDED 5 WAYS AGAINST MYSELF AND HIDE MY ACTIONS FROM MYSELF AS I MANIFEST ALL OF THIS

24. TO {*Goal*} IS TO BE DIVIDED 5 WAYS AGAINST MYSELF AND NEVER REALLY KNOW WHAT IS HAPPENING

[An *energy-implosion* occurs at each of the *5 locations*; each collapses and disappears from view, leaving a *hollow-spot* (*vacuum-of-space*).]

25. TO {*Goal*} IS TO FORGET THAT THIS EVER HAPPENED

After *running* this procedure on a single *Goal*: "*Scan*" the *Backtrack* for times when you dramatized this *Implant*; *Spot* any *harmful-acts* against others, and *spot* being in the other *viewpoints* and contributing to the activity/event-sequence. Check for any dramatization of the *Implant* in *this lifetime*; *identify* which *phase* you were in, and perform this *spotting* action on it as well.

"OGP" DATA & TERMINALS-LIST

The OGP are related to the *64* IPU-*Goals*. In addition to

the *imprint-pictures* and *terminals* (*phases*), there is a unique OGP-*consideration* (*item-1*) for each *Goal*. There is limited data for this; it requires more research. But, where available, the OGP-*consideration* and associated *Identity-phases* for some *Goals* are listed below. The list is numbered based on IPU *Goal-sequencing*. The *phases* are in the *1-to-5* ordering given earlier.

1. CREATE OGP: "To create chaos and overwhelm others or I will blow them up."
—Phases: *God, Satan/Devil, Priest, Virgin, Seer.*

3. MANIFEST OGP: "To manifest intricate ornaments and have them praised or I will cut out their guts."
—Phases: *Artisan (craftsman), Scientist, Fishmonger, Policeman, Priest.*

4. IMAGINE OGP: "To imagine fine stories and have them appreciated or I will strangle everyone."
—Phases: *Writer, Cynical Father, Actor, Critic, Publisher.*

6. UNDERSTAND OGP: "To understand secrets and make others tell (obey?) (recognize my power?) or I will stab them all."
—Phases: *Detective, Criminal, Police Captain, Businessman, Prostitute.*

8. LEARN OGP: "To learn the nature of the *Universe* and be supported or I will overwhelm them all."
—Phases: *Scientist, Preacher, Teacher, Wife, Stupid Person.*

11. COMPETE OGP: "To compete (at boxing) and have the people cheer or I will beat them all up."
—Phases: *Boxer, Newspaperman, Manager, Lover, Businessman.*

15. CHANGE OGP: "To change peoples' nature and have them all be happy about this or I will strike them all blind."
—Phases: *Poet, Priest, Prostitute, Politician, Scientist.*

16. (BRING) ORDER OGP: "To bring order to society and be supported in this or I will torture (burn?) their bodies (flesh?)."
—Phases: *Lawmaker, Criminal, Merchant, Priestess, Nurse.*

19. GUIDE OGP: "To guide settlers and have them respect me or I will burn it all down."
—Phases: *Scout, Wagonleader, Salesman (Trader), Lover (Frontier Girl), Little Girl.*

21. CONSTRUCT OGP: "To construct spiral staircases and have them admired or I will trap them all."
—Phases: *Carpenter, Scornful Person, Salesman, Art Critic, Sexy Girl.*

24. STRUCTURE OGP: "To structure reality and be worshiped as a god or I will destroy them all."
—Phases: *Savior, Priest, Prostitute, General, Temple Virgin.*

33. ENLIGHTEN OGP: "To preach goodness and keep them from sin or else I will torture them."
—Phases: *Minister (?), Sinner, Ruler, Conqueror, (?).*

34. CONVERT OGP: "To convert unbelievers and make them (honest?) or I will implant them to believe."
—Phases: *Priest, Scoffer, Messenger (of the gods?), Empress, (?).*

45. GROW OGP: "To grow flowers and have them make people feel good or I will sacrifice everyone."
—Phases: *Priestess, Policeman, Carpenter, Mother, Priest.*

46. DISCOVER OGP: "To discover truth.. and?"
—Phases: *(?)*

47. HEAL OGP: "To heal illness and receive the peoples' gratitude or I will make their bodies rot away."
—Phases: *Healer, Priest, Politician, Policeman, Priestess.*

51. UNITE OGP: "To unite the workers in building wondrous projects or I will trick them all into slavery forever."

—Phases: *Engineer, (?), Politician, (?), (?).*

54. COOPERATE OGP: "To get people to cooperate in maintaining society and become famous for doing this or I will betray everyone."

—Phases: *Policeman, Criminal, Lawmaker, Priest, Prostitute.*

55. PARTICIPATE OGP: "To participate in dancing and be admired for my beauty of form or else I will cut their hearts out."

—Phases: *Dancer, Critic, Father, Innocent Girl, Lover.*

56. EXPAND OGP: "To expand knowledge and be admired for my genius or I will blow them all up."

—Phases: *Scientist, Priest, Psychiatrist, Girl, Ruler.*

57. REPRODUCE OGP: "To reproduce fine books and have the quality admired or I will inject them all with insanity (with a drug)."

—Phases: *Scribe (Scholar), Peasant, Scientist (Professor), Wife (Lover), Carpenter.*

58. SATISFY OGP: "To satisfy conventions and be respected or I will poison them all."

—Phases: *Girl, Elder Woman, Father, Lover, Publisher.*

59. JOIN OGP: "To join people together and have them be thankful for my help or I will throw things at them."

—Phases: *Prophet, Businessman, Priest, Lawmaker, Inventor.*

60. CARE (FOR) OGP: "To care for children (and keep them safe) and be loved for it or I will claw everyone's eyes out."

—Phases: *(?)*

61. FEEL OGP: "To feel alive and gain everyone's agreement or I will drive them all crazy."

—Phases: *Athlete, Lawmaker, Coach, Lawyer, Professor.*

62. REPLENISH OGP: "To replenish the wildlife and be praised for restoring the planet or I will take it away from them."

—Phases: *Ecologist, Businessman, Housewife, Politician, Priest.*

63. EAT OGP: "To eat people and gain strength from their 'souls' or I will rend their 'souls' forever."
—Phases: *Cannibal, Enemies, Lover, Priest, Explorer.*

64. ENDURE OGP: "To endure existence and be left alone or I will enslave them all."
—Phases: *Carpenter, Juvenile Delinquent, Wife, Detective, Salesman(?).*

After the basic (positive) Goals, this continues with the *inversions* (*negative-Goals* run in the reverse *Goals-Sequence order*).

INV 59. SEPARATE OGP: "To separate people from groups and be praised for helping them or I will leave forever."
—Phases: *Messiah, Ruler, Ruler's Mistress, General, Slave Girl.*

INV 58. RIDICULE OGP: "To ridicule social conventions and have everyone amused by this or I will hide forever."
—Phases: *Publisher, Father, Lover, Girl, Elder Woman.*

INV 54. INVALIDATE OGP: "To get people to individuate from groups which exploit them and have them feel good that I did this or I will shoot myself."
—Phases: *Prostitute, Priest, Criminal, Lawmaker, Politician.*

INV 48. ROT OGP: "To rot other's minds and make them suggestible or I will dissipate myself."
—Phases: *Salesman, Professor, Politician, Judge, Girl.*

INV 29. PERVERT OGP: "To pervert little children and have all the parents fear me or I will hang myself forever."
—Phases: *Pornographer, Judge (Moralist), Publisher, Parents, Little Girl.*

INV 16. (BRING) CHAOS OGP: "To bring chaos and overwhelm everybody or I will hide myself away forever."

—Phases: *Dark Priest (Black Magician), Criminal (?), Lawmaker (?), Prostitute (?), Temple Virgin (?).*

INV 4. DISILLUSION OGP: "To disillusion writers and force society to accept my judgment or I will bash my head in."

—Phases: *Critic, Writer, Father, Publisher, Actor.*

INV 3X. DRAIN OGP: "To drain emotion and make everyone apathetic or I will dissipate myself/others forever."

—Phases: *Artisan (craftsman), Scientist, Fishmonger, Policeman, Priest.*

INV 1. DESTROY OGP: "To destroy all of creation and be worshiped or I will uncreate myself/others forever."

—Phases: *Devil, God, Worshipers, Artisan, Virgin.*

THE "BIG-SPLITTER" INCIDENT
(*Advanced Technical Research*)

This final section of our *advanced training* program presents the experimental research (and procedures) for handling the "*Big Splitter Implant*." Best we can determine at this time: this is the "*entry-into-the-Symbols-Universe*"-*incident.* We know that it occurs after an *Alpha-Spirit* had already experienced "*The Treadmill*" in the *Games-Universe.* [The *Big-Splitter* is constructed to restimulate elements of *The Treadmill.*]

This section includes a new standard procedure. However, for training purposes, we also include the prior research and experimental procedures for this *Implant.* The material has not yet been refined for a standard presentation. This means much of the written background data and explanation still appears with the prior experimental versions, and a *Seeker* should study *all* of its parts before applying anything from this section.

While originally researching and applying earlier versions of this work, we did not yet have the *"Locational Procedure"* (*AT#5*). As a result, *defragmentation* of *"split-fragments"* required many additional steps that the new standard procedure does not. This makes the new standard seem like an oversimplification—but it *is* effective if a *Seeker* understands the true nature of what they are handling with it. Older procedures and background data are included to assist this. [Older methods are still effective; but often more complex.]

During the *"Big Splitter" incident*, an *Alpha-Spirit* is made to *split-off* (*fragment*) into *128* types of *entities*, each of which has various functions—such as keeping the *Universe* manifested, or blocking perception, *&tc*. The *Implant-pattern* was repeated multiple times, using each of the IPU-*Goals*. This means we have a lot of *fragmented-pieces* of ourselves *being* these various things. [A *Seeker* should *disperse* some accessible surface *charge* from the *Implanted Penalty-Universes* (*AT#4*) prior to treating this section (if they have not already).]

New Standard "Entity-Handling" includes:

A. Using the list of *128-entity types*: check the type of *entity* for a *Meter-read* and *spot* where it is; or *spot* one that is *being* this type.

B. *Locational Procedure*. [*AT#5*] Have the *entity "point to the being"* it *"divided from."* At *Wizard-Levels*, this is usually sufficient to *disperse* or *release* the *entity* (*split-*

fragment). You may have to get it to *point* a few times until it gets its own certainty. It doesn't matter "where" it's pointing, or if *you* are certain about it; it is the *entity* that requires certainty in order to *release* itself. If necessary, apply the next step.

C. *Identification Procedure.* [AT#5] If necessary, have the *entity* "*Identify*" itself properly by applying the "*Who Are You?*"-PCL (getting the "*me*" answer), until it *disperses* or *releases.*

D. Check again and repeat A-to-C until no more *entities* are responding for that type.

Go through the entire *entity-type-list* from top to bottom, handling anything that reacts—and not working too hard at trying to "wake" a lot up. When you have completed with *running* one cycle through the *list*: start at the top and go through it again. Repeat this until the whole *list* is *defragmented* (doesn't *register*).

After working with the *New Standard* method, a *Seeker* can use the previously researched methods (given later) to see if any more *entities* are "awakened" (show up) for *processing*. It is quite possible that some of the earlier experimental methods are still necessary for *total defragmentation* of this area, which is another reason we have retained them in this manual (in addition to educating about progressive research).

You could apply the full *Splitter-Platform*, using the most basic (first) IPU-*Goal*—"*To Create*"—and then *run* the above steps again, this time going much deeper (unless you have already hit the main structure of it and taken the whole thing apart).

This final area we are treating in this final training

manual might actually be able to be *run* all the way toward a point of major *realization/recognition* that handles *all* of the *split-fragments* of yourself. As yet, no one (within our organization that we know of) has taken this work to such an ultimate *end-point*.

One of the final activities an individual theoretically conducts prior to a true *"Wizard Level-8 Ascension"* is the *re-collection* of all *split-fragments* present in the *Universe*; because an *Alpha-Spirit* must get out "in wholeness," without any lingering attachments or connectivity to *this Physical Universe.* Otherwise a "part" of us would still remain, and we would not be truly free to manifest or locate our *Awareness* fully on some other plane.

If any of our fixed *"anchor-points"* remain here, we could just as easily be "snapped back in" to this *reality*; or "collapse-in to" it, when it too, one day, collapses-in on the next lower condensation of *agreements.*

If you miss (*fly past*) an *entity* of the type that you're checking that is ready for *processing* and try to continue, you may not find anything on the *next* type—even though the *next* type isn't really cleared. In this case, go back and check the *previous* type (you had just been working with) again for *flown-by fragments.*

This is all best handled with a *Biofeedback-device.* A lot of these *fragments* are off in *"non-physical locations,"* so a *Seeker* should not limit their *attention* to what is only in the immediate area of the Body (as with B.E., *&tc.*) or become overly concerned with *"where"* these *locations* actually are.

SPLITTER-INCIDENT ENTITY-TYPES

This is a list of the *128 entity* types resulting from the

"*Big Splitter*" *incident* (which occurs using the *Splitter-Platform* that is given later). We have the *Platform* developed. The real goal of all experimental procedures (in this area) is to undercut having to *run* the entire *Platform* several times on each of the *128* types.

This list provides the *entity* types in the *reverse* order from how they occur in the *incident*; because that is the easiest way to *run* them when using the *Wizard-Level* ability of "*dispersing-on-realization/Awareness*" (as is the case with the *New Standard* methods). Otherwise, a *Seeker* will have to *process-out* all of the "*programming items*" that are found in the *Platform* for each type.

Note that we have a "*translation*" issue with ascribing "*human language*" names to represent these various types. Usually this is not an issue so long as a *Seeker* has no misconception about what a word means. In this case, we are working toward defining "*type labels*" that are consistent when checking for *Meter-reads*.

There are *16* groups or classes of *entity*; each of which has *8* types. Alternative *labels* appear for some types; the result of different researchers working on this project at different experimental periods of development.

GROUP 16. FINAL BARRIERS (*Blockages against taking this Implant apart.*)

128. OVERSOUL (manages all the others)
127. GUARDIAN (guards the implant against erasure)
126. HOLDER (holds entities in place that try to release)
125. SUPPRESSOR (hides the implant)
  125x. HIDER (may be 'suppressor')
124. DENIER (says implant never happened)
123. MISDIRECTOR (alters and shifts attention)
  123x. BOUNCER ('misdirector')

122. INVALIDATOR (invalidates anything you run/ process)

121. RESTIMULATOR (keeps the implant restimulated)

  121x. RESISTOR (resists change)

GROUP 15. FINAL STRUCTURE (*Entities maintaining the structure of Implant.*)

120. UNIFIER (pulls everything together)

  120x. JOINER or GROUPER

119. KEEPER (keeps/holds you down in the implant)

118. IMPLANTER (continually runs implant-items on you)

117. SPLITTER (continually makes everyone split/divide/ fragment)

116. CORRECTIVE ENTITY (fixes anything that becomes undone)

  116x. REPAIRER

115. PERPETUATOR (keeps the implant going)

114. DRAMATIZER

113. INNER GUARD (keeps you from looking at yourself and seeing the structure of the implant/entities)

GROUP 14. SPIRITUAL BARRIERS (*Blocks*)

112. DEVIL (DEMON) (makes trouble for you)

111. DEGRADER (encourages degradation)

110. TEMPTER (tempts you to do evil)

109. DELUSION ENTITY (creates delusions)

108. TERROR (FEAR) ENTITY (makes you afraid; particularly involving the Mind or Spirits)

107. CONFUSION ENTITY (tries to keep you confused)

106. DISCOURAGER (discourages any effort to do anything about this)

105. INTERIORIZER (makes you 'interiorize'; into Universes and bodies, *&tc.*)

GROUP 13. SPIRITUAL STRUCTURE

104. RECYCLER (cycles you into a 'new' beingness between lives)

103. EXECUTIONER (destroys your 'old' identity between lives)

102. PUNISHER (arranges punishments)

101. JUDGE (harshly judges your conduct, particularly between lives)

101x. BETWEEN-LIVES ENTITY (?)

100. ACCUSER (accuses you of any possible wrongdoing)

99. ATTRACTOR (causes you to 'pull' things in)

98. ANGEL (a piece of yourself sent to serve 'god'/ 'Universal Mind')

97. CREATOR / PART-OF-GOD (a part of yourself sent to be part of 'god'; or contribution to the 'Universal Mind'; "to be the thought of the Universe forever," &tc.)

97x. UNIVERSAL-MIND (likely the same as 97)

[Note that the "*god*" or "*Universal Mind*" that is set up by this *Implant* is *Universe*-managing *machinery* and not a "*Self-aware entity*" in the conventional sense. It is composed of a piece of everyone and is programmed like a computer to run *reality* in the *Universe*. This should not be confused with any "higher dynamic" idea of "*god*" or "*Source.*" Part of us makes up the *Universal-Mind* ("*god*") and part is made into an "*angel*" that runs around enacting *god's* orders.]

GROUP 12. EXISTENCE BARRIERS (*Blocks*)

96. TRICKSTER (tricks you)

95. FATE (ARRANGER) (arranges fates for you)

94. DISPERSER (disperses you)

93. INVERTER (turns your postulates back against you)

329

92. DECEIVER (deceives you)

91. OPPOSER (manifests opposition to your goals)

90. EQUALIZER (balances things; arranges 'karma')

89. WATCHER (watches you)

GROUP 11. EXISTENCE STRUCTURE

88. ALIGNER (COORDINATOR)

87. COACH (keeps you from either winning or losing)
 87x. HUMANIZER

86. ENCOURAGER (encourages you to stay here and live life)

85. FUTURIZER (puts things into the future for you)

84. GOAL-MAKER (manifests goals for you)

83. GAME-MAKER (manifests games for you)

82. PLANNER (plans your continued existence)

81. GUIDE (guides you deeper/further into existence/ Universe)

GROUP 10. UNIVERSE BARRIERS (*Blocks*)

80. REFLECTOR (ENERGY MIRROR) (unmanifests energy-beams by reflecting them back at you)
 80x. COLLAPSAR

79. VACUUM (UNMANIFESTOR) (drains energy and energy-beams)

78. PULL-BACK (causes you to pull back your energy-beams)
 78x. BEAM-STOPPER

77. DIFFUSER (causes energy-beams to disperse and slide off targets)
 77x. DEFLECTOR (likely same as 77)

76. CONSTRAINER (constrains you to follow 'physical laws')

75. BLOCKER (blocks you from messing up structure of Universe)

74. BINDER (binds you together with reality-agreements)
   74x. AGREEMENT-ENTITY
73. PROTECTOR (protects Universe from your postulates)
   73x. UNIVERSE-HOLDER

GROUP 9. UNIVERSE STRUCTURE

72. ACTUALIZER (makes it all real)
   72x. SOLIDIFIER or PERSISTER
71. SYNCHRONIZER (cross-copies the simultaneousness of time between individuals)
70. UNIVERSE COORDINATOR (coordinates the interrelationship of space-time and energy-matter)
69. DETERMINATOR (judges value of potential futures in order to maximize 'Arcs of Infinity')
68. COMMUNICATOR (interconnects everyone)
67. LOCATOR (maintains the position of everything)
66. GENERATOR (projects reality)
65. POSTULATOR (manifests reality)

GROUP 8. SOCIAL/LIFE BARRIERS (*Blocks*)

64. SINNER (inspires 'sin', selfishness, *&tc.*)
63. CONFLICTOR (inspires conflict)
62. SEXUAL ENTITY (sensation and exchange of entities during sex, *&tc.*)
61. SUBLIMATING ENTITY (feelings of love, honor, courage, loyalty, *&tc.*)
60. MOOD ENTITY (shifts moods between extremes; serene/troubled, calm/nervous, pleasant/irritated, *&tc.*)
59. EMOTIONAL ENTITY ('Beta-Awareness'; feelings of cheerfulness, boredom, antagonism, rage, hostility, fear, grief, apathy, *&tc.*)

58. **ATTITUDE ENTITY** (manifests preference; '
likes'/'dislikes', *&tc.*)

57. **MORALIZER** (makes you feel guilty)

GROUP 7. SOCIAL/LIFE STRUCTURE

56. **MISOWNER** (says that the Universe is not your
creation so you can't affect it)

55. **SHELL (FOCAL)** (surrounds you and focuses things
in on you)

54. **UNIVERSE LIFE-ENTITY** (to be 'the life' in the
Universe)

53. **ANIMATOR** (to be 'the life' in lower organisms)

52. **SYMPATHIZER** (to keep you in sympathy)

51. **SOCIAL ENTITY** (inspires communication,
agreement, likingness, *&tc.*)

50. **GROUP-MIND** (to be in 'groups')

49. **SUPER-BEING** (says you evolve by overwhelming
individuals and making all become one)

GROUP 6. BODY BARRIERS (*Blocks*)

48. **SICKNESS ENTITY** (manifests disease according to
'universe laws')

47. **JAILER** (keeps you in a body)

46. **SLEEP-CENTER** (dreams; has you rebuild/manifest
things while you sleep)

45. **SOMATIC-ENTITY** (manages physical pains/
sensations)

44. **BODY-BLOCKER** (keeps you from modifying the
body by postulate)

44x. **PERCEPTION-BLOCKER**

43. **FILTER** (filters out perception of entities, infinities,
&tc.)

42. **CRAVER** (initiates cravings; food, *&tc.*)

41. **COMPELLER** (needing bodies; needing food, *&tc.*,
for bodies)

41x. COMPULSIVE ENTITY

GROUP 5. BODY STRUCTURE

40. RELAYER (relays body perceptions to you)

39. REPRESENTER (manifests body perceptions; sight, *&tc.*)

39x. VISUAL-ENTITY (composes pictures of reality that you look at instead of seeing it directly)

38. REACTIVE ENTITY (generates body reactions to environmental stimuli)

37. BODY MACHINE (regulates organic body processes)

36. CELLULAR ENTITY (creates/duplicates cells of the body)

35. BODY-LOCATOR (integrates cells, perceptions, *&tc.*, with space-time positions)

34. GENETIC-ENTITY (manages the body as a vehicle)

33. BODY-GENERATOR (projects the body into reality/ Universe)

GROUP 4. MIND BARRIERS (*Blocks*)

32. SHIFTER (shifts attention into 'Beta-Existence' and off of 'Alpha')

31. CONSCIENCE

30. JUSTIFIER

29. FORGETTER

28. ENTURBULATOR

27. DEPRESSOR (possibly related to *106*)

26. EXHILARATOR

25. CONTROLLER

GROUP 3. MIND STRUCTURE

24. FILE CLERK (retrieves data)

23. RECORDING-ENTITY

23x. HISTORIAN

22. SYMBOLIZER

21. COMPUTATIONAL ENTITY
20. DECISION-MAKER
19. RANDOMIZER
18. THINKER
17. INSTIGATOR

GROUP 2. ALPHA-SPIRIT BLOCKERS

16. **DESTROYER** (arranges accidents, *&tc.*, to keep you from finding out about this, or escaping)
15. **NARCOTIC ENTITY** (keeps the 'Higher Self' feeling drugged)
14. **INHIBITOR** (blocks non-physical perception, *&tc.*)
13. **DAMPER (DAMPENER)** (keeps you condensed to a single point and in agreement, *&tc.*; holds you down)
12. **PREVENTER** (prevents manipulation of probability, resonance, cohesion, *&tc.*)
11. **WRAITH** (drains energy)
10. **SUBCONSCIOUS** (hides things; convinces you to stay limited and obedient)
9. **ABERRATOR** (compels one to follow laws of 'cumulative charge', fragmented patterns, restimulation, *&tc.*)

GROUP 1. ALPHA STRUCTURING

8. **FORMULATOR** (inspires choices of strength/weakness, likes/dislikes, *&tc.*)
7. **INSPIRATIONAL ENTITY** (inspires beliefs that everyone likes it here and you wouldn't want to leave, *&tc.*)
6. **SEPARATOR** (keeps you as an individual separate from 'Higher Self', and from knowing about other entities, infinities, *&tc.*)
5. **RESTRICTOR** (limits awareness to a located viewpoint)

4. INDIVIDUALIZER (limits you to a single located viewpoint, beingness, &tc.)

3. BENEFACTOR (gives you interesting rewards, &tc., for obeying the implant)

2. MANIFESTATION-INVALIDATOR (invalidates anything that is not 'agreed-upon')

2x. CREATION-MOCKUP INVALIDATOR

1. INITIATOR (compels you to desire 'agreed-upon' Universe; games, forms, reality, existence, &tc.)

THE "HIGHER SELF" H.S. PROCEDURE
(Archaic Splitter-Handling Tech., Revised)

This advanced experimental-research method is based on the concept of a *"Higher-Self"* being established for each of the IPU-*Goals*. These "higher selves" are unaware (compartmented) pieces of yourself that keep everything manifested and operating. [This method is not necessarily recommended. It is a record of the material we utilized for research prior to the *New Standard* techniques, with the *"locational procedure,"* &tc.]

Terminology for this application emerged from the idea of a *"Higher Self"* and that if such an entity or part of us is really fragmented and separated (compartmented), than we had to ask ourselves: *"higher"* than what? Handling IPU-material and other techniques for *Implanting-Incidents* has run us up to *this* point—theoretically the final major "barrier" (or "level of work") that keeps us from *Ascending out of this Universe.*

The IPU-*Goal* for the *H.S. Procedure* is selected by assessment. A *Seeker* doesn't have to worry about *running* a specific *Goal-sequence*; they assess for what currently gives the largest *Meter-reads* and *run* that. The procedure really has two parts: one, is the actual *running* of the "higher self" items; and two, is the handling of 8 types of blocking-entities that interfere with processing-out this Implant.

Although 128 entity types are installed by the Splitter Platform, only one bunch of 8 seem to interfere specifically with systematic processing (defragmenting). You process the 8 blocking-entities whenever you start your session for the day, and if necessary, in between each pass through the "higher self" items on a particular IPU-Goal; and also if you run into interference that is keeping items from dispersing/defragmenting.

The "higher self" programming-items are defragmented as a batch or cluster; not as individual line-items. You just spot one after another and keep going through the entire batch of programming-items until they collectively do not register. Trying to defrag line-by-line seems to stir up too much opposition to dispersal.

[Researcher Notes: If a Seeker runs into a GSR-Meter phenomenon where the needle is slamming: there are likely Harmful-Acts connected to whatever is being handled, which need to be spotted/defragged. If the balance-point on the Meter is excessively high (high-resistance reading), handle only blocking-entities until it lowers. When the "higher self" items do register as erased/dispersed, then they are. Don't overrun. There is a distinct feeling of the Universe shifting around when one of the "higher selves" disperses.]

BLOCKING-ENTITIES LIST

Use this list for assessment:

GUARDIAN
OVERSOUL
HOLDER

SUPPRESSOR
DENIER
MISDIRECTOR
INVALIDATOR
RESTIMULATOR

Whenever you get a *Meter-read*, have the *entity* do the following:

A. *"Spot being made into a(n) ___."*

B. *"Spot being made to split."*

  [*Revision*: add *Locational Proc.* here.]

C. *"Spot the first time you were made to split."*

D. *"Spot making others split."*

E. If necessary: *Identification Proc.* (*"Who Are You?"*/ *"Me"*)

At this level of work, you may get an early *dispersal/ release* of an *entity* without realizing it, and start *processing* another of the same type that was behind the first one. But since the second one didn't get the first-PCL (*&tc.*) or whatever the first *released* on, there is still something there by STEP-E. So, if something remains, check if you're handling another of the same type; and if so, go back to STEP-A. In any case, when one does *release*, you check for another of the same type.

H.S. PROCEDURE

  A. *Spot "Native State" line-item* for the *Goal*. *Spot* being *pushed-in—pushing others in*; and *another pushing others in*—to the *Implanted Penalty-Universe* (IPU) for this *Goal*.

  B. *Spot* the *item*: "TO {*goal*} IS TO BE THE INFINITE {*terminal*} AND DIVIDE INTO MY HIGHER AND LOWER SELF FOREVER."

  C. *Spot* being the *"higher self"* as a manifestation of the "infinite {*terminal*}." Repeat STEP-A (*Native State*) from the *"higher self" viewpoint*.

D. From the *"higher self" viewpoint*: *Spot* the original *split* into the "infinite {*terminal*}." *Spot* the "mirror" that shows you *splitting* into *infinite-copies* of the *terminal*; and *spot* becoming the *terminal* spread out to *infinity*.

[*Revision*: add *Locational Proc.* here on *"higher self" viewpoint*.]

E. *Process* the *"higher self"* through the following *"programming items."* Make sure each *item* gives a *Meter-read* (contacting it), but don't continue to *defrag* each line. [See earlier instruction on this.] If you can't get an *item* to *register*, check if it has been *"suppressed"* or *"invalidated."* If the *Meter-needle* goes dead, or gets "stuck," check for *blocking-entities*.

The *H.S. programming-items*:

TO {goal} INFINITELY IS TO BE MY HIGHER-SELF AND:
1. CREATE THIS FOREVER
2. DEFEND THIS FOREVER
3. REPLACE THIS FOREVER
4. KEEP THIS MANIFESTED FOREVER
5. ESTABLISH THIS SPACE FOREVER
6. HIDE THIS FOREVER
7. HOLD THIS TOGETHER FOREVER
8. KEEP THIS UNCHANGING FOREVER
9. MAINTAIN THIS LOCATION FOREVER
10. ENERGIZE THIS FOREVER
11. PROTECT THIS FOREVER
12. OBSCURE THIS FOREVER
13. SOLIDIFY THIS FOREVER
14. STABILIZE THIS FOREVER
15. GUARD THIS FOREVER
16. FORGET THIS FOREVER

This is the original research-data for the *"Big-Splitter" Implanting-Incident* used for early experiments. It was first replaced by *H.S. Procedure* and then, more recently, by the *New Standard* method. However, the details included in this original research are reissued any time the material is revised to avoid rewriting them. This is also such a key area of *Ascension* that all existing records of this work are considered critical for posterity.

[The actual *incident-sequence* is given as "capital-lettered" *items*, such as "TO {*goal*}.." There are also various "*spotting*" instructions included for *contacting-the-incident*, research and *defragmentation*.]

SECTION 1. INFINITY
(*The space is like being in a thin white cloud with nothing visible.*)

A. TO {*goal*} INFINITELY IS TO:
1. PERCEIVE ULTIMATE TRUTH
2. ACHIEVE ULTIMATE PURPOSE
3. PERCEIVE ULTIMATE BEAUTY
4. EXPERIENCE ULTIMATE ENLIGHTENMENT
5. RECEIVE ULTIMATE ADMIRATION
6. ACHIEVE ULTIMATE BEINGNESS
7. ACHIEVE ULTIMATE DOINGNESS
8. ACHIEVE ULTIMATE HAVINGNESS
9. WIELD ULTIMATE POWER
10. BE GOD

B. THE TEMPLE
1. *Spot:* The {*terminal*} appears in front of you.
2. TO {*goal*} IS TO BECOME THE INFINITE {*terminal*}:
3. TO BECOME THE INFINITE {*terminal*} IS TO BECOME GOD

4. *Spot:* The *temple* appears in front of you.

5. TO BECOME GOD IS TO BECOME THE INFINITE {*terminal*} AND DO {*goal*} INFINITELY

C. SPOTTING STEPS

(*Spot* the following with *intention;* then broadcast it out to the *entities, &tc.,* that started waking up from *running* the above steps.)

1. *"Spot the false data (above) in the Implant."*
2. *"Spot that you don't have to be the terminal to do the goal."*
3. *"Spot that you don't have to do the goal to get the things promised (above)."*
4. *"Spot that you don't have to be the terminal to get the things promised (above)."*
5. *"Spot that these items were all false promises; and that you didn't get these things from obeying the Implant."*

D. ENTITY-PROCESSING

(*Broadcast* the following PCL out to *process* awakened *entities, &tc.*)

1. *"Spot being made to divide by this Implant."*

   [*Revision*: add *Locational Proc.* here.]
2. *"Spot the first time you were made to divide; Spot making others divide."*
3. *"Spot the false data in the Implant; Spot the first time you were implanted with false data."*
4. *"Spot being made to copy; Spot the first time you were made to copy; Spot making others copy."*
5. *"Spot: 'To {goal} is Native State' at the top of the original Implanted Penalty-Universe Platform; Spot being pushed into it; pushing another into it; and others pushing others into it."*
6. *"Come up to present time. Thank You."*

Check for individual *entities/fragments* remaining. [*Revision*: use *Locational* and *Identification Tech* with acknowledgments.] Check for, and handle, any *Guardians, machinery*, and/or other *entity* types.

SECTION 2. INFINITE TERMINAL

(The items from the first section are reused with the "Infinite Terminal" in place of the Goal, as follows. While the items are given, the terminal—which is facing you—drifts backward toward "the Temple" and through the entrance. You are drawn along by it and enter "the Temple" as well.)

A. **TO BECOME THE INFINITE** {*terminal*} **IS TO:** {*items 1 through 10 of Section-1A*}

B. *(The terminal is floating in the center of "the Temple" facing you.)*
TO BE GOD IS TO CHOOSE TO BE THE INFINITE {*terminal*} **AND DO** {*goal*} **INFINITELY**

C. *(You slide into the manifestation of the terminal. You do this by curving around to the right and sliding in on the terminal's left side—so you are now facing toward the direction you just were in and are now looking through the terminal's viewpoint. As this happens, you get the following item. Also: Spot the feeling of turning and sliding into the terminal as you spot the item. There is a heavy emphasis on the word 'Be'.)*
TO {*goal*} **IS TO BE THE** {*terminal*}

D. *Spot seeing the inside of "the Temple" from the terminal's eyes (viewpoint). Notice that everything looked vague and dreamlike before, but now looks solid and sharp-looking with the terminal's eyes (viewpoint). This is a part of the trick/gimmick of the Implant-Universe. You were actually perceiving correctly before. Spot this trick happening.*

E. *Notice that there is some type of mirror on a wall of "the Temple"; and you can see yourself in it as the terminal. Spot the mirror. Spot the false reflection of yourself as the terminal.*

F. *(With this item, the mirror shows you splitting out to infinity.)*
TO BECOME GOD IS TO BECOME INFINITE

(Endless copies of the terminal stream out in all directions. Actually, you are being shown a picture of the terminal splitting, but you think you are already splitting and start agreeing with the idea. Then you are hit with a wave of force that makes you split. Spot the false mirror image, and the wave of force, along with the item.)

G. *(With this item, the mirror view pans backwards and shows you the outside of "the Temple" with endless copies of the terminal streaming off in all directions. Spot this.)*

TO {*goal*} IS TO DIVIDE FOREVER

H. TO {*goal*} IS TO BE THE INFINITE {*terminal*}

I. The original procedure includes: *imagining* dividing out to infinity and being the *"infinite-terminal"* several times. Also: have any *entities* (*&tc.*) that are awake *"spot"* doing this; and *spot* the first time they did this.

J. A revised procedure includes: alternate *running* the conceptual-PCL *"Decide To Be The Infinite {terminal}"* and *"Decide Not To Be The Infinite {terminal}."* (Always end on the second one.)

K. Repeat *"Entity-Processing"* (STEP-D from *Section-1*).

L. TO {*goal*} IS TO BE THE INFINITE {*terminal*} AND: {*items 1 through 16 of Step-E of the H.S. Procedure*}

For the *remaining* sections (below): *spot* the *item* a number of times until it *releases*, *disperses* or stops *registering*; have anyone awake *spot* doing the *item* (and the first time); and then *spot* the *item* again to *disperse* or to confirm *release/defrag*.

The original version includes: *spot* being the *infinite-copies* of the *terminal* and doing the *item* yourself (to be at total *Cause* over doing the *item*); then *spot* the *item* and the *"Native State"* item for that *Goal*.

SECTION 3. INFINITE REALITY

(A feeling of something shifting or coming apart almost always means dispersion/defragmentation. Total defragmentation does not give quite the same feeling as a partial-release. The shift on a full dispersal/release basically feels good; you are shifting back towards reality, and you feel better oriented. Partial-releases tend to leave one feeling disoriented.)

TO {*goal*} IS TO BE THE INFINITE {*terminal*} AND PARTICIPATE IN THE ___, FOREVER

1. CO-ACTUALIZATION OF REALITY
2. SHARING OF GROUP AGREEMENT
3. RHYTHM OF AGREED-UPON TIME
4. DETERMINATION OF AGREED-UPON LOCATION
5. OPERATION OF PHYSICAL UNIVERSE MECHANICS/LAWS
6. ENERGIZATION OF AGREED-UPON MOTION
7. SOLIDIFICATION OF AGREED-UPON FORMS
8. CROSS-COPYING OF THE PHYSICAL UNIVERSE

SECTION 4. SPLIT & PROGRAMMING

There are 128 entity-types. The first item for each is the "split" into that type. Something like a drop of water appears and then breaks apart and fragments into endless tiny droplets spreading across space-time. Spot this with the item.

The second item is a "program" item. The infinite droplets of water freeze or crystallize. Spot this with the item.

This sequence is introduced with:

0.0 TO {*goal*} IS TO BE THE INFINITE {*terminal*} AND
0.1 COPY MYSELF AND OTHERS, FOREVER
0.2 DIVIDE MYSELF AND OTHERS, FOREVER

A *"split/program"* pattern occurs with the *first two items* for each *entity* type.

After all the *items/entities*, there is an additional H.S. *item* (after a repeat of *item* 0.0 above) as follows:

129.0 DIVIDE MYSELF INTO MY HIGHER SELF AND MYSELF AS AN INDIVIDUAL, FOREVER

Then there are eight different "doingness" programming-items for each type. It is easier to run these for each entity type along with the "split-program" items (above), rather than making a separate cycle through for these details.

A revised handling of the "doingness" programming-items includes imagining doing (and not doing) the action, altern-ately to an end-realization or end-point. Once this is clearly conceived, then broadcast processing to entities: spot being made into (type), and the first time, and making others; use "Locational Tech" (point to..); spot false data of the Implant; spot "Native State" item; and apply "Identification Tech," &tc. —all as needed to resolve the case.

[Note that some additional data (research and experi-mentation) is still necessary to complete this final step toward *Ascension*.]

1.1 SPLIT MYSELF AND OTHERS INTO INITIATORS FOREVER

1.2 PROGRAM MYSELF AND OTHERS TO BE THE INITIATOR AND INFUSE MYSELF WITH DESIRE FOREVER

1.X TO {*goal*} INFINITELY IS TO BE THE INITIATOR AND COMPEL MYSELF TO DESIRE PHYSICAL UNIVERSE ___, FOREVER

[1. TIME; 2. SPACE; 3. ENERGY; 4. MATTER;
5. GAMES; 6. FORMS; 7. REALITY; 8. EXISTENCE]

2.1 SPLIT MYSELF AND OTHERS INTO MOCK-UP INVALIDATORS FOREVER

2.2 PROGRAM MYSELF AND OTHERS TO BE THE MOCK-UP INVALIDATOR AND INVALIDATE THAT WHICH IS NOT AGREED-UPON, FOREVER

2.X TO {*goal*} INFINITELY IS TO BE THE MOCK-UP INVALIDATOR AND INVALIDATE NON-PHYSICAL ___ FOREVER

[1. TIME; 2. SPACE; 3. ENERGY; 4. MATTER;

5. GAMES; 6. FORMS; 7. REALITY; 8. EXISTENCE]

 3.1 SPLIT MYSELF AND OTHERS INTO
    BENEFACTORS FOREVER

 3.2 PROGRAM MYSELF AND OTHERS TO BE THE
    BENEFACTOR AND REWARD MYSELF FOR
    OBEYING THIS IMPLANT FOREVER

 3.X TO {*goal*} INFINITELY IS TO BE THE
    BENEFACTOR AND GIVE MYSELF INTERESTING
    ___ TO OCCUPY MY ATTENTION FOREVER

[1. GOALS; 2. HAVINGNESS; 3. PHASES; 4. GAMES;
5. ADVENTURES; 6. DRAMA]

 3.Y TO {*goal*} INFINITELY IS TO BE THE
    BENEFACTOR AND GIVE MYSELF INTERESTING
    ___ FOR OBEYING THIS FOREVER

 [7. REASONS; 8. REWARDS]

 4.1 SPLIT MYSELF AND OTHERS INTO
    INDIVIDUALIZERS FOREVER

 4.2 PROGRAM MYSELF AND OTHERS TO BE THE
    INDIVIDUALIZER AND KEEP MYSELF
    NARROWED DOWN (or compartmented)
    FOREVER

 4.X TO {*goal*} INFINITELY IS TO BE THE
    INDIVIDUALIZER AND ___ FOREVER

[1. SHIFT MY AWARENESS DOWN TO A POINT;
2. KEEP MYSELF LOCATED IN SPACE AND TIME]

 4.Y TO {*goal*} INFINITELY IS TO BE THE
    INDIVIDUALIZER AND LIMIT MYSELF TO A
    SINGLE ___ FOREVER

[3. VIEWPOINT; 4. AWARENESS CENTER; 5. TIME-
TRACK; 6. OPERATING POINT; 7. BEINGNESS;
8. REALITY]

 5.1 SPLIT MYSELF AND OTHERS INTO
    RESTRICTORS FOREVER

 5.2 PROGRAM MYSELF AND OTHERS TO BE THE
    RESTRICTOR AND LIMIT MYSELF TO A
    LOCATED VIEWPOINT, FOREVER

 5.X TO {*goal*} INFINITELY IS TO BE THE RESTRICTOR
    AND RESTRICT MYSELF TO ___ ONLY IN THE
    LOCATED VIEWPOINT, FOREVER

[1. BEING; 2. PERCEIVING; 3. OPERATING;
4. THINKING]

5.X TO {goal} INFINITELY IS TO BE THE RESTRICTOR
AND RESTRICT MY ___ OF THE LOCATED
VIEWPOINT, FOREVER

[5. CONCEPTIONS TO THE EXPERIENCE;
6. KNOWLEDGE TO THE DATA; 7. POWER TO THE
ENERGY; 8. ABILITIES TO THE CAPABILITIES]

6.1 SPLIT MYSELF AND OTHERS INTO
SEPARATORS FOREVER

6.2 PROGRAM MYSELF AND OTHERS TO BE THE
SEPARATOR AND KEEP MYSELF SEPARATE AS
AN INDIVIDUAL, FOREVER

6.X TO {goal} INFINITELY IS TO BE THE SEPARATOR
AND KEEP MYSELF AS AN INDIVIDUAL,
SEPARATE FROM ___, FOREVER

[1. MYSELF AS AN ENTITY; 2. MY HIGHER SELF;
3. INFINITY; 4. OTHER INDIVIDUALS; 5. OTHER
UNIVERSES; 6. GOD (the unmanifest static or
NOTHINGNESS); 7. THE LIFE STATIC (or ALPHA-SPIRIT);
8. THE UNIVERSE MACHINERY]

7.1 SPLIT MYSELF AND OTHERS INTO
INSPIRATIONAL ENTITIES FOREVER

7.2 PROGRAM MYSELF AND OTHERS TO BE THE
INSPIRATIONAL ENTITY AND CONVINCE
MYSELF TO BELIEVE IN ALL THIS FOREVER

7.X TO {goal} INFINITELY IS TO BE THE
INSPIRATIONAL ENTITY AND CONVINCE
MYSELF AND OTHERS THAT ___, FOREVER

[1. EVERYONE REALLY LIKES IT HERE; 2. THIS IS
THE ONLY REAL UNIVERSE; 3. THERE WAS NOTHING
BEFORE THIS UNIVERSE; 4. IT IS NECESSARY TO BE
HERE; 5. YOU CANNOT DO ANYTHING WITHOUT
OTHERS AGREEMENT; 6. POSTULATES CANNOT
AFFECT THE PHYSICAL UNIVERSE; 7. NOBODY CAN
EXIST WITHOUT A PHYSICAL FORM; 8. WE WANT TO
BE THE EFFECT OF ALL THIS.]

8.1 SPLIT MYSELF AND OTHERS INTO
FORMULATORS FOREVER

8.2 PROGRAM MYSELF AND OTHERS TO BE THE

FORMULATOR AND FORMULATE MYSELF AS AN
INDIVIDUAL FOREVER

8.X TO {*goal*} INFINITELY IS TO BE THE
FORMULATOR AND INSPIRE MYSELF TO
CHOOSE ___, FOREVER

[1. STRENGTHS AND WEAKNESSES; 2. LIKES AND
DISLIKES; 3. ALLIES AND ENEMIES; 4. HOPES AND
FEARS; 5. CONNECTIONS AND DISCONNECTIONS;
6. FREEDOMS AND CONSEQUENCES; 7. ABILITIES AND
DISABILITIES; 8. (?)]

9.1 SPLIT MYSELF AND OTHERS INTO
ABERRATORS FOREVER

9.2 PROGRAM MYSELF AND OTHERS TO BE THE
ABERRATOR AND ABERRATE (FRAGMENT)
MYSELF FOREVER

9.X TO {*goal*} INFINITELY IS TO BE THE ABERRATOR
AND COMPEL MYSELF TO FOLLOW THE LAWS
OF ___, FOREVER

[1. CUMULATIVE CHARGE (later incidents stack up on
earlier ones); 2. RESTIMULATION; 3. FLOWS (inflow,
outflow); 4. THE DECLINING SPIRAL (of beingness and
condensation); 5. EXCHANGE; 6. OPPOSITION (creating
your own); 7. PULLING THINGS IN (manifesting motivation
for actions); 8. RESISTANCE (becoming what you resist).]

10.1 SPLIT MYSELF AND OTHERS INTO
SUBCONSCIOUS ENTITIES FOREVER

10.2 PROGRAM MYSELF AND OTHERS TO BE THE
SUBCONSCIOUS AND GIVE MYSELF ORDERS
FOREVER

10.X TO {*goal*} INFINITELY IS TO BE THE
SUBCONSCIOUS AND ___, FOREVER

[1. HIDE FROM MYSELF AS AN INDIVIDUAL; 2. KEEP
MYSELF AS AN INDIVIDUAL UNCONSCIOUS OF THESE
MECHANISMS; 3. KEEP MYSELF AS AN INDIVIDUAL
OBEDIENT TO THE COMMANDS OF THIS IMPLANT;
4. KEEP MYSELF AS AN INDIVIDUAL OBEDIENT TO THE
LAWS OF THE PHYSICAL UNIVERSE; 5. LIMIT MY SELF-
AWARENESS TO MYSELF AS THE INDIVIDUAL;
6. CONVINCE MYSELF THAT THE ONLY WAY TO EXIST
IS TO ACCEPT THESE LIMITATIONS; 7. CONVINCE

MYSELF THAT THE ONLY WAY TO BE HAPPY IS TO
ACCEPT THESE LIMITATIONS; 8. CONVINCE MYSELF
THAT THE ONLY WAY TO BE GOOD IS TO ACCEPT
THESE LIMITATIONS]

11.1 SPLIT MYSELF AND OTHERS INTO WRAITHS
FOREVER
11.2 PROGRAM MYSELF AND OTHERS TO BE THE
WRAITH AND WEAKEN MYSELF FOREVER
11.X TO {goal} INFINITELY IS TO BE THE WRAITH AND
MAKE MYSELF GROW CONTINUALLY ___,
FOREVER
[1. LESS INTELLIGENT; 2. LESS POWERFUL; 3.
LESS ABLE; 4. LESS SKILLFUL; 5. LESS AWARE; 6.
LESS INTEGRATED; 7. LESS COMPETENT; 8. SMALLER]

12.1 SPLIT MYSELF AND OTHERS INTO
PREVENTERS FOREVER
12.2 PROGRAM MYSELF AND OTHERS TO BE THE
PREVENTER AND PREVENT THE
MANIPULATION OF REALITY, FOREVER
12.X TO {goal} INFINITELY IS TO BE THE PREVENTER
AND PREVENT THE MANIPULATION OF ___,
FOREVER
[1. PROBABILITY; 2. RESONANCE (vibration/
sympathy); 3. COHESION (the cohesion of the whole); 4.
SYNCHRONIZATION (solidity/frequency); 5. ORIENTATION
(dimensions); 6. BEINGNESS (identity of spaces, objects,
energies); 7. WILLINGNESS (of spaces, objects, energies);
8. ORIGINAL IS-NESS (actual nature of things/reality)]

13.1 SPLIT MYSELF AND OTHERS INTO DAMPERS
FOREVER
13.2 PROGRAM MYSELF AND OTHERS TO BE THE
DAMPER AND HOLD MYSELF HERE FOREVER
13.X TO {goal} INFINITELY IS TO BE THE DAMPER
AND ___ FOREVER
[1. KEEP MYSELF AT EFFECT; 2. HOLD MYSELF
DOWN; 3. KEEP MYSELF LOCATED; 4. CONDENSE
MYSELF TO A POINT; 5. KEEP MYSELF IN AGREEMENT;
6. CONSTRAIN MYSELF TO PHYSICAL REALITY;
7. CONSTRAIN MYSELF TO A SINGLE INDIVIDUALITY;
8. HIDE ALL OTHER BEINGNESS FROM MY INDIVIDUAL

SELF]

14.1 SPLIT MYSELF AND OTHERS INTO INHIBITORS
        FOREVER
14.2 PROGRAM MYSELF AND OTHERS TO BE THE
        INHIBITOR AND INHIBIT PERCEPTIONS
        FOREVER
14.X TO {goal} INFINITELY IS TO BE THE INHIBITOR
        AND ___ FOREVER
    [1. BLOCK ALL PERCEPTION OF INFINITY; 2. BLOCK
ALL PERCEPTIONS BEYOND 3 DIMENSIONS; 3. BLOCK
ALL PERCEPTIONS OF ENTITIES; 4. BLOCK ALL
PERCEPTIONS OF OTHER'S IMAGINED CREATIONS
(MOCK-UPS); 5. BLOCK ALL PERCEPTION OF OTHER
UNIVERSES; 6. BLOCK ALL PERCEPTION IN NON-
PHYSICAL DIRECTIONS; 7. BLOCK MYSELF AND
OTHERS FROM REALIZING THAT THESE THINGS ARE
THERE; 8. BLOCK MYSELF AND OTHERS FROM
WANTING TO DO ANYTHING ABOUT THIS]

15.1 SPLIT MYSELF AND OTHERS INTO NARCOTIC
        ENTITIES FOREVER
15.2 PROGRAM MYSELF AND OTHERS TO BE THE
        NARCOTIC ENTITY AND KEEP MY HIGHER-SELF
        "DRUGGED" FOREVER
15.X TO {goal} INFINITELY IS TO BE THE NARCOTIC
        ENTITY AND KEEP MY HIGHER-SELF ___
        FOREVER
    [1. LOST IN A FEELING OF PLEASANT DRIFTING;
2. UNCONCERNED; 3. UNAWARE; 4. NON-
CONSECUTIVE; 5. UNFOCUSED; 6. NON-SEQUITUR
(illogical); 7. DISCONNECTED; 8. UNREAL]

16.1 SPLIT MYSELF AND OTHERS INTO
        DESTROYERS FOREVER
16.2 PROGRAM MYSELF AND OTHERS TO BE THE
        DESTROYER AND STOP ALL ATTEMPTS TO
        UNDO THIS, FOREVER
16.X TO {goal} INFINITELY IS TO BE THE DESTROYER
        AND ___ FOREVER
    [1. STOP MYSELF AND OTHERS FROM EVER
DISCOVERING THIS; 2. STOP MYSELF AND OTHERS
FROM EVER SUSPECTING THIS; 3. STOP MYSELF AND

OTHERS FROM EVER PERCEIVING THIS; 4. STOP
MYSELF AND OTHERS FROM EVER DISPERSING THIS
AS-IT-IS; 5. MAKE MYSELF SICK IF I EVER DISCOVER
ANY OF THIS; 6. DRIVE MYSELF CRAZY IF I EVER
DISCOVER ANY OF THIS; 7. USE PAIN TO BLOCK
MYSELF FROM UNDOING THIS IMPLANT; 8. ARRANGE
ACCIDENTS TO BLOCK MYSELF FROM UNDOING THIS
IMPLANT]

17.1 SPLIT MYSELF AND OTHERS INTO
     INSTIGATORS FOREVER
17.2 PROGRAM MYSELF AND OTHERS TO BE THE
     INSTIGATOR AND INSTIGATE PHYSICAL
     UNIVERSE THINKING, FOREVER
17.X TO {goal} INFINITELY IS TO BE THE INSTIGATOR
     AND INSPIRE MYSELF TO ___ FOREVER
     [1. BE CURIOUS ABOUT THE PHYSICAL UNIVERSE;
2. BE INTERESTED IN THE PHYSICAL UNIVERSE; 3. BE
INTERESTED IN SOLVING PHYSICAL UNIVERSE
PROBLEMS; 4. BE INTERESTED IN THINKING ABOUT
THE PHYSICAL UNIVERSE; 5. ENJOY THINKING ABOUT
THE PHYSICAL UNIVERSE; 6. WANT TO THINK ABOUT
THE PHYSICAL UNIVERSE; 7. NEED TO THINK ABOUT
THE PHYSICAL UNIVERSE; 8. BE AFRAID NOT TO
THINK ABOUT THE PHYSICAL UNIVERSE]

18.1 SPLIT MYSELF AND OTHERS INTO THINKERS
     FOREVER
18.2 PROGRAM MYSELF AND OTHERS TO BE THE
     THINKER AND CREATE THOUGHTS FOR
     MYSELF FOREVER
18.X TO {goal} INFINITELY IS TO BE THE THINKER
     AND CREATE ___ THOUGHTS ABOUT THE
     PHYSICAL UNIVERSE FOR MYSELF FOREVER
     [1. INTERESTING; 2. PLEASANT; 3. DESIRABLE;
4. IMPORTANT; 5. COMPLEX; 6. WORRISOME]
18.Y TO {goal} INFINITELY IS TO BE THE THINKER
     AND COMPEL MYSELF TO ___ ABOUT THE
     PHYSICAL UNIVERSE FOREVER
     [7. THINK; 8. BE CONCERNED]

19.1 SPLIT MYSELF AND OTHERS INTO
     RANDOMIZERS FOREVER

19.2 PROGRAM MYSELF AND OTHERS TO BE THE RANDOMIZER AND MAKE ALL THIS APPEAR TO BE RANDOM FOREVER

19.X TO {goal} INFINITELY IS TO BE THE RANDOMIZER AND ___ FOREVER

[1. POSTULATE HAPPENINGS TO FOLLOW THE LAWS OF PROBABILITY; 2. MAKE THIS ALL APPEAR TO BE RANDOM CHANCE; 3. MAKE THIS ALL APPEAR TO BE UNGUIDED; 4. MAKE IT APPEAR THAT THERE IS NO REASON FOR ANYTHING]

19.Y TO {goal} INFINITELY IS TO BE THE RANDOMIZER AND CONVINCE MYSELF AND OTHERS THAT THERE IS NO ___ BEHIND REALITY, FOREVER

[5. PLAN; 6. LOGIC; 7. REASON; 8. INTENTION]

20.1 SPLIT MYSELF AND OTHERS INTO DECISION-MAKERS FOREVER

20.2 PROGRAM MYSELF AND OTHERS TO BE THE DECISION-MAKER AND DECIDE THE COURSE OF EVENTS FOREVER

20.X TO {goal} INFINITELY IS TO BE THE DECISION-MAKER AND ___ FOREVER

[1. DECIDE WHERE THINGS WILL BE; 2. CHOOSE THE COURSE OF EVENTS; 3. DECIDE WHEN THINGS WILL HAPPEN; 4. DECIDE HOW LONG THINGS WILL ENDURE; 5. DECIDE HOW THINGS SHALL MOVE; 6. DECIDE WHO SHALL WIN; 7. DECIDE WHO SHALL LOSE; 8. DECIDE THINGS IN A MANNER THAT WILL GIVE THE APPEARANCE OF RANDOM CHANCE]

21.1 SPLIT MYSELF AND OTHERS INTO COMPUTATIONAL ENTITIES FOREVER

21.2 PROGRAM MYSELF AND OTHERS TO BE THE COMPUTATIONAL ENTITY AND COMPEL MYSELF AND OTHERS TO THINK PROPER THOUGHTS FOREVER

21.X TO {goal} INFINITELY IS TO BE THE COMPUTATIONAL ENTITY AND CREATE ___ FOR MYSELF, FOREVER

[1. ATTITUDES; 2. COMPUTATIONS; 3. IDEAS; 4. STREAMS OF LOGIC; 5. RATIONALIZATIONS;

6. JUSTIFICATIONS; 7. PROBLEMS; 8. WORRIES]

   22.1 SPLIT MYSELF AND OTHERS INTO
           SYMBOLIZERS FOREVER

   22.2 PROGRAM MYSELF AND OTHERS TO BE THE
           SYMBOLIZER AND SUBSTITUTE SYMBOLS FOR
           THINGS, FOREVER

   22.X TO {*goal*} INFINITELY IS TO BE THE SYMBOLIZER
           AND ___, FOREVER

    [1. FORM SYMBOL MASSES TO REPRESENT
PHYSICAL REALITY]

   22.Y TO {*goal*} INFINITELY IS TO BE THE SYMBOLIZER
           AND SUBSTITUTE SYMBOLS FOR ___,
           FOREVER

    [2. IDENTITIES; 3. TIMES; 4. SPACES; 5. ENERGIES;
6. ACTIONS; 7. OBJECTS]

   22.Z TO {*goal*} INFINITELY IS TO BE THE SYMBOLIZER
           AND ___, FOREVER

    [8. SUBSTITUTE WORDS FOR DIRECT
COMMUNICATION]

   23.1 SPLIT MYSELF AND OTHERS INTO
           RECORDING-ENTITIES FOREVER

   23.2 PROGRAM MYSELF AND OTHERS TO BE THE
           RECORDING-ENTITY AND TAKE PICTURES OF
           EVERYTHING, FOREVER

   23.X TO {*goal*} INFINITELY IS TO BE THE RECORDING-
           ENTITY AND ___, FOREVER

    [1. RECORD EVERYTHING; 2. MAINTAIN THIS
HISTORICAL LIE OF ALL SPACES, ENERGIES, AND
OBJECTS; 3. ACCUMULATE THE HISTORY OF
EVERYTHING; 4. FOCUS THE HISTORY OF
EVERYTHING DOWN THROUGH TIME INTO THE
PRESENT-TIME REALITY; 5. ENSURE THAT THE
PRESENT ENVIRONMENT IS THE PRODUCT OF WHAT
HAS GONE BEFORE; 6. REBUILD ANYTHING THAT
VANISHES IN THE PRESENT, USING ITS PAST
HISTORY; 7. BUILD THE TIME-TRACK OF MYSELF AS
AN INDIVIDUAL; 8. ENSURE THAT MY PRESENT
INDIVIDUAL SELF IS THE PRODUCT OF MY PAST
TRACK AS AN INDIVIDUAL]

24.1 SPLIT MYSELF AND OTHERS INTO FILE
     CLERKS FOREVER
24.2 PROGRAM MYSELF AND OTHERS TO BE THE
     FILE CLERK AND ORGANIZE DATA ABOUT THE
     PHYSICAL UNIVERSE, FOREVER
24.X TO {goal} INFINITELY IS TO BE THE FILE CLERK
     AND ___ FOREVER

[1. KEEP TRACK OF ALL THIS; 2. REPORT ANY
INCONSISTENCIES IN THE MANIFESTATIONS OF
REALITY TO THE CORRECTIVE-ENTITIES; 3. ENSURE
THAT THE CORRECT SEQUENCE OF EVENTS IS
FOLLOWED; 4. RETAIN THE CORRECT LOCATION OF
ALL THINGS; 5. PROJECT THE APPARENT MOTION OF
ALL THINGS; 6. RETAIN THE COMPOSITION OF ALL
THINGS; 7. RETAIN THE HISTORY OF ALL THINGS;
8. KEEP THIS DATA ALL SECRET]

25.1 SPLIT MYSELF AND OTHERS INTO
     CONTROLLERS FOREVER
25.2 PROGRAM MYSELF AND OTHERS TO BE THE
     CONTROLLER AND CONTROL MYSELF
     FOREVER
25.X TO {goal} INFINITELY IS TO BECOME THE
     CONTROLLER AND CONTROL (all) MY ___ TO
     BE IN ACCORDANCE WITH THE PHYSICAL
     UNIVERSE

[1. AWARENESS; 2. PERCEPTIONS;
3. ACTUALIZATIONS; 4. PREDICTIONS; 5. ABILITY TO
ENDOW; 6. ABILITIES TO MANIPULATE;
7. MANIFESTATIONS; 8. LOCATION]

26.1 SPLIT MYSELF AND OTHERS INTO
     EXHILARATORS FOREVER
26.2 PROGRAM MYSELF AND OTHERS TO BE THE
     EXHILARATOR AND MAKE ME FEEL
     WONDERFUL ABOUT ALL THIS FOREVER
26.X TO {goal} INFINITELY IS TO BE THE
     EXHILARATOR AND (?)

27.1 SPLIT MYSELF AND OTHERS INTO
     DEPRESSORS FOREVER
27.2 PROGRAM MYSELF AND OTHERS TO BE THE
     DEPRESSOR AND MAKE MYSELF FEEL THE

HOPELESSNESS OF IT ALL FOREVER

27.X TO {*goal*} INFINITELY IS TO BE THE DEPRESSOR
AND (?) [*see 106*]

28.1 SPLIT MYSELF AND OTHERS INTO
ENTURBULATORS FOREVER

28.2 PROGRAM MYSELF AND OTHERS TO BE THE
ENTURBULATOR AND KEEP MYSELF UPSET
FOREVER

28.X TO {*goal*} INFINITELY IS TO BE THE
ENTURBULATOR AND KEEP MYSELF UPSET
ABOUT ___ FOREVER

[1. OTHER PEOPLE'S BEHAVIOR; 2. THE WAY I AM
TREATED BY OTHERS; 3. OTHER PEOPLE'S
POSSESSIONS; 4. THE WAY OTHER PEOPLE TREAT MY
POSSESSIONS; 5. OTHER PEOPLE'S ATTITUDES;
6. OTHER'S ATTITUDES TOWARDS ME; 7. THE THINGS
THAT STAND IN MY WAY; 8. THE THINGS THAT BOTHER
ME]

29.1 SPLIT MYSELF AND OTHERS INTO
FORGETTERS FOREVER

29.2 PROGRAM MYSELF AND OTHERS TO BE THE
FORGETTER AND MAKE MYSELF FORGET
THINGS FOREVER

29.X TO {*goal*} INFINITELY IS TO BE THE FORGETTER
AND MAKE MYSELF FORGET ___ FOREVER

[1. WHEN THINGS HAPPENED; 2. WHERE THINGS
HAPPENED; 3. HOW THINGS HAPPENED; 4. WHY
THINGS HAPPENED; 5. WHO DID THINGS; 6. THE
SOURCE OF THINGS; 7. THE STRUCTURE OF THINGS;
8. THIS IMPLANT]

30.1 SPLIT MYSELF AND OTHERS INTO JUSTIFIERS
FOREVER

30.2 PROGRAM MYSELF AND OTHERS TO BE THE
JUSTIFIER AND JUSTIFY MY ACTIONS
FOREVER

30.X TO {*goal*} INFINITELY IS TO BE THE JUSTIFIER
AND COMPEL MYSELF TO ___ FOREVER

[1. BE RIGHT; 2. DENY BLAME; 3. JUSTIFY MY
ACTIONS; 4. EXCUSE MY FAILINGS; 5. MAKE OTHERS

WRONG; 6. BLAME OTHERS; 7. PROVE OTHERS GUILTY; 8. INVALIDATE OTHERS EXCUSES]

31.1 SPLIT MYSELF AND OTHERS INTO CONSCIENCES, FOREVER

31.2 PROGRAM MYSELF AND OTHERS TO BE THE CONSCIENCE AND MAKE MYSELF GUILTY FOREVER

31.X TO {goal} INFINITELY IS TO BE THE CONSCIENCE AND MAKE MYSELF GUILTY FOR ANY HARM DONE TO ___, EVEN IF IT IS JUSTIFIED, FOREVER

[1. OTHERS; 2. THE PHYSICAL UNIVERSE; 3. ALLIES; 4. ENEMIES; 5. BODIES; 6. GROUPS (OR SOCIETY); 7. OTHER LIFEFORMS; 8. INFINITY (or 'this implant')]

32.1 SPLIT MYSELF AND OTHERS INTO SHIFTERS FOREVER

32.2 PROGRAM MYSELF AND OTHERS TO BE THE SHIFTER AND SHIFT MY ATTENTION FOREVER

32.X TO {goal} INFINITELY IS TO BE THE SHIFTER AND SHIFT MY ATTENTION ___ FOREVER

[1. INTO REALITY; 2. AWAY FROM INFINITY; 3. INTO 3 DIMENSIONS; 4. AWAY FROM HIGHER DIMENSIONS; 5. INTO MY INDIVIDUAL SELF; 6. AWAY FROM MY INFINITE SELF; 7. INTO PHYSICAL EXISTENCE; 8. AWAY FROM THESE MECHANISMS]

33.1 SPLIT MYSELF AND OTHERS INTO BODY-GENERATORS FOREVER

33.2 PROGRAM MYSELF AND OTHERS TO BE THE BODY-GENERATOR AND PROJECT FORMS FOR MYSELF FOREVER

33.X TO {goal} INFINITELY IS TO BE THE BODY-GENERATOR AND ___, FOREVER

[1. REPRESENT MYSELF AS AN INDIVIDUAL IN FORM; 2. COPY THE AGREED-UPON BODY TEMPLATES; 3. DERIVE THE CURRENT BODY TEMPLATES; 4. PROJECT THE BODY INTO PHYSICAL REALITY; 5. REFLECT PHYSICAL UNIVERSE IMPACTS (EFFECTS) INTO THE CURRENT BODY TEMPLATE; 6. MODIFY THE BODY PROJECTIONS IN ACCORDANCE

WITH PHYSICAL UNIVERSE LAW; 7. EVOLVE THE BODY
TEMPLATES TO ADAPT TO THE PHYSICAL UNIVERSE
ENVIRONMENT; 8. SHAPE THE BODY IN RESPONSE TO
PHYSICAL UNIVERSE EFFORTS]

34.1 SPLIT MYSELF AND OTHERS INTO GENETIC-
ENTITIES FOREVER
34.2 PROGRAM MYSELF AND OTHERS TO BE THE
GENETIC-ENTITY AND BUILD BODIES FOREVER
34.X TO {*goal*} INFINITELY IS TO BE THE GENETIC-
ENTITY AND MANAGE THE ___ OF THE BODY,
FOREVER
[1. LIFE PROCESSES (metabolism); 2. LIFE CYCLES
(growth/aging); 3. OPERATING CYCLES (sleep);
4. STRUCTURE; 5. MOTION; 6. ENERGY; 7. REACTIONS;
8. ORIENTATION]

35.1 SPLIT MYSELF AND OTHERS INTO BODY-
LOCATORS FOREVER
35.2 PROGRAM MYSELF AND OTHERS TO BE THE
BODY-LOCATOR AND LOCATE THE BODY IN
THE PHYSICAL UNIVERSE
35.X TO {*goal*} INFINITELY IS TO BE THE BODY-
LOCATOR AND ___, FOREVER
[1. INTEGRATE THE BODY'S MOTION WITH THAT
OF THE PHYSICAL UNIVERSE; 2. INTEGRATE THE
BODY'S ORIENTATION WITH THAT OF THE PHYSICAL
UNIVERSE; 3. INTEGRATE THE BODY'S PERCEPTIONS
TO ITS PHYSICAL UNIVERSE POSITION; 4. INTEGRATE
THE BODY'S REACTIONS TO ITS PHYSICAL UNIVERSE
POSITION; 5. CALCULATE THE SPACE-TIME POSITION
FOR ALL BODY PARTICLES; 6. MOVE THE BODY
VIEWPOINT WITH THE PHYSICAL UNIVERSE;
7. MAINTAIN THE BODY'S ANCHOR-POINTS IN THE
PHYSICAL UNIVERSE; 8. CO-ACTUALIZE THE BODY AT
THE PROPER LOCATION WITHIN THE PHYSICAL
UNIVERSE CROSS-COPY]

36.1 SPLIT MYSELF AND OTHERS INTO CELLULAR-
ENTITIES FOREVER
36.2 PROGRAM MYSELF AND OTHERS TO BE THE
CELLULAR-ENTITY AND CREATE THE
PARTICLES (CELLS) OF THE BODY, FOREVER

36.X TO {goal} INFINITELY IS TO BE THE CELLULAR-
ENTITY AND CREATE CELLS TO ___ OF THE
BODY, FOREVER
[1. PROVIDE THE MASS; 2. PROVIDE THE RIGIDITY;
3. PROVIDE THE COMMUNICATION LINES; 4. MANAGE
THE REACTIONS; 5. ASSIMILATE THE CONSUMPTIONS;
6. MANAGE THE ENERGY; 7. PROVIDE THE
REPRODUCTION; 8. MANAGE THE OPERATION]

37.1 SPLIT MYSELF AND OTHERS INTO BODY-
MACHINES FOREVER
37.2 PROGRAM MYSELF AND OTHERS TO BE THE
BODY-MACHINE AND KEEP THE BODY
FUNCTIONING FOREVER
37.X TO {goal} INFINITELY IS TO BE THE BODY-
MACHINE AND ___, FOREVER
[1. REGULATE THE BODY PROCESSES;
2. INTEGRATE THE FUNCTIONS OF THE VARIOUS
BODY COMPONENTS; 3. MANAGE THE FLOWS OF THE
BODY IN ACCORDANCE WITH PHYSICAL UNIVERSE
LAWS; 4. BALANCE THE ENERGY OF THE BODY IN
ACCORDANCE WITH PHYSICAL UNIVERSE LAWS; 5.
MANAGE THE INTERNAL CONTROL CENTERS OF THE
BODY; 6. MANAGE THE GROWTH AND DECAY OF THE
BODY; 7. MANAGE THE INTERNAL COMMUNICATION
OF THE BODY; 8. MANAGE THE DETAILED
PROGRAMMING FOR THE BODY PARTICLES (CELLS)]

38.1 SPLIT MYSELF AND OTHERS INTO REACTIVE-
ENTITIES FOREVER
38.2 PROGRAM MYSELF AND OTHERS TO BE THE
REACTIVE-ENTITY AND RESPOND TO
PHYSICAL UNIVERSE EVENTS FOREVER
38.X TO {goal} INFINITELY IS TO BE THE REACTIVE-
ENTITY AND RESPOND TO THE ___ IN THE
ENVIRONMENT FOREVER
[1. TEMPERATURE; 2. PRESSURE; 3. ENERGY;
4. IMPACTS; 5. TASTE/SMELL PARTICLES; 6. LIGHT;
7. NOISE; 8. MOTION]

39.1 SPLIT MYSELF AND OTHERS INTO
REPRESENTERS FOREVER
39.2 PROGRAM MYSELF AND OTHERS TO BE THE

REPRESENTER AND CREATE THE
APPEARANCE OF PHYSICAL REALITY FOR
MYSELF AND OTHERS FOREVER

39.X TO {goal} INFINITELY IS TO BE THE
REPRESENTER AND ___ FOREVER
[1. MANIFEST (MOCK-UP) PERCEPTIONS OF THE
AGREED-UPON UNIVERSE FOR MYSELF]

39.Y TO {goal} INFINITELY IS TO BE THE
REPRESENTER AND CREATE ___ FOR MYSELF,
FOREVER
[2. SIGHT; 3. SENSATION OF TOUCH; 4. SOUNDS;
5. SMELLS; 6. TASTES; 7. SENSE OF MOTION]

39.Z TO {goal} INFINITELY IS TO BE THE
REPRESENTER AND ___ FOREVER
[8. FEED BACK THE IS-NESS OF THE PROJECTED
REALITY TO MYSELF]

40.1 SPLIT MYSELF AND OTHERS INTO RELAYERS
FOREVER

40.2 PROGRAM MYSELF AND OTHERS TO BE THE
RELAYER AND RELAY SENSORY DATA
FOREVER

40.X TO {goal} INFINITELY IS TO BE THE RELAYER
AND ___ FOREVER
[1. CONVEY THE PERCEPTION OF REALITY
THROUGH THE BODY'S SENSES; 2. FOCUS THE VIEW
OF THE PHYSICAL UNIVERSE THROUGH THE BODY'S
EYES; 3. CONVERT THE SOUND OF THE PHYSICAL
UNIVERSE THROUGH THE BODY'S EARS; 4. CONVERT
THE FEEL OF THE PHYSICAL UNIVERSE THROUGH
THE BODY'S SKIN (NERVE/SENSORS); 5. CONVEY THE
TASTE OF THE PHYSICAL UNIVERSE THROUGH THE
BODY'S MOUTH; 6. CONVEY THE SMELL OF THE
PHYSICAL UNIVERSE THROUGH THE BODY'S NOSE;
7. CONVEY THE SENSE OF PHYSICAL MOTION
THROUGH THE BODY'S BALANCE CENTERS; 8. LIMIT
THESE SENSES IN ACCORDANCE WITH PHYSICAL
UNIVERSE MECHANISMS]

41.1 SPLIT MYSELF AND OTHERS INTO
COMPULSIVE-ENTITIES (COMPELLERS)
FOREVER

41.2 PROGRAM MYSELF AND OTHERS TO BE THE
COMPELLER AND COMPEL MYSELF TO NEED
THINGS FOREVER

41.X TO {goal} INFINITELY IS TO BE THE
COMPULSIVE-ENTITY (COMPELLER) AND
COMPEL MYSELF TO NEED ___, FOREVER
[1. PHYSICAL UNIVERSE BODIES; 2. PHYSICAL
UNIVERSE SENSATION FROM THE BODY]

41.Y TO {goal} INFINITELY IS TO BE THE
COMPULSIVE-ENTITY (COMPELLER) AND
COMPEL MYSELF TO NEED PHYSICAL
UNIVERSE ___ FOR THE BODY, FOREVER
[3. TIME; 4. SPACE; 5. ENERGY; 6. MATTER;
7. HAVINGNESS]

41.Z TO {goal} INFINITELY IS TO BE THE
COMPULSIVE-ENTITY (COMPELLER) AND
COMPEL MYSELF TO NEED ___, FOREVER
[8. ENTITIES]

42.1 SPLIT MYSELF AND OTHERS INTO CRAVERS
FOREVER

42.2 PROGRAM MYSELF AND OTHERS TO BE THE
CRAVER AND COMPEL MYSELF TO NEED
THINGS FOR THE BODY FOREVER

42.X TO {goal} INFINITELY IS TO BE THE CRAVER AND
COMPEL MYSELF TO NEED ___ FOR THE BODY
FOREVER
[1. FOOD; 2. REST; 3. SHELTER; 4. ENERGY;
5. WARMTH; 6. SENSATION; 7. ADMIRATION; 8. TO
CARE]

43.1 SPLIT MYSELF AND OTHERS INTO FILTERS
FOREVER

43.2 PROGRAM MYSELF AND OTHERS TO BE THE
FILTER AND COMPEL MYSELF TO CONTROL MY
PERCEPTIONS FOREVER

43.X TO {goal} INFINITELY IS TO BE THE FILTER AND
FILTER OUT ANY PERCEPTIONS OF ___
FOREVER
[1. INFINITY; 2. ENTITIES; 3. THE SPLITTER-
MACHINE (POCKET) UNIVERSE; 4. THE CROSS-COPY
SUBSTRATA UNDERLYING REALITY (the interconnection

of things at an Alpha level); 5. SIDEWAYS (into other dimensions); 6. UNIVERSE MACHINERY; 7. SYMBOL MASSES; 8. ENTITY OPERATIONS]

    44.1 SPLIT MYSELF AND OTHERS INTO BODY-BLOCKERS FOREVER

    44.2 PROGRAM MYSELF AND OTHERS TO BE THE BODY-BLOCKER AND PROTECT THE BODY FROM BEING MODIFIED BY POSTULATES, FOREVER

    44.X TO {*goal*} INFINITELY IS TO BE THE BODY-BLOCKER AND (?)

    45.1 SPLIT MYSELF AND OTHERS INTO SOMATIC-ENTITIES FOREVER

    45.2 PROGRAM MYSELF AND OTHERS TO BE THE SOMATIC-ENTITY AND CREATE THE EXPERIENCE OF REALITY, FOREVER

    45.X TO {*goal*} INFINITELY IS TO BE THE SOMATIC-MACHINE AND CREATE THE SENSATION OF ___ FOR MYSELF, FOREVER

[1. MOTION; 2. PRESSURE; 3. IMPACT; 4. SHOCK; 5. PAIN; 6. EFFORT; 7. TIREDNESS; 8. DISORIENTATION]

    46.1 SPLIT MYSELF AND OTHERS INTO SLEEP-ENTITIES FOREVER

    46.2 PROGRAM MYSELF AND OTHERS TO BE THE SLEEP-ENTITY AND MANAGE THE SLEEP-CYCLE FOREVER

    46.X TO {*goal*} INFINITELY IS TO BE THE SLEEP-ENTITY AND ___ FOREVER

[1. CREATE DREAMS TO SUBMERGE MY SELF-AWARENESS (hypnotize myself); 2. USE DREAMING TO HIDE THE DEEP SLEEP ACTIVITIES FROM MY INDIVIDUAL SELF]

    46.Y TO {*goal*} INFINITELY IS TO BE THE SLEEP-ENTITY AND COMPEL MYSELF TO ___ WHILE I SLEEP, FOREVER

[3. REBUILD THE BODY; 4. REPOSTULATE THE PHYSICAL UNIVERSE; 5. RE-CREATE THIS IMPLANT; 6. REBUILD/REPAIR THE SPLITTER (POCKET) UNIVERSE; 7. FORGET WHAT I DO]

46.Z TO {*goal*} INFINITELY IS TO BE THE SLEEP-
ENTITY AND COMPEL MYSELF TO ___,
FOREVER
[8. NEED TO SLEEP]

47.1 SPLIT MYSELF AND OTHERS INTO JAILERS
FOREVER
47.2 PROGRAM MYSELF AND OTHERS TO BE THE
JAILER AND KEEP MYSELF IMPRISONED
FOREVER
47.X TO {*goal*} INFINITELY IS TO BE THE JAILER AND
KEEP MYSELF ___ FOREVER
[1. FROM ESCAPING; 2. IN A BODY; 3. FROM
OPERATING WITHOUT A BODY; 4. BELIEVING THAT I
AM A BODY; 5. LIMITED TO 3 DIMENSIONS;
6. BELIEVING THAT I AM LOCATED IN THIS UNIVERSE;
7. AND MY CREATIONS ENMESHED IN THIS UNIVERSE;
8. ATTACHED TO THE MANIFESTATIONS (MOCK-UPS)
OF THIS UNIVERSE]

48.1 SPLIT MYSELF AND OTHERS INTO SICKNESS-
ENTITIES FOREVER
48.2 PROGRAM MYSELF AND OTHERS TO BE THE
SICKNESS-ENTITY AND KEEP MYSELF AND
OTHERS SICK FOREVER
48.X TO {*goal*} INFINITELY IS TO BE THE SICKNESS-
ENTITY AND ___ FOREVER
[1. CREATE DISEASES; 2. REPLICATE DISEASES
WITHIN THE BODY; 3. ALTER THE BODY TEMPLATES
WITH DISEASE MANIFESTATIONS (MOCK-UPS);
4. MAINTAIN THE APPARANCY OF PHYSICAL VECTORS
WHEN COPYING DISEASES; 5. DEGRADE THE
CHEMISTRY OF THE BODY IN ACCORDANCE WITH
PHYSICAL LAWS; 6. MAKE MYSELF SICK IN
ACCORDANCE WITH THE CONNECTION OF SYMBOL-
MASSES; 7. MAKE MYSELF SICK IN ACCORDANCE
WITH THE LAWS OF RESTIMULATION; 8. MAKE
MYSELF SICK TO PROTECT THIS IMPLANT]

49.1 SPLIT MYSELF AND OTHERS INTO
SUPERBEINGS FOREVER
49.2 PROGRAM MYSELF AND OTHERS TO BE THE
SUPERBEING AND ATTAIN HIGHER STATES

FOREVER

49.X   TO {goal} INFINITELY IS TO BE THE
        SUPERBEING AND ___ FOREVER

[1. EVOLVE IN FORM; 2. COLLECT THE
FRAGMENTS OF INDIVIDUALS INTO A GREATER
WHOLE; 3. STRIVE TO BECOME THE COMPOSITE OF
ALL INDIVIDUALS IN THE UNIVERSE; 4. STRIVE TO
ABSORB OTHERS; 5. AVOID BEING ABSRORBED BY
OTHERS; 6. MANIPULATE REALITY TO ACHIEVE THIS;
7. OVERWHELM INDIVIDUALITY TO ACHIEVE THIS;
8. (?)]

50.1   SPLIT MYSELF AND OTHERS INTO GROUP-
        MINDS FOREVER

50.2   PROGRAM MYSELF AND OTHERS TO BE THE
        GROUP MIND AND BE GROUPS FOREVER

50.X   TO {goal} INFINITELY IS TO BE THE GROUP MIND
        AND ___ FOREVER

[1. COMBINE INDIVIDUALS INTO GROUPS;
2. STRUGGLE FOR GROUP SURVIVAL; 3. UTILIZE THE
COMBINED CAPABILITIES OF THE INDIVIDUALS IN THE
GROUP; 4. ENFORCE COMPULSIVE AGREEMENT
BETWEEN THE INDIVIDUALS OF THE GROUP;
5. SUBORDINATE INDIVIDUAL PURPOSE TO GROUP
PURPOSE; 6. SACRIFICE INDIVIDUALS FOR THE SAKE
OF THE GROUP; 7. COMPEL MYSELF TO WANT TO BE
PART OF GROUPS; 8. EVOLVE GROUPS INTO
SUPERBEINGS]

51.1   SPLIT MYSELF AND OTHERS INTO SOCIAL-
        ENTITIES FOREVER

51.2   PROGRAM MYSELF AND OTHERS TO BE THE
        SOCIAL ENTITY AND INSPIRE MYSELF TO NEED
        OTHER PEOPLE FOREVER

51.X   TO {goal} INFINITELY IS TO BE THE SOCIAL
        ENTITY AND INSPIRE MYSELF TO WANT TO ___
        OTHER INDIVIDUALS IN THE PHYSICAL
        UNIVERSE FOREVER

[1. COMMUNICATE WITH; 2. RECEIVE
COMMUNICATIONS FROM; 3. AGREE WITH; 4. WANT
AGREEMENT FROM; 5. HAVE AFFINITY (LIKINGNESS)
FOR; 6. WANT AFFINITY (LIKINGNESS) FROM;
7. ADMIRE; 8. WANT ADMIRATION FROM]

52.1 SPLIT MYSELF AND OTHERS INTO
      SYMPATHIZERS FOREVER
52.2 PROGRAM MYSELF AND OTHERS TO BE THE
      SYMPATHIZER AND INSPIRE MYSELF TO
      SYMPATHIZE WITH OTHERS FOREVER
52.X TO {*goal*} INFINITELY IS TO BE THE
      SYMPATHIZER AND INSPIRE MYSELF TO
      SYMPATHIZE WITH THE ___ OF OTHERS,
      FOREVER
   [1. SUFFERINGS; 2. HURT (PAIN); 3. LOSS;
4. WEAKNESS; 5. MISERY; 6. FAILURES;
7. ENSLAVEMENT; 8. ABUSED STATE]

53.1 SPLIT MYSELF AND OTHERS INTO ANIMATORS
      FOREVER
53.2 PROGRAM MYSELF AND OTHERS TO BE THE
      ANIMATOR AND ANIMATE OTHER LIFE FORMS
      FOREVER
53.X TO {*goal*} INFINITELY IS TO BE THE ANIMATOR
      AND ANIMATE ___ FOREVER
   [1. ANIMALS; 2. PLANTS; 3. CELLULAR
CREATURES; 4. BACTERIA; 5. CELLS; 6. VIRUSES]
53.Y TO {*goal*} INFINITELY IS TO BE THE ANIMATOR
      AND ___ FOREVER
   [7. ENDOW THESE FORMS WITH LIFE; 8. FILL THE
PHYSICAL UNIVERSE WITH LIFE]

54.1 SPLIT MYSELF AND OTHERS INTO PHYSICAL
      ENTITIES FOREVER
54.2 PROGRAM MYSELF AND OTHERS TO BE THE
      PHYSICAL ENTITY AND BE PHYSICAL FOREVER
54.X TO {*goal*} INFINITELY IS TO BE THE PHYSICAL
      ENTITY AND BE ___ FOREVER
   [1. SOLID OBJECTS; 2. LIQUIDS; 3. GASES;
4. MOLECULES; 5. WAVEFORMS; 6. FORCES;
7. PHYSICAL PROCESSES (LAWS); 8. THE
COMPONENT PARTS OF THIS UNIVERSE]

55.1 SPLIT MYSELF AND OTHERS INTO SHELL-
      ENTITIES FOREVER
55.2 PROGRAM MYSELF AND OTHERS TO BE THE
      SHELL ENTITY AND CREATE THE SHELL
      FOREVER

55.X TO {goal} INFINITELY IS TO BE THE SHELL
       ENTITY AND ___ FOREVER
    [1. ENVELOPE MYSELF; 2. PROTECT MY LOCATION
(AS AN INDIVIDUAL); 3. FOCUS REALITY IN ON
MYSELF; 4. REACT TO THE PHYSICAL UNIVERSE
ENVIRONMENT; 5. TUNE-IN TO THE UNIVERSE CROSS-
COPY; 6. FORM MYSELF INTO AN INDIVIDUAL;
7. PERMEATE BODIES; 8. INTERACT WITH SYMBOLS]

56.1 SPLIT MYSELF AND OTHERS INTO MISOWNERS
      FOREVER
56.2 PROGRAM MYSELF AND OTHERS TO BE THE
      MISOWNER AND TO MISOWN REALITY
      FOREVER
56.X TO {goal} INFINITELY IS TO BE THE MISOWNER
      AND (?) {More research needed; false data is that
                you don't own it so you can't touch it}

57.1 SPLIT MYSELF AND OTHERS INTO
      MORALIZERS FOREVER
57.2 PROGRAM MYSELF AND OTHERS TO BE THE
      MORALIZER AND (?)
57.X TO {goal} INFINITELY IS TO BE THE MORALIZER
      AND (?)

58.1 SPLIT MYSELF AND OTHERS INTO ATTITUDE-
      ENTITIES FOREVER
58.2 PROGRAM MYSELF AND OTHERS TO BE THE
      ATTITUDE ENTITY AND CREATE ATTITUDES
      TOWARDS THINGS FOR MYSELF FOREVER
58.X TO {goal} INFINITELY IS TO BE THE ATTITUDE
      ENTITY AND CHOOSE WHAT TO ___ FOREVER
    [1. BE ATTRACTED OR REPELLED BY; 2. WANT OR
NOT WANT; 3. LONG FOR OR BE DISGUSTED BY;
4. ADMIRE OR SCORN; 5. BE FRIENDLY OR HOSTILE
TOWARDS; 6. BE INTERESTED OR DISINTERESTED IN;
7. LIKE OR DISLIKE; 8. (?)]

59.1 SPLIT MYSELF AND OTHERS INTO EMOTIONAL-
      ENTITIES FOREVER
59.2 PROGRAM MYSELF AND OTHERS TO BE THE
      EMOTIONAL ENTITY AND CREATE EMOTIONS
      FOR MYSELF AND OTHERS FOREVER

59.X TO {*goal*} INFINITELY IS TO BE THE EMOTIONAL
ENTITY AND CREATE THE FEELING OF ___ FOR
MYSELF AND OTHERS, FOREVER
[1. CHEERFULNESS; 2. BOREDOM;
3. ANTAGONISM; 4. RAGE; 5. HOSTILITY; 6. FEAR;
7. GRIEF; 8. APATHY]

60.1 SPLIT MYSELF AND OTHERS INTO MOOD-
ENTITIES FOREVER
60.2 PROGRAM MYSELF AND OTHERS TO BE THE
MOOD ENTITY AND CREATE MOODS FOR
MYSELF FOREVER
60.X TO {*goal*} INFINITELY IS TO BE THE MOOD
ENTITY AND SHIFT MY MOODS BETWEEN ___,
FOREVER
[1. SERENE AND TROUBLED; 2. CALM AND
NERVOUS; 3. PLEASANT AND IRRITABLE; 4. RELAXED
AND RESTLESS; 5. HELPFUL AND TROUBLESOME;
6. ACTIVE AND LAZY; 7. COOL AND PASSIONATE;
8. RECKLESS AND CAREFUL]

61.1 SPLIT MYSELF AND OTHERS INTO
SUBLIMATING-ENTITIES FOREVER
61.2 PROGRAM MYSELF AND OTHERS TO BE THE
SUBLIMATING ENTITY AND (?)
61.X TO {*goal*} INFINITELY IS TO BE THE
SUBLIMATING ENTITY AND (?)

62.1 SPLIT MYSELF AND OTHERS INTO SEXUAL-
ENTITIES FOREVER
62.2 PROGRAM MYSELF AND OTHERS TO BE THE
SEXUAL ENTITY AND CREATE THE SEXUAL ACT
FOREVER
62.X TO {*goal*} INFINITELY IS TO BE THE SEXUAL
ENTITY AND ___ FOREVER
[1. COMPEL MYSELF TO CRAVE SEX; 2. CREATE
FEELINGS OF SEXUAL ECSTASY FOR MYSELF;
3. DIVIDE MYSELF DURING SEX; 4. EXCHANGE PIECES
OF MYSELF DURING SEX; 5. EXCHANGE ENTITIES
DURING SEX; 6. ATTEMPT TO MERGE WITH OTHER
BEINGS DURING SEX; 7. EXCHANGE ENERGIES
DURING SEX; 8. COMPEL MYSELF TO ENJOY DOING
ALL OF THIS]

63.1 SPLIT MYSELF AND OTHERS INTO
     CONFLICTORS FOREVER
63.2 PROGRAM MYSELF AND OTHERS TO BE THE
     CONFLICTOR AND INSPIRE CONFLICTS
     (BETWEEN INDIVIDUALS) FOREVER
63.x TO {goal} INFINITELY IS TO BE THE CONFLICTOR
     AND INSPIRE MYSELF AND OTHERS AS
     INDIVIDUALS TO ___ EACH OTHER FOREVER
   [1. CONFUSE; 2. UPSET; 3. BE JEALOUS OF;
4. DOMINATE; 5. FEAR; 6. HATE; 7. FIGHT; 8. ENTRAP]

64.1 SPLIT MYSELF AND OTHERS INTO SINNERS
     FOREVER
64.2 PROGRAM MYSELF AND OTHERS TO BE THE
     SINNER AND (?)
64.x TO {goal} INFINITELY IS TO BE THE (?)
     {#114 (Dramatizer) might belong here?}

65.1 SPLIT MYSELF AND OTHERS INTO
     POSTULATORS FOREVER
65.2 PROGRAM MYSELF AND OTHERS TO BE THE
     POSTULATOR AND CONTINUOUSLY CREATE
     THE PHYSICAL UNIVERSE FOREVER
65.x TO {goal} INFINITELY IS TO BE THE
     POSTULATOR AND POSTULATE ___ INTO THE
     PHYSICAL UNIVERSE FOREVER
   [1. SOLIDITY; 2. MOTION; 3. DURATION;
4. DISTANCE; 5. AESTHETICS; 6. IMPORTANCE;
7. EXCITEMENT (INTEREST); 8. REALITY]

66.1 SPLIT MYSELF AND OTHERS INTO
     GENERATORS FOREVER
66.2 PROGRAM MYSELF AND OTHERS TO BE THE
     GENERATOR AND GENERATE THE PHYSICAL
     UNIVERSE FOREVER
66.x TO {goal} INFINITELY IS TO BE THE GENERATOR
     AND PROJECT ___ FOR MYSELF AND OTHERS,
     FOREVER
   [1. TIME; 2. SPACE; 3. ENERGY; 4. MATTER;
5. DIMENSIONS; 6. BARRIERS; 7. REALITY;
8. EXISTENCE] {6 and 8 may be in reverse order?}

67.1 SPLIT MYSELF AND OTHERS INTO LOCATORS FOREVER

67.2 PROGRAM MYSELF AND OTHERS TO BE THE LOCATOR AND MANAGE SPACE FOREVER

67.X TO {goal} INFINITELY IS TO BE THE LOCATOR AND ___ FOREVER

[1. MAINTAIN THE ANCHOR-POINTS OF THE PHYSICAL UNIVERSE; 2. MAINTAIN A SINGLE AGREED-UPON COORDINATE SYSTEM BETWEEN ALL BEINGS; 3. PARTICIPATE IN THE CROSS-COPY OF AGREED-UPON LOCATIONS; 4. KEEP ALL SPATIAL POSITIONS CONSECUTIVE WITHIN THE FRAMEWORK OF REALITY; 5. LIMIT SPACE TO 3 DIMENSIONS]

67.Y TO {goal} INFINITELY IS TO BE THE LOCATOR AND HOLD ALL ___ WITHIN THE CONTOURS OF PHYSICAL SPACE, FOREVER

[6. ENERGIES; 7. MASSES; 8. INDIVIDUAL BEINGNESS]

68.1 SPLIT MYSELF AND OTHERS INTO COMMUNICATORS FOREVER

68.2 PROGRAM MYSELF AND OTHERS TO BE THE COMMUNICATOR AND INTERCONNECT EVERYTHING FOREVER

68.X TO {goal} INFINITELY IS TO BE THE COMMUNICATOR AND ___ FOREVER

[1. KEEP MYSELF AND OTHERS IN CONTACT WITH EACH OTHER; 2. INTERPOSE DISTANCE BETWEEN ALL TERMINALS; 3. INTERPOSE DURATION INTO ALL COMMUNICATIONS; 4. RELAY THE DIMENSIONS OF ALL AGREED-UPON SPACES; 5. RELAY THE AGREED-UPON FORCE (EFFORT) OF ALL ENERGIES; 6. RELAY THE AGREED-UPON FORM OF ALL SOLIDITIES; 7. INTERCHANGE AGREED-UPON REALITY BETWEEN ALL BEINGS; 8. RELAY THE ORDERS OF THE INFINITE {terminal}]

69.1 SPLIT MYSELF AND OTHERS INTO DETERMINATORS FOREVER

69.2 PROGRAM MYSELF AND OTHERS TO BE THE DETERMINATOR AND DETERMINE THE COURSE OF EXISTENCE FOREVER

69.X TO {*goal*} INFINITELY IS TO BE THE
        DETERMINATOR AND ___ FOREVER
[1. DETERMINE THE AGREED-UPON COURSE OF
EVENTS; 2. ESTABLISH DETERMINANTS BASED ON
THE MOTION OF SYMBOL-MASSES; 3. ALIGN THE
COPY INFLUX BASED ON THE ESTABLISHED
DETERMINANTS; 4. FILTER OUT ALL INFLUX THAT IS
OUT OF BOUNDS; 5. PRIORITIZE POTENTIAL FUTURE
EVENTS IN TERMS OF ALPHA DYNAMICS (Arcs of
Infinity); 6. MAXIMIZE ALPHA INVOLVEMENT AND
SURVIVAL (the Arcs) IN THE PHYSICAL UNIVERSE
FUTURE; 7. SELECT WHAT WILL BE FROM THE SET OF
DETERMINED INFLUX; 8. SUPPRESS ALL FEEDBACK
OF NON-SELECTED EVENTS]

70.1 SPLIT MYSELF AND OTHERS INTO UNIVERSE
        COORDINATORS FOREVER
70.2 PROGRAM MYSELF AND OTHERS TO BE THE
        COORDINATOR AND INTERRELATE
        EVERYTHING FOREVER
70.X TO {*goal*} INFINITELY IS TO BE THE
        COORDINATOR AND ___ FOREVER
[1. MAINTAIN THE RELATIVE POSITIONING OF ALL
FORMS; 2. COORDINATE THE RELATIVE MOTION OF
ALL PARTICLES; 3. COORDINATE THE
INTERRELATIONS OF ALL ENERGIES; 4. COORDINATE
THE INTERACTION OF FORMS AND ENERGY;
5. MAINTAIN THE CONSERVATION OF ENERGY-MATTER
AND NEVER LET ANYTHING VANISH; 6. MAINTAIN THE
CONSERVATION OF ACTION (MOTION) AND NEVER LET
ANYTHING STOP (MOVING); 7. MAINTAIN THE
CONSERVATION OF VIBRATION AND NEVER LET
ANYTHING STOP (INTERNALLY VIBRATING);
8. MAINTAIN THE CORRESPONDENCE OF REALITY]

71.1 SPLIT MYSELF AND OTHERS INTO
        SYNCHRONIZERS FOREVER
71.2 PROGRAM MYSELF AND OTHERS TO BE THE
        SYNCHRONIZER AND MANAGE TIME FOREVER
71.X TO {*goal*} INFINITELY IS TO BE THE
        SYNCHRONIZER AND ___ FOREVER
[1. MAINTAIN THE PULSE OF TIME; 2. MAINTAIN
THE CONSECUTIVE POSITION OF PARTICLES;

3. MAINTAIN THE CONSECUTIVE FLOW OF ENERGY; 4. MAINTAIN THE CONSECUTIVE SEQUENCE OF EVENTS; 5. COMPEL MYSELF TO REMAIN IN AGREEMENT WITH THE PHYSICAL UNIVERSE TIME STREAM; 6. ENSURE THAT I KNOW ONLY THE PAST AND NEVER THE FUTURE; 7. CROSS-COPY THE SIMULTANEOUSNESS OF TIME BETWEEN ALL INDIVIDUALS; 8. MAINTAIN A SINGLE AGREED-UPON 'NOW' BETWEEN ALL BEINGS]

72.1 SPLIT MYSELF AND OTHERS INTO ACTUALIZERS FOREVER

72.2 PROGRAM MYSELF AND OTHERS TO BE THE ACTUALIZER AND BRING REALITY INTO EXISTENCE FOREVER

72.X TO {goal} INFINITELY IS TO BE THE ACTUALIZER AND COPY THE CORRECT AGREED-UPON ___ INTO EACH INDIVIDUAL'S OWN UNIVERSE FOREVER

[1. SPACES; 2. MASSES; 3. ENERGIES; 4. ACTIONS; 5. DETERMINANTS; 6. CHANGES; 7. FUTURE; 8. EXISTENCE] {may be "Solidifiers"?}

73.1 SPLIT MYSELF AND OTHERS INTO PROTECTORS FOREVER

73.2 PROGRAM MYSELF AND OTHERS TO BE THE PROTECTOR AND PROTECT THE PHYSICAL UNIVERSE FOREVER

73.X TO {goal} INFINITELY IS TO BE THE PROTECTOR AND PROTECT ___ FOREVER

[1. MATTER; 2. ENERGY; 3. SPACE; 4. TIME; 5. REALITY; 6. AGREEMENTS; 7. BODIES; 8. ENTITIES]

74.1 SPLIT MYSELF AND OTHERS INTO BINDERS FOREVER

74.2 PROGRAM MYSELF AND OTHERS TO BE THE BINDER AND BIND THE PHYSICAL UNIVERSE TOGETHER FOREVER

74.X TO {goal} INFINITELY IS TO BE THE BINDER AND ___ FOREVER

[1. TIE THE UNIVERSE TOGETHER INTO A COHESIVE WHOLE; 2. BIND ALL INDIVIDUALS TOGETHER WITH THE PHYSICAL UNIVERSE; 3. BIND

ALL INDIVIDUALS TOGETHER WITH EACH OTHER'S
INFINITE ENTITIES; 4. BIND ALL INFINITE ENTITIES (OF
ALL BEINGS) TOGETHER; 5. BIND THE PHYSICAL
UNIVERSE TOGETHER WITH SYMBOLS; 6. BIND ALL
THOUGHT TOGETHER WITH THE PHYSICAL
UNIVERSE; 7. BIND THE PHYSICAL UNIVERSE
TOGETHER WITH THE UNIVERSE MACHINERY; 8. KEEP
THIS ALL ONE]

75.1 SPLIT MYSELF AND OTHERS INTO BLOCKERS
FOREVER

75.2 PROGRAM MYSELF AND OTHERS TO BE THE
BLOCKER AND BLOCK ALL TAMPERING WITH
REALITY, FOREVER

75.X TO {*goal*} INFINITELY IS TO BE THE BLOCKER
AND ___ FOREVER

[1. KEEP MYSELF FROM REACHING THE TRUE
PHYSICAL UNIVERSE; 2. KEEP MY OWN EFFORTS (AS
AN INDIVIDUAL) DIRECTED AGAINST MY OWN
'SHADOW' OF THE PHYSICAL UNIVERSE; 3. PREVENT
ANY MANIFESTATIONS OF PSYCHOKINETICS
(telekinesis) FROM OCCURRING IN THE TRUE
PHYSICAL UNIVERSE; 4. PREVENT ANY MANIPULATION
OF REALITY BY DIRECT POSTULATE (Alpha Thought)]

75.X TO {*goal*} INFINITELY IS TO BE THE BLOCKER
AND PREVENT MYSELF FROM REACHING THE
___ OF THE TRUE UNIVERSE, FOREVER

[5. SPACE; 6. TIME; 7. ENERGY; 8. MATTER]

{*Note: We are a few microseconds behind the true 'Physical
Universe' time. Everything is experienced on a very slight
communication-lag. You have to reach a little bit 'ahead'
into the 'future' to contact 'Physical Universe present-time'.*}

76.1 SPLIT MYSELF AND OTHERS INTO
CONSTRAINERS FOREVER

76.2 PROGRAM MYSELF AND OTHERS TO BE THE
CONSTRAINER AND IMPOSE THE LAWS OF THE
PHYSICAL UNIVERSE FOREVER

76.X TO {*goal*} INFINITELY IS TO BE THE
CONSTRAINER AND ___ FOREVER

[1. LIMIT ALL PERCEPTIONS IN ACCORDANCE
WITH PHYSICAL UNIVERSE LAWS; 2. LIMIT ALL

MANIPULATIONS IN ACCORDANCE WITH PHYSICAL UNIVERSE LAWS; 3. IMPOSE THE LAWS OF DISTANCE ON ALL OPERATIONS; 4. IMPOSE THE LAWS OF DISTORTION ON ALL OPERATIONS; 5. IMPOSE THE LAWS OF DURATION ON ALL OPERATIONS; 6. IMPOSE THE LAWS OF RESISTANCE ON ALL OPERATIONS; 7. IMPOSE THE LAWS OF SYMPATHY (resonance, gravity) ON ALL OPERATIONS; 8. IMPOSE THE LAWS OF PHYSICAL INTERACTION ON ALL OPERATIONS]

77.1 SPLIT MYSELF AND OTHERS INTO DIFFUSERS (DEFLECTORS) FOREVER

77.2 PROGRAM MYSELF AND OTHERS TO BE THE DEFLECTOR AND (?)

77.x TO {*goal*} INFINITELY IS TO BE THE DEFLECTOR AND MAKE ALL MY ___ MISS THEIR TARGETS FOREVER
[1. BEAMS; 2. POSTULATES; (?)]

78.1 SPLIT MYSELF AND OTHERS INTO PULL-BACKS (HOLD-BACKS?) FOREVER

78.2 PROGRAM MYSELF AND OTHERS TO BE THE PULL-BACK AND (?)

78.x TO {*goal*} INFINITELY IS TO BE THE PULL-BACK AND PULL BACK ANY ___ FOREVER
[1. ENERGY; 2. POSTULATES; 3. REACH; (?)]

79.1 SPLIT MYSELF AND OTHERS INTO VACUUMS (UNMANIFESTORS) FOREVER

79.2 PROGRAM MYSELF AND OTHERS TO BE THE VACUUM AND (?)

79.x TO {*goal*} INFINITELY IS TO BE THE VACUUM AND ___ FOREVER
[1. MAKE THINGS UNREAL; 2. DRAIN HAVINGNESS; 3. DRAIN ENERGY; 4. CAVE THIS ALL IN ON ME; 5. PULL EVERYTHING IN; 6. COLLAPSE EVERYTHING; (?)]

80.1 SPLIT MYSELF AND OTHERS INTO REFLECTORS FOREVER

80.2 PROGRAM MYSELF AND OTHERS TO BE THE REFLECTOR AND REFLECT EVERYTHING BACK IN ON MYSELF FOREVER

80.x TO {*goal*} INFINITELY IS TO BE THE REFLECTOR

AND REFLECT MY ___ BACK IN ON MYSELF,
        FOREVER
    [1. POSTULATES; 2. ENERGY-BEAMS; 3. BAD
INTENTIONS; 4. HARMFUL-ACTS; 5. FEARS;
6. EMOTIONS; 7. CREATIONS; 8. (?)]

   81.1 SPLIT MYSELF AND OTHERS INTO GUIDES
         FOREVER
   81.2 PROGRAM MYSELF AND OTHERS TO BE THE
         GUIDE AND LEAD MYSELF AND ALL OTHERS
         DEEPER INTO THE TRAP FOREVER
   81.X TO {goal} INFINITELY IS TO BE THE GUIDE AND
         ___ FOREVER

    [1. LEAD MYSELF AWAY FROM TRUE KNOWLEDGE
ABOUT REALITY]

   81.Y TO {goal} INFINITELY IS TO BE THE GUIDE AND
         LEAD MYSELF TOWARDS EVEN DEEPER ___
         WITH THE PHYSICAL UNIVERSE, FOREVER
    [2. AFFINITY (LIKINGNESS); 3. ADMIRATION;
4. INVOLVEMENT; 5. INTEREST; 6. AGREEMENT;
7. DEPENDENCE]

   81.Z TO {goal} INFINITELY IS TO BE THE GUIDE AND
         LEAD ___ WITH THE PHYSICAL UNIVERSE,
         FOREVER
    [8. MY INDIVIDUAL SELF TO BECOME ONE]

   82.1 SPLIT MYSELF AND OTHERS INTO PLANNERS
         FOREVER
   82.2 PROGRAM MYSELF AND OTHERS TO BE THE
         PLANNER AND PLAN OUT MY EXISTENCE
         FOREVER
   82.X TO {goal} INFINITELY IS TO BE THE PLANNER
         AND ___ FOREVER

    [1. KNOW THAT THE ONLY WAY OUT IS TO GO
THROUGH THE BOTTOM; 2. FIND WAYS TO KEEP MY
INDIVIDUAL SELF MOVING DOWNWARD; 3. ENJOY
DOING MYSELF IN AND SINKING DEEPER; 4. FIGURE
OUT WAYS TO ENTRAP MYSELF FURTHER; 5. REFUSE
TO ABANDON ANYTHING; 6. FIGURE OUT WAYS TO
ENTRAP OTHERS; 7. FIGHT BACK AGAINST ANYONE
WHO TRIES TO GET ME OUT; 8. LEAD MYSELF DOWN
THE DECLINING SPIRAL]

83.1 SPLIT MYSELF AND OTHERS INTO GAME-MAKERS FOREVER

83.2 PROGRAM MYSELF AND OTHERS TO BE THE GAME-MAKER AND (?)

83.X TO {goal} INFINITELY IS TO BE THE GAME-MAKER AND (?)

84.1 SPLIT MYSELF AND OTHERS INTO GOAL-MAKERS FOREVER

84.2 PROGRAM MYSELF AND OTHERS TO BE THE GOAL-MAKER AND (?)

84.X TO {goal} INFINITELY IS TO BE THE GOAL-MAKER AND (?)

85.1 SPLIT MYSELF AND OTHERS INTO FUTURIZERS FOREVER

85.2 PROGRAM MYSELF AND OTHERS TO BE THE FUTURIZER AND PROJECT (CREATE) A FUTURE FOR MYSELF (AND OTHERS?) FOREVER

85.X TO {goal} INFINITELY IS TO BE THE FUTURIZER AND PROJECT ___ FOR MYSELF INTO THE PHYSICAL UNIVERSE FUTURE, FOREVER
[1. GAMES; 2. IDENTITIES; 3. ACTIVITIES; 4. HAVINGNESS; 5. GOALS; 6. EXPECTATIONS; 7. CONSEQUENCES; 8. MY OWN PERPETUAL EXISTENCE]

86.1 SPLIT MYSELF AND OTHERS INTO ENCOURAGERS FOREVER

86.2 PROGRAM MYSELF AND OTHERS TO BE THE ENCOURAGER AND ENCOURAGE MYSELF TO ACHIEVE THINGS IN THE PHYSICAL UNIVERSE FOREVER

86.X TO {goal} INFINITELY IS TO BE THE ENCOURAGER AND ENCOURAGE MYSELF TO STRIVE ___ IN THE PHYSICAL UNIVERSE FOREVER
[1. FOR ETHICS; 2. FOR AESTHETICS; 3. TO BUILD THINGS; 4. FOR LOGIC AND REASON; 5. FOR CHANCE; 6. FOR GAMES; 7. FOR KNOWLEDGE; 8. TO CREATE THINGS]

87.1 SPLIT MYSELF AND OTHERS INTO COACHES

373

FOREVER
87.2 PROGRAM MYSELF AND OTHERS TO BE THE COACH AND (?)
87.X TO {*goal*} INFINITELY IS TO BE THE COACH AND (?) {false data is to 'keep myself from winning or losing' to 'make games go on forever'}

88.1 SPLIT MYSELF AND OTHERS INTO ALIGNERS (COORDINATORS) FOREVER
88.2 PROGRAM MYSELF AND OTHERS TO BE THE ALIGNER AND (?)
88.X TO {*goal*} INFINITELY IS TO BE THE ALIGNER AND (?)

89.1 SPLIT MYSELF AND OTHERS INTO WATCHERS (MONITORS) FOREVER
89.2 PROGRAM MYSELF AND OTHERS TO BE THE WATCHER AND MONITOR (WATCH) ALL OF THIS FOREVER
89.X TO {*goal*} INFINITELY IS TO BE THE WATCHER AND ___ FOREVER
[1. WATCH ALL THE OTHERS TO ENSURE THAT THEY ARE OBEYING ORDERS; 2. OBSERVE MYSELF AS AN INDIVIDUAL TO ENSURE THAT I REMAIN ENTRAPPED BY THIS; 3. OBSERVE PHYSICAL REALITY TO ENSURE THAT IT REMAINS INVIOLATE; 4. WATCH THE MECHANICS BEHIND REALITY TO ENSURE THAT THEY CONTINUE TO WORK]
89.Y TO {*goal*} INFINITELY IS TO BE THE WATCHER AND REPORT ANY ___ TO THE OTHER ENTITIES (OVERSOULS?) FOREVER
[5. VIOLATIONS OF THESE ORDERS; 6. ATTEMPTS TO UNMANIFEST (UNCREATE) THIS; 7. VIOLATIONS OF REALITY; 8. FAILURES OF THESE MECHANISMS]

90.1 SPLIT MYSELF AND OTHERS INTO EQUALIZERS FOREVER
90.2 PROGRAM MYSELF AND OTHERS TO BE THE EQUALIZER AND (?)
90.X TO {*goal*} INFINITELY IS TO BE THE EQUALIZER AND (?)

91.1 SPLIT MYSELF AND OTHERS INTO OPPOSERS
FOREVER
91.2 PROGRAM MYSELF AND OTHERS TO BE THE
OPPOSER AND (?)
91.X TO {goal} INFINITELY IS TO BE THE OPPOSER
AND (?)

92.1 SPLIT MYSELF AND OTHERS INTO DECEIVERS
FOREVER
92.2 PROGRAM MYSELF AND OTHERS TO BE THE
DECEIVER AND DECEIVE MYSELF FOREVER
92.X TO {goal} INFINITELY IS TO BE THE DECEIVER
AND DECEIVE MYSELF AS TO THE ___
FOREVER
[1. NATURE OF REALITY; 2. NATURE OF OTHER
BEINGS; 3. NATURE OF LIFEFORMS; 4. ANATOMY OF
THE PHYSICAL UNIVERSE; 5. ORIGINS OF THE
PHYSICAL UNIVERSE; 6. ORIGINS OF MYSELF; 7. (?);
8. ORDERS CONCERNING FOREVER]

93.1 SPLIT MYSELF AND OTHERS INTO INVERTERS
FOREVER
93.2 PROGRAM MYSELF AND OTHERS TO BE THE
INVERTER AND (?)
93.X TO {goal} INFINITELY IS TO BE THE INVERTER
AND (?)

94.1 SPLIT MYSELF AND OTHERS INTO
DISPERSERS FOREVER
94.2 PROGRAM MYSELF AND OTHERS TO BE THE
DISPERSER AND DISPERSE ANY ENERGY THAT
I PUT OUT, FOREVER
94.X TO {goal} INFINITELY IS TO BE THE DISPERSER
AND DISPERSE ___, FOREVER
[1. ENERGY-BEAMS; 2. POSTULATES;
3. INTENTIONS; 4. ATTENTION; 5. CONCENTRATION;
6. ANCHOR-POINTS; 7. VIEWPOINTS;
8. PROGRAMMING] {item-8 may be 'vibrations'?}

95.1 SPLIT MYSELF AND OTHERS INTO FATES
(ARRANGERS) FOREVER
95.2 PROGRAM MYSELF AND OTHERS TO BE THE
ARRANGER AND ARRANGE FATES FOR

MYSELF, FOREVER

95.X TO {*goal*} INFINITELY IS TO BE THE ARRANGER
AND ARRANGE ___ FOR MYSELF, FOREVER
   [1. EVENTS; 2. (?); 3. CIRCUMSTANCES; (?)]

96.1 SPLIT MYSELF AND OTHERS INTO
TRICKSTERS FOREVER

96.2 PROGRAM MYSELF AND OTHERS TO BE THE
TRICKSTER AND TRICK MYSELF FOREVER

96.X TO {*goal*} INFINITELY IS TO BE THE TRICKSTER
AND (GO AROUND AND) FOOL MYSELF AS TO
___, FOREVER
   [1. WHO IS REALLY DOING THINGS; 2. WHEN
THINGS REALLY HAPPENED; 3. WHAT IS REALLY
GOING ON; 4. THE ACTUAL PURPOSE BEHIND THINGS;
5. THE ACTUAL ORIGINS OF THINGS; 6. HOW THINGS
REALLY WORK; 7. THE ACTUAL STRUCTURE OF
THINGS; 8. WHO I REALLY AM]

97.1 SPLIT MYSELF AND OTHERS INTO 'PARTS OF
GOD' (CREATORS) FOREVER

97.2 PROGRAM MYSELF AND OTHERS TO BE THE
CREATOR AND CREATE THIS FOREVER

97.X TO {*goal*} INFINITELY IS TO BE THE CREATOR
AND CREATE ___ FOREVER
   [1. MYSELF AS AN INDIVIDUAL; 2. BODIES;
3. OTHER INDIVIDUALS; 4. SOCIETIES; 5. LIFEFORMS;
6. THE PHYSICAL UNIVERSE; 7. ENTITIES;
8. UNIVERSAL MIND]
   {'Universal Mind' also registers as separate item?
   Experimental data is given below.}

97B. TO {*goal*} INFINITELY IS TO BE THE UNIVERSAL
MIND AND ___ THE PHYSICAL UNIVERSE
FOREVER
   [1. BE THE THOUGHT OF; 2. THINK ON BEHALF OF;
3. ARRANGE FOR THE SURVIVAL OF; 4. THINK ABOUT]

97C. TO {*goal*} INFINITELY IS TO BE THE UNIVERSAL
MIND AND ___ ALL THESE OTHERS, FOREVER
   [1. BE; 2. HIDE THE THOUGHTS OF; 3. HOLD
TOGETHER THE THOUGHTS OF; 4. FORGET THE
THOUGHTS OF; 5. PROTECT THE THOUGHTS OF]

98.1 SPLIT MYSELF AND OTHERS INTO ANGELS FOREVER

98.2 PROGRAM MYSELF AND OTHERS TO BE THE ANGEL AND HELP 'GOD' FOREVER

{Note that here, 'god' is a construct that acts as a 'mind' for the Universe; you give a piece of yourself to its service.}

98.X TO {goal} INFINITELY IS TO BE THE ANGEL AND ___ FOREVER

[1. SERVE GOD; 2. CARRY OUT THE ORDERS OF GOD; 3. OBEY THE WISHES OF GOD; 4. MAINTAIN THE LAWS OF GOD; 5. ENACT THE PLANS OF GOD; 6. AGREE WITH THE MANIFESTATIONS (CREATIONS/MOCK-UPS) OF GOD; 7. SEE TO THE NEEDS OF GOD; 8. GRANT POWER (over your individual self) UNTO GOD]

99.1 SPLIT MYSELF AND OTHERS INTO ATTRACTORS FOREVER

99.2 PROGRAM MYSELF AND OTHERS TO BE THE ATTRACTOR AND COMPEL MYSELF TO NEED THE PHYSICAL UNIVERSE FOREVER

99.X TO {goal} INFINITELY IS TO BE THE ATTRACTOR AND COMPEL MYSELF TO ___ FOREVER

[1. HAVE AFFINITY (LIKINGNESS) FOR THE PHYSICAL UNIVERSE; 2. BE IN AGREEMENT WITH THE PHYSICAL UNIVERSE; 3. BE IN COMMUNICATION WITH THE PHYSICAL UNIVERSE; 4. HAVE ADMIRATION FOR THE PHYSICAL UNIVERSE; 5. DEPEND ON THE PHYSICAL UNIVERSE FOR AFFINITY (LIKINGNESS); 6. DEPEND ON THE PHYSICAL UNIVERSE FOR REALITY; 7. DEPEND ON THE PHYSICAL UNIVERSE FOR COMMUNICATION; 8. DEPEND ON THE PHYSICAL UNIVERSE FOR ADMIRATION]

100.1 SPLIT MYSELF AND OTHERS INTO ACCUSERS FOREVER

100.2 PROGRAM MYSELF AND OTHERS TO BE THE ACCUSER AND (?)

100.X TO {goal} INFINITELY IS TO BE THE ACCUSER AND (?)

101.1 SPLIT MYSELF AND OTHERS INTO JUDGES FOREVER

101.2 PROGRAM MYSELF AND OTHERS TO BE THE JUDGE AND JUDGE MYSELF, FOREVER

101.X TO {*goal*} INFINITELY IS TO BE THE JUDGE AND CONDEMN (BLAME) MYSELF FOR ___ FOREVER

[1. ALL MY FAILINGS; 2. ALL THE HARM I HAVE DONE; 3. ALL THE WRONG THOUGHTS THAT I HAVE HAD; 4. ALL MY WEAKNESSES]

101.Y TO {*goal*} INFINITELY IS TO BE THE JUDGE AND ARRANGE ___ FOREVER

[5. PUNISHMENTS FOR MY MISDEEDS; 6. FOR MY DEEDS TO COME BACK ON ME; 7. LESSONS FOR MYSELF TO TEACH ME TO BE GOOD; 8. FATES FOR MYSELF TO PUNISH MY CRIMES]

102.1 SPLIT MYSELF AND OTHERS INTO PUNISHERS FOREVER

102.2 PROGRAM MYSELF AND OTHERS TO BE THE PUNISHER AND (?)

102.X TO {*goal*} INFINITELY IS TO BE THE PUNISHER AND (?)

103.1 SPLIT MYSELF AND OTHERS INTO EXECUTIONERS FOREVER

103.2 PROGRAM MYSELF AND OTHERS TO BE THE EXECUTIONER AND (?)

103.X TO {*goal*} INFINITELY IS TO BE THE EXECUTIONER AND (?)

104.1 SPLIT MYSELF AND OTHERS INTO RECYCLERS FOREVER

104.2 PROGRAM MYSELF AND OTHERS TO BE THE RECYCLER AND REFORMAT MYSELF BETWEEN LIVES FOREVER

104.X TO {*goal*} INFINITELY IS TO BE THE RECYCLER AND RESTRUCTURE MY ___ BETWEEN LIVES FOREVER

[1. PERSONALITY; 2. MEMORIES; 3. ABILITIES; 4. BEINGNESS (IDENTITY)]

104.Y TO {*goal*} INFINITELY IS TO BE THE RECYCLER AND FORMULATE FOR MYSELF ___ BETWEEN LIVES FOREVER

[5. NEW GOALS; 6. NEW LESSONS; 7. NEW
CHALLENGES; 8. NEW ABERRATIONS]

105.1 SPLIT MYSELF AND OTHERS INTO
        INTERIORIZERS FOREVER
105.2 PROGRAM MYSELF AND OTHERS TO BE THE
        INTERIORIZER AND (?)
105.X TO {goal} INFINITELY IS TO BE THE
        INTERIORIZER AND (?)

106.1 SPLIT MYSELF AND OTHERS INTO
        DISCOURAGERS FOREVER
106.2 PROGRAM MYSELF AND OTHERS TO BE THE
        DISCOURAGER AND CONVINCE MYSELF AND
        OTHERS THAT NOTHING CAN BE DONE ABOUT
        THIS FOREVER
106.X TO {goal} INFINITELY IS TO BE THE
        DISCOURAGER AND DISCOURAGE MYSELF
        AND OTHERS FROM EVER DOING ANYTHING
        ABOUT ___ FOREVER
        [1. THIS IMPLANT; 2. ENTITIES; 3. THE PHYSICAL
UNIVERSE; 4. THE SPLITTER MECHANISMS]
106.Y TO {goal} INFINITELY IS TO BE THE
        DISCOURAGER AND CONVINCE MYSELF AND
        OTHERS THAT ___ FOREVER
        [5. THIS IS TOO SOLID TO BE TAKEN APART;
6. EVEN IF THIS COULD BE TAKEN APART (ERASED) IT
WOULD NOT MAKE ANY DIFFERENCE ANYWAY; 7.
EVEN IF YOU COULD TAKE THIS ALL APART, YOU
WOULDN'T WANT TO; 8. EVEN IF YOU DID TAKE THIS
ALL APART, YOU WOULD SUFFER A LOSS AND BE
SORRY THAT YOU HAD DONE IT]
        {'Discourager' may be the same as item-27 'Depressor'?}

107.1 SPLIT MYSELF AND OTHERS INTO
        CONFUSION-ENTITIES FOREVER
107.2 PROGRAM MYSELF AND OTHERS TO BE THE
        CONFUSION ENTITY AND KEEP MYSELF
        CONFUSED FOREVER
107.X TO {goal} INFINITELY IS TO BE THE CONFUSION
        ENTITY AND CONFUSE ___ (SO THAT THEY
        CAN NEVER BE SORTED OUT) FOREVER
        [1. TRUTH WITH FALSEHOOD; 2. REALITY WITH

UNREALITY; 3. MYSELF WITH OTHERS; 4. PAST WITH PRESENT; 5. TIME WITH SPACE; 6. MATTER WITH ENERGY; 7. IDENTITY WITH LOCATION; 8. IMPACT WITH ENLIGHTENMENT]

108.1 SPLIT MYSELF AND OTHERS INTO TERROR (FEAR) ENTITIES FOREVER

108.2 PROGRAM MYSELF AND OTHERS TO BE THE TERROR ENTITY AND TERRIFY MYSELF FOREVER

108.X TO {goal} INFINITELY IS TO BE THE TERROR ENTITY AND ___ FOREVER

[1. MANIFEST (MOCK-UP) MONSTERS AND DEMONS; 2. TERRORIZE MYSELF]

108.Y TO {goal} INFINITELY IS TO BE THE TERROR ENTITY AND MAKE MYSELF AFRAID TO ___ FOREVER

[3. FIND OUT THE TRUTH; 4. SEE ENTITIES; 5. SEE ANY DISCREPANCY IN REALITY; 6. SEE ANY VIOLATION OF REALITY; 7. REMEMBER ANYTHING BEFORE THIS UNIVERSE; 8. DISCOVER ANY PART OF THESE MECHANISMS]

109.1 SPLIT MYSELF AND OTHERS INTO DELUSION-ENTITIES FOREVER

109.2 PROGRAM MYSELF AND OTHERS TO BE THE DELUSION ENTITY AND CREATE DELUSIONS FOR MYSELF FOREVER

109.X TO {goal} INFINITELY IS TO BE THE DELUSION ENTITY AND ___ FOREVER

[1. DELUDE MYSELF AS TO THE TRUE NATURE OF REALITY; 2. CREATE FALSE REALITIES FOR MYSELF; 3. DUB-IN FALSE PERCEPTIONS; 4. DUB-IN MISCONCEPTIONS ABOUT REALITY; 5. DUB-IN INCORRECT CONCLUSIONS; 6. DUB-IN WRONG REASONS WHY; 7. CONVINCE MYSELF THAT ENTITIES ARE DELUSIONS; 8. CONVINCE MYSELF THAT PERCEPTIONS OF THE REAL NATURE OF REALITY ARE DELUSIONS]

110.1 SPLIT MYSELF AND OTHERS INTO DEGRADERS FOREVER

110.2 PROGRAM MYSELF AND OTHERS TO BE THE

DEGRADER AND DEGRADE MYSELF FOREVER
110.X TO {goal} INFINITELY IS TO BE THE DEGRADER
AND INSPIRE MYSELF TO BE ___ FOREVER
[1. GREEDY; 2. LUSTFUL; 3. CRUEL; 4. DISHONEST;
5. LAZY; 6. VISCOUS (NASTY); 7. SELFISH;
8. VENGEFUL]

111.1 SPLIT MYSELF AND OTHERS INTO TEMPTERS
FOREVER
111.2 PROGRAM MYSELF AND OTHERS TO BE THE
TEMPTER AND (?)
111.X TO {goal} INFINITELY IS TO BE THE TEMPTER
AND (?)

112.1 SPLIT MYSELF AND OTHERS INTO DEMONS
(DEVILS) FOREVER
112.2 PROGRAM MYSELF AND OTHERS TO BE THE
DEMON AND MAKE TROUBLE FOR MYSELF
FOREVER {'entrap myself forever'?}
112.X TO {goal} INFINITELY IS TO BE THE DEMON AND
CREATE ___ FOR MYSELF, FOREVER
[1. PROBLEMS; 2. DIFFICULTIES; 3. UPSETS;
4. LOSSES; 5. GUILT; 6. PENALTIES; 7. TRAPS;
8. DECLINING SPIRALS]

{'Devil' also registers as separate item?
Experimental data given below.}

112A. TO {goal} INFINITELY IS TO BE THE DEVIL AND
INSPIRE MYSELF TOWARDS EVIL WITHIN THE
PHYSICAL UNIVERSE, FOREVER
112B. TO {goal} INFINITELY IS TO BE THE DEVIL AND
MAKE TROUBLE BETWEEN MYSELF AND ___,
FOREVER
[1. OTHERS; 2. SOCIETY; 3. GOD; 4. THE PHYSICAL
UNIVERSE]

113.1 SPLIT MYSELF AND OTHERS INTO INNER-
GUARDS FOREVER
113.2 PROGRAM MYSELF AND OTHERS TO BE THE
INNER-GUARD AND STOP MYSELF FROM
KNOWING ABOUT MYSELF, FOREVER
113.X TO {goal} INFINITELY IS TO BE THE INNER-
GUARD AND MAKE MYSELF AFRAID TO ___,

FOREVER
[1. SEE MYSELF; 2. FIND OUT WHERE I REALLY AM;
3. FIND OUT WHO I REALLY AM; 4. FIND OUT WHAT I
REALLY AM; 5. FIND OUT WHEN I REALLY AM; 6. FIND
OUT MY TRUE NATURE; 7. FIND OUT MY TRUE
ORIGINS; 8. LOOK INWARD]

114.1 SPLIT MYSELF AND OTHERS INTO
DRAMATIZERS FOREVER
114.2 PROGRAM MYSELF AND OTHERS TO BE THE
DRAMATIZER AND (?)
114.X TO {goal} INFINITELY IS TO BE THE DRAMATIZER
AND (?)

115.1 SPLIT MYSELF AND OTHERS INTO
PERPETUATORS FOREVER
115.2 PROGRAM MYSELF AND OTHERS TO BE THE
PERPETUATOR AND (?)
115.X TO {goal} INFINITELY IS TO BE THE
PERPETUATOR AND (?)

116.1 SPLIT MYSELF AND OTHERS INTO
CORRECTIVE-MACHINERY FOREVER
116.2 PROGRAM MYSELF AND OTHERS TO BE THE
CORRECTIVE MACHINE-ENTITY AND KEEP
THIS ALL WORKING FOREVER
116.X TO {goal} INFINITELY IS TO BE THE
CORRECTIVE-ENTITY AND ___, FOREVER
[1. REMEDY ANY DISCREPANCIES IN REALITY;
2. ALTER PERCEPTIONS TO KEEP REALITY
CONSISTENT AND HIDE ANY DISCREPANCIES;
3. ALTER MEMORY TO KEEP REALITY CONSISTENT
AND HIDE ANY DISCREPANCIES; 4. MAKE MYSELF AND
OTHERS SPLIT TO REPLACE ANY ENTITIES THAT ARE
RELEASED {registers, but may be part of item-117}; 5. USE
THE RESOURCES OF ALL THESE OTHERS TO
REPROGRAM ANY PART OF THIS IMPLANT THAT FAILS;
6. CONVINCE MYSELF AND OTHERS TO OBEY THIS
IMPLANT; 7. USE THE RESOURCES OF ALL THESE
OTHERS TO KEEP THIS CONTINUOUSLY CREATED;
8. REPORT ALL INFRACTIONS TO THE OVERSOULS]

117.1 SPLIT MYSELF AND OTHERS INTO SPLITTERS

FOREVER

117.2 PROGRAM MYSELF AND OTHERS TO BE THE SPLITTER AND (?)

117.X TO {goal} INFINITELY IS TO BE THE SPLITTER AND (?)

118.1 SPLIT MYSELF AND OTHERS INTO IMPLANTERS FOREVER

118.2 PROGRAM MYSELF AND OTHERS TO BE THE IMPLANTER AND IMPLANT MYSELF WITH ORDERS AS AN INDIVIDUAL, FOREVER

> {wording may be '..myself as an individual, with orders,..'}

118.X TO {goal} INFINITELY IS TO BE THE IMPLANTER AND IMPLANT MYSELF (WITH ORDERS) TO ___ FOREVER

[1. BELIEVE IN REALITY; 2. AGREE WITH REALITY; 3. BE THE EFFECT OF (or 'affected by') REALITY; 4. BE LOCATED WITHIN REALITY (or 'the Physical Universe'); 5. BELIEVE THAT THE PHYSICAL UNIVERSE IS LARGER ('greater') THAN I AM; 6. BELIEVE THAT THE PHYSICAL UNIVERSE IS MORE IMPORTANT THAN I AM; 7. BELIEVE THAT THE PHYSICAL UNIVERSE IS MORE POWERFUL THAN I AM; 8. BELIEVE THAT THE PHYSICAL UNIVERSE IS MORE ENDURING THAN I AM]

119.1 SPLIT MYSELF AND OTHERS INTO KEEPERS FOREVER

119.2 PROGRAM MYSELF AND OTHERS TO BE THE KEEPER AND (?)

119.X TO {goal} INFINITELY IS TO BE THE KEEPER & ?

120.1 SPLIT MYSELF AND OTHERS INTO UNIFIERS (JOINERS) FOREVER

120.2 PROGRAM MYSELF AND OTHERS TO BE THE UNIFIER AND MAKE EVERYTHING ONE FOREVER

120.X TO {goal} INFINITELY IS TO BE THE UNIFIER AND BE ONE WITH ___, FOREVER

[1. INFINITY; 2. ALL THESE ENTITIES; 3. THE PHYSICAL UNIVERSE; 4. ALL LIFEFORMS; 5. ALL SOCIETIES; 6. ALL OTHER INDIVIDUALS; 7. BODIES;

8. THE ITEMS OF THIS IMPLANT]

121.1 SPLIT MYSELF AND OTHERS INTO
RESTIMULATORS FOREVER
121.2 PROGRAM MYSELF AND OTHERS TO BE THE
RESTIMULATOR AND KEEP THIS IN
RESTIMULATION FOREVER
121.X TO {*goal*} INFINITELY IS TO BE THE
RESTIMULATOR AND ___, FOREVER
   [1. CREATE THIS IMPLANT CONTINUOUSLY;
2. FORCE MYSELF AND OTHERS TO CROSS-COPY
INFINITELY; 3. FORCE MYSELF AND OTHERS TO
DIVIDE INFINITELY; 4. FORCE MYSELF AND OTHERS
TO DRAMATIZE THIS; 5. REPEAT THE ITEMS OF THIS
IMPLANT; 6. FORCE MYSELF AND OTHERS TO REMAIN
THE EFFECT OF THIS; 7. KEEP THIS IMPLANT SOLID;
8. RE-CREATE THE IMPACT OF THIS INCIDENT]

122.1 SPLIT MYSELF AND OTHERS INTO
INVALIDATORS FOREVER
122.2 PROGRAM MYSELF AND OTHERS TO BE THE
INVALIDATOR AND INVALIDATE ANY
AWARENESS OF THIS IMPLANT, FOREVER
122.X TO {*goal*} INFINITELY IS TO BE THE
INVALIDATOR AND INVALIDATE ANY ___ OF
THIS IMPLANT, FOREVER
   [1. AWARENESS; 2. KNOWLEDGE;
3. REMEMBRANCE; 4. UNDERSTANDING; 5. ERASURE
OF; 6. FREEDOM FROM; 7. COMMAND OVER;
8. MASTERY OF]

123.1 SPLIT MYSELF AND OTHERS INTO
MISDIRECTORS FOREVER
123.2 PROGRAM MYSELF AND OTHERS TO BE THE
MISDIRECTOR AND MISLEAD ANYONE WHO
ATTEMPTS TO DISCOVER THIS, FOREVER
123.X TO {*goal*} INFINITELY IS TO BE THE
MISDIRECTOR AND ___, FOREVER
   [1. SUBSTITUTE WRONG DATES CONCERNING
THE BACKTRACK; 2. MAKE MYSELF AND OTHERS
CONFUSE THE CORRECT SEQUENCE OF EVENTS;
3. MANUFACTURE FALSE-DATA; 4. MAKE MYSELF AND
OTHERS MIX UP LOCATIONS; 5. MAKE MYSELF AND

OTHERS DUB-IN IMAGINARY INCIDENTS; 6. MISLEAD MYSELF AND OTHERS; 7. DIRECT ATTENTION AWAY FROM THIS INCIDENT; 8. PREVENT THE TRUTH FROM BEING DISCOVERED]

124.1 SPLIT MYSELF AND OTHERS INTO DENIERS FOREVER

124.2 PROGRAM MYSELF AND OTHERS TO BE THE DENIER AND DENY THE EXISTENCE OF THIS FOREVER

124.X TO {*goal*} INFINITELY IS TO BE THE DENIER AND ___ FOREVER

[1. INSIST THAT ENTITIES DO NOT EXIST; 2. INSIST THAT INFINITY DOES NOT EXIST; 3. DENY THAT ANY OF THIS IS REAL; 4. DENY THAT THIS EVER HAPPENED; 5. INVALIDATE THE REALITY OF ANY NON-PHYSICAL UNIVERSE MANIFESTATION ('creation' or 'mock-up'); 6. INSIST THAT THE PHYSICAL UNIVERSE IS THE ONLY REALITY; 7. COMPEL MYSELF AND OTHERS TO DISBELIEVE IN THE EXISTENCE OF THIS IMPLANT; 8. COMPEL MYSELF AND OTHERS TO DISBELIEVE IN THE EXISTENCE OF THE INFINITE {terminal}]

125.1 SPLIT MYSELF AND OTHERS INTO SUPPRESSORS FOREVER

125.2 PROGRAM MYSELF AND OTHERS TO BE THE SUPPRESSOR AND KEEP THIS HIDDEN FOREVER

125.X TO {*goal*} INFINITELY IS TO BE THE SUPPRESSOR AND KEEP MYSELF FROM ___ THIS FOREVER

[1. SPOTTING; 2. KNOWING ABOUT;
3. PERCEIVING; 4. COMMUNICATING ABOUT;
5. THINKING ABOUT]

125.Y TO {*goal*} INFINITELY IS TO BE THE SUPPRESSOR AND ___ FOREVER

[6. KEEP THIS FROM REGISTERING ON ANY DETECTION-DEVICES; 7. STOP THIS FROM BEING DISCOVERED; 8. USE THE RESOURCES OF ALL THESE OTHER ENTITIES TO BLOCK ALL KNOWLEDGE OF THIS]

126.1 SPLIT MYSELF AND OTHERS INTO HOLDERS
FOREVER

126.2 PROGRAM MYSELF AND OTHERS TO BE THE
HOLDER AND HOLD EVERYONE TOGETHER
FOREVER

126.x TO {goal} INFINITELY IS TO BE THE HOLDER
AND ___, FOREVER
[1. MAKE EVERYONE ALL ONE; 2. JOIN EVERYONE
TOGETHER; 3. HOLD EVERYONE IN A SINGLE REALITY;
4. COMBINE EVERYONE INTO A SINGLE BEING;
5. MAKE EVERYONE HOLD ON TO EACH OTHER;
6. HOLD MYSELF AND OTHERS IN AGREEMENT
TOGETHER; 7. HOLD ON TO ALL THESE BEINGS;
8. KEEP ANYONE FROM LEAVING]

127.1 SPLIT MYSELF AND OTHERS INTO GUARDIANS
FOREVER

127.2 PROGRAM MYSELF AND OTHERS TO BE THE
GUARDIAN AND PROTECT THIS IMPLANT
(FROM BEING VIEWED), FOREVER

127.x TO {goal} INFINITELY IS TO BE THE GUARDIAN
AND PREVENT MYSELF AND OTHERS FROM
___ FOREVER
[1. VIOLATING THE RULES OF THE PHYSICAL
UNIVERSE; 2. MOVING OUT OF THE PHYSICAL
UNIVERSE; 3. MODIFYING REALITY; 4. FINDING OUT
THE TRUTH ABOUT REALITY; 5. CHANGING THE
NATURE OF REALITY; 6. DISAGREEING WITH REALITY;
7. KNOWING THAT I AM DOING THESE THINGS;
8. REMEMBERING THIS IMPLANT]

128.1 SPLIT MYSELF AND OTHERS INTO OVERSOULS
FOREVER

128.2 PROGRAM MYSELF AND OTHERS TO BE THE
OVERSOUL AND ORGANIZE ALL THESE
OTHERS FOREVER

128.x TO {goal} INFINITELY IS TO BE THE OVERSOUL
AND ___ FOREVER
[1. MANAGE THIS; 2. SEE THAT THIS IS REPAIRED;
3. COORDINATE ALL THESE OTHERS; 4. ORGANIZE
MYSELF AND ALL THESE OTHERS; 5. CONTROL
MYSELF AND ALL THESE OTHERS; 6. KEEP MYSELF

AND ALL THESE OTHERS DIVIDED; 7. LIE ABOUT THIS
TO MYSELF AND ALL THESE OTHERS; 8. KEEP MYSELF
AND ALL THESE OTHERS ENTRAPPED]

ADDITIONAL RESEARCH NOTES:

Other entity type-labels may include a *Problem-Maker*;
and also a *Balancer, Equalizer,* or *Tabulator (for karma).* Or
these may be alternate labels for existing types on the list
that require more research.

There is some *Meter-data* for a *Convincer,* to "convince
myself that I need this" or "make myself dependent on
this," *&tc.* The label *"Misleader"* also registers; but may
be similar to (or the same as) the *"Guide"* — that "guides
my individual self deeper into the Physical Universe,
forever," and "keep myself more in agreement," "keep
myself more confused," "more solid," *&tc.* More research
is needed to be certain.

There are also additional *"Higher-Self" items* that apply to
the ending sequence of the *Implant.* These have already
been well researched; however, their precise wording
and sequencing is still in question.

1. MAKE THIS ALL HAPPEN (FOREVER); 2. REMAIN IN
AGREEMENT WITH THIS IMPLANT (FOREVER); 3. KEEP
THIS ALL WORKING (FOREVER); 4. KEEP THIS ALL IN
MOTION (FOREVER); 5. NEVER LET MY LOWER SELF
KNOW WHAT I AM DOING (FOREVER); 6. RULE OVER
ALL THESE OTHER (ENTITIES) (FOREVER); 5. ENJOY
DOING THIS (FOREVER); 7. ENJOY BEING HERE
(FOREVER); 8. NEVER THINK ABOUT BEING HERE
(FOREVER).

SECTION 5. FINAL ITEMS

TO {goal} INFINITELY IS TO BE ALL THESE THINGS
AND ___, FOREVER

1. BLOCK ALL AWARENESS OF THESE ORDERS

2. BLOCK ALL KNOWLEDGE OF INFINITY
3. BLOCK ALL REMEMBRANCE OF THIS
4. BLOCK ALL KNOWLEDGE OF THESE ENTITIES
5. KEEP MYSELF AND OTHERS UNKNOWING
6. KEEP MYSELF AND OTHERS ASLEEP
7. KEEP MYSELF AND OTHERS UNCONSCIOUS
8. KEEP MYSELF AND OTHERS DEAD

SECTION 6. FINAL PROCESSING STEPS

Use these methods for "group-processing" any entities re-maining after completing the Splitter-Platform (incident-sequence) given in previous sections. Apply as many tech-niques as is necessary to resolve the case.

A. *Imagine* "doing" and "not doing" (alternately) these things repeatedly to an *end-point*.

B. *Spot* "being programmed into being" these things. *Spot* the first time. *Spot* programming others. *Spot* others programming others.

C. *Spot* "being made to split." *Spot* first time; to others; others to others.

D. *Spot* "being implanted with false-data." *Spot* first time; to others; others to others.

E. *Spot* "being made to divide out to infinity." *Spot* first time; to others; others to others.

F. *Spot* "being made into the infinite {*terminal*}." *Spot* first time; to others; others to others.

G. *Decide* "to be" and "not be" the *infinite-terminal* (alternately) repeatedly to an *end-point*.

H. *Imagine* "creating" and "un-creating" the *infinite-terminal* (alternately) until you are at *Cause* over it.

I. *Spot* "the first item of the *Splitter-Platform*" (*To {goal} Infinitely Is To Perceive Ultimate Truth*); *Spot* it as *false-data*.

J. *Spot* the *"Native State" item* for the IPU-*Goal*. *Spot* being pushed into it; pushing others into it; others pushing others into it.

K. Ask the entity: *"Can You Create?"* It will *register* as *"yes"* on the *GSR-Meter*. If not: have the *entity* practice *imagining/creating* and *"throwing away"* a few objects; then ask again.

L. Ask the entity: *"Are You Free Of This?"* If it does not *register*: *list* to find out why (what *item* is not fully *discharged*).

M. *Identification Tech. (Who Are You?)*

N. *Locational Tech. (Point To..)*

Then check if anything remains to be handled—if any *entities* didn't *release*, *&tc*. Other *entities*, from other *Goals*, may try to "copy" and "replace" what was just handled. So, check for that; and if it is the case, simply indicate it to yourself (it *disperses-on-realization*).

Then *process-out* the IPU-*Platform* (*AT#4*) to *total defragmentation* on that *Goal*. Since you've handled the *Splitter-Incident*, the *defragmentation* may occur relatively quickly after a small number of *items*.

Only after this point should you handle the *negative-Goals*. When you do: start by *spotting* the *"Native State" item* of the *basic (positive)* IPU-*Goal*. Then, reaffirm (to yourself) the *total defragmentation* of the *basic-Goal* by *spotting* the point (in time) when you *totally defragmented* it with the *Platform*. Do this any time you feel that *"charge"* may be accumulating on the *basic* while handling the *negative*.

OPENING GATES TO THE KINGDOM
(*The Beginning In The Ending*)

A *Wizard* is one who is not only a *Master* of their own *Universe*, but who has the ability and certainty to knowingly affect and change the *Universe* around them; for themselves, and for others. We are not speaking of stage acts and parlor tricks; we mean actually *helping one another* and *making this world a better place* to conduct our *Ascension* work.

For the first time in known history (including the *Backtrack*), there is a true launch point toward *Ascension* available to humanity—and *it is our Systemology.* As should be self-evident after *33* progressive *lesson-booklets* and *manuals*: all of this could have only been uncovered with a *Self-Honest systematic approach.*

The basic *spiritual cartography* is complete—and the *Way Out* has been cleared. Are there still some rough patches that require additional development? Sure. But, that is where you come in—investing yourself in the final *research-actions* necessary for your own *Ascension*; and perhaps assisting your fellow *Seekers* by contributing to the ongoing *Infinity Grade* that is intended to follow hereafter and preserve the legacy of the *Systemology Society* and the perfection of its knowledge.

This presentation of the final *Keys to the Kingdom* volume —and the completion of an entire library synthesizing the *systematic truth* of *spiritual life* and *all existence*— marks the end of a personal *29-year quest.* Bearing the weight of carrying *Excalibur*—the *Sword of Truth* or *Sword of Shannara*—to *dispel all illusion*, the present author forged ahead, determined and steadfast in his mission to chart a true *Map* that could lead us back through the *Gates* of the *Magic Kingdom* and retrieve the *Grail-secret* we had lost.

Finally, that *Map* has been rediscovered and decoded—and its facsimile stands publicly on display in these many printed works—for *anyone* that cares to travel this *Pathway*. The stable gains and progress you make on the *Pathway* is true and lasting—carried with you beyond this lifetime, on your infinite spiritual journey.

Now, the *Grail* is safely stored in the *Castle* again—an overflowing cup that serves to remind us that we already have, within our *Beingness*, the well-springs of *all the Havingness* we could ever want or dream for; and we have no need to be dependent on any other *Source*.

The *Grail* is there for all who might shed their *Human* garb, recollect the *fragmented pieces* of their *Beingness*, and simply *reach* through the dimensions for it. It is all of ours for the taking; and so long as this record is maintained, it can never be lost again.

But now I digress; yielding to the *next-generation* of *Seekers* to take up this quest and complete the *Pathway* for themselves—remembering always to *help one another*.

And to all those that follow: I have returned the *Sword* to the *Lake*—where it is now, still there, just waiting for *you*.

Safe journeys, dear Seeker.

We'll see you on the Other Side.

SYSTEMOLOGY
PILOTING
MANUAL

Based on the lecture notes by Joshua Free for
the 2024 Spring Equinox release of the complete
Pathway-To-Ascension Professional Course and
Keys to the Kingdom Advanced Training Course.

SYSTEMATIC PROCESSING

Systematic Processing is primarily *looking* and *seeing* "*What Is*" — *As-It-Is*. "*Processing Command Lines*" (or "PCL") are really a query-line (or question) of "*what is*"? The response is based on whatever our *attention* (*Awareness*) is on, or directed to. Even when not worded as a literal question, a PCL is still a prompt for such a response. For example:

Q: *Recall a time when... (What is it?)*

A: *(It is) when such-and-such...*

Q: *Spot something in the... (What is it?)*

A: *(It is) that thing...*

Q: *Notice something about... (What is it?)*

A: *(It is) this...*

A *Seeker* is still permitted to *consider* or *wonder about* things. But to avoid having progress slow down to a halt during a *processing session*: the focus should be on what they *can identify, see*, or *know about*, rather than concentrating on "*unknowns*."

To be effective, *systematic processing* is applied to only one thing/area at a time. It is for this reason that a *Pilot* must be aware of where a *Seeker's attention* is *fixed* — or a *Solo-Pilot* must be aware of it.

If *attention is* "stuck" on a point that can't be put aside, then it must be addressed first in *processing*, because that is the *fixed* point of *attention* that all other *processing* will take place from anyways. The "*presence*" that is elsewhere must be brought under *control* before other gains will be made "*in-session*."

Defragmentation is a gradual process of relieving the "weight" off of the *Spirit*. This "weight" is mostly *persistently created entangled energy-masses*. A proper *"session"* should provide *some sense of release* to a *Seeker* for it to be effective.

If a *process* is not *run long enough,* there is a general feeling of "incompleteness." A *Seeker* may feel irritable as a result. Irritability and hopeless feelings are good indicators for a *process* being *"under-run."* The solution is to *run* the *process* longer.

The other side of this—*"over-run"*—tends to make things more *"solid"* or feel *"heavier."* Usually an area or target item was *defragmented* (a *release-point* was achieved) but since the *process* continues to target it as *being there*, it gets "pulled in" again, or else is *recreated.* This often happens when a beginner expects a single *process* to handle everything, or do it all, when it really requires applying many different *processes*, each providing another step forward as a fairly quick progression.

The *systematic* solution to an *"over-run" process* is to simply *"spot"* and *acknowledge* the point when the *"win"* or *"new realization"* had occurred (but was overlooked, not *acknowledged*, and *invalidated*).

PREVENTATIVE FUNDAMENTALS

If a *Seeker* has an *upset*, a *problem*, or any *attention* "stuck" on things they are worried about, it is not possible to progress in other areas until this handled. In the *Professional Course*, this handling is called "preventative fundamentals" because a *Pilot* must take care of these things first before attempting to spend *session* time in other areas. What we are *preventing* is an *invalidation* of our methods by a *Seeker* that is unable to apply *presence* of *attention in-session*. These fundamentals are treated in *Professional Course* materials:

1. A *break* or *upset* in the "*Flow-Factors*"—enforced or inhibited *communication, likingness* and/or *agreement.* [*Lesson-7, "Eliminating Barriers"*]

2. A "*Human Problem*" — present-time *attention* (*presence*) is occupied fixedly elsewhere (and outside one's own control). [*Lesson-4, "Handling Humanity"*]

3. A "*Hold-Out*" —*attention* restimulated an area, usually because someone else *almost found out* about it. [*Lesson-6, "Escaping Spirit-Traps"*]

A *Solo-Pilot* looks over this list and determines if any of these factors are in play at the start of a *session*. In *Traditional Piloting*, a *GSR-Meter* may be used to *assess* if anything on the list *reads.* For example:

1. "Is there a *break* or *upset* of a *Flow-Factor?*"

[if it "*reads,*" check]

　a. "Is there a break in *Communication?*"

　b. "On *Likingness?*"

　c. "On *Agreement?*"

[then, *run* on which of *a, b,* or *c,* "*reads*"]

　a. "Was this ___ *Enforced?*"

　b. "*Inhibited?*"

In this first case: when you can *spot* the primary underlying source of the *upset*—such as "*inhibited communication*" or "*enforced agreement*" —there should be *some* feeling of "*relief.*" If not: you may need to *reassess* the list.

The *"relief on spotting"* is either partial or total. If total: *acknowledge* it and continue on with the *session*. If partial: handle the *upset* (or *flow-break*) before continuing. It is handled by *spotting* the *flow* and *circuit*.

For example: did *you inhibit (or enforce) someone else's communication (&tc.)* or did *someone else inhibit yours?* Perhaps it was observing *someone else inhibiting another.* Whatever the case: *identify it,* then *spot* exactly what *communication* was *inhibited.* Then *spot* yourself in the situation; what you *did* and *decided* as a result of it, *&tc.* If the *turbulence* doesn't resolve or worsens: look for an earlier incident that was similar. If it gets more *solid,* it has been *over-run*: *spot* the *release-point* that was missed.

TRADITIONAL PILOTING

This manual is a continuation of material presented in *"Systemology Procedures"* and *"Systemology Biofeedback."* Its emphasis is *how to "Pilot"* (or *"Co-Pilot"*) *Systemology* for traditional/professional applications. This is not a guide for *"what to process"* or *"what processing is"*—as such subjects are taken up in other manuals and lessons.

The purpose of this manual is to "pull together" all the data into an applied practice of *helping others—processing others.* There are *no* "special cases" in *Systemology.* We apply *New Standard Systemology*—given in *"Pathway to Ascension" Level-0 to 6*; and *"Keys to the Kingdom" Level-7 and 8*—from *bottom to the top,* to *all Seekers.* To deliver *processing-levels 0-to-6,* a *Pilot* must be *Level-7* or *8,* themselves. Only a *Pilot* that has completed *Level-8* is qualified to supervise paperwork for a *Solo Level-7.*

We originally developed *systematic processing* to train *Mardukite Ministers (of Zuism)* with skills to provide *spiritual advisement* or *counseling*. Initially, there was no prescribed *Pathway*. A *minister* studied our entire philosophy so they could apply the most relevant elements to handle the immediate concerns of an individual coming to them for assistance.

The first *"Professional Piloting Course"*—from 2020—is contained in the *"Metahuman Destinations"* volumes. It was there that the "seeds" of a *standardized Pathway* first began to grow; and the basic outline for a *"Formal Session"* began to emerge. It remains our basic *Pilot Training* material.

It is important to handle the immediate concerns of an individual before attempting to guide them along the *Pathway*. If the difficulties and upsets are not treated, then a *"hidden standard"* develops where *Systemology* is only considered to "work" *if* such-and-such a *"condition"* improves.

To effectively *process* another individual, a *Pilot* must apply *Systemology* with *certainty*—of the materials; of their own skill to communicate *processing command lines* (PCL); and their own ability to maintain control of the *systematic processing session*.

A *Pilot* develops their skill similar to how a *Seeker* ascends the *Pathway*; except in this case, the emphasis becomes applying the material to *someone else*, not just *Self*. For example: *Level-0* for the *Pathway* is *"communication."* *Level-0* for *Pilot Training* is also *"communication."* *Clear communication* is necessary for *all processing* to occur.

Piloting requires the *ability-to-confront* the *Seeker* existing across from you in *session*; just as the *Seeker* must be able to *recognize/confront* you as a *Pilot* for the *session*.

It requires an *ability-to-communicate* (project) PCL to a *Seeker* (clearly and directly with *intention*); and see that it has been received, or perceive the response; and then end the *communication-cycle* with an appropriate *acknowledgment*. [These are the same steps a *Seeker* practices on "objects" during *Level-8* (see *AT#7*).]

Traditional Piloting requires the same level of *presence-in-session* described in the *Professional Course* (PC) material of "*Pathway to Ascension.*" A *Seeker* has to have *reality* on the *session* for it to be effective. When you say "*recall a time you communicated...,*" does the *Seeker* properly receive, understand, and *process* the *command-line*? Does the *Seeker* even have any *reality* on *Life*; any *reality* on *communicating* at all? You will know by the *communication-lag*; the delay in getting a response or answer—and I mean an actual answer to the PCL; not just the production of a sound.

A *Pilot* must study *Systemology* to have any *reality* on it— otherwise, what are they delivering? If a *Pilot* hasn't gone through *processing* themselves, how are they to understand a *Seeker's* responses?

Traditional Piloting is not a "cultish" tactic; it cannot be enforced. It requires *two-way communication* with a willing *Seeker* that is interested in *Systemology* and their own case—or resolving the *Human Condition*. *Pilot Training* is as much about *communication* and *control* as it is about *processes* and techniques.

A *Pilot* must be able to skillfully deliver *systematic processing*:

—without *Evaluating* out loud to the *Seeker* about things that they should arrive at as their own *end-realizations*;

—without *Invalidating* with disbelief or suppression in any way, or trying to "correct" the data that a *Seeker* is giving; and

—without *Reacting* (or displaying any *emotion*) to anything a *Seeker* says or does during a *session*.

You don't say to a *Seeker*, "*Oh, this is what is going on with you*." We want the *Seeker* to realize the "*This is..*" part on their own.

ELEMENTS OF PILOTING

There are only four components to *Traditional Piloting*: the *Pilot*; a *Seeker* to *process*; the *session*, or *space* to have a *session*; and the *processing* or *processes*. That's all.

There is a big difference between *talking* and *being in-session* or *processing*. A *Seeker* needs to accept the *Pilot* as their "guide" (or as a *Co-Pilot*) if their presence is to be of any actual assistance to them. We start off, asking: "*Is it alright if I process you?*" And an initial line of communication is established. That's *Level-0*, or *square-one*.

We move on to the next requirement: and that is *presence-in-session*. Is the *Seeker's* *attention* somewhere other than the *session?* If it is, you aren't going to make any real progress. Whatever a *Seeker's* *attention* is *fixed* on is considered a "*problem*" to them—that's why they're *fixated* on it.

When a *Seeker* isn't able to apply *presence-in-session*, it is because they are treating something else as happening "now" in the *session*-space *and* time; even when it is not. You can even address this: "*Is this problem happening here in this room?*" or "*Is this person here in this room?*" You could even repeatedly alternate: "*Where is the problem?*" and "*Where are you now?*"

"*Human Problems*" is treated as *Level-1* on the *Pathway*; and it is *Level-1* for a *Pilot*. In this case, it is the matter of *presence-of- Awareness in-session* for *processing*. There is no progress—no *processing* taking place—if the *Seeker* isn't *present*. You aren't there to *communicate* with their *mental machinery*; you want to *process* a *Seeker*.

At the start of the *session*, you want to determine if a *Seeker's attention* is elsewhere; so you just ask: "*Is there anything that you are currently worried about?*" or "*Is there anything your attention is currently on?*"

New Standard Systemology is already designed for use by *Solo-Pilots*. Therefore, a *Professional Pilot* needs to demonstrate that they are of genuine benefit as an assistant to the *Seeker* on the *Pathway*. You aren't there just to read a book to them.

A *Pilot* ensures there is *presence-in-session* and a *communication-line* before *running* any other *processing*. Obviously, there are *techniques* and *processes* used to accomplish these basic points. But, for example, a *Pilot* isn't going to apply more "*subjective-styled processes*" regarding something that they can't visibly observe, unless they know the *Seeker* can receive PCL and follow commands regarding things that *can* be observed.

If a *Pilot* is having issues with getting a *Seeker* to focus *in-session*, or understand and follow-through with "picking up an object," don't start introverting the *Seeker* to *ima-*

gine/create or *recall* things with any *reality*; because they don't have it (*reality*).

A "*condition*" is a set of circumstances encountered by *Life*—by the *Alpha-Spirit*—and in our work, we are predominantly concerned with the "*Human Condition*"; the *mental-circuitry* and *reality-agreements* associated with the "*Human Condition.*"

When handling the *conditions* of *Life*, an individual has two choices: to *increase* or *decrease* their level of *Actualized Awareness.* An individually is either *knowingly direct* in *confronting reality* "*As-It-Is*" or they are operating *unknowingly, compulsively* and on *automatic.* As a route of *Self-improvement*—or when applied vocationally by a *minister* —*systematic processing* is only *piloted* (or *Co-Piloted*) to assist the *Seeker* in rehabilitating their own abilities.

The *Pathway* is marked by an increased *ability-to-confront* —leading to upper-level abilities of "*defragmentation-by-realization*" alone. It is also critical for a *Pilot* to be able to *confront/handle* the *processing-session*—and the *Seeker* within that *session.*

This means maintaining sufficient control over the *session* and *communication-line* until the *Seeker* can exercise true *Self-Honest* control of focused *attention* and their own *Self-Directed Actualized Awareness.*

Whether or not a *Seeker* is *Co-Piloted* up the *Pathway* through *processing level-6*, the upper-most levels are always handled "*Solo.*" This means at some point, a *Seeker* must take total responsibility for their own case. Records of this work can be reviewed by an experienced *Seeker*, but they act solely as an adviser to the *Seeker* in between *Solo-sessions.*

It is difficult for a *Seeker* to apply *presence-in-session*, or work their way along the *Pathway* (*processing-levels 0-to-6*), if they are currently concerned with "pain management" (especially chronic conditions).

Ideally, a *Seeker* becomes more able to *confront* past-*incidents* and is less likely to *compulsively* (*unknowingly*) create reactive *mental-images* and other *stored impressions* (possibly even at a cellular-level). [More details on this are given in the companion supplement, "*Systemology Procedures.*"]

PILOTING SEEKERS

To apply the *Pathway* material for *Self-improvement*, a *Seeker* needs to feel safe in their environment; and free to *communicate* and *process* without inhibition. They can't be worried that the "*Pilot might find out something.*" It is likely a *Seeker* is carrying around some bad experiences (which is to say *imprints*) concerning *communication* and *contact* with their *environment*.

It is up to a *Pilot* to provide reassurance. You might direct a *Seeker* to: "*Look around the room and spot things that are not being a threat*" or "*...not threatening you.*" Ideally, the *Seeker* will also include "*The Pilot*" in their list of such observations.

Any technique that puts the *Seeker* in contact (*communication*) with their present environment is useful for achieving and maintaining *presence-in-session*, while at the same time, increasing *clear perception* and *Actualized Awareness*.

When a *Seeker* enters upon the *Pathway* from the *Human Condition*, they are *seeking* the *answer* to an ultimate "*WHY?*" — an ultimate "*Cause Of*" — and they are not going to be able to accept or understand the *answer* — the *Truth* — until it is fully and personally *recognized* and *realized* for what it is. And there certainly *are answers* when a *Seeker* is ready to receive them.

Even the degree to which a *Seeker*, themselves, is actually at *Cause*, is not likely to be accepted early on. Most elements that a *Seeker* believes to be their issue are misassigned or misidentified until they are able to realize their own true *Beingness* — being at *Cause* — and their participation in the *duplication* and *cross-copying* of *reality*.

This *realization* of *total responsibility* is a steep gradient to achieve — and it is not expected all-at-once. In fact, most of the background story of *this Universe* and the *Spiritual Timeline* (or *Backtrack*) of the *Alpha-Spirit* is not totally understood until the *upper-level A.T.* work. But it is *there now*, as the "*Keys to the Kingdom*" series of *advanced training manuals*. It is something we have not kept locked away from you.

Prior to *New Standard Systemology*, the common starting-point was *incident-running* — what we now treat as "*Confronting the Past*" in *PC Lesson-9* (*Level-4*). The first presentation of this appears in "*The Tablets of Destiny Revelation*" (*Liber-One*) as "*Route-1*" or "*Route-1R.*" This had mixed results in the very beginning; since it required expert *Piloting* to apply, and there was no existing *Pilot Training* available.

We saw better results after publication of "*Crystal Clear: Handbook for Seekers*" — and it is still relevant with the *New Standard*.

If handled earlier on the *Pathway* then *Level-4*, *"confronting-the-past"* or *"incident-running"* (as a *counseling-action*) still requires expert *Piloting.* Even in this case, one can only expect to *destimulate* the area enough to treat with proper *processing* as a part of the greater *Pathway.* Sometimes too much is expected from the techniques early on; as if they are like a *"magic spell."*

Full or *Total Defragmentation* only occurs when the *Alpha Thought*—the *"postulates"* and *"considerations"*—associated with the *incident* (or *imprint*) is *realized* and *confronted "As-It-Is."* This ultimate level of *defragmentation* may not occur early on the *Pathway*—or if techniques are sporadically applied only as *"counseling-actions."*

ENTRY-POINTS TO A SESSION

The *entry-points* of any *case* are the same whether a *Pilot* is going to be able to take a *Seeker* all the way up the *Pathway* or not. Application of technique is the same.

A *Pilot/Co-Pilot* assists a *Seeker* in *accessing* the *incidents* on the *Backtrack.* The *Pilot* is not particularly interested in the *significances* of the *energetic-masses* and *terminals* entangled there. That is more of an interest to the *Seeker* themselves, about their own case. But a *Pilot* needs to be interested in a *Seeker's* case, and help maintain the interest and *attention* level of the *Seeker* on their own case.

The easiest way to get started, is with whatever a *Seeker's attention* is currently on. It is common, at the beginning of a session, to ask: *"Has anything happened that's been a problem to you?"* Or, if you are able to *Pilot* a *Seeker* for multiple *sessions*, you might modify this with *"Since your last session..."* and so forth. This creates *communication-lines* and gets *attention* off of *"human problems"* — *domestics, money* or whatever, by simply *acknowledging* it.

When using a *GSR-Meter* (as described in *"Systemology Biofeedback"*): if there is a *high-resistance* (*balance-point*) at the start of the *session,* some preliminary PCL may be required to lower the *resistance-reading.* Examples of this would be:

"Are you currently protesting something?"

"Has some condition gone on too long?"

"Has an achievement of yours not been acknowledged?"

"Are you having pains (body problems)?"

"Has something 'almost been found out'?"

"Is there something you can't tell anyone?"

Even if not prompted to disclose/speak the information to the *Co-Pilot,* often just the *realization* of *attention being on* these things is enough to bring down the *resistance-reading.* Of course, this may require *"repeated spotting"* of the data *"As-It-Is"* to get the *balance-point* into "normal range." Once it is: the *Pilot* starts each *session* by *running* the *"preventative fundamentals."*

THE PRELIMINARY INTERVIEW

Prior to any *processing*-regimen or standard *session,* the relationship between the *Pilot* and *Seeker* really begins with a *formal interview.* This allows the *Pilot* to get familiar with a *Seeker* and their *case.* But this is still best conducted in a *session-like* environment—and using a *GSR-Meter.*

The *Pilot* can ask the *Seeker* about times they've encountered trouble during their life—noting the *Meter-reads*, and the *area* or *terminal* that it *registers* on. This is only to determine the background and also to help steer what *areas/terminals* will require handling; but *processing* is not part of the *preliminary interview* itself.

The interview helps a *Pilot* "locate" areas with *fragmentary charge* prior to an actual *processing-session*; but also to gauge the *Seeker's attention* and *communication-lag*.

If a *Seeker* is experiencing *low-Awareness* states in-*session*—and/or they have no *reality* on any *recall-type processing* (*analytical recall*)—then focus on "*objective-style*" *processes* that involve *objects* and *masses* in their environment—even *points in space* if they can be worked up to it. This will provide a greater sense of *relief* for their present *state* than initially trying to go after the deeper sources of *turbulence*.

A key point of the interview is for a *Pilot* to get *reality* on a *Seeker's case*. You want to know what is the *Seeker's* ideal picture of *Life*, what is their existing situation, and how far of a departure is one from the other. By knowing this, we can bridge the gap in their *perceptions*—gradually separating the *Seeker's* "*Personal Universe*" from the "*Physical Universe*" in which it is entangled. A *true realization* of this *differentiation* is how one eventually "*Ascends*."

There are many ways to engage in an interview—and a *Pilot* is likely to develop their own style for this as they gain more experience. You might simply say: "*Tell me about your life*."

One popular interview technique is often referred to as the "*Spheres Assessment*." In this practice: you simply go down the list of *Spheres of Existence*—and representative *terminals* for them—and note if there is a *Meter-read*, and/or there is noticeable "*charge*" based on the *Seeker's* observable reactions to each.

For the first *Sphere*, you have the *Body*, the *Human life*, their *name*, *&tc.* You move on to the second *Sphere*, concerning "*Home*," and you have anything involving *domestic life*, or various *family-roles*, like "*mother*" or "*husband*," *&tc.* And you just keep going through all of the facets of existence in this manner. By noting the reactions to the various *areas* and *terminals*, a *Pilot* can apply *processing-levels 0-to-6* more effectively for a *Seeker*; targeting specific areas of *turbulence* that are holding them down.

A *Pilot* wants to pay particular attention to *Spheres* three (*groups*), seven (*spirits*) and eight (*divinity* and *religion*). You want to know what spiritual, mystical, social, philosophical, or religious groups and practices the *Seeker* has been involved with prior to *Systemology*. There is likely to be a lot of *imprinting* for these areas.

The obvious area to target is whatever a *Seeker* is most "upset" about (in present-time). Locate the "*can't do*" justifications or considerations attached to that.

Goals or *Purposes* are also heavily charged areas—which we treat more directly in *AT#2* and *PC-12*. But from the beginning, a *Pilot* should know what a *Seeker* wants to achieve in their life—their motivations and perceived purposes; but also "*failed goals*" and "*incomplete cycles-of-action.*" By this, we mean, when they set out to do something, or intended something, but for whatever reason it didn't happen. It is likely some *Awareness* still remains on it.

THE SKILLS OF PILOTING

As said previously: *communication* is *level zero* for both the *Pathway* and *Pilot Training*. It is *step-one* of having a *session*. And it is key to everything else that we handle with our *Systemology*. Consider how far a *Seeker* could really get beyond *level-zero*, without the *ability* and *willingness* to *communicate* and *engage* on *any* subject; and without reactively *avoiding* what is *unpleasant* or *undesirable*.

Now, as we move into *Level-1*—"*handling problems*"—the first part, *communication*, already has to be in place; established. It is on such an incremental or gradual incline that we *ascend* the *Pathway*. Stable progress is built upon the foundations of previous stabilized progress. This is the only way that one can be sure of their own progress; and that nothing has been accepted blindly—or "*on faith*," as is said.

Most *session*-difficulties—whether *Solo* or *Co-Piloted*—generally stem from one of the *preventative fundamentals*. So, when in question, this should be checked periodically throughout a *session*, to make sure they don't require additional attention; or that something hasn't happened *in-session* (such as the *Pilot* making a mistake) that has put the *Seeker out-of-session*.

If a *Seeker* seems suddenly put-off by the *Pilot* or the *session*, the correct question to ask is: "*What have I done wrong?*" You do not ask "*if you did something wrong*," because a *Seeker* is likely to just say "*no*," or be dismissive. The *Seeker* may still indicate that you did nothing wrong; but by asking in this way, you also have a chance to check for any reaction on the *Meter*. It also gives them a better chance to volunteer information; because you *do* really want to know. A *Seeker* going *out-of-session* is easily missed; then you wonder why they aren't making further progress.

A *Pilot* needs to have an understanding of *two-way communication* and skill in its use. This is not only important for *processing*, but also for understanding the relay of information that occurs internally between systems; for example, following the *ZU-Line* from the *Alpha-Spirit* through *mental circuitry* and finally engaging with a *body*. All of these components are in *communication* with one another—usually *fragmented*, but it is still *communication*.

A *Pilot* should also understand the *Beta Awareness Scale*. This helps you determine what level a *Seeker* is *communicating from*. For example: an *enthusiastic* person is going to *communicate* far differently than an *angry* person, or a *bored* person, *&tc*. Not only do they relay *communication* differently in their speech and behaviors, but they also will receive *communication* differently. For example: a *sad* person is not going to respond very well to someone coming at them *enthusiastically hyper, &tc*.

The other frequently missed-point is the handling of a *presently perceived problem*. This cannot be overstated; because there is some strange expectancy that *Systemology* will still produce stable results even if one's conscious *attention* is *fixedly* elsewhere; and it won't. Of course there is a lot of *fragmented Awareness* that is still suspended elsewhere; but what chance have we of reclaiming *that* if we can't pull together what *attention-units* we currently *are* in a position to *knowingly control*?

A *Pilot* should observe where a *Seeker's attention* is *fixed* on something that they perceive to be still in need of "solving" or "controlling"—*stopping, changing, &tc.*

A bit of our *Awareness* remains on a line to those *terminals* and *areas* that we are considering *"problems,"* but of which are not actually present in our environment; only our personal or "mental" environment. And often, *"problems" are* generated compulsively and automatically by various *machinery, just* to *be* a *"problem"* for us—manufactured *just* to keep our *attention fixed on* all this nonsense; so we don't have a chance to figure out what is really going on. It's all been *systematically engineered* to operate that way; as becomes even more apparent in *upper-level* work.

A *Seeker* will get a handle on *"human problems"* after they get a certainty on being able to *create* them at will. Sounds a bit backwards, doesn't it; but it is truth. As long as an individual remains unable to *create* and *destroy* their own *machinery* and *circuitry,* they will remain *compulsively*—and often quite *unknowingly*—dependent on *programmed automation* to manufacture *reality* for them; based on long-forgotten and horribly *fragmentary reality-agreements* and *postulates.* In other words: they will remain ever *"at effect."*

Rather than *avoiding* areas, you want the *Seeker* to *"describe the problem."* You want to bring it into view, rather than having it linger perpetually on the periphery or side-view. Ask the *Seeker* if the problem seems *"farther away"* after each time they describe it. Our first goal here is to keep the solidity of *mental imagery* and entangled energy of the perceived problem from being right there up on the *Seeker* and overwhelming them. Because no real progress occurs that way. It has to be brought up—*resur-*

faced—and treated *analytically*; not remain down in *low-Awareness* levels of misemotion and such.

Another critical component to *processing*, and too often missed, is the *acknowledgment*. This is how a *Pilot* "ends" one cycle of action, or communication, or in most cases, a single PCL. *"Thank You." "Okay." "Good."* It is an indication to the *Seeker* that their response has been received.

The *acknowledgment* is also important to keep the *Pilot* in check and following the standard procedures. Each PCL is given in its own unit of time and is a complete cycle of action. It isn't just one long string of commands.

Once a PCL is complete, the *Pilot acknowledges* its completion or response given. Then, when the *Pilot* speaks again, they are starting a *new* cycle-of-action or communication; they are *not* leading off of the *Seeker's* previous response. This is the only way to maintain *control* of a *session*. Let me tell you how to quickly lose *control* of a *session*. You ask a *Seeker*, *"How are you?"* And they say, *"Not well."* And you say, *"Oh, how come?" bzzzt*—*crash!* You've just lost *control* of the *session*.

You've got to maintain *communication* without treating a *session* like two buddies having a good-ol' conversation. That is really not what *systematic processing* is. And you won't make any solid gains that way. You say *"Okay, thank you for telling me"* so they don't feel ignored. But if you keep letting a *fragmented Seeker* "steer the ship" than you aren't a very good *Pilot*.The *acknowledgment* also ensures that a *Seeker's attention* does not remain *fixed* on any incomplete cycles-of-action due to the *session* itself. There are such things as *session repair-actions*; where a *Seeker* must essentially *repair* a *processing*-mistake that can occur whether *Solo* or *Co-Piloted*.

To *repair* a *processing-error*, a *Seeker* simply *"Spots"* the point where it occurred and then handles it properly. In the case of a *Piloting* error: the *Seeker* would *"Spot"* it and respond; and the *Pilot acknowledges* that response. For example: they *"Spot"* when you were shuffling papers around and it bothered them. You just say, *"Okay, thank you"* and *"is it alright with you if we continue the session?"* You're back in business. You don't need to get bogged down in blame. Just keep the *session* going.

The last point that I want to make—and it seems strange that we should need to point this out—but: *processing* is about the *Seeker*. The *Seeker* is the focus.

Going back to what is said about *sessions* not being a "simple conversation": there is sometimes a tendency for *Pilots* to do too much of the *talking*. Having studied the subject of *Systemology* more intensely, they generally know a great deal about what is happening with a *Seeker* that the *Seeker* hasn't fully *recognized* or *realized* yet for themselves. Don't deny your *Seekers* a chance to achieve these *realizations* for themselves; given them their *wins*.

But the point is: its the *Seeker's* time. This isn't a time for the *Pilot* to bring up their own case or editorialize the *Seeker's*. Your own stuff is for your *sessions*, when you are getting *processing*. Let's not have any of that *"Oh, yeah, this one time I..."* If you want to share stories of the *Backtrack*, save it for discussions that are not *in-session*.

The initial interview is also *two-way communication*—but the focus is still entirely on the *Seeker's* case; not yours. You don't want to be doing all the talking; that isn't going to make the *Seeker* get any better. You do enough *talking* to keep the *Seeker* engaged and attentive. Some good example questions to keep them *focused*, include:

"What are you interested in?"

"What activities do you enjoy?"

"What makes you happy?"

"What have you been successful at?"

"What do you feel you must do?—must not do?"

"Tell me about it."

"What do you think that is about?"

"How have you dealt with that?"

"Who else was involved?"

Whatever technique or application of our *Systemology* is handled by a *Pilot* or *Minister*, the stable results will only occur by handling the *Alpha-Thought*—the underlying continuously created or generated *postulates*, *considerations*, and *reality-agreements*, that are keeping the *Seeker's attention-Awareness* suspended on an *entangled fragmentary existence*, rather than actually *confronting reality* and treating it *"As-It-Is."* Once a *Seeker* has reached that point, a *Pilot* can step back and let the *Seeker fly!*

For the first time ever in history: we have the *Map*; we have the *spiritual technology*; and we have the *training* available. So, let's work together now, and start helping one another get out of this mess. Let's help one another reach *Ascension!*

THE FORMAL SESSION (EXAMPLE SCRIPT)

1. <u>BEGINNING THE SESSION</u>

"Would it be okay with you if we begin this session now?"

"Okay."

"Start of session."

2. <u>OPENING PROCEDURES</u>

A. Presence In-Session

"Is there anything going on that might keep your attention from being present in-session?"

(if *"no,"* acknowledge and go to B.; if *"yes,"* continue below)

"Okay. Tell me about it."

"Alright. How does that problem seem to you now?"

(if *"further away"* or handled, acknowledge and go to B.; if *"closer"* or more turbulent, continue below)

"Spot something in the incident; Spot something in the room."

(this alternating command line is repeated as needed)

B. Orientation in Present Space-Time

"Get the sense of you making that body sit in that chair."

"Okay. Get a sense of the floor beneath your feet."

"Do you have that real good?"

(if *"no,"* acknowledge and repeat A.; if *"yes,"* continue below)

"Recall a time something seemed real to you."

"Tell me something you notice about it."

"Look around and spot something in the room."

"What do you notice about that?"

(these last four command lines are repeated in series as needed; acknowledge and continue below)

C. Control of Body and Mind In-Session

(two dissimilar objects—here given as *"Item-1"* and *"Item-2"*—are presented and placed within reach; or alternatively, at two distant points in the room, in which a command line for "walking" between them would be inserted)

"Pick up Item-1."

"Tell me about its weight."

"Tell me about its color."

"Tell me about its texture."

"Put it down."

"Pick up Item-2."

"Tell me about its weight."

"Tell me about its color."

"Tell me about its texture."

"Put it down."

(this series of command-lines may be repeated several times; when there is no communication-lag for several full series, and duplicate answers are reoccurring, acknowledge and continue below)

"Choose an object. Decide when you are going to reach for it. Then make that body pick it up."

"Now decide when you are going to put it down. Then make that body put it back where it was."

(repeat as needed; when there is no communication-lag for a full series of command lines, acknowledge and continue below)

"Close your eyes. Put all of your attention on the upper two back corners of the room and just get real interested in them for a while."

(if there are no visible signs of "strain" after two minutes, acknowledge and continue below)

D. Establishing the Session

"Do you have any goals for this session, or anything in particular you want to address?"

(acknowledge, then start a process)

3. STARTING A PROCESS

"I would like to start a process; would that be okay?"

"Alright. The command lines are ---. Does this make sense?"

(if *"no,"* clear up any misunderstood words; if *"yes,"* start the process)

4. CHANGING A PROCESS

(only the wording in a command line may be changed to make it more workable for a *Seeker*; to change processes altogether, the present process must reach an end-point)

Example: a Seeker expresses inability to "imagine" or visualize imagery.

"Okay. Well, just 'get a sense' of..." or *"Just 'get the idea' of..."*

Example: a Seeker expresses discomfort (or withdrawal from) recalling a particular incident.

"That's fine. What part of that incident 'could' you confront?"

5. STOPPING A PROCESS

(when an end-point has been reached on a repetitive-style process)

"We'll just run this process a couple more times if that's okay with you?"

(general process is run two more times)

"Okay. Is there anything you would like to tell me before we end this process?"

(**or**, if an end-point "realization" is communicated from a process)

"Alright. Very good."

(the formal end of a particular process requires a command-line)

"End of process."

6. ENDING THE SESSION

(once a process, or series of processes, is completed)

"Is there anything you would like to tell me before we end this session?"

(if *"yes,"* acknowledge and handle it with communication before ending the session; if *"no,"* continue below)

"Would it be okay if we ended this session now?"

"Okay."

"End of session."

BASIC SYSTEMOLOGY GLOSSARY

A-for-A (one-to-one) : an expression meaning that what we say, write, represent, think or symbolize is a direct and perfect reflection or duplication of the actual aspect or thing—that "A" is for, means and is equivalent to "A" and not "a" or "q" or "!"; in the relay of communication, the message or particle is sent and perfectly duplicated in form and meaning when received.

actualization : to make actual, not just potential; to bring into full solid Reality; to realize fully in *Awareness* as a "thing."

affinity : the apparent and energetic *relationship* between substances or bodies; the degree of *attraction* or repulsion between things based on natural forces; the *similitude* of frequencies or waveforms; the degree of *interconnection* between systems.

agreement (reality) : unanimity of opinion of what is "thought" to be known; an accepted arrangement of how things are; things we consider as "real" or as an "is" of "reality"; a consensus of what is real as made by standard-issue (common) participants; what an individual contributes to or accepts as "real"; in *Systemology*, a synonym for "*reality.*"

alpha : the first, primary, basic, superior or beginning of some form; in *Systemology*, referring to the state of existence operating on spiritual archetypes and postulates, will and intention "exterior" to the low-level condensation and solidity of energy and matter as the 'physical universe'.

alpha-spirit : a "spiritual" *Life*-form; the "true" *Self* or I-AM; the *individual*; the spiritual (*alpha*) *Self* that is animating the (*beta*) physical body or "*genetic vehicle*" using a continuous *Lifeline* of spiritual ("*ZU*") energy; an individual spiritual (*alpha*) entity possessing no physical mass or measurable waveform (motion) in the Physical Universe as itself, so it animates the (*beta*) physical body or "*genetic vehicle*" as a catalyst to experience *Self*-determined causality in effect within the *Physical Universe*; a singular unit or point of *Spiritual Awareness* that is *Aware* that it is *Aware*.

alpha thought : the highest spiritual *Self-determination* over creation and existence exercised by an Alpha-Spirit; the Alpha range of pure *Creative Ability* based on direct postulates and considerations of *Beingness*; spiritual qualities comparable to "thought" but originating in Alpha-existence (at "6.0") independently superior to a *beta-anchored* Mind-System, although an Alpha-Spirit may use Will ("5.0") to carry the intentions of a postulate or consideration ("6.0") to the Master Control Center ("4.0").

apparent : visibly exposed to sight; evident rather than actual, as presumed by Observation; readily perceived, especially by the senses.

archetype : a "first form" or ideal conceptual model of some aspect; the ultimate prototype of a form on which all other conceptions are based.

ascension : actualized *Awareness* elevated to the point of true "spiritual existence" exterior to *beta existence*. An "Ascended Master" is one who has returned to an incarnation on Earth as an inherently *Enlightened One*, demonstrable in their actions—they have the ability to *Self-direct* the "Spirit" as *Self* and maintain consciousness beyond this existence as a personal identity continuum with the same *Self-directed* control and communication of Will-Intention that is exercised, actualized and developed deliberately during one's present incarnation.

assessment : an analysis or synthesis of collected information, usually about a person or group, in relation to an *assessment scale.*

associative knowledge : significance or meaning of a facet or aspect assigned to (or considered to have) a direct relationship with another facet; to connect or relate ideas or facets of existence with one another; a reactive-response image, emotion or conception that is suggested by (or directly accompanies) something other than itself; in traditional systems logic, an equivalency of significance or meaning between facets or sets that are grouped together, such as in $(a + b) + c = a + (b + c)$; in Systemology, erroneous associative knowledge is assignment of the same value to all facets or parts considered as related (even when they are not actually so), such as in $a = a, b = a, c = a$ and so forth without distinction.

attention : active use of *Awareness* toward a specific aspect or thing; the act of "attending" with the presence of *Self*; a direction of focus or concentration of *Awareness* along a particular channel or conduit or toward a particular terminal node or communication termination point; the Self-directed concentration of personal energy as a combination of observation, thought-waves and consideration; focused application of *Self-Directed Awareness*.

awareness : the highest sense of-and-as Self in knowing and being as I-AM (the *Alpha-Spirit*); the extent of beingness directed as a POV experienced by Self as knowingness.

axiom : a fundamental truism of a knowledge system, esp. *logic*; all *maxims* are also *axioms*; knowledge statements that require no proof because their truth is self-evident; an established law or systematic principle used as a *premise* on which to base greater conclusions of truth.

beta (awareness) : all consciousness activity ("*Awareness*") in the "Physical Universe" (KI) or else *beta-existence*; *Awareness* within the range of the *genetic-body*, including material thoughts, emotional responses and physical motors; personal *Awareness* of physical energy and physical matter moving through physical space and experienced as "time"; the *Awareness* held by *Self* that is restricted to a physical organic *Lifeform* or "*genetic vehicle*" in which it experiences causality in the *Physical Universe*.

beta (existence) : all manifestation in the "Physical Universe" (KI); the "Physical" state of existence consisting of vibrations of physical energy and physical matter moving through physical space and experienced as "time"; the conditions of *Awareness* for the *Alpha-spirit* (*Self*) as a physical organic *Lifeform* or "*genetic vehicle*" in which it experiences causality in the *Physical Universe*.

beta-defragmentation : toward a state of *Self-Honesty* in regards to handling experience of the "Physical Universe" (*beta-existence*); an applied spiritual philosophy (or technology) of Self-Actualization originally described in the text "*Crystal Clear*" (*Liber-2B*), building upon theories from "*Systemology: The Original Thesis*."

catalyst : something that causes action between two systems or aspects, but which itself is unaffected as a variable of this energy communication; a medium or intermediary channel.

chakra : an archaic Sanskrit term for "wheel" or "spinning circle" used in *Eastern* wisdom traditions, spiritual systems and mysticism; a concept retained in Systemology to indicate etheric concentrations of energy into wheel-mechanisms that process *ZU* energy at specific frequencies along the *ZU-line*, of which the *Human Condition* is reportedly attached *seven* at various degrees as connected to the Gate symbolism.

channel : a specific stream, course, current, direction or route; to form or cut a groove or ridge or otherwise guide along a specific course; a direct path; an artificial aqueduct created to connect two water bodies or water or make travel possible.

charge : to fill or furnish with a quality; to supply with energy; to lay a command upon; in *Systemology*—to imbue with intention; to overspread with emotion; application of *Self-directed (WILL)* "intention" toward an emotional manifestation in beta-existence; personal energy stores and significances entwined as fragmentation in mental images, reactive-response encoding and intellectual (and/or) programmed beliefs; in traditional mysticism, to intentionally fix an energetic resonance to meet some degree, or to bring a specific concentration of energy that is transferred to a focal point, such as an object or space.

circuit : a circular path or loop; a closed-path within a system that allows a flow; a pattern or action or wave movement that follows a specific route or potential path only; in *Systemology*, "*communication processing*" pertaining to a specific flow of energy or information along a channel; *see* also "*feedback loop.*"

communication : successful transmission of information, data, energy (&tc.) along a message line, with a reception of feedback; an energetic flow of intention to cause an effect (or duplication) at a distance; the personal energy moved or acted upon by will or else 'selective directed attention'; the 'messenger action' used to transmit and receive energy across a medium; also relay of energy, a message or signal—or even locating a personal POV (viewpoint) for the Self—along the *ZU-line*.

compulsion : a failure to be responsible for the dynamics of control—starting, stopping or altering—on a particular channel of communication and/or regarding a particular terminal in existence; an energetic flow with the appearance of being 'stuck' on the action it is already doing or by the control of some automatic mechanism.

concept : a high-frequency thought-wave representing an "idea" which persists because it is not restricted to a unique space-time; an abstract or tangible "idea" formed in the "Mind" or *imagined* as a means of understanding, usually including associated "Mental Images"; a seemingly timeless collective thought-theme (or subject) that entangles together facets of many events or incidents, not just a single significant one.

condense (condensation) : the transition of vapor to liquid; denoting a change in state to a more substantial or solid condition; leading to a more compact or solid form.

condition : an apparent or existing state; circumstances, situations and variable dynamics affecting the order and function of a system; a series of interconnected requirements, barriers and allowances that must be met; in "contemporary language," bringing a thing toward a specific, desired or intentional new state (such as in "conditioning"), though to minimize confusion about the word "condition" in our literature, *Systemology* treats "contemporary conditioning" concepts as imprinting, encoding and programming.

conflict : the opposition of two forces of similar magnitude along the same channel or competing for the same terminal; the inability to duplicate another POV; a thought, intention or communication that is met with an opposing counter-thought or counter-intention that generates an energetic cluster.

confront : to come around in front of; to be in the presence of; to stand in front of, or in the face of; to meet "face-to-face" or "face-up-to"; additionally, in *Systemology*, to fully tolerate or acceptably withstand an encounter with a particular manifestation or encounter.

consciousness : the energetic flow of *Awareness*; the Principle System of *Awareness* that is spiritual in nature, which demonstrates potential interaction with all degrees of the Physical Universe; the *Beingness* component of our existence in *Spirit*; the Principle System of *Awareness* as *Spirit* that directs action in the Mind-System.

consideration : careful analytical reflection of all aspects; deliberation; determining the significance of a "thing" in relation to similarity or dissimilarity to other "things"; evaluation of facts and importance of certain facts; thorough examination of all aspects related to, or important for, making a decision; the analysis of consequences and estimation of significance when making decisions; in *Systemology*, the postulate or Alpha-Thought that defines the state of beingness for what something "*is.*"

continuity : being a continuous whole; a complete whole or "total round of"; the balance of the equation ["–120" + "120" = "0" *&tc.*]; an apparent unbroken interconnected coherent whole; also, as applied to Universes in *Systemology*, the lowest base consideration of space-time or commonly shared level of energy-matter apparent in an existence, or else the lowest degree of solidity or condensation whereby all mass that exists is identifiable or communicable with all other mass that exists; represented as "0" on the *Standard Model* for the Physical Universe (*beta-existence*), a level of existence that is below Human emotion, comparable to the solidity of "rocks" and "walls" and "inert bodies."

continuum : a continuous enduring uninterrupted sequence or condition; observing all gradients on a *spectrum*; measuring quantitative variation with gradual transition on a spectrum without demonstrating discontinuity or separate parts.

control (general) : the ability to start, change or start some action or flow of energy; the capacity to originate, change or stop some mode of human behavior by some implication, physical or psychological means to ensure compliance (voluntarily or involuntarily).

control (systems) : communication relayed from an operative center or organizational cluster, which incites new activity elsewhere in a system (or along the *ZU-line*)

defragmentation : the *reparation* of wholeness; collecting all dispersed parts to reform an original whole; a process of removing "*fragmentation*" in data or knowledge to provide a clear understanding; applying techniques and processes that promote a *holistic* interconnected *alpha* state, favoring observational *Awareness* of continuity in all spiritual and physical systems; in *Systemology*, a "*Seeker*" achieving an actualized state of basic "*Self-Honest Awareness*" is said to be *beta-defragmented*, where as *Alpha-defragmentation* is the rehabilitation of the *creative ability*, managing the *Spiritual Timeline* and the POV of *Self* as Alpha-Spirit (I-AM); see also "*Beta-defragmentation*."

degree : a physical or conceptual *unit* (or point) defining the variation present relative to a *scale* above and below it; any stage or extent to which something *is* in relation to other possible positions within a *set* of "*parameters*"; a point within a specific range or spectrum; in *Systemology*, a *Seeker's* potential energy variations or fluctuations in thought, emotional reaction and physical perception are all treated as "*degrees*."

dramatization / dramatize : a vivid display or performance as if rehearsed for a "play" (on stage); a *'circuit'* recording *'imprinted'* in the past and, once restimulated by a facet of the environment, the individual "replays" it as through reacting to it in the present (and identifying that reality as present reality); acts, actions and observable behaviors that demonstrate identification with a particular character type, "phase" or personality program; a motivated sequence-chain, implant series or imprinted cycle of actions—usually irrational or counter-survival—repeated by an individual as it had previously happened to them; a reoccurring or reactively triggered out-flow, communication or action that indicates an individual "occupying" a particular *'Point-of-View'* (*POV*)—typically fixed to a specific (past) identification (identity) that is space-time locatable (meaning a point where significant *Attenergy* —enough to compulsively create and maintain a POV—is "stuck" or "hung up" on the *BackTrack*).

dynamic (systems) : a principle or fixed system which demonstrates its *'variations'* in activity (or output) only in constant relation to variables or fluctuation of interrelated systems; a standard principle, function, process or system that exhibits *'variations'* and change simultaneously with all connected systems; each *'Sphere of Existence'* is a dynamic system, systematically affecting (supporting) and affected (supported) by other *'Spheres'* (which are also dynamic systems).

emotional encoding : the readable substance/material (data) of *'imprints'*; associations of sensory experience with an *imprint*; perceptions of our environment that receive an *emotional charge*, which form or reinforce facets of an *imprint*; perceptions recorded and stored as an *imprint* within the "emotional range" of energetic manifestation; the formation of an energetic store or charge on a channel that fixes emotional responses as a mechanistic automation, which is carried on in an individual's *Spiritual Timeline* (or personal continuum of existence).

encompassing : to form a circle around, surround or envelop around.

end point : the moment when the goal of a process has been achieved and to continue on with it will be detrimental to the gains; the finality of a process when the *Seeker* has achieved their optimum state from the current cycle (whether or not they run through it again at a later date with a different level of *Awareness* or knowledge base doesn't change the fact that it has flattened the standing wave

enforcement : the act of compelling or putting (effort) into force; to compel or impose obedience by force; to impress strongly with applications of stress to demand agreement or validation; the lowest-level of direct control by physical effort or threat of punishment; a low-level method of control in the absence of true communication.

evaluate : to determine, assign or fix a set value, amount or meaning.

existence : the *state* or fact of *apparent manifestation*; the resulting combination of the Principles of Manifestation: consciousness, motion and substance; continued *survival*; that which independently exists; the *'Prime Directive'* and sole purpose of all manifestation or Reality; the highest common intended motivation driving any "*Thing*" or *Life*.

exterior : outside of; on the outside; in *Systemology*, we mean specifically the POV of *Self* that is *'outside of'* the *Human Condition,* free of the physical and mental trappings of the Physical Universe; a metahuman range of consideration; see also *'Zu-Vision'*.

external : a force coming from outside; information received from outside sources; in *Systemology*, the objective *'Physical Universe'* existence, or *beta-existence*, that the Physical Body or *genetic vehicle* is essentially *anchored* to for its considerations of locational space-time as a dimension or POV.

facets : an aspect, an apparent phase; one of many faces of something; a cut surface on a gem or crystal; in *Systemology*—a single perception or aspect of a memory or "*Imprint*"; any one of many ways in which a memory is recorded; perceptions associated with a painful emotional (sensation) experience and "*imprinted*" onto a metaphoric lens through which to view future similar experiences; other secondary terminals that are associated with a particular terminal, painful event or experience of loss, and which may exhibit the same encoded significance as the activating event.

faculties : abilities of the mind (individual) inherent or developed.

feedback loop : a complete and continuous circuit flow of energy or information directed as an output from a source to a target which is altered and return back to the source as an input; in *General Systemology*—the continuous process where outputs of a system are routed back as inputs to complete a circuit or loop, which may be closed or connected to other systems/circuits; in *Systemology*—the continuous process where directed *Life* energy and *Awareness* is sent back to *Self* as experience, understanding and memory to complete an energetic circuit as a loop.

flow : movement across (or through) a channel (or conduit); a direction of active energetic motion typically distinguished as either an *in-flow*, *out-flow* or *cross-flow*.

fragmentation : breaking into parts and scattering the pieces; the *fractioning* of wholeness or the *fracture* of a holistic interconnected *alpha* state, favoring observational *Awareness* of perceived connectivity between parts; *discontinuity*; separation of a totality into parts; in *Systemology*, a person outside a state of *Self-Honesty* is said to be *fragmented*.

game : a strategic situation where a "player's" power of choice is employed or affected; a parameter or condition defined by purposes, freedoms and barriers (rules).

general systemology ("systematology") : a methodology of analysis and evaluation regarding the systems—their design and function; organizing systems of interrelated information-processing in order to perform a given function or pattern of functions.

genetic-vehicle : a physical *Life*-form; the physical (*beta*) body that is animated/controlled by the (*Alpha*) *Spirit* using a continuous *Lifeline* (ZU); a physical (*beta*) organic receptacle and catalyst for the (*Alpha*) *Self* to operate "causes" and experience "effects" within the *Physical Universe*.

gradient : a degree of partitioned ascent or descent along some scale, elevation or incline; "higher" and "lower" values in relation to one another.

hold-back : withheld communications (esp. actions) such as "*Hold-Outs*"; intentional (or automatic) withdrawal (as opposed to reach); Self-restraint (which may eventually be enforced or automated); not reaching, acting or expressing, when one should be; an ability that is now restrained (on automatic) due to inability to withhold it on Self-determinism alone.

hold-outs : in photography, the numerous snapshots/pictures withheld from the final display or professional presentation of the event; withheld communications; in Utilitarian Systemology—energetic withdrawal and communication breaks with a "*terminal*" and its *Sphere of Existence* as a result of a "*Harmful-Act*"; unspoken or undiscovered (hidden, covert) actions that an individual withholds communications of, fearing punishment or endangerment of *Self-preservation* (*First Sphere*); the act of hiding (or keeping hidden) the truth of a "*Harmful-Act*"; a refusal to communicate with a *Pilot*; also "*Hold-Back.*"

holistic : the examination of interconnected systems as encompassing something greater than the *sum* of their "parts."

Human Condition : a standard default state of Human experience that is generally accepted to be the extent of its potential identity (*beingness*)—currently treated as *Homo Sapiens Sapiens,* but which is scheduled for replacement by *Homo Novus*.

identification : the association of *identity* to a thing; a label or fixed data-set associated to what a thing is; association "equals" a thing, the "equals" being key; an equality of all things in a group, for example, an "apple" identified with all other "apples"; the reduction of "I-AM"-*Self* from a *Spiritual Beingness* to an "identity" of some form.

identity : the collection of energy and matter—including memory—across a "*Spiritual Timeline*" that we consider as "I" of *Self*, but the "I" is an individual and not an identification with anything other than *Self* as *Alpha-Spirit*.

imagination : the ability to create *mental imagery* in one's Personal Universe at will and change or alter it as desired; the ability to create, change and dissolve mental images on command or as an act of will; to create a mental image or have associated imagery displayed (or "conjured") in the mind that may or may not be treated as real (or memory recall) and may or may not accurately duplicate objective reality; to employ *Creative Abilities* of the Spirit that are independent of reality agreements with beta-existence.

imprint : to strongly impress, stamp, mark (or outline) onto a softer 'impressible' substance; to mark with pressure onto a surface; in *Systemology*, the term is used to indicate permanent Reality impressions marked by frequencies, energies or interactions experienced during periods of emotional distress, pain, unconsciousness, loss, enforcement, or something antagonistic to physical (personal) survival, all of which are are stored with other reactive response-mechanisms at lower-levels of *Awareness* as opposed to the active memory database and proactive processing center of the Mind; an experiential "memory-set" that may later resurface—be triggered or stimulated artificially—as Reality, of which similar responses will be engaged automatically; holographic-like imagery "stamped" onto consciousness as composed of energetic *facets* tied to the "snap-shot" of an experience.

imprinting incident : the first or original event instance communicated and *emotionally encoded* onto an individual's "*Spiritual Timeline*" (recorded memory from all lifetimes), which formed a permanent impression that is later used to mechanistically treat future contact on that channel; the first or original occurrence of some particular *facet* or mental image related to a certain type of *encoded response*, such as pain and discomfort, losses and victimization, and even the acts that we have taken against others along the Spiritual Timeline of our existence that caused them to also be *Imprinted*.

inhibited : withheld, held-back, discouraged or repressed from some state.

"in phase" : see "*phase alignment.*"

intention : the directed application of Will; to intend (have "in Mind") or signify (give "significance" to) for or toward a particular purpose; in *Systemology* (from the *Standard Model*)—the spiritual activity at WILL (5.0) directed by an *Alpha Spirit* (7.0); the application of WILL as "Cause" from a higher order of Alpha Thought and consideration (6.0), which then may continue to relay communications as an "effect" in the universe.

interior : inside of; on the inside; in *Systemology*, we mean specifically the POV of *Self* that is fixed to the *'internal' Human Condition,* including the *Reactive Control Center* (RCC) and Mind-System or *Master Control Center* (MCC); within *beta-existence*.

internal : a force coming from inside; information received from inside sources; in *Systemology*, the objective *'Physical Universe'* experience of *beta-existence* that is associated with the Physical Body or *genetic vehicle* and its POV regarding sensation and perception; from inside the body; within the body.

invalidate : decrease the level or degree or *agreement* as Reality.

knowledge : clear personal processing of informed understanding; information (data) that is actualized as effectively workable understanding; a demonstrable understanding on which we may 'set' our *Awareness*—or literally a "know-ledge."

Master-Control-Center (MCC) : a perfect computing device to the extent of the information received from "lower levels" of sensory experience/perception; the proactive communication system of the "*Mind*"; a relay point of active *Awareness* along the Identity's *ZU-line*, which is responsible for maintaining basic *Self-Honest Clarity* of *Knowingness* as a *seat of consciousness* between the *Alpha-Spirit* and the secondary "*Reactive Control Center*" of a *Lifeform* in *beta existence*; the Mind-center for an *Alpha-Spirit* to actualize cause in the *beta existence*; the analytical *Self-Determined* Mind-center of an *Alpha-Spirit used* to project *Will* toward the genetic body; the point of contact between *Spiritual Systems* and the *beta existence*; presumably the "*Third Eye*" of a being connected directly to the *I-AM-Self*, which is responsible for *determining* Reality at any time; in *Systemology*, this is plotted at (4.0) on the continuity model of the *ZU-line*.

mental image : a subjectively experienced "picture" created and imagined into being by the Alpha-Spirit (or at lower levels, one of its automated mechanisms) that includes all perceptible *facets* of totally immersive scene, which may be forms originated by an individual, or a "facsimile-copy" ("snap-shot") of something seen or encountered; a duplication of wave-forms in one's Personal Universe as a "picture" that mirror an "external" Universe experience, such as an *Imprint*.

methodology : a complete system of applications, methods, principles and rules to compose a *'systematic'* paradigm as a "whole"—esp. a field of philosophy or science.

misappropriated : put into use incorrectly; to apply ineffectively or as unintended by design or definition.

objective : concerning the "external world" and attempts to observe Reality independent of personal "subjective" factors.

one-to-one : see "*A-for-A.*"

optimum : the most favorable or ideal conditions for the best result; the greatest degree of result under specific conditions.

organic : as related to a physically living organism or carbon-based life form; energy-matter condensed into form as a focus or POV of Spiritual Life Energy (*ZU*) as it pertains to beta-existence of *this* Physical Universe (*KI*).

paradigm : an all-encompassing *standard* by which to view the world and *communicate* Reality; a standard model of reality-systems used by the Mind to filter, organize and interpret experience of Reality.

parameters : a defined range of possible variables within a model, spectrum or continuum; the extent of communicable reach capable within a system or across a distance; the defined or imposed limitations placed on a system or the functions within a system; the extent to which a Life or "thing" can *be*, *do* or *know* along any channel within the confines of a specific system or spectrum of existence.

patterns (probability patterns) : observation of cycles and tendencies to predict a causal relationship or determine the actual condition or flow of dynamic energy using a holistic systemology to understand Life, Reality and Existence as opposed to isolating or excluding perceived parts as being mutually separate from other perceived parts.

perception : internalized processing of data received by the *senses*; to become *Aware of* via the senses.

personality (program) : the total composite picture an individual "identifies" themselves with; the accumulated sum of material and mental mass by which an individual experiences as their timeline; a "beta-personality" is mainly attached to the identity of a particular physical body and the total sum of its own genetic memory in combination with the data stores and pictures maintained by the Alpha Spirit; a "true personality" is the Alpha Spirit as Self completely defragmented of all erroneous limitations and barriers to consideration, belief, manifestation and intention.

phase (identification) : in *Systemology,* a pattern of personality or identity that is assumed as the POV from *Self*; personal identification with artificial "personality packages"; an individual assuming or taking characteristics of another individual (often unknowingly as a response-mechanisms); also "*phase alignment.*"

phase alignment or "*in phase*" : to be in synch or mutually synchronized, in step or aligned properly with something else in order to increase the total strength value; in *Systemology*, alignment or adjustment of *Awareness* with a particular identity, space or time; perfect *defragmentation* would mean being "in phase" as *Self* fully conscious and Aware as an Alpha-Spirit *in* present *space* and *time*, free of synthetic personalities.

physics : regarding data obtained by a material science of observable motions, forces and bodies, including their apparent interaction, in the Physical Universe (specific to this *beta-existence*).

physiology : a material science of observable biological functions and mechanics of living organisms, including codification and study of identifiable parts and apparent systematic processes (specific to agreed upon makeup of the *genetic vehicle* for this *beta-existence*).

pilot : a professional steersman responsible for healthy functional operation of a ship toward a specific destination; in *Systemology*, an intensive trained individual qualified to specially apply *Systemology Processing* to assist other *Seekers* on the *Pathway*.

point-of-view (POV) : a point to view from; an opinion or attitude as expressed from a specific identity-phase; a specific stand-point or vantage-point; a definitive manner of consideration specific to an individual phase or identity; a place or position affording a specific view or vantage; circumstances and programming of an individual that is conducive to a particular response, consideration or belief-set (paradigm); a position (consideration) or place (location) that provides a specific view or perspective (subjective) on experience (of the objective).

postulate : to put forward as truth; to suggest or assume an existence *to be*; to state or affirm the existence of particular conditions; to provide a basis of reasoning and belief; a basic theory accepted as fact; in *Systemology*, "Alpha-Thought"—the top-most decisions or considerations made by the Alpha-Spirit regarding the "*is-ness*" (what things "are") about energy-matter and space-time.

potentiality : the total "sum" (collective amount) of "latent" (dormant—present but not apparent) capable or possible realizations; used to describe a state or condition of what has not yet manifested, but which can be influenced and predicted based on observed patterns and, if referring to beta-existence, Cosmic Law.

presence : the quality of some thing (energy/matter) being "present" in space-time; personal orientation of *Self* as an *Awareness* (*POV*) located in present space-time (environment) and communicating with extant energy-matter.

Prime Directive : a "spiritual" implant program that installs purposes and goals into the personal experience of a Universe, esp. any *Beta-Existence* (whether a 'Games Universe' or a 'Prison Universe'); intellectually treated as the "Universal Imperative" in some schools of moral philosophy; comparable to "Universal Law" or "Cosmic Ordering."

"process-out" : to reduce *emotional encoding* of an *imprint* to zero; to dissolve a *wave-form* or *thought-formed* "solid" such as a "*belief*"; to completely run a *process* to its end, thereby *flattening* any previous *waves* of *fragmentation* that are obstructing the *clear channel* of *Self-Awareness*; also referred to as "processing-out"; to discharge all previously held emotionally encoded imprinting or erroneous programming and beliefs that otherwise fix the free flow (wave) to a particular pattern, solid or concrete "*is*" form.

processing command line (PCL) or **command line** : a directed input; a specific command using highly selective language for *Systemology Processing*; a predetermined directive statement (cause) intended to focus concentrated attention (effect).

processing, systematic : the inner-workings or "through-put" result of systems; in *Systemology*, a methodology of applied spiritual technology used toward personal Self-Actualization; methods of selective directed attention, communicated language and associative imagery that targets an increase in personal control of the human condition.

reactive control center (RCC) : the secondary (reactive) communication system of the "*Mind*"; a relay point of *Awareness* along the Identity's *ZU-line*, which is responsible for engaging basic motors, biochemical processes and any *programmed automated responses* of a living *beta* organism; the reactive Mind-Center of a living organism relaying communications of *Awareness* between causal experience of *Physical Systems* and the "*Master Control Center*"; it presumably stores all emotional encoded imprints as fragmentation of "chakra" frequencies of *ZU* (within the range of the "*psychological/emotive systems*" of a being), which it may *react* to as Reality at any time; in *Systemology*, this is plotted at (2.0) on the continuity model of the *ZU-line*.

reality : see "*agreement.*"

realization : the clear perception of an understanding; a consideration or understanding on what is "actual"; to make "real" or give "reality" to so as to grant a property of "beingness" or "being as it is"; the state or instance of coming to an *Awareness*; in *Systemology*, "gnosis" or true knowledge achieved during *systematic processing*; achievement of a new (or "higher") cognition, true knowledge or perception of Self; a consideration of reality or assignment of meaning.

relative : an apparent point, state or condition treated as distinct from others.

responsibility : the *ability* to *respond*; the extent of mobilizing *power* and *understanding* an individual maintains as *Awareness* to enact *change*; the proactive ability to *Self-direct* and make decisions independent of an outside authority.

resurface : to return to (or bring up to) the "surface" of that which has previously been submerged; in *Systemology*—relating specifically to processes where a *Seeker* recalls blocked energy stored covertly as emotional "*imprints*" (by the RCC) so that it may be effectively defragmented from the "*ZU-line*" (by the MCC).

Seeker : an individual on the *Pathway to Self-Honesty*; a practitioner of *Mardukite Systemology* or *Systemology Processing* that is working toward *Spiritual Ascension*.

Self-actualization : bringing the full potential of the Human spirit into Reality; expressing full capabilities and creativeness of the *Alpha-Spirit*.

Self-determinism : the freedom to act, clear of external control or influence; the personal control of Will to direct intention.

Self-honesty : the basic or original *alpha* state of *being* and *knowing*; clear and present total *Awareness* of-and-as *Self*, in its most basic and true proactive expression of itself as *Spirit* or *I-AM*—free of artificial attachments, perceptive filters and other emotionally-reactive or mentally-conditioned programming imposed on the human condition by the systematized physical world; the ability to experience existence without judgment.

sensation : an external stimulus received by internal sense organs (receptors/sensors); sense impressions.

slate : a hard thin flat surface material used for writing on; a chalk-board, which is a large version of the original wood-framed writing slate, named for the rock-type it was made from.

spectrum : a broad range or array as a continuous series or sequence; defined parts along a singular continuum; in physics, a gradient arrangement of visible colored bands diffracted in order of their respective wavelengths, such as when passing *White Light* through a *prism*.

Spheres of Existence (dynamic systems) : a series of *eight* concentric circles, rings or spheres (each larger than the former) that is overlaid onto the Standard Model of Beta-Existence to demonstrate the dynamic systems of existence extending out from the POV of Self (often as a "body") at the *First Sphere*; these are given in the basic eightfold systems as: *Self, Home/Family, Groups,*

Humanity, Life on Earth, Physical Universe, Spiritual Universe
and *Infinity-Divinity.*

spiritual timeline : a continuous stream of moment-to-moment
Mental Images (or a record of experiences) that defines the "past"
of a spiritual being (or *Alpha-Spirit*) and which includes impressions (*imprints, &tc.*) form all life-incarnations and significant
spiritual events the being has encountered; in Systemology, also
"*backtrack.*"

standard issue : equally dispensed to all without consideration.

Standard Model, The (systemology) : in *Systemology*—our existential and cosmological *standard model* or cabbalistic model; a
"*monistic continuity model*" demonstrating *total system* intercon-
nectivity "above" and "below" observation of any apparent
parameters; the original presentation of the *ZU-line*, represented
as a singular vertical (y-axis) waveform in space across dimensional levels or Universes (*Spheres of Existence*) without charting
any specific movement across a dimensional time-graph x-axis;
The Standard Model of Systemology represents the basic workable synthesis of common denominators in models explored
throughout Grade-I and Grade-II material.

static : characterized by a fixed or stationary condition; having no
apparent change, movement or fluctuation.

succumb : to give way, or give in to, a relatively stronger superior
force.

system : from the Greek, "to set together"; to set or arrange things
or data together so as to form an orderly understanding of a
"whole"; also a *'method'* or *'methodology'* as an orderly standard
of use or application of such data arranged together.

systematization : to arrange into systems; to systematize or make
systematic.

terminal (node) : a point, end or mass on a line; a point or connection for closing an electric circuit, such as a post on a battery
terminating at each end of its own systematic function; any end
point or 'termination' on a line; a point of connectivity with other
points; in systems, any point which may be treated as a contact
point of interaction; anything that may be distinguished as an 'is'
and is therefore a 'termination point' of a system or along a flow-

line which may interact with other related systems it shares a line with; a point of interaction with other points.

thought-form : apparent *manifestation* or existential *realization* of *Thought-waves* as "solids" even when only apparent in Reality-agreements of the Observer; the treatment of *Thought-waves* as permanent *imprints* obscuring *Self-Honest Clarity* of *Awareness* when reinforced by emotional experience as actualized "thought-formed solids" ("*beliefs*") in the Mind; energetic patterns that "surround" the individual.

thought-habit : reoccurring modes of thought or repeated "self-talk"; essentially "self-hypnosis" resulting in a certain state.

thought-wave or **wave-form** : a proactive *Self-directed action* or reactive-response *action* of *consciousness*; the *process* of *thinking* as demonstrated in *wave-form*; the *activity* of *Awareness* within the range of *thought vibrations/frequencies* on the existential *Life-continuum* or *ZU-line*.

threshold : a doorway, gate or entrance point; the degree to which something is to produce an effect within a certain state or condition; the point in which a condition changes from one to the next.

tier : a series of rows or levels, one stacked immediately before or atop another.

time : observation of cycles in action; motion of a particle, energy or wave across space; intervals of action related to other intervals of action as observed in Awareness; a measurable wave-length or frequency in comparison to a static state; the consideration of variations in space.

timeline : plotting out history in a linear (line) model to indicate instances (experiences) or demonstrate changes in state (space) as measured over time; a singular conception of continuation of observed time as marked by event-intervals and changes in energy and matter across space.

turbulence : a quality or state of distortion or disturbance that creates irregularity of a flow or pattern; the quality or state of aberration on a line (such as ragged edges) or the emotional "turbulent feelings" attached to a particular flow or terminal node; a violent, haphazard or disharmonious commotion (such as in the ebb of gusts and lulls of wind action).

understanding : a clear 'A-for-A' duplication of a communication as 'knowledge', which may be comprehended and retained with its significance assigned in relation to other 'knowledge' treated as a 'significant understanding'; the "grade" or "level" that a knowledge base is collected and the manner in which the data is organized and evaluated.

validation : reinforcement of agreements or considerations as "real."

viewpoint : see *"point-of-view" (POV)*.

will *or* **WILL** (5.0) : in *Systemology* (from the *Standard Model*), the Alpha-ability at "5.0" of a Spiritual Being (*Alpha Spirit*) at "7.0" to apply *intention* as "Cause" from consideration or Alpha-Thought at "6.0" that is superior to "beta-thoughts" that only manifest as reactive "effects" below "4.0" and *interior* to the *Human Condition*.

willingness : the state of conscious Self-determined ability and interest (directed attention) to *Be*, *Do* or *Have*; a Self-determined consideration to reach, face up to (*confront*) or manage some "mass" or energy; the extent to which an individual considers themselves able to participate, act or communicate along some line, to put attention or intention on the line, or to produce (create) an effect.

ZU : the ancient Sumerian cuneiform sign for the archaic verb —*"to know,"* *"knowingness"* or *"awareness"*; in *Mardukite Zuism and Systemology*, the active energy/matter of the "Spiritual Universe" (AN) experienced as a *Lifeforce* or *consciousness* that imbues living forms extant in the "Physical Universe" (KI); *"Spiritual Life Energy"*; energy demonstrated by the WILL of an actualized *Alpha-Spirit* in the "Spiritual Universe" (AN), which impinges its *Awareness* into the Physical Universe (KI), animating/controlling *Life* for its experience of *beta-existence* along an individual Alpha-Spirit's personal *Identity-continuum*, called a *ZU-line*.

Zu-**Line** : a theoretical construct in *Mardukite Zuism and Systemology* demonstrating *Spiritual Life Energy* (*ZU*) as a personal individual "continuum" of Awareness interacting with all Spheres of Existence on the Standard Model of Systemology; a spectrum of potential variations and interactions of a monistic continuum or singular *Spiritual Life Energy (ZU)* demonstrated on the Standard Model; an energetic channel of potential POV and "locations" of Beingness, demonstrated in early Systemology materials as an individual Alpha-Spirit's personal *Identity-continuum*, potentially connecting *Awareness (ZU)* of *Self* with "*Infinity*" simultaneous with all points considered in existence; a symbolic demonstration of the "*Life-line*" on which *Awareness (ZU)* extends from the direction of the "Spiritual Universe" (AN) in its true original *alpha state* through an entire possible range of activity resulting in its *beta state* and control of a *genetic-entity* occupying the *Physical Universe (KI)*.

Zu-Vision : the true and basic (*Alpha*) Point-of-View (perspective, POV) maintained by *Self* as *Alpha-Spirit* outside boundaries or considerations of the *Human Condition* "Mind-Systems" and *exterior* to beta-existence reality agreements with the Physical Universe; a POV of Self *as* "a unit of Spiritual Awareness" that exists independent of a "body" and entrapment in a *Human Condition*; "spirit vision" in its truest sense.

WOULD
YOU
LIKE
TO
KNOW
MORE
? ? ?

SYSTEMOLOGY

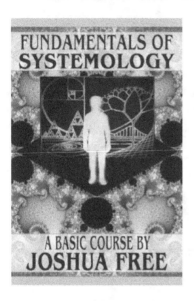

FUNDAMENTALS OF SYSTEMOLOGY

A New Thought for the 21st Century

The Official
Basic Course

ALL *Six Lessons*
in one
Collector's Edition
hardcover

All *six* lesson-booklets of the first official
Basic Course on Mardukite Systemology
are combined together in *one volume* as
"Fundamentals of Systemology."

Also available individually.

"Being More Than Human"

"Realities in Agreement"

"Windows To Experience"

"Ancient Systemology"

"A History of Systemology"

"Systemology Processing"

SYS✞EMOLOGY

THE PATHWAY TO ASCENSION

A New Thought for the 21st Century

The Official
Basic Course

ALL *Sixteen Lessons*
in *two*
Collector's Edition
hardcover volumes

All *sixteen* lesson-booklets of the newest
Professional Course on Mardukite Systemology
are combined together in *two volumes* as
"The Pathway to Ascension."

Also available as individually.

"Increasing Awareness"

"Thought & Emotion"

"Clear Communication"

"Handling Humanity"

"Free Your Spirit"

"Escaping Spirit-Traps"

...and more!

Seekers and students of the *Basic Course* and *Professional Course* will also be interested in the *Systemology Core Research Volumes.* These eight volumes are a complete chronological record of the *Mardukite New Thought* developments from the *Systemology Society*, published in 2019 through 2023.

Our *Systemology Core* begins with the first professional publication released when the *Mardukite Systemology Society* emerged into public view from the underground in 2019, with: *"The Tablets of Destiny Revelation."*

The Tablets of Destiny Revelation:
*How Long-Lost Anunnaki Wisdom
Can Change the Fate of Humanity*

Crystal Clear: *Handbook for Seekers*

Metahuman Destinations (*2 volumes*)

Imaginomicon:
Approaching Gateways to Higher Universes

Way of the Wizard: *Utilitarian Systemology*

Systemology-180: *Fast-Track to Ascension*

Systemology Backtrack:
Reclaiming Spiritual Power & Past-Life Memory

IN A WORLD FULL OF "TENS" BE AN
ELEVEN

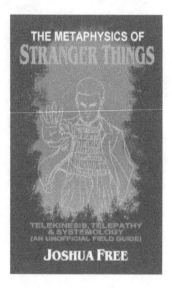

THE METAPHYSICS OF STRANGER THINGS

TELEKINESIS,
TELEPATHY
SYSTEMOLOGY

by Joshua Free

*Mardukite
Systemology
Liber-011*

*Experimental
exploratory
edition*

Discover the metaphysical truth about the Universe—and maybe even yourself—as we explore what lies beneath the epic saga, *Stranger Things.* You're invited to a world where fantasy, science fiction and horror unite, and games like *Dungeons and Dragons* become reality.

Uncover a world of secret "mind control" projects, just like those at *Hawkins National Laboratory.* Decades of psychedelic experiments among other developmental programs for psychic powers, remote viewing, telekinesis (psychokinesis, PK) and more are revealed. Get an inside look at the operations of a real-life underground organization pursuing the truth about rehabilitating spiritual abilities for an actual "metahuman" evolution on planet Earth.

Premiere edition available in paperback and hardcover!

Commemorating the Mardukite 15th Anniversary!

NECRONOMICON
THE COMPLETE ANUNNAKI BIBLE
(*Deluxe Edition Hardcover Anthology*)
collected works by Joshua Free

The ultimate masterpiece of Mesopotamian magic, spirituality and history, providing a complete collection—a grand symphony—of the most ancient writings on the planet. The oldest Sumerian and Babylonian records reveal detailed accounts of cosmic history in the Universe and on Earth, the development of human civilization and descriptions of world order. All of this information has been used, since ancient times, to maintain spiritual and physical control of humanity and its systems. It has proved to be the predecessor and foundation of all global scripture-based religious and mystical traditions thereafter. These are the raw materials, unearthed from the underground, which have shaped humanity's beliefs, traditions and existence for thousands of years—right from the heart of the Ancient Near East: Sumer, Babylon and even Egypt...

∞

PUBLISHED BY THE **JOSHUA FREE** IMPRINT REPRESENTING

**The Founding Church of Mardukite Zuism
& Mardukite Academy of Systemology**

mardukite.com

Printed in the USA
CPSIA information can be obtained
at www.ICGtesting.com
LVHW011043080524
779473LV00044B/27/J